CHILD LABOUR AND HUMAN RIGHTS

CHILD LABOUR AND HUMAN RIGHTS:
A Prospective

NANJUNDA D. C

KALPAZ PUBLICATIONS
DELHI-110052

Child Labour and Human Rights : A Prospective

Rs.1200

ISBN: 9788178356457

Published in 2015 in India by
Kalpaz Publications
C-30, Satyawati Nagar,
Delhi-110052
E-mail: kalpaz@hotmail.com
Phone : 9212729499

Lasser Type Setting by: Rudra Computer Graphics, Delhi
Printed at : Vishal Kaushik Printers, Delhi

Content

Preface

Child labour is one of the worst forms of violation of child rights and also the most widespread. The International Labour Organization (ILO) has estimated that 250 million children between the ages of five and fourteen work in developing countries-at least 120 million on a full time basis. Sixty-one per cent of these are in Asia, 32 percent in Africa, and 7 percent in Latin America. Most working children in rural areas are found in agriculture; many children work as domestics; urban children work in trade and services, with fewer in manufacturing and construction. Child labour ranges from four-year-olds tied to rug looms to keep them from running away, to seventeen-year-olds helping out on the family farm. In some cases, a child's work can be helpful to him or her and to the family; working and earning can be a positive experience in a child's growing up. This depends largely on the age of the child, the conditions in which the child works, and whether work prevents the child from going to school.

Child Labour is increasingly becoming an important issue of concern for the world community, with over 250 million children working around the world. India is one of the worlds' leading countries in terms of employing children with an estimated number between 60 and 115 million working children. Most of these children work in the agricultural sector, leaving about 15 per cent of these children in the service and small-scale industries."

Bonded labour is also becoming a major problem in India. Families who cannot pay their debt sell or trade their children to their debtors in exchange for the money they owe. The local moneylender who takes labour in exchange usually manages money owed to rural banks, the government, or local creditors. Human Rights Watch estimates that about 15 million children work under these conditions. Children are forced to work to help pay for their families' debt, and have absolutely no say in voicing whether they agree to working under the presented circumstances. They are sold like objects, and are submitted to working under terrible conditions. Bonded labour is clearly an abuse of their basic rights as humans.

The issue of child labour is sometimes debated on the basis of a cultural framework. More precisely, child activities are perceived either as a socializing way for children or an apprenticeship way of life. In a certain meaning these arguments deny the value of human rights. If Sen (2005) does not focus particularly on child labour, he rejects clearly the cultural point of view. Moreover, in its discussion about human rights Sen (2005) establishes a distinction between substantive opportunities and freedom of processes. He focuses essentially on substantive opportunities, as the capability approach seems more in phase with this way of thinking. Human rights become entitlements to capability.

The attempts to assert human rights or child's rights are often confronted with the accusation of violation and non-respect of countries cultural specificity's. This inquisition is too excessive and most of the time does not rest on any foundation. To us, three arguments clearly reject a "caricatured" conception of defense of cultural specificity's. Firstly, as Sen (1999) underlines, if we have to consider these specificity's, then they indeed do not concern countries but even more restrained geographical areas and sometimes do concern only with some individuals. It is in fact impossible in most cases to consider that the individuals of the same country have homogenous cultural traits. Significative differences between the regions or States, as well as within the same region or country really exist. And these differences do not limit themselves to large countries like India or the USA, but also affect countries of small size like France or Togo. The defenders of cultural specificities should agree that cultural specificities have to be maintained at the finest level that could lead to accept specificities applying to restricted individual groups. But under no circumstances, they can be considered valid for a given country.

Secondly, specificities saying "cultural" constitute a serious attack for human life. Let us imagine that a cultural specificity in a given geographical area consists in mutilating children severely at birth, for instance by cutting them a hand. On what foundation this specificity could be defended? It is clear that the defenders of cultural specificities are badly comfortable to defend cases affecting seriously human life. But they do not provide any appropriate criteria for distinguishing the specificities that can be rejected from those that can be accepted. Unless they accept that some individuals may attack human life, whereas others do not. Many countries experience dramatic practices. Let us choose two examples: the in fibulation and the cramming (force feeding) are both practices having destructive impacts on children. The former, a deeper and serious form of excision consists of the ablation of clitoris with the suture of sex. The latter practiced essentially in West Africa consists in forcing young girls to eat a huge amount of food (more often, it is poor) in order that they gain weight substantially and become enough fat to respect the standards of beauty and perform a "good and nice" marriage. This practice leads inmost cases to serious problems of obesity and health and invalidates severely the young girls, who indeed are subjected to their husband.

Moreover, various practices, saying cultural traits, are indeed not as ancient as it appears and are the results of socioeconomic evolution. They have no only "cultural" foundations since they result from economic strategies in a context of survival or wealth rising. The dowry issue in India illustrates perfectly this specificity. Marriage and the practice of dowry are strongly embedded in a rigid social context of norms and caste rules. At the same time, new economic and development opportunities have a considerable impact on social organisations in Indian society. The social status of a person is determined by his caste. Within a context of economic development, particularly in urban areas, the social status takes into account of several elements: caste, education, nature of the occupation, and income. Within such context, the identity, and therefore the social status, of an individual is not determined by rigid, hereditary factors such as community and caste affiliation, but by economic factors (particular, the fact that some families pay higher dowries is for them a way of entering into a prestigious alliance and of distinguishing themselves within their own community. income, education, occupation). In well-developed urban areas, this leads to a bigger socio-economic heterogenity within a given caste. So, a striking social change is operated across India and implies new strategies notably within the family. The changes in social status play indeed a major role in the marriage institution, which is regarded as a mean to strike up family relations and to enhance social mobility.

Any work and writing a book can rarely be done individually. It is only with the inspiration, guidance and cooperation of individuals that such an effort is possible. It would therefore, be failing if I do not acknowledge the valuable contributions of the very persons and friends who have helped me in completing this endeavor. First of all I would like to be greatful to the Human Right water for their Report. I owe a special debt **Prof. Steven wind** (USA), **Prof. Fleming Just** (Denmark), **Prof. Srinivas Mani** (USA), **Prof. Annapurna M, Dr. Midatala Rani** and **Dr. Nagrathna K R** for their inspiration. I also owe deep sense of gratitude to **Jyothi Lakshmi S,** (ROAD TRUST), **Venu Gopal K (Research Scholar), Dr. Pavithra (UGC), Shyam Sunder H (IPS), Bhasker M, Suresh Kumar M S, Nagesha D and Linga Raju** and to my parents for their vital role. I also extend my hurtful thanks to concerned organisation my beloved parents and to my research staff of the institute sharing their knowledge.

More important, I express my heartfelt thanks to Kalpaz Publication, and New Delhi for gladly publishing this book.

Nanjunda D. C

Introduction

"We are guilty of many errors and many faults, but our worse crime is abandoning the child, neglected the fountain of life. Many of the things we need can wait. The child cannot. Right now is the time his/her bones are being formed, his/her blood is being made and his senses are being developed. To child we cannot answer Tomorrow. His/her name is Today" (Mistrale, 1977).

The occasional spurts of attention that child labour has gained in the recent past following the debates on globalization and its impact have often raised only a cacophonic noise instead of a coherent understand of the issues. The issue of child labour is hardly an issue in a country that houses the largest numbers of child labourers in the world. But it is less upraise when one learns that the official position of the country has been insouciant, accepting it as a has *harsh reality*, intrinsic to its status as developing country.

If we go back, from the time of shift from an agricultural and commercial society to an industrialized one has been one of the most important developments in modern times. It has modified many social relationships and broken others completely, as the members of an industrial society have been forced to adjust to new ways of life. Researchers have examined some of the aspects of social disorganization as they have affected first men and then women in industry. Industrialization has also made a serious impact upon the status and role of children. In many ways the latter are the most vulnerable of all when they leave the shelter of their homes and enter the factory, office, field or City Street.

Labour effort is the first and prime condition for man's existence. Labour helped the socio-economic development of human beings and social evolution from the primitive animal stage of man to the modern civilized society. Without labour, production is inconceivable. It is the principal creator of all the wealth possessed by human society. Labour is a great creative force. Technology improves labour productivity. Child labour has been an integral part of labour force, especially in third world countries and enters labour market at tender age. It is liable to sharp exploitation by the owners of means of production in the poor countries (Kant, 2001).

In the ancient time, people all over the world were generally indifferent to the all round development of children. Then the children didn't get necessary freedom and opportunity for their natural development. Of course attention was paid to their physical development through physical exercise, hard discipline and self-control. Childhood is an important phase of human life. The entire life structure will be based on it. The knowledge of the importance of childhood is necessary for the community. Repression of instinctive desires of children may develop complexes and lead undesirable behaviour. The development of child is conditioned both by heredity and environment. A child is a future asset or capital for development of the society. If a society burden, by the work may be physical or mental and overburdened it may be curse for the society.

Experts fell poverty and inquiring dependency ratio on account of population explosion since 1950s are major pushing factors in sending children to the labour market. More than that, India's unique cultural background accounts for son-preference and a vital discrimination against girl child. This kind of gender discrimination is more prevalent in India. Enormous supply of labour force means hectic labour market in developing and under developed countries in spite of increased demand generated by the different developmental programmes (Dharma, 1999).

Children under the age of 15 years constitute a substantial portion of any country. Some time even exceeding more than forty per cent. Child labour constitute the most deprived section of the community forced to earn a pittance or to contribute to family work sacrificing personnel development at prime age for want of opportunity. There is no doubt that the iniquitous and exploitative nature of the economy and socio-economic milieu lead to this harsh reality of child labour. Also it has been noted that the socio-economic milieu determines to a significant extent the working and living conditions of child workers. Social scientists have argued that the socio economic parameters like survival strategy, place of origin, caste and religion, the existence of clear nexus between occupational profiles of parents and child labour caste and tradition and family sizes are some of the basic anthropological factors embedded in this chronic melody (Mohanty, 2001).

The issue of child labour is the major human rights issue and at the same time it is highly an emotional one. These emotions tend to be coupled with very strong views both on what the child labour problem is and what ought to be done for its elimination. Although the predominance of the child labour has to be quite prevalent among all the developing and under developed countries, it is a global phenomenon which exists in almost all the countries of the world the difference if any, is of degree only (Shandilya, 2003).

The existence of child labour is a blot of slur on a modern welfare state, which seeks to promote the all round development of citizens. Children are the future hope of the nation. They are like buds, which need to be properly nursed and well taken care. So that they bloom fully and grow in to able human beings and on the contrary, instead of being sent to schools and properly educated, they are made to work, and this amounts to squeezing the bud before it blooms. It also not only threats the development of children but of the society as, well, since only able children can shape the future of the society. Thus, child labour has become a chronic problem and has deepened into the Indian social fabrics. The problem has changed its venues from public platforms, it has reached the inner circle of legislative, executive and judicial chamber (Sharma, 2001).

The recent trend in the global system is to evaluate the development of any country, not in terms of their military or economic strength or the splendour of their capital cities and public buildings, but also in terms of human development or the well being of its people. Against this back drop, the existence and perpetuation of child labour have been one of the main limiting factors in the way of human development in almost all the developing countries including India.

Child labour is also rooted in the traditions and an attitude of the regions where it is practices, as a remnant of the past, a kind of resistance to change. In many societies even though child working in most hazardous sectors can not be considered as a problem because that kind of society think that this kind of work is highly essential in child's normal socialization. Also it is most unfortunate that many elite's of the community and policy makers, who belong to the upper class have attitude and beliefs that children of the poor family should prepare for their future from an early age (Wood, 1997).

In every nation, the welfare of the entire community depends on the health and welfare of the child. The child welfare policy should acknowledge the fact that the personality of a human being is built up in the formative years of child. The physical, social and cultural health of the nation determined by the manner in which the life of the child is shaped in early stages. Child welfare includes the total well being of the child. It not only includes care of the malnourished child, delinquent and the disabled child, but also the development of the normal child's physical, mental, emotional and social faculties. Immoral society has accepted child labour in different forms and it is common knowledge that children are the wealth of a nation, so no nation can afford to ignore the welfare of this human wealth (Pandey, 2001)

Progress for children should be a key goal of overall national development. As today's children are the future citizen of this nation. But we should not forget that, their survival, protection and development is the prerequisite for the overall development of the country. Empowerment of younger generation with knowledge and resource to meet their basic human needs and to grow to their full potential should be a primary goal of our national development as their individual development and social contribution will shape the future of the world, investment in children's health, emotional development, nutrition and education is the foundation stone for our future human resource development (Tripathy, 2003).

Child labour has drawn increasing international attention and condemnation since the 1970s. During the same period many international NGOs and agencies have began to speak out against the inhuman conditions under which children work in many developing countries. The issue of child labour has generated renewed interest because of the new economic policies formulated in line with the structural adjustment programmes developing countries have adopted hoping to help them integrate into the global market economy. Hence, the long neglected topic of child labour has suddenly attracted worldwide interest as a subject of research and analysis, particularly regarding the supply and demand sides of the problem (Bon,1996).

This interest among economists and social scientists began during a transition period in which the incidence of child labour had been declining for more decades among developed countries and increased among third world countries. This pattern may be a source of optimism that signals the spread of science and technology that have little use for child labour and values that endorse the preservation and protection of childhood. Nevertheless, why does child labour remain an issue of intense concern around the world? One reason may be because there is an ongoing worldwide debate on poverty reduction among the vulnerable sections of the society, where a large proportion of working children is found. In the same way, it is revealed that child labour is viewed as a major hurdle to the overall development of an economy. It is also known that dependence on child labour minimizes the human capital accumulation, which is a prerequisite for development. The early 20th century witnessed the sharp and sudden reduction in child labour in western industrialized countries. But unfortunately the same period saw the expansion of the problem in the third world (Rao, 2001).

The problem of child labour is the curse for humanity. The problem is concerned with the children whose childhood is lost and they live in poverty. It is the problem of those children who instead of playing and studying bear the responsibility of eradicating poverty of their family, being themselves in the tremendous 'working poverty'. The prevalence of child labour is the most striking issue in human resources development now-a-days. Those lovely and innocent children are not only engaged hard and hazardous works but they become prey of sexual abuses too. (Naresh,1993)

The World Bank Report published in the first week of January, 2000 has revealed that there are six crore working children in India which is largest in times of any country in the World. These six crore working children include the one and a half crore bonded working children. No doubt, the elimination of child labour is a challenge for the country. The Union Labour Minister once said, in the recent Parliament session that the Government for elimination of child labour in the country has adopted a progressive as well as integrated approach. In order to resolve this intense socio-economic problem, a multidimensional action plan to create awareness among all sections of the society is required. In the national awareness campaign for the elimination of child labour, along with the efforts made by the government side, the non-government organisations and the mass media have also to play an important role (*The Hindu).*

With the heralding of the new millennium, the burning challenges that have appeared globally, the problem of child labour stands as one of the most acute among them. More than a billion of children in the world today turned into child labour because of their non-schooling or because of their dropping out of school at the initial stage. Child labour may normally be defined as a child who has not attained the age of fourteen years, whose physical, mental and social development has languished due to employment in organized as well as unorganized sectors.

In the densely populated poor and developing countries, the child labour problem is passing through a miserable state and India is also regarded as one among those countries. The real number of working children in the country is very large. People at large as well as the public representatives are greatly concerned with the magnitude of the child labour problem in the country in the new millennium. This concern was also expressed in December 2001 before both the houses of Parliament when issues relating to the child labour were raised in different ways during Parliament session. The given by the Labour Minister in LokSabha and Rajya Sabha is very much appreciative particularly for those who are more concerned with this problem. The minister said that Government is considering the nature, magnitude and the intensity of the child labour problem. He stated that 'a progressive and integrated approach has been adopted to tackle the problem starting from relieving the child labour from the hazardous occupation and to rehabilitating them'.

India is obviously keen to improve its image under international pressure with regard to child labour. The Governament asserts that children are forced to work because their parents are poor. Here lies the actual problem. Child labour keeps children out of school and contributes to the growth of the illiteracy rate of the country. Industrial employers compete with schools for children. Middlemen for the commission generally recruit those school age children. Official policy, in all developed and some developing countries dictates that 'no employer is permitted to employ child labour and no matter how poor, cannot keep children out of school'. Hence they have succeeded in eradicating this problem up to certain extent. The Indian laws prohibit the employment of children in factories. But not in cottage industries, household enterprises, hotels, and mainly in agriculture sectors. The absence of stricter child labour laws, or the implementation of existing laws or provisions for compulsory education, has meant that a little less than half of India's children between ages 6-14 are not in school (Nayem,2001). Ironically, since independence the Indian government, every Government has formed many inquiring commissions and all political parties have/had promised of ending child labour and impairing compulsory education to all children upto 14 years. Yet no improvement.

How ever Kerala State is a very good example with respect to the issue of child labour. Though it's per capita income is not higher than the rest of the country, the intensity of the child labour in this state is very low. Because this state is investing more money on primary education. The problem is that India is spending a lower proportion of its gross national product (GDP) on education than most of the other developing countries. A larger proportion of the money is investing only on higher education. Further western expert opines that a major reason behind the persistence of child labour in India is strong prevalence of caste and class system (Wood, 1999).

Higher castes feels education as a menace to maintain difference among social classes, believes in reinforcing down divisions among people. And this higher caste people may expect better social dealings, respectable place in society and improvement in their living standard. This aspect of socio-anthropological enquire is of vital importance in the present study because it facilitates a socio-anthropological probe into the working of a social system and the functional and unfunctional aspects of various social institutions and sub systems (Eggan, 1990). Many researchers have shown that of the child labour issue and intensity of the problem is depended upon various social and cultural factors in third world countries. Since culture is an integrated functional unit of a society, the anthropologist's tries to find out the nature of the phenomenon, related with the child labour and how this problem is interlocked with the culture (Sinha, 2001).

According to the Foster, the anthropological studies tries to identify the social issues in the following ways: 1. The logical reasoning of the society or the social philosophy of the problem 2. Social facts pertaining to the particular social issues and 3. Appropriate research techniques used to get original and reliable field data. Anthropologist generally uses participant observation and interview methods to get fist hand informations of the social problems. Field data obtained by using above-mentioned methodologies would be highly useful document in encountering with this kind of social problem.

Anthropologists working on developmental programmes have produced adequate theories and research methodologies dealing with the processes of change that are vitally important to policy makers and administrators in charge of the welfare of the weaker sections of the society. (Sharma, 2003). These theories and research methodologies are potential tools to the planners in identifying the ongoing changes to understand better the community which is prone to either resist or accept the change in the face of social and technological innovations.

The study on child labour has taken considerable attention in recent times, every where in the world and in India also which accounts for a significant proportion of the worlds child labour force. Most of these studies have attempted to give detailed description of the various manifestation of child labour. A few have attempted to understand the underlying forces caused for the persistence of child labour despite its universal condemnation and the various legislative and administrative measures introduced by the Governament to deal with the problem. While some have treated child labour as an evil to be eliminated others have viewed it from the prospective of socio-economic significances of a society at a particular stage of transformation. They try to assert that the very persistence of child labour is an indicative of the crucial role that it plays and consequently it cannot be eradicated by enacting legislation's (Naidu, 2003).

So, it is highly desirable at this stage to study the conditions of child workers in different urban settings especially after the Globalization. In-depth Anthropological study has acquired a great relevance to the present day problem emphasizing on, how community evaluates the risks associated with child labour. It is also most important to know the extent to which the people are responsive to the different policies and programmes of both Governament and different NGOs. The differences in the mental attitudes and outlooks regarding with the causes for the existences of the child labour in traditional societies and the modern societies is of so important for the social scientists. The study demands not only a deep analysis of the broader frame work of community norms regarding childhood as a life phase, human rights, the rights of children and also the age and gender appropriateness for different types of work.

Traditional factors are also important. The established female role in certain countries dictates that women will not fit into traditional roles if they become educated. There is a pervasive notion in some nations that educated females will not get married nor have children. Therefore, many families raise daughters solely to take over the household duties in order release the mother for paid labour. Such cultural practices restrict the education of females and promote child employment. The acceptance of social class separation perpetuates child labour as well. For example, people of India's lower castes are expected to perform manual labour and therefore are more apt not to attend school (Dak, 2004).

Often parents in developing countries assign different roles to their children. This has been called child specialization, and may increase the number of working children. This phenomenon involves certain siblings going to school while others work. Many times this depends on the birth order where the oldest is the one who attends school. Studies find that the number of siblings does not have much of an effect on school enrollment, although it does have a significant effect on child labour. This exclusive effect is not inconsistent with the idea of specialization (Vergees,1995).

Rapid rural-to-urban migration is the cause for the increasing rate of child labour in urban areas of developing countries. Families leave the severity of agricultural working conditions for cities in order to search for economic opportunities that often do not exist. In the last 40 years, this movement has been drastic. In 1950, 17 per cent of the population of the developing world lived in urban areas. This increased to 32 per cent in 1988. By the year 2000 it is estimated that this proportion will increase to 40 per cent, and to 57 per cent by the year 2025 (United Nations 1989). Such increases coupled with worsening economic trends, force children and their families into urban poverty where children are soon required to work.

Despite the attention devoted to child labour in recent years, those addressing the issue were divided on how to proceed and considered a range of different approaches. Some urged that child labour be eliminated quickly and aggressively, including through the use of trade sanctions when countries or industries failed to act decisively. Others called for reforming the conditions in which children worked with a view toward gradual elimination. Some believed that work plays an important and positive role in children's lives and in their relations with their families, and sought reform, but not an end to child labour.

In tackling the issue of child labour, consideration of the immediate and direct consequences for children and their families could not be underestimated. The removal of children from the workforce had devastating results for some children when not accompanied with nuanced adjustment programs for their rehabilitation and education, and direct assistance. Children discharged from work found themselves on the street in prostitution or crime, or working in even worse conditions and for less pay.

The trade sanction approach seeking boycotts of employers or governments who permitted the use of child labour, or banning the importation of goods made with child labour was extremely difficult to monitor. Employers' assurances that they did not use child labour in manufacturing workplaces around the world were meaningless without effective and independent monitoring mechanisms in place. And trade sanctions or boycotts narrowly targeted to particular export industries, even when effective, had small impact, as only a small portion of child labourers worked in these industries.

Child labour included a range of situations from the clearly hazardous and exploitative, as in the case of four-year-old children tied to rug looms to keep them from running away, to the benign or positive, seventeen-year-olds helping out on the family farm or working after school to earn some pocket money. In many cases, as in the latter examples, children's work was helpful to them and their families, and contributed positively to their development into responsible adults. This depended largely on the age of the child, the conditions in which the child worked, and whether work prevented the child from going to school.

What was clear, and what the international community agreed on, was that certain types of child labour were categorically hazardous to the health, safety, and morals of children and should be banned. The ILO Convention Concerning the Prohibition and Immediate Action for the Elimination of the Worst Forms of Child Labour (ILO Convention 182), adopted unanimously by the 174 member states of the ILO in June 1999, committed states party to take immediate steps to prevent, prohibit, and eliminate "the worst forms of child labour." The term child referred to anyone under the age of eighteen. Under the convention, the worst forms of child labour included the sale and trafficking of children, debt bondage, forced or compulsory labour (including the forced recruitment of children for use in armed conflict), using children for prostitution or production of pornography, using children for illegal activities, particularly drug trafficking, and other work likely to "harm the health, safety or morals of children."

Cognizant of the dangers of banning child labour without also providing children with alternatives to labour, the convention obligates states parties to ensure that children removed from the worst forms of child labour be given direct assistance to ensure their removal, rehabilitation,and social reintegration. Most importantly, the convention mandated that children removed from labour ensured access to free basic education, and wherever possible and appropriate, vocational training.

Human Rights Watch worked on the issue of child labour in areas where the rights abuses were clear and acute, and which fell within the new ILO Convention's definition of "worst forms of child labour." We worked on bonded child labourers in India; the use of children as soldiers in armed conflicts around the world; and the employment of live-in domestic child servants in Sri Lanka. Throughout, Human Rights Watch emphasized the importance of providing education and rehabilitation in assisting children removed from these worst forms of child labour to truly end the practice.

Violence Against Children in School

For many children around the world, violence was a regular part of the school experience. In some countries, school officials routinely used corporal punishment to maintain classroom discipline and to punish children for poor academic performance. In other countries, authorities failed to intervene to protect minority children from harassment and attacks by other students. The failure of school officials to protect children from violence in school denied them their right to be free from all forms of physical or mental violence and the full enjoyment of their right to education.

School Corporal Punishment

School corporal punishment remained widespread and an accepted part of the class room experience for millions of children around the world, where the human rights violations inherent in its use went unrecognized. In many countries, the use of corporal punishment by teachers against children was explicitly authorized by law, making it a legalized form of violence against children.

The U.N. Committee on the Rights of the Child, the U.N. Committee against torture, the U.N. Human Rights Committee, and the European Court and Commission of Human Rights took a strong stand against corporal punishment in schools on the grounds that it may rise to the level of torture or cruel, inhuman or degrading treatment or punishment. The Committee on the Rights of the Child was particularly outspoken, stating that the use of corporal punishment against children was incompatible with the Convention on the Rights of the Child, and it frequently proposed the revision of existing legislation and the development of education campaigns to prevent the physical punishment of children. The use of corporal punishment violated the right of children to be free from violence, debased their dignity and physical integrity, interfered with the development of their physical and mental health, and infringed on their basic right to education. Human Rights Watch worked to highlight these abuses, undertaking a fact-finding mission to Kenya and issuing its findings in August 1999. Kenya's School Discipline Regulations authorized the use of corporal punishment in schools but failed effectively to regulate its use. Nominal restraints were routinely ignored by teachers and the regulations rarely enforced. Teachers caned children for "offenses" such as tardiness, talking in class, wearing torn or dirty uniforms, being unable to answer a question, or failing to achieve target marks set on exams. These measures often resulted in bruising, swelling, and small cuts; at times, however, children suffered more serious injuries such as sprained or broken fingers or wrists, knocked-out teeth, internal injuries, and even death.

Unsurprisingly, school corporal punishment did little to further its supposed educative purpose and had far-reaching and harmful consequences for children. Aside from the common physical injuries and the extreme cases of death which resulted, the practice produced psychological scars that stayed with children for the rest of their lives. Research in Kenya found that the use of corporal punishment instilled a fear of the classroom for some children that impaired learning and at times led children to drop out of school altogether. Other research showed that corporal punishment could be a significant factor in the development of violent attitudes and actions in childhood and later life.

Violence Based on Sexual Orientation

In the United States and in other countries around the world, gay, lesbian, bisexual, and transgendered students too often experienced school as a place that accepted intolerance, ostracization, and violence against those perceived to be different. For the most part, school officials refused to intervene to protect these students, allowing what began as harassment to escalate to physical violence. Studies by the U.S. Department of Health and Human Services, the states of Massachusetts and Vermont, and the Seattle, Washington school district found that students who were subjected to harassment and violence at the hands of their peers frequently suffered from depression, low self-esteem, and an inability to focus on schoolwork; most alarmingly, the studies concluded that gay, lesbian, bisexual, and transgendered students were two to three times more likely to attempt suicide than their heterosexual counterparts.

1

Child Labour Through Ages

History of Child Labour

In ancient societies, the daily occupation entrusted to the adults and the children were gradual; learning the skills, socialized children and customs so that by the time they pass through the *rite de passage*, they had become fully accomplished adults. The transitions in to the modern industrial society changed all the traditional factors for at least two basic reasons: the initiation of formal education turned childhood into a distinct phase of life and work done by the children changed its character from family employment to the sale of labour power (Liten, 2001)

During the pre-industrial period child labour had been prevalent in Germany in, a) workshops and in factories of post industrial and early industrial phase between 1750-1850 b) and in the factories after industrial revolution. Further there are evidences to prove that the existence of child labour even as early as in 16th and 17th centuries, in orphanages and workhouses. In 1667, for instance, children worked together with convicts at the loom in the orphanage of Basel, in order to turn out products of sale. (Arno herzing, 1990).

Even in 1536 England had an Act on the practice of child labour. According to this Act, children who are between the age of 5-14 could work in agriculture and cottage industries to improve their skills for their adult life. Also there was a plan to fix the minimum wage for different labourers. In 1601 Queen Elizabeth implemented a new Act. Through this Act there was a clear direction to the parents to look after their children well.

Further there was a provision in the Act to appoint some officers at local level to implement the Act. In 1667, the Board of Trade requested William III to constitute a committee to investigate into the present conditions of poor and destitute children in the country. These committees recommended establishing informal schools to the working children with free supply of food and some other benefits to the poor parents. (Ahmed Shah, 1992).

In 1784 the board of juries sent a proposal to the King to take appropriate action to improve the present condition of the child labourers. Next, there was a provision in the proposal to provide all available facilities to the existing child workers. In 1795 the Board of Health was established to keep an eye on the health of the children working in hazardous sectors. In 1802, Robert had conducted a survey on children working in different factories and recommended to implement a new Act called Apprentices Act 1801. This Act made provisions to provide education to working children including moral and spiritual education.

According to this Act

1 There was a ban on different factories to hire apprentices to work during nightime.

2 Apprentices should not work more than 12 hours a day and

3 Factories should not hire children who are below 9 years.

Since this Act had a lot of drawbacks, again in 1819, a new Act was passed. Actually it was a modified version of the1802 Act. According to the new Act, factories should have arrange lunch and other facilities to the children. But this Act also failed in avoiding the exploitations of the children. So in 1833, a new Factory Act was enacted

According to this Act

- Children who are below 13 years old could work upto 8\9 hours a day and not more than 48 hours in a weak;
- Child labourers should attend school atleast for about 2 hours a day and;
- Fixes holiday and other benefits should be provided to child labourers. During the early part of 19th century, New England mills employed children 8 to 9 years old, to work often for 12-13 hours a day. Soon local Government recognized that these children would grow up illiterate. In 1836, Massachusetts enacted a law requiring all children under15 to receive education for at least three months a year. Other New England states enacted compulsory school laws and passed restrictions on children's working more than ten hours a day.

In 1844, a new Act was passed in favour of child labourers to fix minimum wage and hours of work in factories. In 1847 a new Act was again brought to improve the conditions of women and children working in cotton industries. In 1850 and 1853 there were many laws and Acts in favour of working children.

In 1860, a new Printing Press Act was implemented. In 1870 England brought a historical Act to provide free and compulsory education to all the children who are in between 5 to 10 years. This Act gave permission to the owners to hire children who are above 15 years old to work in households, construction sites and cleaning etc.

Out side England there was no great mass employment of children until the Civil War, which gave impetus to large-scale production. Children then became an important part of toll of machine methods. As early as in 1881, adult workers were aroused with references to both the disorganization of the child labourers and the "Unfair Competition" which the children posed for adult labour. Children could operate many machines with various facilities. In that year, the newly founded American Federation of Labour urged the abolition of child labour. Until such claim however, the effort to restrain employers from exploiting young children gain momentum (U.S.A. Department of Labour, 1959).

During the period from 1885 onwards-European immigration flooded the country to participate in the vast industrial development. Industrialists sponsored immigration to promote surplus supply of labour, so that they might keep wage low for all labour and operate their businesses at higher profits. It was most common in USA, UK and Germany. The children of such labourers had little alternative but to seek work in order to contribute towards their family income.

After World War I, the number of children employed in industry decreased sharply, largely because of the decline in industrial production worldwide. Also there were some movements in USA, UK and Germany to impose ban on child labour. The US Congress enacted a child labour amendment in 1924, and it had been ratified by 28 states. This is the first Act against child labour in the history of the child labour. In consequent of the generally aroused opinion, the number of employed children from 10 to 15 decreased by 46.7 per cent between 1910 and 1920 and 37.1 per cent in 1930 (Greene, 1954).

During the depression years of the thirties, in the USA, the problem of child labour took serious turns. Because of the vast number of unemployed breadwinners, many children left school to help and support their families or themselves. Quite often such cases have not been reported to any statistical bureau. There were other trends accompanying the employment of children during the depression. Children drifted to the less desirable, lower -paid and generally unregulated industries. Many young persons were out of school because they could not afford the cost of education.

At the same time, social sentiment was mounting against child labourers. The new National Recovery Act (NRA) was in force in the USA between 1933 and 1935 which prohibited children under sixteen years of age from working in industry and those between sixteen and eighteen from employment in the hazardous industries. Children were practically eliminated from the labour scene temporarily. The NRA was declared unconstitutional in 1935 and the number of children working soon mounted as an adverse effect (WEBSITE).

In 1937, however, the "Sugar Act,"(USA) which prohibited children under fourteen from working in the beet fields, went into effect. Those from fourteen to sixteen were not allowed to work more than eight hours a day in the beet industry and were to receive the same wages as adults. The new Act of 1940 severely penalized all beet growers hiring children by making them ineligible from marketing benefits. Children were virtually eliminated from one of the industries in which they were most seriously exploited. Meanwhile in USA, the Fair Labour Standards Act of 1938 often designated the "Wage and Hour Act," prohibited the shipment in interstate or foreign commerce of any article/s produced under conditions of "oppressive child labour." (Lumpkin and wolff, 1969).

The Fair Labour Standards Act, as amended in 1957, sets sixteen years as the limit for any employment during school hours or for any time and in manufacturing, mining, or processing occupations requiring duties in work rooms or factories and for power-driven machinery. Children were prohibited employment in explosives, manufacturing, driving or helping on motor vehicles, coal mining, exposure to radioactive substances, operating hoisting apparatus or metal forming, punching, and shearing machines, mining in non-coal industries, work in slaughtering and meat packing and rendering plants and on power-driven bakery machinery—and other work considered particularly hazardous. In these industries children must have been eighteen before they can be employed. They must also be eighteen before they can be employed as public messengers or as operators of vehicles. (Markoff, Sol, 1957).

The Labour Standards Act was declared constitutional in 1941 in the case of the USA vs. Derby. The right of the Government to restrict child labour and to enforce standards was no longer to be questioned, so for as industries involved in interstate commerce were concerned. Then in many vital industries, child labour was very nearly disappeared. Those certain industries, which violated the child existing labour Act/s were penalized. The Public Contracts Act (1952) also forbid hiring of boys under sixteen and girls under eighteen in the manufacture of goods under contract to the Government (Website).

During World War II, child labour laws were relaxed in order to increase the number of available workers in the factories and to meet the demands for labour on the home front. So, much of the normal labour force was absorbed either in the armed services or in the production of materials that there was a real difficulty in meeting essential civilian needs. Children were recruited on every hand and in many instances were illegally employed under the coverage of existent State and Federal laws (Bon,1998).

"Only a small percentage of these violations ever came to public attention; people winked at the hiring of children because there was often no other help available. Even so, the increases reported were an index to the general situation. In North Carolina (USA), in 1943, for example, there were fourteen times as many violations of the State child labour laws reported as in 1940. And in the first half of 1944, twenty-two times as many violations were reported as in the first half of 1940. In Illinois State, less than forty establishments were found guilty of evading child labour laws from January through June in 1941, and more than 500 were guilty for the same period in 1944" (Wind, 1999).

Moreover, the legal standards for the employment of children were also relaxed. "Over half legal standards for the employment of child labourers during the war period, with reference to one or more provisions affecting children under eighteen. Three other States operated under laws allowing wartime emergency employment of children which hand never been repealed following World War I"(Bon, 1998). Further, in 1960, Western Europe and Canada started to think seriously towards the problem of child labour. Juvenile delinquency was a major problem among some of the European nations by that time.

Former USSR also had many noted laws and Acts to safeguard women and children. In 1932, Code of Labour Act was passed. According to this Act Govt. had a provision to impose ban on employers' to hiring children below 15 years to work in hazardous sectors. Also, there was no provision for children to work during nightime. Next, USSR brought some guidelines to avoid exploitations such as;

Ban on hiring children below 16 years except for academic or education related work;

- Compulsory medical examinations before hiring children below 16 years;

Below 16 years old children should not be asked to work not exceeding 6 hours a day as three should be a provision to provide holiday and other facilities.

In 1971 an Act was passed to restrict children to work in hazardous sectors like garage, mining etc. Also Government constituted a watching committee to keep an eye on the labour market. In 1988, USSR brought a powerful Act, which bans on hiring children between 6 to 14 years. Also a lot of stress were given to provide free education, dress, food etc to the children and also some guidelines to the parents. But after the disintegration of former

USSR, due to severe economic depression, the rate of working children are getting increasing (Perasthroyeeka, USSR, 1980).

History of Child Rights and Child Labour

Every country in the world except for the United States and the collapsed state Somali has ratified the Convention on the Rights of the Child and pledged to uphold its protections for children. In 1999, the convention stood as the single most widely ratified treaty in existence. Adopted by the United Nations General Assembly on November 20, 1989, the promises of this historic document included children's rights to life; to be free from discrimination; to be free from military recruitment and to be protected in armed conflicts; to be protected from torture or cruel, inhuman, or degrading treatment or punishment; to be free from arbitrary deprivation of liberty; to special treatment within the justice system; and the rights to education, health care, an adequate standard of living, and freedom from economic exploitation and other abuse.

Some significant advances on behalf of children marked the decade since the adoption of the Convention on the Rights of the Child. Many countries used the convention as the basis on which to revise domestic legislation and improve protections for children, or have appointed special ombudspersons or envoys for children. As the Committee on the Rights of the Child evaluated country reports under the convention, it developed new standards of protection and pressed governments for specific reforms.

A 1996 United Nations report on the impact of armed conflict on children raised international concern about the plight of children in war, prompting varied initiatives to end the use of child soldiers and other wartime abuses. The number of children killed every year by antipersonnel landmines dropped in the wake of massive efforts to end the use of the weapon and the adoption of the1997 Mine Ban Treaty. The adoption of the statute for the International Criminal Court held out the hope of ending the impunity of those responsible for the recruitment of children under the age of fifteen in armed conflicts, as well as those who commit other war crimes, crimes against humanity, and genocide.

However, despite these advances, the promises of the Convention on the Rights of the Child were broken for countless children around the world. The armed conflicts that raged in all quarters of the world produced appalling abuses of children's rights. Hundreds of thousands of children were pressed into service as soldiers. Millions became refugees displaced from their homes, often separated from their families, their future and safety uncertain.

Children living outside war zones were also subjected to routine violence. Street children on every continent endured harassment and physical abuse by police. Even schools, intended to promote the healthy development of children, were the site of abuse. In some countries, the use of corporal punishment by teachers resulted in injury and even death. In others, gay and lesbian students endured harassment and violence by their peers while school authorities failed to intervene.

Millions of children had no access to education, worked long hours under hazardous conditions, or languished in orphanages or detention centers where they endured inhuman conditions and daily assaults on their dignity, in violation of the rights guaranteed to them under the convention. The issues selected for attention below represent those which were the focus of Human Rights Watch investigation and advocacy over the past half-decade.

The tenth anniversary of the Convention on the Rights of the Child marked an important milestone. The rights of children were recognized as never before. But it also posed a challenge for governments and civil society to take stronger action to implement its provisions, strengthen protections, and fulfill the promises made to the children of the world.

The Use of Children as Soldiers

In dozens of countries around the world, children were direct participants in war. Denied a childhood and often subjected to horrific violence, some 300,000 children served as soldiers in current armed conflicts. These young combatants participated in all aspects of contemporary warfare. They wielded AK-47s and M-16s on the front lines of combat, served as human mine detectors, participated in suicide missions, carried supplies, and acted as spies, messengers, or lookouts.

Physically vulnerable and easily intimidated, children typically made obedient soldiers. Many were abducted or recruited by force and often compelled to follow orders under threat of death. Others joined armed groups out of desperation. As society broke down during conflict, leaving children with no access to school, driving them from their homes, or separating them from family members, many children perceived armed groups as their best chance for survival. Others sought escape from poverty or joined military forces to avenge family members who had been killed.

Child soldiers were used in more than thirty countries around the world. Human Rights Watch investigated the use of child soldiers in some of these conflicts, including in Angola, Colombia, the Democratic Republic of Congo, Lebanon, Liberia, Sierra Leone, Sri Lanka, Sudan and Uganda. In Sierra Leone, thousands of children abducted by rebel forces witnessed and participated in horrible atrocities against civilians, including beheadings, amputations, rape, and burning people alive. Children forced to take part in atrocities were often given drugs to overcome their fear or reluctance to do so. In Colombia, tens of thousands of children were used as soldiers by all sides to the country's ongoing bloody conflict. In southern Lebanon, when boys fled to desert or avoid conscription by the South Lebanon Army, an Israeli auxiliary militia, their entire families were subject to expulsion from the occupied zone.

Girls were also used as soldiers in many parts of the world. In addition to combat duties, Human Rights Watch found that girls were subject to sexual abuse and taken as "wives" by armed groups in Angola, Sierra Leone, and Uganda. Girls who were impregnated by rebel commanders were sometimes forced to strap their babies on their backs shortly after giving birth and take up arms against opposing forces.

Some governments took positive steps. Colombia significantly reduced the number of under-eighteen's in its national security forces after pledging to uphold a minimum recruitment age of eighteen. The Sierra Leonean government excluded under-eighteen's from its newly-formed military, based on pledges made to Olara Otunnu, the special representative for the secretary-general on armed conflict and children. The U.K. government made a military aid agreement to the Sierra Leonine government contingent on non-recruitment of children and the demobilization and rehabilitation of former child soldiers, although it continued to use sixteen-and seventeen-year-olds in its own military force. Other states, including the Czech Republic, Germany, Norway, Portugal, and South Africa, passed legislation or introduced measures to exclude under-eighteen's from their military forces.

Under the Convention on the Rights of the Child, the general definition of a child is any person under the age of eighteen. However, Article 38, governing children and armed conflict, uses fifteen as the minimum age for recruitment and participation in hostilities. This low standard of protection remained a glaring and troubling anomaly among the convention's other strong provisions.

Several years after the convention's adoption, a U.N. working group was created to draft an optional protocol to the convention that would raise the minimum age for recruitment and participation in hostilities to eighteen. However, as the tenth anniversary of the convention's adoption arrived, agreement on the optional protocol still had not been reached, largely because of opposition by governments who continued to recruit minors, notably the United States.

Despite these obstacles, efforts to stop the use of child soldiers continued to grow. In 1998, the recruitment of children under the age of fifteen and their use in hostilities was identified as a war crime in the statute of the International Criminal Court. Once established, the court will have jurisdiction to prosecute those responsible for the use of child soldiers. The use of children as soldiers was also recognized as a child labour issue. A labour treaty banning the worst forms of child labour, adopted in June 1999, prohibited the forced recruitment of children for use in armed conflicts.

In 1998, the Coalition to Stop the Use of Child Soldiers formed in order to campaign for a strong optional protocol to the Convention on the Rights of the Child which would prohibit any recruitment of children under the age of eighteen or their use in armed conflict. Established by six international NGOs, the coalition worked with national campaigns in more than thirty countries around the world, mobilizing political will and public pressure to end the use of children as soldiers. In addition to media campaigns, the publication of new research, and advocacy within regional and international fora, its activities included a series of high profile regional conferences focused on the use of children as soldiers in Africa, Latin America, and Europe. (See Special Issues and Campaigns.) Despite this growing momentum, efforts to stop the use of child soldier did not reach fruition. Recruitment of child soldiers continued around the world, those responsible for their recruitment escaped justice, and key governments continued to resist efforts to establish and enforce the prohibitions necessary to end the use of children as soldiers.

The International Criminal Court

On July 17, 1998, in Rome, delegates representing 160 countries voted by an overwhelming majority to establish a permanent International Criminal Court (ICC) to try persons charged with committing war crimes, crimes against humanity, and genocide. Upon its establishment, the court will provide a powerful deterrent to the conscription, enlistment, or use in hostilities of children under the age of fifteen years conduct defined as a war crime in the ICC statute. The statute also included other important measures to protect children in armed conflict: it recognized intentional attacks on educational institutions as a war crime, provided special arrangements for children as victims and witnesses, and exempted children below the age of eighteen from prosecution by the court.

Delegates reconvened at the United Nations headquarters for three weeks in July and August of 1999 to draft the rules of procedure and evidence for the court and the elements of the crimes covered by the statute. (See Special Issues and Campaigns). Two proposals introduced by the United States and by Costa Rica, Switzerland, and Hungary would have restricted the scope of the statute's provisions on the war crime of conscripting, enlisting, or using children in hostilities. The U.S. proposal would have required the prosecutor to prove that the accused knew the child in question was below the age of fifteen. The proposal by Costa Rica, Switzerland, and Hungary would have required a showing that the accused knew of or was "willfully blind" to the child's minority. In addition, both proposals would have required proof that the accused caused the child's conscription, enlistment, or use in hostilities.

Human Rights Watch said that the court should have jurisdiction over cases in which the accused recklessly failed to take steps to ascertain the child's age. Such a position, we argued, would be consistent with Protocol I. Additional to the Geneva Conventions, which requires states to "take all feasible measures" to ensure that children under the age of fifteen do not take an active part in hostilities. Human Rights Watch also pointed out that encouragement, acceptance, or authorization of a child's enlistment or participation in hostilities should be sufficient conduct for the court to exercise jurisdiction.

A subsequent discussion paper, produced by the coordinator of the delegates' working group on the element of crimes, reflected these recommendations. It required prosecutors to show that the accused "knew or should have known" that the child in question was under the age of fifteen years phrasing that recognizes an obligation to attempt to determine the child's age. The discussion paper did not reflect a consensus among delegates, and was introduced to provide a basis for further discussion. It nevertheless reflected an awareness that the court must have adequate discretion to interpret the statute's language for the benefit of children in armed conflict.

Refugee Children

Refugee children were among the most vulnerable children in the world. Not only had they suffered from war or other forms of persecution in their countries of origin, but many refugee children continued to suffer human rights abuses in countries of asylum. Children made up more than half of all refugees around the world, yet their rights and special protection needs as children were frequently neglected.

The human rights abuses that drove children into flight were only the first chapter of hardship for many refugee children. Even after travelling across an international border to seek refuge, they remained vulnerable to hazardous labour exploitation, physical abuse, denial of education, sexual violence and exploitation, cross-border attacks, militarization of refugee camps, and recruitment as child soldiers.

Article 22 of the Convention on the Rights of the Child grants special protection to refugee children. Children who are not being cared for by their parents, known as "separated children," are entitled to special protections under Articles 20 and 22. Refugee children fleeing war are also entitled to special protection under Article 38 of the convention, as children affected by armed conflict. Refugee children, like all children, are entitled to all other rights granted under the convention including the rights to life, physical integrity, adequate food and medical care, education, and to be free from discrimination, exploitation, and abuse.

Separated and unaccompanied children were particularly vulnerable. In the United States, Human Rights Watch found that unaccompanied children were held by the U.S. Immigration and Naturalization Service in detention facilities where some were confined for lengthy periods of time before being released to family members or appropriate guardians. Rarely understanding what was happening to them, children were often denied information about their detention and their right to be represented by an attorney in immigration proceedings in a language they understood. In some cases they were housed with juvenile offenders and subjected to a rigid and punitive environment.

In 1999, Human Rights Watch conducted an in-depth investigation into the protection of Sierra Leonean refugee children in Guinea, where children made up 65 percent of the 300,000 Sierra Leonean refugees there. Most of the children interviewed by Human Rights Watch had been in refugee camps in Guinea just over a year, with little hope of returning home in the near future. Internally displaced children within Sierra Leone were thought to suffer many of the same problems on an even larger scale.

The plight of separated children and girls in the Guinean refugee camps was found to be particularly severe and warranted special attention. Separated children were taken in by families along the way, while fleeing, or in the camps. These families acted as care givers, or foster families. However, some children in such care were neglected, physically or sexually abused, denied food, denied education, or exploited for their labour. Social workers charged with protection of separated children in the refugee camps in Guinea had not even identified most children of concern, much less monitored their care and protection.

Human Rights Watch found that Sierra Leonean refugee girls as young as twelve felt they had no choice but to work as child prostitutes in order to support themselves and, in some cases, their families. These girls had little or no access to education or health care and little hope for their future. Better identification and monitoring systems were clearly needed to ensure effective interventions.

Refugee children who lived in camps close to the porous Sierra Leone-Guinea border were vulnerable to cross border armed raids which resulted in murder, mutilation, and abduction of dozens of refugees over the past year.

According to international law and standards, as well as United Nations High Commissioner for Refugees (UNHCR) policy, the refugees should not have been in camps located dangerously close to the border in the first place. Refugee children were also at risk of being recruited and used as child soldiers. In Guinea, Sierra Leonean refugee children as young as seven risked being abducted by raiding rebel forces or being used by the government civil defense forces, known as Kamajors.

Despite the fact that these children suffered enormously and remained extremely vulnerable, their plight was largely ignored by the international community. UNHCR faced substantial political, financial, and logistical challenges in protecting the human rights of refugee children in Guinea. The focus of international attention on refugee crises in Europe, as well as "donor fatigue" with respect to African refugees, served to limit resources available for Guinea. One manifestation of this was a grossly insufficient number of staff present inside or near camps. UNHCR also faced severe logistical constraints in the Gueckedou area of Guinea, which housed more than sixty camps. One was the poor state of the unpaved roads, which were often impassable during Guinea's June to November rainy season. However, the failure to adequately protect the rights of refugee children was only partially attributable to a lack of resources.

Although UNHCR had used the Convention on the Rights of the Child as the basis for extensive policies and guidelines designed to protect the rights of refugee children, in many cases these policies were not implemented. For Sierra Leonean children in Guinea, the international community failed to identify vulnerable children; to monitor for abuse and labour exploitation; to protect girls from sexual abuse and exploitation; to move the refugees to safe locations away from the border; to preserve the humanitarian character of the refugee camps; and to prevent refugee children from serving as child soldiers.

Police Abuse and Arbitrary Detention of Street Children

Attention to street children focused largely on their pressing economic and social plight poverty, lack of shelter, denial of education, AIDS, prostitution, and substance abuse. With the exception of mass killings of street children in Brazil and Colombia, little attention was paid to the police violence and abuse inflicted on these children, or their treatment within the justice system through which they regularly passed. Civil and political rights violations against street children were largely overlooked, symptomatic of the larger failure to take seriously the full scope of children's rights enshrined in the Convention on the Rights of the Child.

Viewed as "anti-social" or criminal elements, or a scourge on a city's tourist-filled streets and business districts, many police and ordinary citizens simply wished street children would disappear, by whatever means. Street children throughout the world were subjected to routine harassment and physical abuse by police, government, and private security forces, out to wipe the streets clean of a perceived social blight. Street children faced extortion, theft, severe beatings, mutilation, sexual abuse, and even death.

They were often arrested and jailed because of their homelessness (on vague grounds such as vagrancy or loitering) or their involvement in small businesses deemed to be illegal, such as unlicensed hawking, or were accused of petty theft, drug-related crimes, or prostitution. Some were arrested as scapegoats, or in order to finger or catch others. Many police believed street children had information about crimes committed on their beat, or attributed crimes in the area to them directly, imputing criminal associations and activities to the children generally.

They were held for excessive periods of time in police lockups, for days and even weeks, usually mixed with adults. In jails they were sometimes further beaten by police, or forced to pay bribes in order to be released. Girls were sometimes coerced into providing sexual services to police in exchange for release, or were raped. From jails, street children were transferred eventually to long-term penal institutions, sometimes euphemistically called "homes" or "schools" where they languished out of sight, for years.

Few advocates spoke up for these children, let alone lawyers or prosecutors, and street children rarely had family members or other concerned adults able to intervene on their behalf. Often, family members were not informed of their children's arrest and detention in the first place. Contrary to popular belief, many street children actually had family members and homes to which they returned periodically, and were not orphans.

Over the years, Human Rights Watch had attempted to highlight the serious nature of the human rights abuses committed against street children by law enforcement personnel in Brazil, Bulgaria, Colombia, Guatemala, India, Kenya, and Sudan, and on the gross lack of police accountability for abusive actions. Widespread impunity and the slowness of law enforcement bodies to investigate and prosecute cases of abuses against street children allowed violence against street children to continue unchecked.

Even in Guatemala, where the NGO Casa Alianza had been singularly active in seeking police accountability for the rape, torture, and killing of street children, only a handful of prosecutions resulted out of hundreds of criminal complaints filed. Frustrated with the failure of the national judicial system to address these cases, Casa Alianza and the Center for Justice and

International Law brought a landmark case involving the police killings of five street youth in 1990 to the Inter-American Commission on Human Rights and subsequently to the Inter-American Court of Human Rights, where the case was pending at the time of this writing. Still, violence against street children in Guatemala continued and the government was as slow as ever in responding to the abuse.

The case of Guatemala demonstrated that even where there were strong advocates willing and able to assist street children in seeking justice, without the commitment of governments, the judiciary, and most importantly law enforcement itself, the abuses would continue.

Children in Conflict with the Law

In the ten years following the adoption and near-universal ratification of the Convention on the Rights of the Child, a growing number of countries modified their juvenile justice laws to guarantee children the rights set forth in the convention and in other international instruments.

This trend was most evident in Latin America, where many countries enacted reforms to bring their legislation into compliance with the convention. Brazil, one of the first to reform its national laws comprehensively in response to the Convention on the Rights of the Child, adopted its Children's and Adolescent's Statute in 1990. Ecuador and Peru passed Juveniles Acts in 1992, Mexico adopted its Law on the Treatment of Juvenile Offenders in 1991, El Salvador enacted a new juvenile justice law in 1995, and Nicaragua adopted a Children's Legal Code in 1998 after a two-year delay Grounded in the principle that all children possessed rights which must be respected by the state, these reform efforts represented a significant departure from earlier legislation directed exclusively at "minors" in "irregular situations" and in need of protection.

In other countries, reforms were under consideration but had not yet been enacted into law. Efforts to reform Guatemala's juvenile justice system stalled in early 1998, when the government delayed for the second time the implementation of a new Minors' Code that would represent a vast improvement over current legislation. Among other protections, the code would guarantee the right to a lawyer at government expense to children accused of crimes, would forbid placing children in protective custody in juvenile detention centers, and would end the practice of imprisoning children for "status offenses" such as running away or being homeless. A similar proposal was pending in Venezuela.

Nevertheless, a large number of countries in the region and elsewhere in the world had not taken action to bring their legislation into compliance with the convention. In the Americas, Argentina and Paraguay, among others, retained outdated juvenile laws that did not adequately protect children's rights; in Colombia, the 1989 Juveniles Act was little more than a repackaging of earlier legislation.

Where legislative reforms had taken place, the practices in many countries fell far short of their new legal standards. In Mexico, as the U.N. Committee on the Rights of the Child observed in 1994, a large number of children complained of ill-treatment at the hands of police and military personnel. In Nicaragua, although the law provided that children should be housed separately from adults, children continued to be commingled with adults because of the lack of appropriate juvenile facilities. In the Dominican Republic, the government's near-complete failure to enforce the country's 1994 minor's code led to the confinement of hundreds of adolescents in adult prisons, where youth were not afforded sufficient protection, education, or rehabilitation.

Trial and Sentencing Practices

Far too often, children around the world were brought to trial and sentenced in ways that volated their rights. Human Rights Watch documented systemic failures to guarantee children legal representation and otherwise provide them with fair hearings in Brazil, Bulgaria, Guatemala, India, Jamaica, Kenya, Pakistan, and Russia. Of particular concern were sentences that violated the International principle that deprivation of liberty should be a measure of last resort and for the shortest appropriate period of time and prohibiting measures that constituted torture or cruel, inhuman, or degrading treatment.

In many cases, children were detained arbitrarily or indefinitely on the basis of vague legalprovisions. In Kenya, Human Rights Watch's investigation found that street children were committed for years to juvenile correctional institutions after they were found to be "in need of protection or discipline" in summary proceedings without legal representation. Similarly, in Paraguay and other countries in the Americas that had not brought their laws into conformity with the Convention on the Rights of the Child, children were detained on the ill-defined basis that they were in a "state of danger."

In other instances, state authorities simply flouted laws intended to protect the due process rights of juveniles. Our 1996 investigation of Bulgaria found that children were often detained in police lockups far longer than the legally permissible periods, without being formally charged, and without any judicial review. In India, we found that police regularly detained street children without giving them any grounds for arrest and failed to bring them before magistrates in the time period required under India's Juvenile Justice Act. In a

1999 investigation of police practices in Russia, adolescents in various cities told Human Rights Watch that police routinely violated Russian law and international standards by interrogating them sometimes under torture in the absence of attorneys.

In Jamaica, Trinidad and Tobago, and elsewhere in the English-speaking Caribbean, juvenile court judges were authorized to impose sentences of flogging for certain crimes. In addition, children in detention in these countries were subjected to corporal punishment as a method of discipline. Similarly, Pakistan's Hudood Ordinances permitted judges to include whipping, usually between fifteen and thirty lashes, as part of children's sentences; in practice, however, that portion of the sentence appeared to be routinely overturned on appeal. In Kenya too, corporal punishment by cane or rod is authorized by law in sentencing children and as a disciplinary measure in correctional institutions for children. The imposition of corporal punishment is prohibited by international standards. Moreover, the U.N. bodies charged with monitoring states parties' compliance with the International Covenant on Civil and Political Rights, the Convention against Torture and Other Cruel, Inhuman or Degrading Treatment or Punishment, and the Convention on the Rights of the Child have all indicated that corporal punishment is incompatible with those human rights treaties.

Conditions of Confinement

Throughout the world, children were subjected to appalling conditions of confinement that violated international standards. Often held with adults and subjected to beatings at the hands of guards and other detainees, children in confinement were frequently denied adequate food, medical and mental health care, education, and access to basic sanitary facilities. All of these children would eventually return to society, meaning that the failure to prepare them for their return was shortsighted as well as cruel, carrying enormous social costs.

The practice of holding children in adult facilities, common in many parts of the world, exposed children to abusive conditions including physical and sexual abuse far worse than those they would have experienced in juvenile facilities. In Cambodia, for example, children were housed indiscriminately with adult detainees and reportedly sexually abused and subjected to other forms of physical and psychological violence at the hands of adults. In Guatemala, Human Rights Watch interviewed children commingled with adults who reported beatings and rapes by adults, and being forced to give up their clothing to adults, or to pay money to adults in order to get a place to sleep.

The United States continued to incarcerate large numbers of children in response to a perceived upsurge in violent juvenile crime. In fact, the number of juvenile offenders consistently fell from 1994 to 1997; according to U.S. Federal Bureau of Investigation data, juvenile arrests declined each year, with an overall decrease of nearly 4 percent for the period. Juvenile arrests for violent crimes were down by 6 percent during the same time period.

Many youth in the United States were charged in the adult criminal system under state laws that made it easier for children to be tried as adults. Between 1992 and 1998, at least forty U.S. states adopted such legislation. A similar measure was pending at the federal level in 1999. Forty-two U.S. states detained youth in adult jails while they awaited trial. As a result, whether or not they would ultimately be found innocent, many children faced the prospect of spending six months to one year or more of their formative adolescent years behind bars pending trial.

In the U.S. state of Maryland, Human Rights Watch found that youth held in adult jails were subjected to the risk of violence at the hands of other juveniles and, in some facilities, from adult detainees. These risks were particularly high in the Baltimore City Detention Center, where some 150 adolescents faced daily risks to their personal safety, at times from fights condoned or even organized by corrections officers. Disciplinary measures there often appeared to be arbitrary and excessive, with many youth, and sometimes the entire juvenile section, receiving the maximum sanction of ninety days confinement to their cells. With few exceptions, the Maryland jails visited by Human Rights Watch suffered from serious deficiencies in the amount of education provided, a dearth of age-appropriate recreational activities, and an apparent lack of specialized training programs for staff in adolescent development and behavior management. In addition, children in all facilities reported that they did not receive enough to eat.

Commendably, some countries took positive steps to acknowledge and correct abusive conditions of confinement. The South African government initiated a program in November 1997 to keep children out of the country's prisons, although delays in implementing the program threatened its effectiveness. Another deficiency in the program was that children between the ages of fifteen and eighteen who were accused of the most serious crimes would remain in adult prisons. In Bangladesh, the government accepted the need for improvements in conditions of confinement for children in conflict with the law, in particular noting in its 1997 supplementary report to the Committee on the Rights of the Child that "Too many minors are held in jails and police stations alongside adult offenders." In Jamaica, following the July 1999 release of the findings of a Human Rights Watch investigation of the practice of detaining children in filthy and overcrowded police lockups, the government announced that it would move all detained children to juvenile facilities.

The Death Penalty and Juvenile Offenders

The Convention on the Rights of the Child unequivocally prohibits the use of the death penalty on juvenile offenders, those who were under the age of eighteen at the time of their crimes. Nevertheless, six countries-Iran, Nigeria, Pakistan, Saudi Arabia, the United States, and Yemen are known to have executed juvenile offenders in the 1990s.

The ten executions of juvenile offenders in the United States during this period represented more than half the known worldwide total, making it the worldwide leader in executing juvenile offenders. Five executions took place in the U.S. state of Texas; the states of Georgia, Louisiana, Missouri, Oklahoma, and Virginia each executed one juvenile offender in the same period. Sean Sellers, executed in Oklahoma in February 1999, was the first sixteen-year-old offender to be put to death in the United States in forty years. Seventy juvenile offenders were on death row in the United States as of July 1, 1999.

In positive developments, the highest court of the U.S. state of Florida ruled that the imposition of the death penalty on sixteen-year-old offenders was cruel and unusual punishment in violation of the state constitution; and effective October 1, 1999, the state of Montana abolished the death penalty for those under eighteen at the time of their crimes. As a result, nineteen of the forty U.S. states that permit capital punishment now prohibit the execution of offenders who were sixteen years old and younger at the time of their crimes; fifteen of the remaining twenty-one states restrict that punishment to adult offenders.

Orphans and Abandoned Children

Throughout the world an unknown number of children, most likely in the hundreds of thousands, if not millions, were kept in orphanages and non-penal custodial institutions. Many were condemned to live a grim existence, and subjected to shocking and at times deadly levels of abuse and neglect.

Many children who ended up in orphanages had at least one living parent but had been abandoned because their families were poor, jobless, ill, or in trouble with the law. In countries that had restrictive population control policies, or where cultural traditions valued boys more highly than girls, babies and girls in particular were abandoned. In other cases, medical personnel pressured parents at birth to give up children born with disabilities, claiming that parents would be ostracized for raising a disabled child. For this reason, healthy children who were given up for financial or domestic reasons were often assumed to be "defective."

In Russia, children were abandoned to the state at a rate of more than 100,000 per year. In a 1998 report, Abandoned by the State: Cruelty and Neglect in Russian Orphanages , Human Rights Watch found that children in Russian orphanages were exposed to appalling levels of cruelty and neglect. They were beaten, locked in freezing rooms for days at a time, or sexually abused, and often subjected to degrading treatment by staff.

Russian babies classified as "disabled" were segregated into separate rooms where they were changed and fed, but were bereft of stimulation and without medical care. At age four, these and other children faced another grave violation of their rights: those labeled retarded or "oligophrenic" ("small-brained") were sent to locked and isolated "psycho-neurological internats," which were little better than prisons.Considered "ineducable," children in these facilities were restrained in cloth sacks, tethered to furniture, denied stimulation, and sometimes left to lie half-naked in their own filth. Orphans who survived to the age of eighteen moved on to an adult internat, removed from public view.

Russian orphans who were not categorized as disabled grow up in Dickensian-like institutions where they suffered ill-treatment at the hands of staff and older children within the institutions. In the orphanages, children were physically punished not only by school staff, but by older children who were encouraged to beat up, bully, and intimidate younger ones. The use of cruel, inhuman and degrading treatment and punishment, including corporal punishment, public shaming, and isolation in freezing rooms was not uncommon. Children had no means of redress or complaint to protest ill-treatment and abuse at the hands of staff and older children.

Shocking abuses were also documented in Chinese orphanages, where infants suffered staggering mortality rates. Deprived of adequate food and basic medical care, orphans admitted into welfare institutions in 1989 faced less than a 50 percent chance of surviving for more than one year. Many institutions appeared to operate as little more than assembly lines for the elimination of unwanted orphans (especially girls), with an annual turnover of admissions and deaths far exceeding the number of beds available. At some facilities, the rate of death reached 90 percent.

In Romania, Human Rights Watch found in 1990 that doctors who were forbidden to acquire medical information from outside the country carried out blood transfusions in a misguided attempt to improve the health of institutionalized orphans. Large numbers of children contracted HIV as a result. Children also suffered from inadequate food, housing, clothing, medical care, lack of stimulation or education, and neglect.

As these conditions came to light, the international community responded. In the past decade, the European Union provided more than (U.S.) $75 million to improve the plight of abandoned Romanian children. Funds were directed not only towards emergency food, clothing, and medical care but also toward creating and implementing policies to prevent child abandonment. In 1999, the United States Agency for International Development developed a program to channel (U.S.) $6 million to Russian organizations working to keep families together and further develop foster care and alternatives to institutional care for orphans and abandoned children. In China, staffing and medical care in orphanages improved, and the government worked to encourage adoption of abandoned children. Despite these encouraging developments, orphans and abandoned children continued to be institutionalized at alarming rates and too often failed to receive adequate care and protection.

Finally, while numerous international standards exist which protected the rights of children confined in penal or correctional institutions and settings, no comparable international standards exist to protect the rights of abandoned or orphaned children. Human Rights Watch advocated the use of alternatives to institutionalization of children wherever possible, including support for families or extended families, and foster care, with placement in small residential care facilities as a measure of last resort.

The Indian Context

In ancient India it was one of the responsibility of the King to provide education to his people. During that time, child labour was exist only in the form of 'child slaves'. Children some times even less than 8 yeas of age, were purchased to do so-called low and dishonourable work Further, during that time, parents were considering the early involvement of their children in the family occupation/s is one part of socialization. So, children were helping their parents in their household work and other traditional activities. They had to learn the skills by observing and participating in such activities.

If we go through the different phases of the Indian history, we can classify the people in two distinct classes; 1 Haves and 2 Havenots. These two types of classes gradually emerged in the society due to the different administrative procedures adopted by many then Indian Kings/Rulers. In the medieval Indian history, it is evidenced that large acres of land were given as a gift to honor courtiers and to other people who had done remarkable achievements in Art, Literature, and Music. Gradually increasing pressure on land led to fragmentation of holdings. Growing families had to look beyond personal cultivation for subsistence. This is the point where large section of landless people emerged in Indian society often bonded to the large landowners. This landless families used their children to help in their economic activities.The rural artisan rarely worked alone. In fact, the entire family was a work unit with the 'pater family" being the master crafts man occupations were determined largely on the basis of heredity, and children were introduced to the traditional craft at a young age. (Shandilya and Khan, 2003)

In the first part of 17 the century, the most significant change was the growth of different organizations involving the employment of large number of Artisans. The Dutch silk factory in Bengal was employed 700-800 hundred weavers. But the characteristic unit of production was still the small one. 'The persistent dominance of family based work units indicates that any disciplined organization of an industrial society was not in sight". (Irfan, 1981).

In mid 19th century, many European owned industries entered to India. They invested a lot of money on coffee tea, indigo and jute. In this point Handy crafts business gradually started to disappear. Later on, cotton, jute industry and coal mining were started in an organised way. Due to the Industrial revolution in early 19th century, more are less Indian agriculture system become mechanized. Number of different factories were increased. Small landholders stared to work as farm labourers on bigger forms as; small land holdings were no longer economically viable by that time. As factories increased in number they started to hire children because of cheap labour force. No demand for more wage, long hours of work for less wage, easy to disciplined were the main reasons behind hiring the children. A considerable amount of children were employed in India particularly in cotton and jute mills in last phase of 19th century. Between 1891 and 1923 the number of children employed in factories increased from 18,880 to 74,290.i.e., an increase of 25%. (Indian labour Year Book, 1953-1954, p, 96.).

In 1919, Inter National Labour Organization (ILO) was set up and it gave an effective guidelines to improve the working condition of children across the globe and ordered to ban on hiring children before the age of fourteen. The percentage of children to total number of workers employed in factories, however, had already begun declining in 1923 and between 1923 to 1955 the decline was not only relative but also absolute. After the Independence, the Indian Constitution has given a lot of constitutional security to the children against various forms of exploitations. In 1986, the Government of India enacted a new Child Labour (Prohibition and Regulation) Act. And National Policy on Child Labour was framed in 1987. A MoU was also signed with ILO. India is also a signatory for the UN Convention on the Right of Child (CRC). In India, International Programme on the Elimination of Child

Labour (IPEC) was established in 1992 with an objective to enhance the capacity of ILO constituents and NGOs to design, implement and social mobilization for securing child labour elimination programmes. The National Authority for the Elimination of the Child Labour was also constituted in 1994. As per the constitutional provisions and new legislative Acts of Government of India, the Government of Karnataka has implemented an Action Plan to make the State as a child labour free state by 2007.

Concept of the Child Labour

The term 'Child Labour' means different things in different societies. A universally accepted definition of child labour is not available. A distinction is often made between child work and child labour. 'Child Work' refers to occasional light work done by children, which in most of the societies is considered to be an integral part of the child's socialization process. While helping parents at home and in family farms, children learn to take responsibility and pride in their own activities acquire certain skills and prepare themselves for the tasks of future adulthood.

'Child Labour' implies something different in which young people are being exploited, or overworked or deprived of their rights to health, education or just to childhood. It impairs their health, their overall physical, mental and social growth. The distinction between both child work and child labour may Be briefly stated as follows;

Child Work

Light work [children learn to take responsibilities]

Respect of Children's right to health & education

- Occasional and legal

Child Labour

- Hard & hazardous work, exploitation
- Deprivation of rights to health & education
- Constant, long hours and Illegal
- Basically to earn some money

Definition of the Child Labour

The measurement of child labour depends, of course, on how it is defined. Ethical and Cultural views influence this in turn. Some analysis, activists and groups take the position that all non-school, non-leisure activates of children constitute child labour. This includes light work after school in household's enterprises or help in domestic work such as house cleaning and watching siblings etc. Others count only full time employment in economic activities by children or focus on bad Child labours, such as child prostitution, scavenging, or backbreaking work in quarries in mines. Like wise, the concept of child differs greatly across societies and cultural settings. In many western countries, chronological age is the sole criteria to define child labour. But in other societies, "cultural and social factors play a vital role as well, and whether a young person is considered a child depends more on social responsibilities than physical age". (Rodgers and Standing, 1981). In many societies, a Ten – year-old child, whose work makes a major contributions to the household income will no longer be considered a child. Hence, the empirical analysis of child labour and the derivation of policy conclusions must be sensitive to the cultural and social setting. ("The Paradox of Anthropology and Child labour", The American Anthropological Review, 1996).

So it is clear that concept of child labour is not as simple and straightforward as it may appear. Urban folk can be defined childhood in terms of age, but the different societies may have different age threshold for demarcating childhood and adulthood. In some societies, age may not be sufficient basis for defining childhood. The fulfillment of certain social rights and traditional obligations is very important requirements in defining adult and child status. In still others, the integration of children in to socio economic life may begin so early and the transition from childhood and adulthood may be so smooth and gradual that it may be virtually impossible to identify clearly the different life phases. (Whoodhead, 1999).

The term 'children labour' is a convenient expression for "the labour of children", has a well recognized though rather vague meaning. Child labour is, at times, used as a synonym for 'employed child' or 'working child'. In this sense it is coextensive with any work done by a child for gain. Homer Folks, the Chairman of the United States National child Labour committee, defined child labour 'any work by children that interferes with their full physical development, their opportunities for a desirable minimum of education or their needed recreation'. Our former President V.V. Giri has distinguished two senses of the term child labour. The term 'child labour' is commonly interpreted in two different ways: First as an economic practice and secondly, as a social evil. In the first context, it signifies employment of children in gain full occupations with a view to adding to the labour income of the family. It is in the second context labour is now more generally used. In assessing the nature and extent of the social evil, it is necessary to take into account the character of the job on which the children are engaged, the dangers to which they are exposed and the opportunities of development which they have been denied.

The above statements clearly shows that, the conceptualization of the 'child status' leads to ambiguity, as it is guided by the individual considerations. So, a set standard has to be accepted to determine an age-range for defining a child or childhood. The Indian Factory Act of 1948, which is an elabourate and highly specific Act relating to child labour, make use of 3 different concepts to classify the workers, i.e., a 'child', a 'young person' or an 'adolescent' and an 'adult'. It has been made explicit in this Act that a person below the age of 15 years is to be regarded as a child. (Khan, 2003). We can say, 'any physical labour undertaken by a child of below 15 years either under compulsion or pressure or voluntarily in an organized or unorganized sector qualifies to be called as child labour'. However, International community recognizes all the children below 18 are child laboures. Recently a lot of NGOs are demanding the Government to follow these international guidelines in India too.

Child labour refers to working of children in gainful occupations away from their family in return for wages. (Gore, 1968). But it is important to distinguish this concept of child labour from the concept of it, which is prevalent in rural and urban areas. In rural area children will participate in family occupation as a part of socialization process to augment family income. Dasguptha (1977) writes "legitimacy to the latter concept of child labour by describing working children as 'intermittent workers' who supplement the adults' income as a regular component of the labour force". Stein (1980), while studying the south Indian agrarian family recognizes the importance of the multi dimensional aspect of a long apprenticeship which younger members of the peasant family under go under the tutelage of their elders. "Child" in terms of his chronological age, and 'labour' i.e., terms of its nature, quantum and income generation capacity. So child labour, however, can broadly be defined as the segment of the child populations which participates in work either paid and unpaid (Kumar and Khan,2003).

The world child labour has been differently defined in various studies. According to the Sen committee (1981), Child labour, however, can broadly be defined as that segment of child population in work either paid or unpaid. In the study of working of children in Bombay. Singh (1991) and others have held a view that 'child labour means a working child who is between 6 and 15 years of age, is not attending school during the day, is working under an employer or learning some trade as an apprentice'. In the study conducted by the Indian Council of Child Welfare (ICCW) in Delhi opines, 'every child below 14 years, who contributed to the family income or treated, as a full-time/ part- time worker is a child labourer'.

According to the UNICEF, it is every important to distinguish between work that is beneficial and work that is intolerable-and to recognize that much chunked work falls into the Grey area between these two extremes. Therefore it believes that child labour is exploitative, if it involves;

(a) Full-time work at an early age;
(b) Too many hours spent working;
(c) Work that exerts undue physical, social or psychological stress;
(d) Work and life on the streets in bad conditions;
(e) Inadequate pays;
(f) Too much responsibility;
(g) Work that hamper access to education
(h) Work that undermines children's dignity and self esteem such as slavery or bonded labour and sexual exploitations;
(i) Work that is detrimental to full social and psychological development.

The term child labour is generally used to refer "any work by children that interface with them in their full physical development, the opportunities for a desirable minimum of education and of their needed recreation. Children aged between 5 to 14 doing work on family farms or in factories or out side home for wages constitute child labour" (Stein and Davis, 1979). The diversity of opinion among researchers in defining child labour is due to differences in social perceptions.

Francis Blanchard, the Director General of the international Labour Organization states that 'a first problem is one of definition inherent in the notions of 'child work' and 'labour'. The most suitable and common definition of child labour is as follows; Child Labour can be conceived to include children under the age of 15 years in work or employment with the aim of earning a livelihood for themselves or for their families.

Census of India has modified the definition of workers and non-worker from one Census to another in enumerating child and adult workers. The reference paired in which a person is considered as worker or non-worker has also changed from time to time. Fortunately, in 1971 and 1981 Census, definitions of worker and non-workers have almost remained the same. These various Census report gives the concept about main activity i.e., 'on the economically productive pursuits in which worker engaged his or herself for most part of the time'. Further, "as for seasonal work is concerned, such as agriculture and ancillary work/activity of a person was defined with reference of his/ her work during the year preceeding the enumeration". Further, if a person participated in economically productive work, not as a main activity, persons attending household duties, beggars, etc. were not treated as workers (Various Census Reports) ILO s recent definition is a sort of restricted use of the term because according to it, unless the labour interferes with the growth of the child, it may be leveled as child labour. The problem with such definition is the question of defining as to when the labour interferes with the physical development or restricts opportunities?. This question may be a culture specific. Such definition shares the basic philosophy that child labour is bad and that it denies the inherent dignity of human being. Social scientists who define child labour in this sense (infact, most of the studies on child labour in India share this view) highlight more on the character of the jobs. This is not to claim that such studies serve no purpose but the author contention is that any pre-conception on the part of social scientist prevents him/her from looking at the phenomenon objectively. (ILO,1986).

Kulshreshtha is the view that child labour in a restricted sense means the employment of child in gainful occupations, which are dangerous to their health and them the opportunities of development. The term child labour not only applies to the children working in the industries but also to the children in all forms of non-industrial occupation which are injurious to their physical mental, moral and social social development According to Al N Sharma, 'child labour means the employment if children in gainful occupations (in industrial as well as non-industrial occupations) which are injurious to their physical, mental, moral and social development'. (Thus, the term includes wage labour as well as self-employed children working independently as well as in family enterprises. Child labour thus can be defined as any work undertaken by children below the age of 15 years in such works which are injurious to their health, and harmful to their proper full physical, mental, moral and social development (Pati , 2001).

The above description shows that age is an important criterion for distinguishing child labour. The Operation Research Group based in Borada defines child labour as 'A working child is one was enumerated during the survey as a child falling within the 5-15 age group and who is at remunerative work, may be paid or unpaid and busy in any our of the day within or outside of the family'.

In India, many labour Acts have fixed the minimum age of employment. But the definition of a child in terms of age differs from Act to Act: The Factories Act prohibits employment of children below the age of 14 in factories. The limit in Mines Act is 15 years, whereas it is 12 in plantation Labour Act. The Child Labour (Prohibition and Regulation) Act, 1986, defines ' child' as a person who has not completed his fourteenth year of age.

Article 24 of the Constitution of India states. " No child below the age of 14 years shall be employed to work in any factory or mines or engaged in any other hazardous employment." Thus, one may broadly say that a child means a person who has not completed his fourteenth year of age.

The term 'work' and labour'have been used interchangeable and synonymously, although a studious critic discerns a semantic difference that has existed throughout. Differentiating work and labour is determined by the particular social context, the quality of the various interactions and dynamics present in the production process. Both labour and work are born out of the ubiquitous human need to survive and much of the ambiguity that exists centers around this commonality. Both labour and work are organised human responses to design ways of securing resources and satisfying human needs for substenance

'Work' is a process which intrinsic to life at all levels, be it plant, animal or human. Since, living organisms are not self-contained, from the every moment of their existence they engage in interactions and exchanges with the larger world around them. Any process aimed at bridging the gap between needs originating in an organism and resources in the organism's environment satisfying these needs may be termed "work". Therefore, work is a natural process. Work insures survival and to cease to work is to cease to live. The emergence of the caste system in India is an example of social stratification determined by occupational stratification. Work in this system is assigned status, with each status being imputed higher or lower, superior or inferior valuations. The original nature of work has undergone a change so that today it is difficult to distinguish between work and labour(UNISEF,2001).

When individuals are engaged in the production process, not primarily to meet their psychological and physiological needs, but to meet the profit-motivated needs of the employer, the process they are engaged in may be called "Labour". Work becomes labour when the individual's capacity to produce a surplus beyond the value of her means of existence is capitalized upon be the employer. Labour denies the producer an opportunity for Self-direction and control (Prasaad, 2001).

Nowadays child labour is a widespread phenomenon. It is not only confined work on family farms or in traditional family jobs and occupations, but it has also extended to other fields. They work in agriculture and allied activities, unorganised small-scale sector and even in organised industries. The notion of child labour is intended to cover children under the age of 15 engaged in work or employment with the aim of earning a livelihood for themselves or for their family or themselves directly or indirectly at the cost of their physical, mental or social development". Thus the term child labour not only applies to the Children working in industries but also to the children working in all forms of non-industrial occupations which are injurious to their physical, mental, moral and social development.

It is has observed that "defining it as that of a child whom deprives the definition of child labour or child work by defining it as that of a child whom of the right to reduction and childhood. The child population can be grouped in to three categories: 1 school going children 2 child labour and 3 nowhere children. The last category of nowhere children forms about 35 per cent and they are potential child labourers. So, the dimensions of the problem should include not only the category of child labour but also the category of nowhere children" (Mahendra, 2001).

In the Indian context, there has been a tendency to formulate the definition of child labour rather loosely. Even in the latest Labour Commission Report (2001), all working children are taken as one hardly differentiated category. It also includes all the children who are out-of-school. Burra (1999) advocate that: a child labouer is "basically a child who is deprived of the right to education and childhood. What makes her definition important is that it makes it unambiguously clear that all out-of – children are working children in one form or another. The nowhere children are stated to be potential Child labourers. And are assumed to be staying home away from school so that they can take over some of the household duties of the parents and allow the latter to go out of and work. According to this redefinition, India has around 100 million child labourers.

These ten millions of children are deprived children, no doubt, but it is unwarranted to classify this childhood time as 'child labour'. One does not have to look for causes as to why they are workers (and what can be done about it), but at reasons why they are not in school (and what can be done about it). The casual factors behind child labour and behind non-enrolment of school dropout are different and should be analytically separated. Analytical clarity is not merely an academic circus. It is "closely related to the pattern of solution to any specific problem. Child labour is an aberration that is to be eliminated forthwith. Scrambling all forms of deprived child hood into one category of child labour is compounding confusion and disagreements rather than being helpful" (Lieten, G K and White, 2001).

The importance of clearly defining what child labour is and what child labour is not relations to the nature of the policy intervention and the setting of the priorities. But it also relates to the explanatory exercise: if we are to assign causes for the existence and the continuation of child labour, it becomes mandatory to clarify what we talk about. If "child labour refers to all children not attending school (which clearly is a trend) then the explanatory factor will differs from the explanations which will come up when the category of child labour is confined to children actually selling their labour power (or having their labour power appropriated) in such a way that it harms a proper development of body and mind" (Lieten, 2005).

Child labour should be treated as one concept rather than as two separate words, which combine in the same way as adult labour. It is not all work done by children, but we can say it is a specific context with a specific duration and with a specific potentially harmful their health. It is a concept, which looks at the point of view of an underaged person from the specific interest of the child rather than from the point of view of economic accounting. Such a usage of child labour as one concept rather than as two words would include certain activities, which until now generally have not been included in the present statistics, and would exclude many activities, which now are included.

For India child labour is not a new phenomenon. Before industrialization also, children were engaged to work in agricultural and trade activities-etc. Also a lot of children were forcefully brought in to the scene in the name of inherited family occupations. But the work performed by them was not so arduous. It formed a part of their socialization and training process.

Radical changes, however, occurred on socio economic front with the advent of industrialization and Urbanisation, under the impact of the newly generated centrifugal and centripetal forces (Raj, 2001). Scene got changed not only in India but also, throughout the world. This industrialization brought fundamental changes in the mode of production and in the relationship of productive factors. The mechanization made agricultural productive as capital-intensive. Family based economy was destroyed. Hence small and ladles formers start migrate to urban areas for their survival. Thus urban industries had surplus labour. Rapid urbanisation, increase in the family size, unemployment and poverty compelled not only the whole family, including their children to work. As a result, the children were in a hectic situation where they had to earn for themselves as well as for the families. Profit oriented traders and other employers attracted towards chief labour force. Children are the cheapest to hire and easiest to fire. Thus began the exploitation of the child labour. They do not resist. The child's ability to grow and to develop into mentally and physically sound adult was severely restricted. The exploitation of children in the labour market continues to go unnoticed and public apathy allows it to be perpetuated (Dak, 2003).

Rodgers and Guy (1981) have observed that "the major analytical problem in devising a valid typology (of child activities) is that the desirable categories depend crucially on the nature of the social system and prevailing mode of production". These two social scientists have distinguished and classified the economic roles of children and their activities. These are;

Domestic Work

It is usually within the family. It is self-employment and is generally time intensive (cleaning, cooking, washing, childcare etc.)

Non Domestic and Non Monetary Work

It is usually found in poor agrarian/ rural economics. This is self-employment, which is a part of family activity and includes work like tending of livestock, protecting crops from birds and animals, hunting, gathering and weeding. This work is also time intensive and is often intermixed with domestic work.

Children also work in the non-agrarian environment, such as artisan production, small scale production and in the informal sector activities in trade, manufacturing and services (such as running errands, looking after goods for short periods and marketing of domestic produce).

The fourth type is the work where children work as bonded labourers and are pledged by their parents in lieu of debt. Although bonded law abolishes labour but still it is in practice.

Wage labour: a child wage labourer is sometime a part of the family labour force where in the entire family works on wages and children become a part of the group. These practices are noted in agricultural field, brick making, carpet making, domestic services and digging operations etc. The other part of the child wage labour is where children are independently employed as wage earners either on fields or in factories or in the service sector. Children are also engaged in economic activities, partly economic but mainly illegal or antisocial.

In addition to the activities mentioned, they are employed in works characterized by irregularity and short term nature and may be termed "marginal semi- economic activities of this type include the selling of newspapers, cleaning of cars, shoe-shining, selling of sweets or other small items, sorting of garbage etc." such work typically does not contribute to capital formation and could be described as the activities of lumped proletariat. It is sure that child activity patterns depend on the demographic variations notably with respect to age, sex and family structure. Almost all of these activities of children either directly deprive the child from opportunities for full physical and mental development or indirectly cause low level of equilibrium in terms of a life time chance (Narendre, 2001).

So it is the point where controversy over the concept of child labour, where the conventional approach distinguishes between child labour and child work exist. While the latter is accepted as a process of socialization, the former is rejected as it is detrimental to children's overall development and negative affects their education (Fyfe and George, 2001). It is said that all the work that children do, does fall under the term 'child labour'. This implies that child work is more generic and child labour is restrictive. One of the reasons the study group on women and child labour employed for rejecting the existing definition of child labour is that it is restricted to paid employment and working for others (Lieten, 2003). Even the NSSO definition restricts the labourers as working for wages when it defines rural labour. When one takes up these restrictive definitions, it excludes even other reportedly working children, especially in unpaid work, as child labourers. In fact, the census defines a worker as one who participates in economically production in economic activities. (Venkatanarayana, 2001). National Sample Servey defines it as a participation in economic activities. i.e. production of goods and services that adds value to national product. In both cases, the definition includes paid and unpaid and participation in household farms and enterprises, self-employed and outside the house holds working for others. Referring to child labour in this context excludes the children who are not working for others and those working in unpaid jobs as per the usual definition of work. It is because of definition of worker is in general restrictive in the sense that it excludes some activities especially unpaid services like household chores and domestic works (Hirway, 2001). When a border definition of worker is considered, the work forces estimation in general and that of child workers in particular will shoot up. As the concept of work is more inclusive, more and more children will be keep included as child labourers.

Occupational Structure

The classification of workers in to various sectors can give an indication of the level of economic development, Colin Clack (1988) has observed that "economic growth is a process of structural transformation of an economy from its substances sector in to the secondary an then in to the territory industrial sectors. The shift of workers from the primary sector in the economy to secondary and tertiary sector follows industrialization and development of the economy.

Primary sectors: This relates to the production of primary goods in agriculture and in the allied pursuits. Workers in this sector includes persons engaged

- as cultivators
- as agricultural labourers
- in livestock, forestry, fishing and
- In mining and quarrying.

Secondary sector :This includes all persons engaged in manufacturing, processing, servicing and repairs in

- house old industry
- other the n house hold industry and construction

* Tertiary sector

This includes

- trade and commerce
- Transport, storage and communication
- Other services.

Child labourers are generally found in all above-mentioned sectors. Also, in number of other economic activities like brick kilns, stone quarries, construction, carpet weaving, handlooms, matches and fireworks, glass, bangles, diamond cutting and polishing, lock making, household activities, hotels and restaurant and the like.

A distinction is made, therefore, between a child working in a silk industry, and one tending cattle owned by the family, the former being considered highly exploitative and so, detrimental to the child. It is argued that it is the degree of exploitation of the child that determines whether or not the work is harmful. Child work, which does not involve an exploitative relationship, should therefore be separated from child labour. Hence, any effort to eliminate children from both hazardous and non-hazardous sectors must and should, therefore, concentrate on child labour rather than child work. A broad consensus should be emerged that the degree of the risk and exploitation should be major criteria to judged in terms of whether the work done is paid or unpaid, as a part of family labour or for an out side employer and the working conditions imposed on the child.

At the for end of the spectrum lies the views that all forms of work are bad for children. Concerned people of this views hold the arguments in favor of children working, whatever their logic, are merely excuses for the perpetration of child labour to the advantage of certain vested interest. According to this view, any distinction between one form of work and another as far as children are concerned is completely arbitrary. It is argued that the concept of segregation of work done by a child into exploitative labour and non-exploitative work suffers from basic flows and raises many more issues than it resolves. "The first issue that has to be sorted out is when, and under what circumstances can work be considered exploitation. For instance, it is quite possible to have a situation where a child is working in less exploitative circumstances on a sericulture than in a family owned field. Hence, no simple method by which some activities indulged in by a child could be classified as work and some as labour. The second issue that arises is why only two categories, namely child work and child labour. One could just as well have a whole range of categories with various forms of work being classified in terms of the degree of perceived exploitation" (Shantha Sinha. 2000).

Organised and Unorganised Sectors

We can classify the child labour in to two types Legal child labour, and illegal child labour. Legal child labour is child labour who is above the minimum age, but is not an adult. Ex in factories, workers in the category of 14-18 years are child labour. On the other hand illegal child labour is one which is below the specified age limit and working in the sectors which is organised themselves. For example hotels, garage, domestic, agriculture, tea shops, house hold industries, and not covered in by child labour legislation (Murthy, S). Million of children are working mainly in unorganised sectors only. Jobs will be easily available in these sectors. Because no need of having any special skills or experiences to the children. Almost all jobs comes under unorganised sector are small activity –oriented one and children would be more suitable to these kind of occupations Since it does not comes under any specific law employers are severely exploiting the children. Low wages, long working hours, working without protection are different types of the difficulties facing by the children working gin the in this sector. Although organised sector is being under constant monitoring under various Government agencies as per the law her too children are exposed to various forms of hazards and are exploited in different ways by the employers. On the other hand in organised sector, is "characterized by large enterprises, using highly mechanized or capital intensive technologies, the scope of children's work relatively declines, vis-à-vis, the smaller enterprises, since child workers appear redundant and uneconomical in a production system using advanced technology and a reduced labour force" (Nadeem Mohsin, 1993)

Child Labour in Hazardous Industries

Like organised and unorganised sectors we can classify the children occupation in to two major types base on level of the risks involved. 1. Hazardous 2. Non hazardous. The recent survey has shown that 91% children are working in hazardous sectors Child labour working in agriculture sector in India is said to be the highest than rest of the sectors. Children working in agriculture through the world and often face hazards through exposure to biological and chemical agents. Children can be found mixing, loading and applying pesticides, fertilizers or herbicides, some of which are highly toxic and potentially carcinogenic (causes cancer).

Not only that mining carpet industry, glass and molding construction work sericulture, beedi rolling, fire work are some of the other most hazardous sectors where most of the children are found employed. A report of The Pioneer said that around 3,00,000 in carpet and 40.000 child workers are employed in glass industries. The kid labourers, who never went to school, draw molten glass from the furnace for making bracelets and glassware. The report also states that child workers in glass industries operate in front of the furnace, where temperature goes up to 1550 degree Celsius. Man of them, due to the harsh working environment, get physically and mental scared and may suffer from chronic illness, destroyed eyesight and even premature death.

A recent survey conducted in Surath City more than 1800 children under age 14 is working in. Hazardous diamond cutting. And these children contribute nearly 1/3rd of their families' total income. In Bangalore City mostly children are working in some hazardous sectors like construction cites, carpet, glass, garage unorganised industries, beedi rolling. Zari and sericulture-etc

The plight of child workers in unorganized industry sector in India is some what better than that of children working in hazardous industries, these child workers are deprived of minimum wags, regular working hours and also job security. Most of thee children are belong to marginal comminutes and socially and economically deprived groups. (Pattnaik and Beedi, 1998)

It may be hazardous or non-hazardous risks will always be embedded with the job. In the above point of dissuasion it will be highly relevant to explore how comminute evaluates the risk associated with each type of work and age being appropriate for each kind of work. Once we could explore the traditional concepts of risks then it will be easy to remove children from hazardous industries.

The involvement of children in work is seen as one of the important survival strategies of the poor. In recent years a distinction has been made between different forms of work where children are concerned. Some forms of work are seen as detrimental to children's developmental and need to be eliminated while others are considered relatively harmless. This understanding underlines the categorization of children's work into that which is hazardous, expletive, intolerance, worst form, as against that which is hazardous, non-hazardous, light and so on (ILO, 1999).

Tradition of the family

Some time early involvement of children in continuing family tradition work also causes child labour problem. Many Anthropological factors too have their share in this scourge. The educational system adds yet another dimension to the prevalence of this problem. Recently ILO has criticized the Indian Governament and said India is not willing to ratify the ILO convention because of fear of vanishing of her traditional cottage industry.

Defective education system, drawbacks in laws and acts low economic growth, breaking of joint families, Urbanisation. migration, corporal punishments at the schools- etc are some of other facts in perpetuating the child labour problem.

In India more than 36 percent of the population is below poverty line. The problem persists in every state of the country, though its concentration is more in certain states and castes. Ideally child labour is an anathema, outrageous to human conscience and dignity. Its abolition is advocated on moral and ethical grounds. But the ground reality of the situation is completely different. As long as poverty exists in all different forms, child labour is bound to exist in either open or disguised form (Rao and Rao, 1999).

Among the reasons for the high incidence of child labour on India, poor implementation of child labour act stands since matters relating to children receive low priority when it comes to implementation. In addition, the existing enforcement machinery very often does not have proper inclination to deal with the problem of child labour, which result in effective implementation Effective of any law depends on its enforcement. The enforcement of the child labour law is vested in machinery controlled by both the central and state Government.

Not only above reasons, it is the whole society is at fault not only under privileged parents, it is the employers who are directors for this whole event. "Even in family run units, where the child is generally better looked after by his parents and may not suffer from any physical hard ship, he goes through mental strain because of problems and anxieties regarding the undertaking which he shares with his/her parents". (Tapan Kumar, 2003),

The largest group of working children is the unpaid family workers. A high proportion of the children gives their wages to their parents or other relatives. Rural children work more then urban children. Large amount of urban children found employed in informal sectors.

Gender Issues and Child Labour.

The status of the girl child constitutes an acid test of social development in the third world. Decrimnation on the basis of sex is a structural feature of tradition cultures. Recent studies have shown that the lower position of girls in the society under value girl child labour compared to the male child labour. Besides occupational hazardous, girl children are vulnerable to sexual abuse both at the place of employment and at home when the are left to themselves. Sinha* depicted in his study reasons other than poverty which causes child labour problem. Gender inequalities, for instance, are not specific to any particular social group but cut across religion, caste and class. They reflect social norms against the education of the children, the early praxes of the family occupations that often foreclose heir educational options. It is more particular to girl child labourers. There are several factors contributing towards low enrollment and high dropout. Usually in case of girl child, low enrollment and high dropout rates are the result of the need felt for her presence at home for household activities. Thus the intellectuals growth is hampered by depriving the girl child of educational opportunities, minimizing her chances for vocational training, condemning to low wages and forcing her work all her life as unskilled labourers (Sinha, 1993). Gender Issues and Child Labour.

While discrimination of girl children in the specific area of child labour does exist, it is often studied only as a part of the overall pattern of discrimination against girls. As far as child labour is concerned, what most writers on the subject stress is that the parameters are often defined in such a manner that discrimination is not even apparent. Thus, a large amount of work in which girl children are engaged does not even figure as child labour. Studies have revealed that in the Indian context, girl children are tragedy engaged in running the household from a very early age, even before they are capable of wage earning activities. This includes collection of water. Fuel and looking after the younger siblings. It is argued that although these activities engage the girl child for a large part of each into the calculation of child labour. Even when the girls reach the older age group of nine and above, a significant portion of their time remains unaccounted for since it is consumed by these activities. The first point that is often stressed in the case of girl children is that there role as child labour is one, which does not receive much attention. (Mrs. Sinha, 2000)

A second aspect that has received attention is the manner in which traditional and cultural factors play a major role in deciding the work patterns of girls in India.. The fact that in most Indian communities it is the son who is expected to assume the dominant role in all traditional activities including festivals and religious occasions results in an almost automatic discrimination against girls. This manifests itself in a number of ways, which have been documented in detail. Adverse sex ratios, female infanticide, deliberate neglect of girl children in the younger years, lower nutritional and educational status and even the nature of work performed by girls are some of the indicators which have been utilized to study discrimination against girls. 1981 census studies has shown that the percentage of girls employed as main workers was considerably higher than boys in almost all the categories of occupations, in both rural and urban areas Boys were employed more as marginal workers than girls. The difference clearly indicates that girls are being pushed to employment for full time more than boys, which further reduces the educational and developmental opportunities for girls. So, third aspect, which has dominated studies in relation to discrimination against girls, is the immense need for promoting literacy and education as a strategy for bringing down the levels of discrimination. The positive role that education has played in this regard has also been widely documented (Usha Nayer). As far as discrimination of girls in the specific context of child labour is concerned, it needs to be set in the context of issues that govern child labour as a whole and cannot be viewed in isolation. In particular, one has to appreciate the key factors, which influence the understanding of child labour in the country.

The macroscopic analysis shows that the concept of child labour is a sex specific and not only is there sex specificity in occupations but there are also differences in the ramifications for girls and boys. Deferent societies and communities have assured and achieved different degrees of equality off status between male and female members depending on their economic and social progress. So we are emphasizing this aspect, namely, the importance of a macro policy for what looks like special issues such as the condition of girl children, is that often we in the womens movement do not excrete our political importance in the in the debate on micro polices. Another neglected aspect is the deeper questions; whether in our quest for equality we wish to transform the girl into a boy in the acculturation or let the boy become more like the girls? Thus it mean the girl, as she is brought up today, in poverty or in wealth, in rural or urban areas, has multiple skills because of the house hold pressure. This generates in her ability or capabilities in manag e ment and a degree of self-reliance. Relative to the girl, young Indian boy is a helpless dependent weak person. In our zeal for equality, should we forefeet this advantage of the womens domain?

Child Abuse

The social problems that are the proper concern of child welfare are as mankind. Among them the problem of child abuse has gained the attention of social scientists, the public and the Govermanent in the western society since 1960s. Abuse of children has increased considerably during the last decade or so and every tenth child in India was victimized. It is noted that child labour is also on form of the worst form of child abuse, There are not many systematic and empirical study on the different forms of the child abuse such as the one propertied in the family, school, in the work place as well as may take a number of forms, including physical, sexual, and emotional. The child abuse is often a symptom of other problems like poverty, weak agencies, dissemination within families, absence of human rights and weak democratic institutions-etc. It is most unfortunate that even though Indian constitution has provided a lot of legislation's to protect children there is no single law where the problems of child abuse could be dealt effectively

A study, which is conducted by one mumbai, based Womens College has shown that 68.5 percent of female criminals had been sexually abused as children. Child abuse is one of the worst, hidden and invisible crime of the civilized society. Child Abuse can be defined as " a condition having to do with those who have been deliberately injured by physical assault". This definition is limited only to physical violence, which produce a diagnostic injury. Thus, it is evident that acts of neglect and maltreatment of children, which do not produce an injury but are equally harmful, cannot be included in this definition. No definition of child abuse can be considered as valid unless it includes physical, physiological and psychological ill treatment of a child. Burgess has given a wider definition of child abuse. According to him, child abuse refers to "any child who receives non-accidental physical and psychological injury as a result of acts and omissions on the part of his parents or guardians or employers..." Verbal abuse, threats of physical violence, and excessive physical punishment are also included in the definition of child abuse. So we can say that the term abuse has different meanings and it varies according to the time and space.

We can say that child abuse is more common among child labourers, children in remand home, physical handicap children, children under mental stress and abandoned children are more vulnerable to different kinds of abuses. This child abuse can be broadly divided in to 3 major types. 1. physical 2. sexual and 3. emotional.

It is more unfortunate to say that it is evident that all above mentioned kinds of abuses exists among child labourers. A number of explanations have been given by social scientists to reveal the major motivational factors behind the child abuse. Psychiatric and Socio Cultural Explanation. Social cultural explanation includes a) social-situational b) social habitability and c) social control explanations. Recently social scientists have added 3 more types of explanations. 1. resource explanation, 2. social interactional and 3. social learning explanations.

Psychiatric explanations : the psychiatric explanation was propounded by many scholars. It links with child abuse factors such as mental illness and personality defects or intra-individual abnormalities. It also links abusive parents' own childhood experiences to the individuals' weak personality development and poor self-control. The thesis that personality disorder is responsible for child abuse was further advanced by reports that abusers often had a propensity for impulsive and/or antisocial acts that extended beyond the preventing role. A parent, according to this explanation, may abuse his/her child due to unmet emotional needs and capabilities with own (parental) expectations, or emotional scars from their own abusive or deprived family background affecting their ability to care for their own offspring (Bhasak, 1998). This explanation initially drew support from many support from many fields, including law-makes and public-interest groups because it directed most of the responsibility for abusive behavior squarely at the individual involved, and absolved society from blame in contributing to the risk of child abuse through lack of education, adequate housing, family support programmes, employment opportunities, and so on. However, recent researches have disproved the role of psychopathology in child abuse (Burgess, 1989).

Socio-cultural explanation says those external forces or a socio-demographic variable within the society causes child abuse. This theory has 3 major sub fields 1. social situational, 2. social habitability and 3. social control. The social-situational explanation proposes that abuse and violence arise out of two factors: structural stress and cultural norms. As the social structure in which a parent lives becomes more stress ridden greater becomes the possibility that family violence will surface as an attempt to gain control over irritating, tense events. Cultural sanctioning of violence as an appropriate conflict resolution technique further provides a foundation for the use of corporal punishment in child rearing. If a parent was frequently exposed to harsh physical punishment as a child, he/she may have great propensity toward viewing such behavior as normative and inhibition against physical force may be lessened (Bendura, 1973).

Some western scientist have maintained that factors such as low income, unemployment, isolation, unwanted pregnancy and conflict with spouse/ inlaws, cause structural stresses which, combined with the cultural acceptance for violence to resolve conflict, lead to the use of force and violence against children at home. Talking of social factors, which cause stress, Gill (1981) has referred to social class and family size. The major problem in this explanation is that it is unable to account for the finding that given the same set of deprivation or advance conditions, many parents do and others do not abuse their children. Gill propounded the social control explanation in 1981. According to him, parents use violence against their children because they have no fear of being hit back, nor of being arrested neighbour lodges thus, violence is used when (I) the cost of being violent is to less than the rewards, (ii) the absence of effective social control over family relations decreases the cost (of one member being violent towards another), and (iii) family structures reduce social control in family relations and, therefore, reduce the costs and increase the rewards of being violent. Recent studies have showed that: (a) inequality in home reduces both social control and the costs of being violent, and (b) the privacy in the family serves to reduce the degree of social control exercised over family relations. In case of social habitability the nature of child maltreatment depends upon the quality of the environment in which the person and family live, or the level of family support in the environment. Maltreatment of children increases when family support decreases.

In Social control view some parents use violence against their children because they have no fear of being hit back. Social interactional explanation approach the etiology of child abuse in terms of the interplay between individual family and social factors in relation to both past and present events. The condition in which children have been raised may help to reveal why some adults are predisposed to abusive behavior, given certain setting conditions. Social learning theory lays emphasis on the learned nature of parenting and the fact that many parents have lack of knowledge and skill to carry out the highly complex task of child-rearing. (Kumar, 2003)

Types of Abuse

Neglect

Child abuse and neglect can be defined as the intentional, non accidental injury, malnutrient of children by parents, caretaker, employers or others including those individuals presenting Government/non Government bodies which may lead to temporary or permanent impairment of their physical, mental, psycho-social development, disability of death (Uma, 1990). Children, particularly infants, are perhaps the most vulnerable victims of crime, because of their very great dependence upon their parents. Its is a tragic fact that children suffer to a fall greater extent as the hands of parents and their friends then they do as the hands of strangers. This type of abuse can be further classified in to physical neglect, emotional neglect, moral neglect and social neglect.

Emotional abuse. Child emotional abuse can be refereed to as a pattern of behavioral that impairs a child emotional development or sense of self worth. This may include constant criticism, threats or rejection as well as withholding love, support, or guidance. Emotional maltreatment is rarely manifest in physical signs. A few physical indicators of emotional maltreatment are speech disorders, lag in physical development and failure-to-thrive syndrome. The behavioral characteristics of emotional maltreatment are habit disorders, conduct disorders neurotic trait psycho-neurotic reaction behaviour extremes (passive, aggressive, rigid reserved, demanding stubborn), lag in emotional and intellectual, and attempted suicide. Four impordent causes emotional abuse are poverty, deficient parental control and non cordial relations within family, maltreatment faced by parents in their child hood or inter generational transmission of child mal treatment, and alcoholism of parents. A significant proportion of abusing parents were themselves abused as children (National Clearinghouse Information, 2004).

Physical abuse. It can be defined a situation in which a child suffers, or is likely to suffer, significant harm from an injury inflicted by the child's parent or caretaker. It is more visible form of abuse among working children than children who normally resides with the parents. If a child failed in execute the order of his boss the boss may get angry and beat, burn, fracture, abrasion etc. Boys are more batten than girls. Also school going children well be more beaten by the other children. The studies have revealed that mothers abuse children physically more than of the fathers. Also this study further says expressive violence is one in which the use of physical is an end in itself. Instrumental or power oriented violence is one in which violence is intended not only as a mean of including the child to alter his behaviour but also to establish parental authority. Child precipitated violence is one in which the victims of violence contribute to their own victimization either through action defined as deviant by the aggressor parent or through provoking their antagonism.

Causes of Physical Abuse

Many social scientists have given different causes of physical abuse. Some consider the psycho-pathology of the individual perpetrators as the primary causes factor, other view the psycho social pathology of family interaction as the main cause, and still others put major emphasis on situations of acute as tress. The situational stresses pointed out four model of dominant causes of a child's physical abuse 1 relation between couples 2 relations between parents and children 3 structural stress, and 4 child-produced stress. Totally we can say that through the role of the personality traits of the abusers cannot be ignored but family environment and stress radian family situations are more crucial in child battering.

Sexual Abuse

It can be defined as 'contacts or interactions between a child and an older or more knowledgeable child or adult, when the child is being used as an object of gratification for the older child's or adult's sexual needs' (Karna, 2006). Or Child sexual abuse can be defined as the involvement of dependent and immature children in sexual active's thay do not fully comprehend, to which they are unable to give informed consent. Sexual abuse is not often identified though physical indicators alone. Frequently, a child confides in a trusted person (parents relatives, friends, teachers etc) that she /he has been sexually assaulted. There are some behavioral indicters too of sexual abuse. The sexually abused child may appear withdrawn or retarded, may have poor peer relationships, may be unwilling to participate in activist, may indulge in delinquent behavior, may runaway etc. (Kiran, 1990).

The recent studies has shown that the lower caste girl children are more frequent victims of sexual abuse and victims age distribution is more homogenous, the assault age distribution is more heterogeneous. Also it is noted that more than 11 percent of child abuse takes place in side the family. Persons having blood relationships constitutes a considerable percentage of perpetrators.

Causes of Sexual Abuse

Literature survive shows that it has 4 main reasons.1 adjustment problems of the perpetrators, family disorganization, victims characteristics, and the psychological disorders of the abusers. The 4 variables related to sexual abuse are family environment, family structure, and individual predispositions and situations factors. The analyze of family environment revealed that congestion in family was not related of sexual abuse but conflict between parents and weakening of inhabitation's leading to neglect of the children, absence of affectionate parent-child relationship within the family that fails to give support and protection to child, alcoholism of the earning male member, lack accountability of the parents, absence of control on children, mass media, male dominate family, extra martial relationship and social isolation of the family are the major factors behind this sexual abuse. The environment in the work place also contributes to sexual molestation. Several cases of assault by employees ad mutation by co-workers of the young victims when they were all alone in the house or work place. The reserved and loneliness of young girls make them more susceptible to the overtures of the perpetrators (ibid).

Sexual abuse is the most common and invisible child abuse more among the girl child labourers. Girls are more vulnerable to the sexual abuse then boys. Usually the victims will be 14 or above 14 years of age and they will be more from lower economic classes and are deprived of all parental care. Basically boys are the victims of employment-related abuse and girls are usually the victims of 'acquaintance related abuse'. Also we can give some other reasons that push children in to commercial sexual exploitation are economic disparities, inequitable socio-economic structure, traditional and religious practice. The circumstance surrounding child abuses are often complex. Thus the most appropriate form of state response whether to impose criminal sanctions or whether to rely intend on some therapeutic alternative- is a difficult decision. Child victims of sexual abuse may experiences enduring feelings of guilty shame, and emotional isolation. The infliction of serious bodily injury upon a child leaves psychological scares, which endure long over after physical wound is healed. The developing of healthy personalities will be seriously jeopardized for a child, who feels unsafe, unwanted and uncared for in its parent's response. This may leads to poor development in terms of initiative and low school performance. In some cases it can be stated that the child survives rather than develops.

The study of sexual abuse of girls in India is in its infancy. The real problem is inadequacies of data relating to sexual abuse of girls because of the secrecy and stigma attached to it (Pradhan). Nevertheless, the notion of the 'girl child' has been reified, as if there is something essential about all female children regardless of wealth or ethnicity, something that makes them more vulnerable than boys in general. This focuses on vulnerability to sexual violation, early marriage, female feticide and infanticide un planned teenage pregnancy and is a new manifestation of the old control over women's sexuality and fertility all over the world, the child's susceptibility to commercial sexual expatriation lies in his or her family circumstances. Study has shown that most of the sexually exploited children re either from marginalised families in the cites, and destitute families in the country, or children of women already for commercial gain can no more be hidden. Recently the increasing incidences of children suffering from sexually transmitted diseases have gradually raised awareness regarding the likelihood of sexual abuse. The literature on child prostates were sought after because they were believed to be free of STDs, including the apparently world wide belief that "penetrative sex with a virgin is a cure" Not only this also some other myths are embedded in this child trafficking since time immoral.

In India, domestic child workers and street children are further vulnerable to sexual abuse more particularly the innocent girls. Incidents where facts are fudged at police station are not uncommon. There is some report that victims raped by the police personnel's (*The Hindu*, 2002). In case India especially girl children are victims of extreme discrimination and neglect by the parents. Latest report says that India has around 4 lakh under 15 child prostitutes for child sex tourism. Thus India has got second place in the world after Thailand with 6-lakh child prostitutes (ILO, 2003). One more study says more than one million sexual exploitation children only in Asia. In Nepal, Bangladesh, Korea, Taiwan child trafficking has become a kind invisible business. It has become a new feature of economic life in several countries.

In India, the demand for children comes mainly from the local population. However, India and other South Asian countries are gradually replacing South East Asia as the venue of choice for foreigners, as there are fewer laws against child sexual abuse, and South Asian children can be bought at more affordable prices. The Convention on Rights of the Child has been rectified and supported by 178 countries including India. It given the NGOs, lawyers, government officials, and police officers, no choice except to take all possible measures in ensuring protection of the rights of children. We do not need more legislation's. We already have a number of laws, which are not being implemented.

The NGOs role has almost become a pattern of speech. The chosen rhetoric is that the NGOs are the closest to the target groups, that the NGO role is the critical and most important one. It is a way of transferring responsibility from one sector to another. The government and we, however, cannot shun the responsibility. NGOs can be partners, not substitutes, in the government's efforts. There isneed to raise public sensitivity and awareness about these problems that confront us in our work. The problem of child prostitution has to be worked out not merely through rehabilitation, but with greater emphasis on prevention. There are backward villages and districts that provide the base for the traffickers. That is where the real problem. NGOs working towards rural development should focus on such poor families that are willy-nilly-forced to send their children to earn. We lack the skills to search the underworld Mafia that is dangerous. There are people who are making a lost of money in trafficking. We have witnessed the power of community action in Manila where the parents of the children came out on the street and demanded justice; and in Goa where protestation are going on; the beach areas of Sri Lanka, where small community groups are committed to monitor the problem in order to protect their own children. The community has to rise up and join hands, though it is not something that is going to be easy.

Recently, there has been increasing awareness, in the country, of the menacing aspects and repercussions of child prostitution. The difference between reality and application of the law shows that the issue of child prostitution is more hidden than exposed. This sorry state of affairs rather compound the problem in the country and the Human Rights Commission has decided to have this issue considered on regular basis by a core group comprising, inter alia, the National Commission for Women, the Department of Women and Child Development, selected NGOs and UNICEF. This group is, among other things considering sufficiency of existing laws and the ways of improving upon their enforcement, necessity of making development on such issues of holding public meetings, seminars in the specific areas and so on in order to eliminate or minimize the child prostitution. There is a strong correlation between family abuse of children, especially girls, and the drive to enter the sex trade. The mother in particular plays a pivotal role in her daughter's life decisions. The record indicates that there is direct commercial sexual exploitation of children because of the family situations (Coleman, 2001).

Poverty, despair and newly dislocating values supports such incidence of sexual exploitation among the children. Even though proverty is often prescribed to be cause of sale of children into labour, actually no poor families sell their children. Some families sell the child due to poverty, unemployment, consumerism and other adverse situations. At time, however, a child is sold into commercial sex by parents who have themselves sexually or otherwise abused the child. The child is prepared and made "ready" for sex and able to earn money for the family. Such parents get lumpsum money for their children and push their children into "bondage", a situation in which the child is forced to provide sex to earn money to repay the family's debt to the exploiter.

Commercial sexual, exploitation of children is above board in an organised industrial sector from small business to larger factories. There are people who use technology to sell the product to increase "good business". This "industry" is on abuse of children involved in fraud enslavement, bribery and corruption at various levels. The impact of commercial sexual exploitation on child has assumed staggering positions. The child loses its childhood, its dignity, often its future. These are unquestionable causes, but these are evil effects of exploitation, which are more miserable. The most obvious of these relates to the health of the child. HIV/AIDS is both reason and consequence of commercial, sexual exploitation of children.

The evidence indicates that the miscreant people who consider sex with a child as "safer" is choosing children as sex partners. Having sex with a child, it is a notion, protects and abuse from HIV/AIDS, because the child is more likely to be "clean". But the fact is otherwise because of their vulnerability and weaknesses. Children in flesh-market who are often forced to take more clients than adult might accept and are generally too weak to protest or avoid the situation. Moreover, children are physically more vulnerable to infection because of their socio-economic weakness. The 'virgin' child is asked by many customers as the "safest". Presently another problem is reconstruction surgery, which promotes commercial exploitation of sex children making multiple operations. Thus, the child is more infected with HIV as is found thorough some studies. Thus, the innocent child is met with death sentence meaning thereby that his/her life, respect and options. There are, besides, various physical and psychological reasons among the children forcing then in to sex. Children trapped in the cycle of commercial sex are frequently abused, beaten, burnt, tortured and deprived of food, air etc. They are also prone to different kind diseases. Drugs are often used to keep children taken into prostitutions easily. They may also be a self-medicating meance to numb the pain of hunger or despair. At the national level, many countries laid down laws making children's abuse a crime. Recently, there has been growing awareness of commercial sexual explorations of children. Children are transferred across borders. Exploiters travel to set up their network. Clients to go buy service on foreign shores for promotion of their trade .It is said that making laws and enforcing them are 2 different things (Razawat , 2003). It is certainly difficult to make laws work well against such odds. It is more difficult when local laws make them scot- free and safeguard the culprits exploiting the children. Indian constitution articles 24 and 39 seek to protect children of tender age from abuse, exploitation, moral and material abandonment, employment of children under 14 years in any factory of hazardous jobs. The national policy for children also seeks to prevent exploitation of children against neglected and abandoning juvenile justice (Care and protection) of children Act also contains measures such as care and protection for abandoned and delinquent children. The Indian penal Code declared kidnapping, maiming, selling or buying, seduction and sexual exploitation of children as an offence liable for punishment (Chaudhary, 1990).

The present day media technology although develop consumption leading to sexual trade, they can erase the mean. The advent of the Internet has opened up new channels of informations of those looking for children for sex. The dark aspect of Internet technology meance that informations can be shared really time and again on special request dealt with by promotes and supplies of children for sex. Pornographic pictures and video clips can be up loaded and down –loaded anonymously. Besides technology, the press and media also play an impordent role in domain of commercial, sexual, exploitation of children, both positive and negative.

On the negative side, the media contributed to the liberation of sexuality explicit imaginary and to shift any moral values. Satellite technology, international travel and support infrastructure means, that such image are quite frequently revised in a non- supportive context. Many TV viewers are adolescent and their attitude to adolescence itself is worthless. On the negative side, many reporters investing commercial, sexual exploitations leading have unwitting corrupted evidence by paying for stores, enabling to escape convection. Press and media can play both positive and negative roles in exploitations of children for sex. The press and media can help immensely to advocacy, highlighting positive moral values and human rights. They can support positive family values and apprise parents when their children are at stake. They can hold children themselves to draw moral values on there on behavior and to identify risk factors of their social situations. According to Rights of the children, child labour may be viewed as denial child rights (Razawath, 2003). Under this right come rehabilitation, protection of child workers and betterment of their working conditions. Hence regulation of these facets of child labour is felt essential. Right to education and access to recreation and to child hood itself is linked with the right of the child. The notion of child hood is relatively of recent significance especially in the context of children rights. The enforcement of economic, social and cultural rights is made conditioned to the availability of the resources while civil and political rights have same obligations and regressive implementation of economic, social and cultural rights. A Country's richness is measured by the norms like maximum extent of utilization of valuable resources in order to tackle child labour more effectively. In this context, child labour is now considered in a humanitarian as well as human rights approach. Child labour is considered as a violation of civil and political rights or a violation of economic, social and cultural rights. Nonetheless, all these rights are interacted and immediate steps need be taken for talking all these facets or effectively breaking a point in the vicious circle.

No doubt, we cannot resolve the problem in while, but no time can be delayed for taking adequate initiation in the matter. Under the Child Rights Convention, there are various sections relating to child labour–discriminations, abuse, encroachment to privacy and recession impeachment on child's education and safely and security of the child. Child labour is attributed mainly exploration discrimination, helpless, caste and gender operation. There are different attitudinal factors which contribute to taking children to hazardous jobs on dignified services and insecure and indeed lie calling. Even the World Bank is setting restrictions on the misuse of child labour. It is surmised that the greater productively of these children who remain in primary schools for sufficient time will enable them to earn over six times the cost of giving them the extra education. Primary education, say the bank. is the largest single contributor to the economic growth rates of high quality. A number of NGOs are now active to control the quantum of child labour and reduce its harmful effects and repercussions. Government has also established a few committees to deal with child rights in its various sections of the society. It has also set up the National Human Rights Commission to examine not only the human rights, in general, but also children's rights in particular (Kumar, 1991)

Trafficking in Children

Child trafficking includes the recruitment, transportation, transfer, harboring or receipt of a child for the purposes of sexual or labour exploitation, forced labour, or slavery. Trafficking in children is a human rights tragedy estimated to involve over a million children worldwide. In Togo, for example, hundreds of children are trafficked annually—sent from, received in, or transited through the country. They are recruited on false promises of education, professional training and paid employment; transported within and across national borders under sometimes life-threatening conditions; ordered into hazardous, exploitative labour; subjected to physical and mental abuse by their employers; and, if they escape or are released, denied the protections necessary to reintegrate them into society.

Both girls and boys are trafficked—in its study of trafficking in Togo, for instance, Human Rights Watch reported on the trafficking of girls into domestic and market work and the trafficking of boys into agricultural work.

Child trafficking is prohibited under international law as both a "practice similar to slavery" and one of the "worst forms of child labour." States have an urgent and immediate obligation to eradicate trafficking in children.

Dansi D., age sixteen, told Human Rights Watch she spent three days on a boat to Gabon, before working as a housemaid there for eighteen months. She said her journey began in the village of Nungbani in Togo, where she and seven other girls boarded a minibus with a woman who said they would be looking after small children in Gabon. The bus drove as far as Lomé, stopped there for five days and then made a one-day journey to Nigeria.

When she arrived in Nigeria, Dansi was abandoned by the woman who brought her and told to wait to be collected by a boat. "I stayed in Nigeria for five months," Dansi told Human Rights Watch. "It was a big house with not many people in it, and [the woman] told me just to wait. I ate *gari* [cassava dough] from the stock [she] had left. After five months, a man came and took me to a boat." Dansi went on to describe the journey from Nigeria to Gabon. "On the boat, there were over a hundred children, Togolese and Nigerian, and there were some adults, but more children than adults," she said. "I talked to some of them, and all the girls were going to Gabon to work. It took three days on the boat to get to Gabon. They gave us *gari* and cassava and sometimes bread to eat."

Area of Concentration

The typical nature of child labour in India is more prevalence in rural areas. As we know three fourth of national income comes from agricultural sector only. More than 75 percent of the people depend on the agriculture for their subsistence. According to the 1991 census more or less 83,56 percent of children are employed in different segment of the agricultural and allied activates. Census data shows that while boys are involved highest in cultivation and girls are the most in agriculture sector. Rural economy, which is characterized by a relatively higher level of poverty, unemployment and illiteracy, compared to urban economy supports 90 percent of the total childlabour in India. Noted percent of children were continue the their respective family \ traditional occupations. Census showed still existence of bonded child labour in many parts of India. Many children are helping their family members in the field. Some work as part of contract family labour whereas some work as part of contract family labour where men, women, and children all work together. Many of them employed in plantation. Rodgers and Standing

(1979) has given useful classification where more prevalence of girl child labourers.1 domestic 2 non-domestic 3 bonded 4 wage labour. The domestic work includes maidservants or domestic servants, where female children have to bear the burden. Non-domestic includes grazing animals, work in the field etc. Recent study has noted rapid raising of female child workers in rural domestic sectors. It is nothing but society treating girls as second grade children. They are being regarded more as a liability rather than asset to their family. So they being made to work instead of sent them to schools. Parents favor male children as more economically valuable than girls. And boys are more or less permanent resource of income. This gender based economic significance of male child is further enhanced in countries where social and cultural taboos restrict women from participating in paid work of family, occupational work (Narayana, 1992)..

In rural areas, girl child workers are readily available for work and it is found very common for school age children to be involved in agricultural work as a part of family labour. Also girls are mostly working in domestic sectors then boys, because these children come largely from land less and semi land less families. Tripaty* found that the total number of hours spent on work increased progressively with age. The study demonstrates that a certain increase in family size, the number of respondents doing wage work increased. Further, this study stressed that over two-thirds of the girl children, whose brothers do not attend to work, were engaged in domestic work only. If the girl child has no sister, she has to perform only domestic work. If the brothers go to work, it was manifested that about 60 per cent of girls did wage work along with domestic work (Tripathy, 2003).

The working conditions of girl children in both organised and unorganised sectors are very ruthless. Long hours of work, low wage, unsafe working conditions, abuse are most common in both the sectors. Children have become victims for this kind of exploitations. Girl child workers face greater exploitation when compare to the boys. Sexual abuse in domestic sector is most common in urban areas. Basically girls performs all domestic work including looking after the children. This work does not comes under the term child labour. This kind of domestic work gives the immense chance to the elder members of the family to go out for work. Girls these kind of work have more significance in rural areas when compare to the urban areas. The reason is that it affects the attitude of parents of female children and confers upon the latter a status that is lower than that of their male siblings (Muthu raja, 2001).

The magnitude and intensity of the involvement of girl child labour differs From different regions, and also, in the same region in rural and urban areas. In all the states except few states like Kerala ,Gujarat and Punjab the growth rate of male worker is lower than the growth of male population, but the growth of female worker is greater then the growth rate of female population. One of the common charectersticts of girl child labour all over India is there concentration in unskilled and simple routine woks which offer little opportunity for innovation or scope transfer to other more remunerative jobs thereby betterment. Also in recent years female work participation has increased due to their increased participation in industries and service sectors due to removal of social taboos regarding male employment, loosening of joint family system etc.

Thus the girls perform economically useful roles at homes not only by undertaking productive works themselves but also making possible for adults to undertaker productive works by shouldering the burden of house hold work and taking care of siblings. In fact many cases people do not recognize many of the tasks undertaken by the girl children as labourer in strict sense of the term. Domestic chore is one such example. Such activates are seen as tasks that the girl's should automatically perform without any monetary compensation. Low values is a accorded to domestic and household work because it does not bring in a wage and is not productivity oriented This affects the attitude of parents of female children and confer on the latter a lower status than that of male siblings (Sinha,1993).

Gender discrimination also plays a vital role in case of girl child labour in India. In Indian society education has become kind untouchable to the girls. Lot of tradition and other cultural factors are embedding in this fact. So that girls starts to work in their very early ages than boys to supplement the inadequate income of the family. Since usually girl's works in unorganised sectors or marginalised work right from the beginning their education opportunity will be nil in the future. So we observe high rate early drops out more among girls than boys. Gender is the major form of inequality in the Indian context, with implication for a varity of outcomes, demographic, economic and social. Girls makeup a disproportionate percentage of out-of-school children and dropout from all social classes. In addition, they are less visible in the official child labour force statistics and over-represented among nowhere children (Chadudhri, 1997). However, unlike the effects of caste, which are constant with, and exacerbate, the consequences of poverty, the relation between poverty and gender is more complex. Also it is points out, cultural constraints against girls education are likely to be more pronounced among upper caste groups, particularly in rural areas. Burra* while explaining the cultural context of child exploitations writes, It needs to be kept in mind that, particularly in the areas of child labour and child trafficking and discrimination against the female child, parents may not be in a position to make judgements because of 'cultural' and 'social' and 'economic' reasons and therefore the state has to take up issues such as elimination of child labour and compulsory education in the larger interests of equity and good citizenship. The veil of tradition and culture is often used to mask systematic exploitation of girl children(Burra, 1996).

While discrimination of girl children in the specific area of child labour does exist, it is often studied only as a part of the overall pattern of discrimination against girls. As far as child labour is concerned, what most writers on the subject stress is that the parameters are often defined in such a manner that discrimination is not even apparent. Thus, a large amount of work in which girl children are engaged does not even figure as child labour. Studies have revealed that in the Indian context, girl children are tragedy engaged in running the household from a very early age, even before they are capable of wage earning activities. This includes collection of water. Fuel and looking after the younger siblings. It is argued that although these activities engage the girl child for a large part of each into the calculation of child labour. Even when the girls reach the older age group of nine and above, a significant portion of their time remains unaccounted for since it is consumed by these activities. The first point that is often stressed in the case of girl children is that there role as child labour is one, which does not receive much attention. (Mrs. Sinha, 2000)

A second aspect that has received attention is the manner in which traditional and cultural factors play a major role in deciding the work patterns of girls in India.. The fact that in most Indian communities it is the son who is expected to assume the dominant role in all traditional activities including festivals and religious occasions results in an almost automatic discrimination against girls. This manifests itself in a number of ways, which have been documented in detail. Adverse sex ratios, female infanticide, deliberate neglect of girl children in the younger years, lower nutritional and educational status and even the nature of work performed by girls are some of the indicators which have been utilized to study discrimination against girls.

1981 census studies has shown that the percentage of girls employed as main workers was considerably higher than boys in almost all the categories of occupations, in both rural and urban areas boys were employed more as marginal workers than girls. The difference clearly indicates that girls are being pushed to employment for full time more than boys, which further reduces the educational and developmental opportunities for girls. So, third aspect, which has dominated studies in relation to discrimination against girls, is the immense need for promoting literacy and education as a strategy for bringing down the levels of discrimination. The positive role that education has played in this regard has also been widely documented (Usha Nayer).

As far as discrimination of girls in the specific context of child labour is concerned, it needs to be set in the context of issues that govern child labour as a whole and cannot be viewed in isolation. In particular, one has to appreciate the key factors, which influence the understanding of child labour in the country

Wrong Concepts on Child Labour

What the informations we have and knowledge regarding child labour is not absolutely correct because there are some mis conceptions.

1 Child labour is not only prevalent not only in underdeveloped or developing countries. Recent UNISEF study has shows that UK has 17 percent of and USA has 36-38 percent of child labour are beyond the age of 15 yeas.

2 Poverty is the basic root for this problem. Without eradication of poverty elimination of child labour is not possible without elimination of poverty. But UNSEF says it is quite possible without eradicating poverty if community decides to do so.

3 Third wrong concept is that child labour is more among export oriented countries. But there is lot of evidence to show that existence of child labour exists even among non exported countries.

4 Eradication of child labour is only possible if government decide. But it is proved that Egos role is vital and with out NGO's help Governament alone can't fight against this evil.(Thakur, R N).

Child Labour: Impact on the Society and Health of the Children

Today's child would construct tomorrow's India. Child is not only the future of a nation but also its future strength in reserve. The future of our Nation is not secure, if the practice of child labour is at alarming rate. Child labour have a for reaching consequences on the human society. The problem of child labour India has of late assumed the proportion of a social menace threading the very fabric of a social milieu. The appalling faces of a vast number of ill-clad. Ill-fed and ill-paid (Datta, S K, 2001) teenaged and mostly under 14 age group of young boys and girls brings to our mind the view of a very skewed distribution of the fruits of development, despite crossing 55 years since independence. Due to involvement of children in different kinds of work in their tender age may be physically and mentally depressed in the yeas to come. So that, Society would loose some productive adults in the future. Karl Marx rightly said that, "The result of buying the children and working persons of under age by the capitalist in physical deterioration and moral degradation's

Already we are facing a massive unemployment problem in our country. Due the practice of child labour adult unemployment problem still increases more. The huge number of child labourers have adversely effected the quality of Indian labour force and narrowed down the scope of adult employment. The lower level of income the huge percentage of adult workers is responsible for the increase of child labour. (Kumar, 1999) Child labour also affects the migration of labour to a certain extent in rural areas. The participation of children in the household and economic activities allows the elder members to migrate to other places in search of seasonal or permanent employment. Besides, the prevalence of child labour leads to formation of delinquent gang's, anti social elements and final end up human resource under development.

1. Causes of illiteracy 2. Reduced income capacity 3. Increased exploitation 3. Further poverty and marginalization which forms a vicious circle along with illiteracy and child labour 4. Human right violation 7 Violation of ILO norms 8 Trade sanctions and social labeling. These are the some other effects directly or indirectly on the society.

As a result, owing to unhygienic condition, several occupations exposes children to different types of health hazards, emanating from the extensive use of chemicals and poisonous substances in industries and the pollution discharged by the, to long hours of work. Such working environment endangers the children's physical and mental growth including lot risks for the normal growth and development of the children.

But in cases of children working in rural areas, the quality of life is better when comparing to the urban working children. Because they work under the compete supervision of their respective parents and relatives. And are in a position tom attend schools too (Ramana and Mrs. Kumari, 2001). Exposures to poor working conditions in hazardous and non-hazardous works have adverse effect on the working children. In the future children may have to suffer with skin problems. Respiratory problem. Malnutrition. Abnormal development, Tuberculosis, joints problems etc Early employment also degenerates the mental health of the child and reduces his earning capacity at later stage of the life. It has impact on the fertility and mortality behaviors. Also Psychologically disturbed children may become short-tempered stubborn, aggressive and more chance to learn bad habits. Also dependence of social service, family problem adjustment problem and irregular jobs may lead them to become antisocial elements.

Child Labour and Child Abuse

Child abuse is one of the worst forms of the child labour. It can be defined as "a condition having to do with those who have been deliberately injured by physical assault". This definition is limited only to physical violence, which produce a diagnostic injury. Thus, it is evident that acts of neglect and maltreatment of children, which do not produce an injury but are equally harmful, cannot be included in this definition. No definition of child abuse can be considered as valid unless it includes physical, physiological and psychological ill treatment of a child. Burgess* has given a wider definition of child abuse. According to him, child abuse refers to "any child who receives non-accidental physical and psychological injury as a result of acts and omissions on the part of his parents or guardians or employers..." Verbal abuse, threats of physical violence, and excessive physical punishment are also included in the definition of child abuse. So we can say that the term abuse has a different meanings and it varies according to time and space.

We can say that child abuse is more common among child labour, children in remand home, physical handicap children, children under mental stress and abandoned children. These children are more vulnerable to different kinds of abuses. This child abuse can be broadly divided in to 3 main major types. 1. physical 2. sexual, and 3. emotional.

It is more unfortunate to say that it is evident that all above mentioned kinds of abuses exists among child labourers. A number of explanations have been given by social scientists to reveal the major motivational factors behind the child abuse. 1. "psychiatric 2. socio cultural including (a) social-situational (b) social habitability (c) social control explanations. 3. resource explanation 4. social intersectional and 5. social learning explanations.

"Socio-cultural explanation says those external forces or a socio-demographic variable within the society causes child abuse Socio-situational explanation proposes two aspects: structural and cultural norms. Social structure meance influence of stress ridden conditions on the parents in their child or adulthood life. Cultural norm means cultural background of the family, marriage, kinship, believes which affects on the attitude of the parents or a parent

Social habitability exploitation says the nature of child ill treatment depends on the quality of the environment in which the person and family live, or the level of family support in the environment.

In Social control some parents use violence against their children because they have no fear of being hit back.

Social intersectional explanation approach the etiology of child abuse in terms of the interplay between individual family and social factors in relation to both past and present events. the condition in which children have been raised may help to reveal why some adults are predisposed to abusive behavior, given certain setting conditions.

Social learning theory lays emphasis on the learned nature of parenting and the fact that many parents have lack of knowledge and skill to carry out the highly complex task of child-rearing.

Physical abuse. It is more visible form of abuse among working children. If a child failed in execute the order of his boss the boss may get angry and beat, burn, fracture, abrasion etc"(Kumar, A 2001).

Sexual Abuse.

Sexual Abuse is the most common child abuse more among the girl child labourers. Girls are more vulnerable to the sexual abuse then boys. Usually the victims will be 14 or above 14 years of age and they will be more from lower economic classes and are deprived of all parental care. Basically boys are the victims of employment-related abuse and girls are usually the victims of 'acquaintance related abuse'. The four causes of sexual abuse mostly given are 1 adjustment of problems of the perpetrators, family disorganization, victim's characteristics, and the psychological disorders of the abuses. The four variables related to sexual abuse are family culture and environment, family structure, individual predispositions and situational factors (Kumar,2003). Also we it some other reasons that push children in to commercial sexual exploitation are economic disparities, inequitable socio-economic structure, traditional and religious practice and finally the Globalization.

The sexual abuse of girls in India is in its infancy. The real problem is inadequacies of data relating to sexual abuse of girls because of the secrecy and stigma attached to it (Pradhan). Nevertheless, the notion of the 'girl child' has been reified, as if there is something essential about all female children regardless of wealth or ethnicity, something that makes them more vulnerable than boys in general. This focuses on vulnerability to sexual violation, early marriage, female feticide and infanticide UN planned teenage pregnancy and is a new manifestation of the old control over women's sexuality and fertility. Recently the increasing incidences of children suffering from sexually transmitted diseases have gradually raised awareness regarding the likelihood of sexual abuse. The literature on child prostates were sought after because they were believed to be free of STDs, including the apparently world wide belief that "penetrative sex with a virgin is a cure" Not only this also some other myths are embedded in this child trafficking since time immoral.

In India, domestic child workers and street children are further vulnerable to sexual abuse more particularly the innocent girls. Incidents where facts are fudged at police station are not uncommon. There is some report that victims raped by the police personnel's. In case India especially girl children are victims of extreme discrimination and neglect by the parents.

Latest report says that India has around 4 lakh under 15 child prostitutes for child sex tourism. Thus India became gas got second place in the world after Thailand with 6-lakh child prostitutes (ILO). One more study says more then one million sexual Exploitation children only in Asia. In Nepal, Bangladesh, Korea, Taiwan child trafficking has become a kind invisible business. It has become a new feature of economic life in several countries. Many noted NGO's are working against this worst form of child labour.

Child Labour—Statistical Profile

If, an action to eradicate child labour is to be effective it must be based on the correct assessment of size and magnitude of the problem. Since it is complex socioeconomic problem it has become a challenge to any social science research methodologies.

For effective implementation of programme and polices good quality of field data is highly essential. Working of major quantity of children in informal sectors has caused a main hurdle in estimating the size of the child labourers around the globe.

Studies on the magnitude of child labour often rely on official figures. Such figures usually have been slanted for various reasons. So the given figure some time is not solid as suggested. Apart from that difficulty with separating child labour from child work. For such reasons, global figures purposing to demonstrate the extent of child labour are not very meaningful (White, Lieten, 2001) At best, for the conceptual and methodological reason the present figures are of a limited reliability. They are also of a limited utility.

The ILO has made some considerable effort over the years in assisting member states and other partners to collect and disseminate information about child labour, using innovative research methods (Bhargava, 2003). This includes time use studies, anthropological micro-studies and community mapping. Since1979, when a large number of country studies were commissioned for the International Year of the Child, their has been an on going programmes of child labour research providing new insights through counting, describing and analyzing the work of children in a Varity of economic setting. In 1998, ILO has established the Statistical Information and Monitoring Programme (SIMPOC) on child labour with the help of international organizations, NGO's and academicians around the world.

Presently, the number of child labourers in the world has been calculated to be around 240 million (IPEC, 2004). Between 1970-1979 the number of working children increased from 43 million to 54 million across the globe. Further ILO states 3.34 million from South America, 11.2 million from Africa. 33.45 million from South Asia and 7.12 million from other third world countries.

According to the 1971 Indian census, there were 10.74 million child workers representing 4.68% of the total child population and 5.81% of the total labour force. But according to the 1984 census it was noticed that 13.57 million children were working in organised and unorganized sectors. More or less 92.23% of the total child labourers are working in rural India. The latest officially report says more than 29.34 million children are working in different parts of India, out of which 6.45 million are girl child workers. National Sample Survey estimates 21.12 million (1993); Operational research Group, Baroda says 44 million (1983); CWC, (Concerned for Working Children) Bangalore (1995) says around 100 million.

As per 1991 censuses, around 28.56 lakhs children, are out of school in the State of Karnataka. Out of which 9.76 lakhs of are child labourers working in various activities including farm labour.

40.529 child labourers are working in both in hazardous and non-hazardous manufacturing and other units (Labour Department –Karnataka)

According to the 2001 census more than 4186743 children are out of school in the state of Karnataka-India. Out of which 14,34 lakhs are child labourers. According to the few noted NGO's more than 1,04 lakh (CWC, 2003) children are working in Bangalore city (Capital City of Karnataka State-India.) only.

The above statements show lot of inconsistency in accurate number of child labourers. Data have been culled from various sources and information on many impordent sources became available only after new estimates were finalized. On the basis of estimates in 200, the ILO concluded that the magnitude of child labour had decreased by almost20 percent since 1995, resulting in a child labour incidence of 20.2 percent as compared to 24,2 percent five ears earlier. Due to the lot of differences in the data collection methodologies however, accuracy is simply impossible.

Extent and Concentration of Child Labour

Despite various acts and legislation along with mammoth effort by many NGO's and other organizations, India is still continues to be one of the high incidence of the child labour. According the global labour force estimates of the ILO every fifth child in the age group of 10-14 years was part of the country's active labour force. The number of child workers in India was estimated at 15.1 million in 1975. The NSS-32 rounds (1977-78) estimated child workers in the age group 5-14 at 16.25 million in 1978.

In 1983 the Planning Commission projected the number of child workers as 17.36 million. The NSS (National Sample Survey) data clearly show, in 1971, children formed about 6 percent of the total force and in 1983 7.4 percent of the total force. As per the 43rd round of NSS (1987-1988), the total number of working children was estimated to be 17.02 million (NSS REPORTS).

According to 1981 census, about 86.4 percent child workforce is employed in agricultural and allied activities in rural sector. This sector is commonly referred as most invisible sector. Most interesting factors is that this agricultural and allied activities does not comes under any specific acts and legislature. Many children work as hired wage labour and even some as bonded labour.

Recognizing the harm done to children who are forced into the labour forces at an early age, Governament all over the world have sought to eradicate child labour by bringing into force legal measures and social policy prescriptions. However, as seen from various labour and education statistics from the developing world, the condition of children remains deplorable.. In India alone it is estimated that 82.3 million children in 1981 were not attending the school and 11.2 million were part of the labour force. Government reports in 1983 showed 17.4million children below the age of 15 in the labour force, constituting 6.8 percent of the rural labour force and 2.4 percent of the urban labour force (Wiener, 1990)

The secondary sector is the next important area of child labour particularly in urban areas, More than one third of the urban workers in this sector are children and more than one fourth of them belong to non- house hold industries and construction. (Dacca, T M, 2003) Usually in urban areas children work in garages, construction cites, shop and commercial establishments pavement selling, rag picking, etc. A lot of children also found employed in many hazardous industries like carpet weaving mining, Zaire weaving, fire works, glass etc. Also some time we can see children engaged in smuggling goods, prostitution and some other illegal activities. Girl child workers usually found employed in domestic work, household and cottage industries etc.

Non Government Organisations (NGOs) and child labour

NGO's are some time called as a fifth unofficial organ of the Government. Numerous NGOs have been working towards find a solution to the child labour problem. Many NGO's have grown in size and capabilities conducting research and training while developing effective and innovative programmes to shift children from work to school. The work of NGO's in the fields of primary education, micro-financing, and alternative income generation programmes have also made an important contribution in the effort to eradicate child labour in both urban and rural India. However, unless NGO's make significant improvement in their performance in promoting sustainable livelihood for the poor their best efforts may not prove sufficient for ending child labour.

Since Government programmes has experienced a mere success in the total eradication of the problem NGO s can play a vital role to solve the problem at least. The effectiveness NGO's is attributed to two major factors.1 they are relatively accepted to the people due to their aversion towards Government Officials in some areas. 2 since they will work at the grass root level they will have an intense knowledge about day-today problems and cultural resistance for the change of the concerned people. They also have the experience in running special schools with certain advantages over Government agencies like having a more committed work force flexibility in operation, through Knowledge and human resources and the preparedness to work with target groups in far flung locations. (Kumar, 1999). So NGO's are believed to be better motivators than the Government machinery with respect to any problem concerning child labour and child abuse. In this regard the service being rendered by NGO's in Karnataka State CRY, CWC, ROAD, CHIGURU, APSA, MAYA, CRY, CACL, and DON BOSCO-etc. and some of the famous International Organisations like ILO, UNISEF, WHO, DFID etc are to mentioned and policies and programmes relating to child labour relief and rehabilitation must be financially and technically supported by both the Government and other funding agencies. But now a days a lot of question have been raised on the validity of the function and financial transferency of the NGO's.

Nowhere Children and Child Labour

Despite progressive laws and policies child labour issue in India is growing more and more. It has remained both an economic and a social problem since a long time. According to the latest report more than 100 million children below 14 years are toiling in different corners of India. Economic compulsion of the family, adult unemployment and growing trend of employers of hiring children to save the different costs are the prime factors for this chronic problem. Basically the magnitude of child labour often rely on official figure. That kind of figures usually overestimated or slanted, for various other reasons.

As per Indian context is concerned there has been trend to formulate the definition of child labour rather loosely. All child labour estimating Organisations keeping all working children in one hardly differentiated category. I e. all out of school children have been categorized under one sub head potential child labourers. Some advocacy says all out of school children are child labourers. Some of the social scientists have given a statement that child labour means denied of education at child hood

(Burra, 1995) has an opinion that a child labour is 'basically, a child who is deprived of the right to children and childhood'. These statements lead to the mind that all out of school children are working in one form or another. The nowhere children are classified as potential child labourers and it is assumed to be staying home from school. So that they can assume the responsibility of the household instead of parents and allow the latter to go out and work. So we say, we have over 100 million child labourers. But, still lots of arguments are going on between the term's child work and child labour. Ambiguities still persist (Venkatanarayana,2001).

It is crystal clear that so many million children are absolutely educationally deprived children, but it is unwarranted to classify this child hood time as 'child labour'. It is necessary to find out the causes why they are workers, but at reasons why they are not in the school (Lieten, 2005). Since real factors behind actual child labourers and behind non-enrollment of school or drop out are absolutely different, it must and should be theoretically, more over analytically separated soon.

As per statistics are concerned on school age children have reveled that a small proportion of the children is reportedly working. However a large proportion of children are reportedly out of school and out of work too. They are refered as 'nowhere children.' What they are keep doing? This is the clear-cut segment where, exactly we need conceptual clarity. Saying that all out-of –children are child labourers are not logic more over it has no concrete evidences and also it is not convincing.

Because existed and restrictive definitions of work excludes many activities in which children are reportedly involved. And parents hesitant to give real fact because of low value attached to it. Also the present definition of work in general has led to neglect of work force, particularly female workers. It is just because of exclusion of certain kinds of jobs or hidden occupations. In the same, we can say there is also an underestimation of child labourers.. Because of limited definition of work as said earlier, many out of school children that are working do not get included in the broad category of working children. So there is a general agreement that all out of school children are a child labourers.

Since, lot of visible and invisible reasons are embed, general usage that all out of school children is child labourers is not appropriate. If, we agree with the above statement for a moment, it sounds as if work and schooling are mutually exclusive activities for children. It, shows that only out-of-school children are no working and school-attending children are not working at all. But it known fact that many children are working while attending school to meet their school expenditures. In the same way if, one can refers out-of-school children as child labourers, one can infer that it may legitimize the work that is combined with schooling (Nieuwenhuys, 1999).

We can say that lot children may not attend the school due to the severe health reasons. It may include congenital problems, undernourished, etc. So any one can say, for such children it is their deprivation of health that deprives them of education. Hence we cannot say all out of school children are working. Illness may cause the gap in schooling, and it may ends with drops out.

Culturally bounded country like India tradition also plays a vital role, which deprives children from school. In many cases parents may don't like to send their children at all. More than that in rural areas usually parents would like to withdraw girl children from school immediately after attaing puberty. Since India is a tropical country usually females attains the puberty stage at the age of 12-13or even soon. No doubt early marriage practice too plays a significant roles in early withdrawing the children from the school and family perceptions of a suitable age for their children to enter school differ, may also leads to the wrong conclusion.

Deprived children, whether employed as child labour or the uncounted 'nowhere children' have become a major focus of attention in police oriented social science research in India. In the interest of the future of the Nation it is highly essential that all children should be at the school in the age of atleast 6-14. All economic oriented including (tradition occupations) at the cost of education and precious education may authentically termed as deprived children. But vast number of children still denied the benefits of schooling and a normal child hood in India. Hence, it is socially imperative to seek new approach and more than better analyze the problem from eyes of children it self. So it is highly essential to find out what is the real factor behind, why children are not going not to school despite free primary education?. What is the impact of non-schooling on involvement in work? Also it is time to determine the household expenditure on education and health among nowhere children families. Are educational market is gradually failing in India.? Satisfactory answer for all these burning questions and to other remaining questions may lead to a solution for the problem of child labour in India, and the issue of the nowhere children could then take place with more insight into the actual process and the resulting causes and consequences.

Globalization and Child Labour

Globalisation is a process that is defined in a number of ways and differently understood. It is defined as the transnational of capital, internationalization of labour, homogenization of culture, Globalisation of production and standardization of consumers' testes. The organizing principle of production or the harnessing of the countries human and natural resources is profit maximization. Globalization is integration of our economy with the global exchange system. "Those who have no exchange entitlements, purchasing capacity and no means of production except labour is automatically exclude from market. Market fundamentals are the key words and not struggling people who basically contribute to the value addition".(REDS- An NGO, WorkShop,1997).

Under such an economic arrangement, the growing expansion of wealth and increasing social exclusion, economic growth and unemployment, rapid technology process, commodification and feminization of poverty to go hand in hand. The emergent global order is not obligated to preserve earth, life supporting systems and more than that the very existence of poor and marginalised section of the community. Totally thorough maximization of profits, exploitation of human and natural resources and monopolization of technology, globalization has pushed aside the human factor. This is nothing but re-colonization and gradual elimination of the vulnerable section of the people, their culture, tradition, and customs.

The advent of globalization has by passed all the basic tenets of a welfare state. By accelerating the process in 1992, the Government of India relaxed the polices and laws in order to permit the transnational /multinational companies to move around freely and have their own business. As a result the multi national companies have appropriated key business sector across the country. The Government new economic polices prompted a drastic reduction in expenditure ion the welfare front such as education, health, sanitation housing and food security. The above sectors have now been privatized and a better parallel service has been established which comes at a heavier price, which can never be afforded by the common citizen.

Intensified with the Structural Adjustment Programme (SAP), globalization has done enough harms to public sectors. The sales of public undertakings and reduction in public investment have left the workers in the lurch (CACL). This has resulted in the closing down of small and medium industrial units throwing the labourers into the streets. The open market policy no reins on the MNC which carry out their profit making market mechanisms This phenomenon has brought in further unemployment in the country followed by extreme poverty and children are the direct victims of this process. They are forced to leave their schools and search foe any job for the sake of their respective families. MNC always claim that they do not employ children for their work. It is good that they realize that children should not be employed. But the stains of the children's sweat and blood get incorporated in the process of manufacture of products for these cooperate. (CACL).

Job security is now a bygone dream. In the new era, jobs are given on contract. Informalisation of jobs was a major aspect of the globalization process of which domestication of sectors is a direct result when the piece rate system was introduced, the work came to homes. It has made all the members of the family as workers. Through women and children work in this process they are not recognized as workers. The dropout rate of children from such families has shown an upward trend. Globalization process thus devastates the economic fabrics of our society and breeds further unemployment resulting in deprivation of basic rights of the millions of children of this country. of the child, the conditions in which the child works, and whether work prevents the child from going to school.

The Children's Rights Division at Human Rights Watch has focused its efforts on the worst forms of child labour, those prohibited by the ILO's Worst Forms of Child Labour Convention. Children who work long hours, often in dangerous and unhealthy conditions, are exposed to lasting physical and psychological harm. Working at rug looms, for example, has left children disabled with eye damage, lung disease, stunted growth, and a susceptibility to arthritis as they grow older. Children making silk thread in India dip their hands into boiling water that burns and blisters them, breath smoke and fumes from machinery, handle dead worms that cause infections, and guide twisting threads that cut their fingers. Children harvesting sugar cane in El Salvador use machetes to cut cane for up to nine hours a day in the hot sun; injuries to their hands and legs are common and medical care is often not available.

Denied an education and a normal childhood, some children are confined and beaten, reduced to slavery. Some are denied freedom of movement—the right to leave the workplace and go home to their families. Some are abducted and forced to work. The human rights abuses in these practices are clear and acute. We have found similar problems in Asia, the Middle East, Latin America, and the United States: children who work for too many hours and too many days, for too little, or sometimes no pay, subject often to physical abuse, exposed to dangerous pesticides, and made to work with too dangerous tools. Our objectives in tackling these aspects of the complex and troubling child labour issue include drawing attention to the plight of child workers, helping to end these appalling practices, and contributing to the debate on the rights dimension of the larger issue of children and work.

2

Child Labour in India

Child Labour: A Global View

The problem of child labour is a universal phenomenon. Since it is inextricably associated with socio economic plight of the people. Children in every society have assisted in the activities, characteristics of their social group. Developed nations have got some control over the social problems, since developed countries have control over poverty and population. Economic development is of very high standard in those countries. Still, one can observe considerable amount of child labour even in the developed nations of the world. But, the developing and underdeveloped nations are facing it very seriously. Because, in these countries usually poverty and population explosion are beyond control. The child labour is a measuring rod for the economy of a country and a black spot on the face value of the so-called modern and civilized society.

The latest International Labour Organisation (ILO) report on the magnitude of child labour has revealed that around 250 million of children are engaged in one or other kinds of works of whom 120 million are working full time workers and 130 million are part time workers. The report says, Asia accounts for 153 million working children, Africa about 80 million and Latin America 17.5 million working children. According to the recent ILO survey, in selected countries like India, Ghana, Indonesia and Senegal 15 per cent children are workers in the total work force. The percentages is as much as 40 per cent in Senegal if seasonal labourers are taken into account. In Ghana more than 75 per cent of working children aged between 10-14 years are girl children and 73 million children in the age group of 10-14 years are workers. There are estimated 250 million child labourers in the age group of 5-14 years in the world, apart from those who work with their families mainly in domestic activities.

Child labour, a form of child exploitation is a worldwide phenomenon. The consideration of age for being child labour is different in different nations and nature of works. In India children below 14 years gainfully engaged physically and or mentally in any occupation either in agriculture or in industry, are called child labourers. The minimum age considered for child labour is 12 years in Egypt, 14 years in Philippines and Hong Kong 13 years percent in Malaysia. In Peru, this age is 14 years for agriculture sector, 15 years for industry, 16 years for ocean fishing and 18 years for working in ports. ILO in its 'Minimum Age (Industrial) Conference (1919)' has determined 12 to 13 years for light works and 18 years for hard and dangerous works. Although the minimum working age determined by ILO is 15 years (as a child is expected to complete his or her primary education). Engaging the children anywhere below this age will be considered as child labour (Murthy)

The problem of child labour is not particularly specific to any culture or geographical areas. It is a world wide problem since a long time. It is prevalent more or less in all the countries of the world. But it is found that Asia has the largest child labourers in the world. Some recent studies shows that even the developed European countries are not exempted from this. Some of the richest countries also have this problem. However, the intensity may be less when compared to other developing countries.

Child Labour Across the Globe

Countries/Continents	*Number of children ('000s)*		*Work ratio*	
	5-9	*10-14*	*5-9*	*10-14*
Developed economies	800	1,700	1.4	2.8
Transition economics	900	1,500	3.1	4.2
Asia and the Pacific	40,000	87,300	12.3	26.5
Latin America & Caribbean	5,800	11,600	10.6	21.5
Sub-Saharan Africa	20,900	27,100	23.6	34.7
Middle East and North Africa	4,800	4,800	10.8	19.6

Of the 10-14 years old children the working children are 41.3 per cent in Kenya, 31.4 per cent in Chile 30.1 per cent in Bangladesh, 25.8 per cent in Nigeria, 24 per cent in Turkey, 20.5 percent in Ivory Cost, 17,7 percent in Pakistan, 16.1 per cent in Brazil, 14.4 per cent in India, 11.5 per cent in Chine, 11.3 percent in Egypt, 6.7 per cent in Mexico, 4.5 per cent in Argentina, 1.8 per cent in Portugal and 0.4 per cent in Italy. In some countries of Eastern Europe the difficulties connected with family income had led to a substantial increase in child labour. (Thakur, R N) It shows child labour has been spread from east to west and south to north without fail. All developed, developing and under developed countries are exhibiting with this problem. But in western countries, children are working more in secondary sectors unlike India.

USA is considered to be a richest country of the world today. It is true that child labour is banned 60 years ago in USA. Still, a survey conducted has revealed that about 3 lakh children in the age group of 5-15 yeas of age work in various occupations even in the hazardous sectors. They are paid less and exploited more. In this country children of any age may be employed by their parents or persons standing in place of their parents at any time and in any occupation on in farm owned or operated by their parents or persons standing in place of their parents, with the implication that these children may engage, in activities that they would not be allowed to undertake in other circumstances. It is an irony that the country which is so vocal for abolition of child labour in India and other under developed countries, often threatening to ban imports of goods manufactured using child labourers itself is infected with this kind of disease.

England is the first country, which imposed ban on child labour. According to the latest ILO report more than 3.5-lakh children are working in different part of the United Kingdom. Mainly children belonging to the migrant families are working for few Pounds. A recent study has shown that more then 3.5 per cent of educated couples have agreed with the concept of socialization of the children through work (Grant). The same study has revealed that people unanimously agreed that parents should provide happy and best childhood to children at any cost. But still the rights of the children are not yet effectively implemented through out the country. Many children are working in rural areas as field workers. More than that, children below the age of 16 years of are working in many hazardous industries.

With the transformation to market economy, new kinds of pressures have emerged on children, especially among the poors, to contribute to family income or to provide for themselves. Countries of the former USSR and those in Central and Eastern Europe have witnessed in varying degrees the increase of poverty, family disintegration, migration and population displacement, erosion of social safety nets, deterioration in health and education services and increases in delinquency and drug use among young people. At the same time, opportunities for children to participate in the largely unregulated labour market have rapidly multiplied, especially in expanding informal (and often illegal) economy. With limited experiences in dealing with child labour, government institutions are ill equipped to devise responses. Greater proportional losses by the poor in times of economic crisis have occurred in other regions as well. In countries like Brazil, Chile and Ecuador, for example, poor children are pulled out of schools. But, it is noted that effects are not uniform across countries or socio-economic groups(Bhargav). But in Asia, household coping strategies appear to be heavily influenced by government policy, especially as regards to social welfare and education pointing to the specific importances of social protection for the poor.

It is reported that more than 250.00 children are working in domestic sector around the globe. In Brazil, Colombia and Ecuador more then 20 per cent of girls in the age group of 10-14 are working in domestic, cocoa, rubber and coffee plantations. In El Salvador, children work in small-scale family based cottage industries for money in which children harvest shellfish and girls also markets the products. This work begins at the age of 10 years. A substantial portion of children is working in fishing and tanning industry in Peru, Mexico etc. It has been observed that many children are working in *ganja* and *hashish* fields in Afghanistan.

In Philippines enrolment of children in schools especially at secondary level declined. At the same time, youth unemployment is increasing. So children are thus more vulnerable to informal, illegal and hazardous economic sectors. Here many of the children are working as swimmers and divers to catch reef fish for marketing. In case of Thailand, the crisis has limited impact on the overall rate of children in schools, but youth unemployment is gradually increasing. In South Thailand, children are working as fish sorters and crews on fishing boats. In Central Java and Sumatra, children are working in fishing industry as divers, draining boats. However, in rural areas school dropout rates are increasing possibly indicating a shift into urban child Labour in many parts Southeast Asia. (ILO, 2001)

Child labour is not just ideologically unacceptable, it had no real place in centrally planned economies operated by controlling labour mobility and by strictly regulated job market. Officially, children could perform works only if they prepare it from the point of view of future employment within the framework of education. To this day, Cuba and China claims that child labour does not exist in their countries. Nonetheless, even in pre-reform socialist countries, child labour existed to some extent.

In most of the African countries, the rate of child labour is considerably high because they are under developed countries. Moreover many countries have recently escaped from the clutches of the colonies. The economic and other resources exploited by other countries have caused much damage to them. Even though, they have got enough natural resources, they could not succeed in over throwing poverty. Some of the African countries like Kenya, Egypt, Zambia and Nigeria etc where rich natural and human resources could play a role in eradicating poverty, three fourth per cent of total population are living still under the acute poverty line. Not only these countries are facing poverty problem, but also population explosition that has pushed them back to dark. Further, many of the African countries are facing acute internal conflicts and civil wars. Many of the children have become child soldiers for food and money. One of the study has shown that "traditional and superstitious believes have blocked their ways to social and economic development" (Verma). Basically, children are found employed largely in agricultural sectors in many African countries. Also a substantial portions among them are in mining and quarries. Bonded labour system is still prevalent in many African countries. Basically, a notable number of children are working in commercial agricultural forms. In Kenya, Rwanda and West Africa children under the age of 15 years form 27-30 per cent of total workforce in agriculture and selling crafts (Bhargav). In central Africa a large number of children are working in plantations. In Madagascar, more than 53 per cent children are working in small-scale mines. In Dominican Republic basically people are living on sugar cane. It is reported that many children under the age group of 15 are working in sugar plantations and largely children are migrated from Haiti. In Tanzania, children work along with their parents in blue metal industry. In South Africa, children are working in diamond mining.

A recent study has proved that countries with relatively high per captia income could succeed in reducing illiteracy rates and poverty ratio. It is important to note that in some of the countries like Korea, Japan, Kuwait and Saudi Arabia, both poverty ratio and incidence of child labour have declined to zero per cent. It shows positive correlation between poverty ratio and incidences of child labour. In some countries like Sri Lanka, Thailand and Vietnam despite of significant reduction in rats of illiteracy rate the child labour still persists.

Girls working as domestic servants away from their homes are frequent victims of physical, mental and sexual abuses, which can have devastating consequences of their health. ILO reports on child labour has mentioned categorically about forced prostitution's or forced sex workers in which girl children are subjected to. 'The AIDS' epidemic is a contributing factor to this trend, as adults see the use of children for sexual purposes as the best means of preventing infection. The full extent of the problem is unknown, but in Thailand an estimated 55,000 to 80,000 underage children are involved in the sex trade. The large number of 'travelers' from industrial countries and other developing countries come to India every year in search of child prostitutes as there is less risk and fear of being defamed and imprisonment. According to the report of "Girls and child prostitutes in Asian Tourism," there are three lakhs of such child prostitutes (girls) in India, one lakh in Thailand, one lakh in

Taiwan, one lakh in Philippines. 40,000 in Vietnam, 30,000 in Sri Lanka and about more than 20,000 in China. Germany, Norway and Sweden have enacted acts to deal with the sex-criminals especially in the tourism industry. Recently Australia, France and Newzland are trying to make such laws (rajjwat)

It is said to be around 2.89 million child labourers are in Nepal. Many of them are under the age group of 14 years and one fourth of the children are below the age of 10 years. Beside domestic sectors children are found employed largely in agriculture and export industries. Carpet industries are well established in Nepal. According to one of the local NGOs working condition of the children are inhuman, underwaged and unhygienic. Many children working in carpet and gem industries are facing acute occupational hazardous health problems.

Not only Nepal, the poor country Bangladesh also is facing acute child labour problem. More than 60 million children are working in many sectors. Since this country is commonly called as a bowl of jute half of the total child labour force are working in garment industry. Most of the children are in between 8-14 years of age. Working condition is below the fused standard. Poor ventilation, and long hours of continuos work are some of the problems faced by the children. One of the studies(hdxbh) has shown that children are facing a lot of health problems due to cotton dust constant clatter of machines and very short breakage for lunch and for bathrooms. A lot of children are working in most of the hazardous sectors even without having any minimum protective measurement. Even the Government does not pay much attention as 12 percent of GDP comes from the sector where children are largely found employed

Basically agriculture is a prime sector in Pakistan like India. So, as usual many children are working in different segments of the agriculture sector. Also children are working in leather, surgical instruments and manufacturing sporting goods. Most of the children employed are below the age of 12 years. More than that, one fourth of the total child labourers are bonded labourers. It is so common in brick industries, fisheries stone crushing shoe making, powers looms Bhargava). Sine carpet industry is basically a cottage industry, many children are working in their family units. Those children who are working out side their family units earn not less than 40 Rs per day and they have to work for about 9-10 hours per day. According to the AMNESTY International 13 to 20 per cent are children are working in sports goods industries. In rural areas it has become a cottage level family units. Here children work for about 10 hours and the wage is Rs 1000 per month. Manufacture of surgical instruments is a well-established industry in Pakistan. Recent study shows that thousand children are working in this industry and all of them are below the age of 17 years. These children are working with out any protective measurements. Recently many western countries have imposed ban on the import of these surgical instruments from Pakistan. Since Pakistan is more or less an agricultural oriented country one fourth of the total child force is working in the agricultural field.

Number of Working Children Less than 15 Years old across the globe

Area	*Total(Million)*	*Unpaid Family Worker*	
		Million	*Percentage of Total*
World	52.0	41.2	80
South-East Assia	29.0	23.2	80
East Asia	9.1	6.4	70
Africa	9.7	9.3	96
Latin America	3.1	2.0	65
Europe	0.7	0.4	50
USSR	----	----	--
North America	0.3	----	10
Oceania	0.1	0.1	85

Child Labour in India: A Retrospective

Inspite of significant achievements in most of the sectors after independence, India is still facing several social hurdles in the way of national development. Child labour is one such problem. It is not a new phenomenon as for as India is concerned. It has been linked with the socio economic development of every society since time immemorial and became more significant after economic revolution. The problem of child labour in India has of late assumed the proportion of a social menace threatening the very fabric of the social milieu. Child labour has become a well explained popular issue ever since many western countries, under the fabric of labour welfare, took it up, targeting developing countries like India and China as the two countries having has very poor record in the sphere of child labour. Despite progressive laws and polices, child labour issue in India is growing more and more. It has remained both an economic and a social problem for a long time. According to the latest report more than 100 million children are toiling in different corners of India. Every one fourth of working child in the world is an Indian. Inspite of industrialization, urbanization, privatization and its various achievements, India ranks first in the world for having the highest number of child workers. Experts assume economic compulsion of the family, adult unemployment and growing trend of employers of hiring children to save the costs production are some of the reasons behind child labour in India.

Child labour was prevalent even in the ancient time in different forms in India. But it was not of so exploitative as of now. Effective socialization was the main motive and concern among the parents and teachers. Their work was favorably related to the overall development of children. Later on the situation changed. During 1860-1870 there was an enormous growth of coffee, tea, indigo and jute industries in northern and central part of India. These industries belonged to many European countries the colonel rulers. During 1940, children accounted for 17 per cent of the labour force in many agricultural and plantation work. After independence, Mukherjee,1951) writes "it was so common in many parts of India that children were found in the coal mines to help the parents in cart pushing or loading. In mica mines also children were found employed" Lieten (2005) writes "the very precise figures that we find in the official accounts of many industries- tea gardens, coal mines, mica industries, bidi industries and the regulated and non regulated factories have been carefully shifted and convey a picture of the reality in those days"

It is a well-known fact that children were found employed in many household works since the ancient time. The main intention was that after the elder's life period the children were supposed to continue the family occupation. These kinds of activities were so common during medieval period also in rural India because small and marginal economic units inevitably characterized a predominantly rural society. Gradually children become an integral part of the house hold economy. They were trained while still young and gradually start contributing individually to the family's income .As a result, the children were in a situation where they had to earn for themselves as well as for the families. Experts say even in family run units, where the child is generally better looked after by is parents and may not suffer from any physical hardship, he goes through mental strain because of problems and anxieties regarding the undertaking which he shares with his parents .

An important issue in human resources development is the prevalence of child labour. Basically child labour can be defined as the engagement of children between the years of 6-14 years (as per Indian context) working in economically gainful works. Even though, child labour is more or less common in many countries, it is most prevalent among the developing countries. India has the largest population of child labourers who contributes nearly 7 per cent of the work force contributing considerable amount to the GDP (Kumar A R). Estimates supplied by various agencies regarding the population of child Labour in India don't depict a uniform picture. According to ILO, India has the dubious distinction of having perhaps the largest child Labour force in the world. Approximately 45 million children are found employed in both organised and unorganised sectors in different corners of India. Among these working children around 24 per cent in urban centers and rest in rural areas. Government statistics in 1986 had shown that that there were 18.4 million children below the age of the 15 in the labour force, constituting 7.8 percent of rural child labour force and 2.9 per cent of urban labour force. Recent World Bank report says that there are 78.5 million working children in India that is the largest in terms of any country include 27 million bonded working children (World Bank Report, 2001). India alone accounts for about 100 million child labourers. If we go for multiplicity of the concept of child labourers it will be around 140 million. Thus, the magnitude of child labour in India varies from sources to sources.

Areas of concentration

The typical nature of child labour in India is more prevalent in rural areas. As we know, three fourth of the national income comes from agricultural sector and more than 75 per cent of the people are depended on agriculture for their subsistence. According to the 1991 Census 85 percent of children are employed in different sectors of the agricultural and allied activities. Rural economy, which is characterized by relatively a higher level of poverty, unemployment and illiteracy when compared to urban economy supports 90 per cent of the total number of child labourers in India. A considerable number of children are engaged in their respective traditional occupations. Many children are helping their family members in the field. Some work as part of contract family labour whereas others work as part of contract family labour where men, women and children all work together. Many of them employed in plantation. Rodgers and Standing (1979) have classified the pattern of child labouer found in rural areas as of domestic, non domestic, bonded and wage labourers. The domestic work includes maidservants or domestic servants, where female children have to bear the burden. Non-domestic works include grazing of animals, working in the field's etc. Gender based economic significance's of male child is further enhanced in countries where social and cultural taboos restrict women from participating in paid work of family, occupational work (Narayana). In rural areas, girl child workers are readily available for work and it is found very common for school aged children to be involved in agricultural works as part of family labour. Girls are mostly engaged in domestic sectors than boys, because these children come largely from land less, small and marginal landholders (Dinesh,1998).

Secondary sectors play a predominant role in case of urban child labourers in India. More than one third of the urban workers are children and more than one fourth of them belong to the non-household industries and construction. Children are found employed in many other sectors like hotel, firework, glass, carpet weaving, automobile etc. In urban areas considerable number of girl children are found to be employed in household works, cottage industries etc. Further children are engaged in many unorganised sectors like shops, pavement selling, dhabas, venders, and porters, scavenging etc. joseph

Estimated Number of Children involved in the Unconditional Worst Forms of Child Labour in India

Type of worst form of child labour Number of Children(in millions) Forced and bonded labourForced recruitment into armed conflictProstitution and pornography Other illicit activities Trafficked children Total 4.70.31.80.6 (1.2)7.4

Bargava 1

Age-specific Work Participation Rates in Indian (1983-2000)

	Age 5-9				*Age 10-14*			
	1983	*1987*	*1993*	*2000*	*1983*	*1987*	*1993*	*2000*
Rural boys	2.5	2.4	1.1	0.6	25.3	19.0	13.9	9.1
Rural girls	2.6	2.3	1.4	0.7	24.0	18.0	14.2	9.6
Urban boys	0.8	0.5	0.5	0.3	11.3	8.5	6.6	4.9
Urban girls	0.7	0.5	0.5	0.2	7.0	6.5	4.5	3.6

Sources: The Indian journal of labour economic, Vol.48, No.1, 2005- (Lieten G.K.)

The sector specific distribution of child workers In India, as per the 1991 Government census reveals that a majority of the children are working in agricultural and its allied activities. The predominance of agriculture is even more pronounced in the case of child workers. More than 80 per cent of the children are working in the major economic sector i. e. agriculture. Agricultural sector can be divided into of cultivators and agricultural labourer. Cultivators constitute 36 per cent and agricultural labourers constitute 45 per cent of total rural child labour force. The table shows more than 3.86 children are working in agricultural activities like live stock, plantation etc. The higher percentage of their employment in cultivation appears to be due to the respondents' bias arising out of higher prestige attached to cultivator category as compared to labourers. The Agricultural Enquiring Committee says "their composition as earners and helpers in the ratio of 11:9. It indicates that majority of child labour working in agriculture, worked for wage and smaller proportion possibly worked as family members and helpers" ((Behor).

Distribution in Different Sectors

Percentage distribution of total working children in different sectors in India, 1991. Percentage distribution, according to the different sectors. (Source: Census Report, 1991)

	Industrial Category	*Percentage distribution of total working children*		
		Male	*Female*	*Total*
1.	Cultivators	38.14	31.10	35.49
2.	Agricultural labourers	39.73	52.27	44.45
	Total	77.87	85.37	79.94
3.	Livestock, forestry, fishing, hunting, plantation, orchard and allied activities	4.55	2.72	3.86
4.	Mining and Quarrying	0.28	0.31	0.29
5.	Household Industry	2.18	4.68	3.12
	Others	6.19	4.65	5.61
	Total	8.37	9.33	8.73
6.	Construction	0.98	0.44	0.78
7.	Trade & Commerce	3.91	0.59	2.66
8.	Transport Storage, etc.	0.52	0.05	0.34
	Other service	3.52	3.19	3.40
	Grand total	100.0	100.0	100.0
	Number in Million	5.66	3.42	9.08

Manufacture and processing units are the third important sector ofter agriculture where a large number of children are found to be employed. Household and other related works accounts for 5.61 per cent of child labourers. Household works are more visible in rural areas than urban and semi urban areas. The major reason is that household work does not come under any specific laws and acts. One-study reports that more than 0.78 percent children are working in construction cite. It is observed that many children start this work during their early age of the life phase. So, that they can learn all essential skills to become an expert mason. In the future. Considerable amount of children are working in transport and storage field. This includes shops and commercial establishments.

It is known that children are found employed in all three sectors of Indian economy. And it has been established that primary sector has highest concentration of child labourers, both in absolute and relative terms. This table show that less number of children is in tertiary sectors, probably this sectors requires more skilled adults.

Child Workers in Different Sectors in India

Sectors	*All works*	*Child workers*
Primary	71.12	86.64
Secondary	12.39	8.57
Territory	16.49	4.56
Others	1.56	2.45

Sources: Census Report, 1981.

Location Specific Occupations

One of the unique features of child labour system in India is the location specific nature of the jobs. Even though, child labourers are spread all through the length and breadth of the country, some specific kind of occupations is observed in some areas only. But, however no one should think (From the table) those lists of occupations found only in those areas only. This table shows some specific occupations found more in those areas as than any other places in India. This table includes only widely known occupations where large number of children is found employed. Carpet industry is more common in J and K, West bangal and U P. Working in the construction cites found in every patches of the country. Glass industry predominately found in U P. Like that concentration of large power loom industry can be seen in both Tamil Nadu and Maharashtra state because of availability of enough raw materials and chief labour. Large numbers of girl worker are found in garment industry in Delhi. Children working in fishing industry are common in all along the costral areas of the country. Garage work and street children are found in many parts of the country. Andra pradesh has the highest number of child labourers. Rural child labour is highest in Karnataka. Rate of child employment is very less in Kerala State.

Geographical Concentration

1. Glass & Bangles – Firozabad (Utter Pradesh)
2. Handloom—Tamil Nadu and Maharastra
3. Powerloom –Bhiwandi in Maharashtra.
4. Carpet weaving – Jammu & Kashmir, Utter Pradesh and Rajasthan.
5. Zari and Embroidery –Lucknow (U.P.).
6. Gem cutting and polishing – Jaipur (Rajasthan)

7. Diamond cutting and polishing—Surat (Gujarat).
8. Match & fire works—Sivakasi (Tamil Nadu).
9. Garages and petrol pumps—Through out India
10. Cashew processing and manufacture of coir products- (Kerala.)
 Helpers in Hotels, Restaurants, Canteens, Tea Stalls, Shops-Through out India
 Rag picking- Predominately in Megacites of the county
 Construction-Throughout India
 Fishing—Kerala, Tamil Nadu, Gujarat
 Pottery Units—Khuraja (U.P.).
 Hawkers, Vendors, Newspaper sellers-through out India
 Coolies—Throughout India
 Lock Industry—Aligarh (UP)
 Bonded Labour- Several patches in India
 19Slate Industry—Mandsaur (M.P.).
 Sources: T. M. Dak (2003) 'Child labour in India.'

Child Labour in Selected Sectors.

MINES

Children formed a large part of the mining labour force in the early years of the century. According to a report during 1901, there were as a many as few thousand children below the age of 12 years who constituted 4.8 per cent of the total labour force engaged in mines. Administration brought many acts to ban child labour in mines like *The Mines act-1901 and The Indian Mines Act 1921.* In the report of labour conditions in the iron and ore industry, the committee observed that "in particular mines employment of children under 15 years in contravention of the law is frequent." Recently an NGO has observed hat large number of tribal children are found employed in many mines in Utter Pradesh, Madhya Pradesh and Bihar. Children engaged in this work usually suffer with harmful dusts, gases, fumes fatigue and endangered by mercury poisoning. It is most common in UP, MP and Bihar.

Plantations

Quite a large number of children are employed in plantations is between the age of 12-14. According to one findings of the *Ad-hoc* enquiry conducted in Assam in 1976, roughly 57 per cent of the children employed in European owned estates and 63 per cent of those employed in Indian owned estates were between the ages of 12 and 14 years. At present the children in the tea plantations earn about 40 Rs per day. Here regular employment will no be available unlike factories and mines. Children employed in tea plantations are so common in Tamil Nadu, Orissa, and W. Bengal, Assam Karnataka State. etc.

Ceramic and Glass work

The children in these works are common. Children must carry molten loads of glass dragged from the tank furnace at a temperature of 1500-1800 degree centigrade. Some times young children of 8-9 years of age carry weight upto 20 kg with their bodies bent and frames trembling with the effort.(Joseph).Some time children have to work with exposed electric wires and sound as high as 100 decibels. Here many children are working like urban bonded labourers. Children get around 35 Rs per day. Poor eyesight, toxic fumes, injures from the flying glass are common health affected problems that children are facing in this sector. It is found very common among Utter Pradesh, Madhya Pradesh, Rajasthan, Karnataka states.

Construction

Owing to a rapid growth of wealth and an ever-expanding need for housing, construction work is undertaken on large scale under private, cooperative and government auspices. This is the only sector in which without any prior conditions one can enter into the work. Large number of rural migrant families is engaged in this sector. When the head of the family is recruited, he moves to the city with his entire family. The construction sites change, the family is constantly on the move and the child cannot take advantage of the existing schooling facilities. Basically children starts as a helper and after some years of experience, one can become a skilled mason and he gets around 175 Rs per day. Children usually get around 45 Rs per day. One can say among all the jobs where children are engaged, construction work is the hardest and most tiresome. Carrying of heavy loads, mixed cements and bricks etc causes a lot health related problem to the children.

Brassware industry

Brassware industries are most common in many parts of central India like Utter pradesh, Madhya Pradesh and Bihar. The subcontractors who are responsible for he jobs of molding, polishing and electroplating mostly child labourers. Children are also engaged in welding and scraping. The other process in which many children work is polishing the semi-finished products. Children are also observed working in electroplating and polishing. They have to work with poison's chemicals and molding hot temperature that naturally may cause unimaginable health hazardous to the children. Main reason for the employment of children is low wages that reduces production cost.

Carpet Industry

Utter Pradesh is commonly known as carpet belt of the country. It has been estimated that more than 4 lakh children are working in carpet industry in Utter Pradesh, Karnataka, Jammu and Kashmir states. Children's nimble fingers play a vital role in carpet weaving. Here wage depends on number of carpet they can weave in a day. Further children work in sorting. Dying and knotting sections. It is found that 8 per cent of the total work force in the hand-knotted carpet industry is child labourers.

Gem polishing industry is popular in Gujarat, Rajasthan and Madhya Pradesh State.95 per cent of all colured gemstones in India are polished in these states only. The gem industry caters of the international market because of the easy availability of child labour. Mostly boys between 12-13 years old, polish diamonds for an average of seven to nine hours in a day including cutting washing and polishing diamond chips. In addition, children also polish emeralds, corals, rubi, and topaz. According to a report more than 15.000 thousand children (22 per cent of total work force) are working in this field in Rajasthan. They have to work for about 10 hours for 30 Rs per day. Wages is based on the number of diamonds that they polish. Some time children do not get paid wags for several years in the gem polishing industry because they are considered as to be learning the craft. People in the industry believe that education is of paramount importance in the gem industry because they have or to deal with dealers and foreign market.

Lock Industry

Aligarh s famous for lock industry. It is estimated that 85 per cent of the locks are made in Aligarh Dist only. It comes under small-scale cottage industry. More than 15000 children below the age of 12 years are working 12-bhours a day. Family based units are very common in this field. The practice of employing children as part of family labour is very common. Children are engaged in hand press, buffing machines, electroplating, painting- etc. which are very dangerous to health. Lack of attention may cause of accidents and often child may loose the tips of the fingers while working with the machine. Usually children will get 900 Rs. per month.

Silk

It has been reported that more than 7.000 thousand children are employed in southern parts of Bangalore-Karnataka. Children found employed in this job usually between the age of 6-12 years. It is because the pretences of nimble fingers are very important for silk weaving. They will work for about 10 hours per day. Girl child labourers found more in this sector. Many children are working as bonded labourers. Children commonly prepare yarns on beams and weave the silk. Majority of the children is from poor Muslim families. Children have to work in all activities like weaving, dying, and rolling and washing etc. Since it comes under house holds industry, employers have narrow chance to escape from the clutches of the law.

Auto Garage

With the emergence of private car and taxi or two/three wheeler vehicles, automobiles repair shops have sprung up in almost all parts of the metropolis. It is the most popular sector for child laboures. More than 12 per cent of the total child labourers are working in this sector. Most of the all parents think children should start this work in the early ages so that he can become a good skilled mechanic. Usually children do their jobs without having any protective measures. Depending upon their knowing to undertake repair works, children get their wages. During apprenticeship, children are not paid any money. Tightening of nuts and bolts, cleaning, oiling, washing is the different kind of this works entrusted them. Some risks are definitely involved in this job. Basically children work as helpers to the adult mechanics that undertakes the main repair work and they are supposed to be the guide to the children. Apart from the physical hazards involved and its unclean nature, the job also entails

Industry wise Distribution of Child Labourers in India

Industry	*Locations (states)*	*Total*
Match and Fireworks processing	Sivakasi	50.000
Stone Quarries	Kerala	20.000
Lead Mines	Meghalaya	28.000
Fish freezing and processing	Kerala	20.000
Handloom Industry.	Kerala, Tripura and Maharashtra	33.000
Bidi Industry	Karnataka, TN, Kerala	25.000
Lock industry	Uthar Pradesh	23.000
Handicraft	Jammu and Kashmir	27.000
Carpet weaving	Kashmir, UP and Rajasthan	2,20,000
Glass Industry	Firozbad (UP)	50,000
Glass Industry	Rajasthan Kerala	34,000
Coir	Kerala	80,000
Pottery	UP	10,000
Brassware	UP Bihar	27,000

Source: Rehabilitation of Child Labour in India-R.N Patil.

elements of exploitation. The master generally has a tendency to protract the period of the so-called training so as to impress on the child that he is only learning and not working and hence is not entitled to any wages or remuneration.

Reported Reasons for Child Labour in India

Child labour is a universal problem, which is more common among developing countries. Social factors, poverty, illiteracy, rural migration, family disintegration, inadequate measures of social security, lack of avenues for education, social choices, social polices and shortcomings in institutional arrangements, and resource constraints are the main reasons for this problem. On other hand, due to technological backwardness and labour intensive technology in these countries, there is a search for cheap labour which is compensated out of child labour. An ILO study shows that

- about 85 per cent of the total child labourers in India are forced work to supplement the income of their families
- about 75 per cent of parents allow their children to work from the economic point of view
- about 50 per cent of parents feel that the income earned by their children is essential for the maintenance of their families
- about 44 per cent of the families have their own cultural and traditional beliefs in maintaining and continuing their family occupations
- about 70 per cent of child labourers want to continue their present job even if they are given the option to leave them (Pandey, S.2001) (The Economic Times, Calcutta, Dak (Ed.)1996)

By and large it observed that social factors, poverty, population explosion, and urbanisation are the real factors behind this child labour problem.

Social and Cultural Factors

A social and cultural concept on child labour has become a more debatable issue of recent time. Culture has its own definition on the term *child* and child labour and it differs greatly across the society. Culture has fixed some functions, which has to be performed by the children in their early ages for the effective socialization. This process of socialization and the cultural objectives to which they are supposed to respond are clearly interdependent with the structural economic system within which the process of socialization occurs. In a culturally bounded society like India, culture plays a vital role on both family structure and sex roles of the every child. Child labour can be seen more among low class people or weaker sections of the society. Due to the unequal distribution of wealth and neglect towards the traditional beliefs among the upper caste people has made domination on low caste group. Hence, child labour can be seen more among low class people or weaker section of the society. In a society like ours sending children to school largely depends on cultural context of the family and basically that decisions will be taken at household level. However, such decisions are not separated from other crucial aspects of household decision making nor are they purely household based. They reflect the norms and values of the wider community within which the household is located and the social and economic possibilities which local contexts offer to different categories of households (Subramaniyan). Some explanation of poverty has focussed on the level of economic development within a given society as the prime cause of poverty. Others have focused on the presumed inferior personnel or cultural traits of the poor. Still others have interpreted poverty as the result of societal conditions that permit or encourage economic deprivation for some societal members.

Poverty

The poverty has two aspects: absolute poverty and relative poverty. In case of absolute poverty the level of the income of people of a country is too low that they cannot meet even their basic minimum requirements, it is called the absolute type of poverty. On the basis of this definition, nearby 27 crores of people which constitutes about 29 per cent of total population fall below this line. Relative poverty means, When we compare incomes of different people we find that some people are poorer than others. This is called Relative poverty. A recent survey on poverty show that, 37 crores of people are living below poverty line. It is most visible, speculative and prime reason for the existence of the problem like child labour. In India basically poor people forces their children to go to the work because augmentation of their income is essential for the survival of the family. The urban poor and rural marginalised and ladles poor people send their children for wage earning.

Rapid Growth of Population

For the most of its 4.000-year history, India has been a rural nation. By 1901,only 27 million people were residing in present day territory, In 2001, 100 crores people are living in India. This represents almost a tenfold increase in less than a century. Now the population of India is increasing rapidly. It is one of the most important causes among others for creating child labour problem Population pressure in India have created widespread misery and suffering for their members and have seriously handicapped their chances to complete economic development. Rapid growth of population in India is a pivotal issue with numerous and far reaching implications on the quality of life economic inequalities and the rate of economic growth. Rapid population growth in India has created gigantic problems, which directly affects on social political and economic aspects of our country. The poor people having low income and who constitute the major portion of the society generally become the victim's of all these phenomena's. For certain extent population growth can be considered as a favourable development. But after crossing the transition point it is a hindrance to economic development of the country and population decreases the per captal income of the nation also constrain the limited resources. Continuous increase in population may lead to excess labour supply and adult unemployment. This high fertility may exert enormous pressure on the parents to save and invest a lot of money on education and health of their respective children.

Urbanisation

Less opportunities, unemployment, drought and unfinished rural development programmes are the main reasons behind rural migration to urban areas. By 1901, 11 percent of total population were lived in cites (Nagpaul, 1988). In 1993, it was 26 percent. However, as incredible as India's urban development has been to date, growth projections for the end of first quarter of the 21st are nothing short of mind boggling. By the 2020, approximately one-half of the country's projected 1,370,000,000 people will be in urban residents (Dogan & Kasarda, 1988). 75 million people will likely to live in India's biggest and Mega cites by the year 2010. India's population is growing at a rate of 2.1 per cent per year, and the cites has been growing at the rate of 3.8 per cent per year, with many urban centers increasing between 4 and 7 percent annually. This rapid urban growth causes many more problems, which led to the existence of childlabour in urban centers. Flow of labour forces in to the urban center leads to the excess availability of labourers for fewer wages to the employers.

These aspects affects in many different ways 1 trance acculturation 2 rising of urban unemployment 3 decrease in living index 4 social disintegration. Some times semi urban areas that very near to border of any villages may emerged as the most important business centers for meeting day-to day requirements of the migrant and slum labourers. The rural migrants working in urban centers and other villagers who visit to semi urban areas would take numerous urban-industrial characteristic with them when they go back to their mother village (Jha, M). This greatly affects the homogeneous rural society mainly to customs, tradition and to beliefs. More or less we can say original rural culture will be under heavy influence of another culture. This change may provoke the parent's either to migrate to the so-called urban centers or send their children to such centers to earn more extra money. This finally leads to the social disintegration.

In recent years there has been a decline in the proportion of child labour in organised sector but it is spreading in many more unorganised sectors like loading and unloading, pavement selling, rag-picking, child prostitution, hawking goods, and daily labourers. This is all due to the uncontrolled and unlimited growth of urban centers in India (Murthy).

Gender Issues

While discrimination of girl children in the specific area of child labour does exist, it is often studied only as a part of the overall pattern of discrimination against girls. As far as child labour is concerned, what most writers on the subject stress is that the parameters are often defined in such a manner that discrimination is not even apparent. Thus, a large amount of work in which girl children are engaged does not even figure as child labour. Studies have reveled that in the India context, girl children are largely engaged in running the household from very early age, even before they are capable of wage earning activities. This includes collection of water, fuel and looking after the younger siblings. It is argued that although these activities engage the girl child for a large part of each day, and ultimately of here life, they very rarely enter into the calculation of child labour. Even when the girls reach the older age group of nine and above, a significant portion of their time remains unaccounted for since it is consumed by these activities. The first point that is often stressed in the case of child children is that their role as child labour is one which does not receive much attention.

A second aspect that has received attention is the manner in which traditional and cultural factors play a major role in deciding the work patterns of girls. The fact that in most Indian communities it is the son who is expected to assume the dominant role in all traditional activities including festivals and religious accessions results in an almost automatic religious occasions results in an almost automatic discrimination against girls. This manifests itself in a number of ways, which have been documented in detail. Adverse sex ratios, female infanticide, deliberate neglect of girl children in the younger years, lower nutritional and educational status and even the nature of work performed by girls are some of the indicators which have been utilized to study discrimination against girls.

Child Labour in Karnataka

Children working in different works of economic activities are observed in almost all the states of the country. Recent survey study shows that Karnataka State has a high incidence of child labour after Andra pradesh. In

Karnataka child workers form about 6.25 per cent of the total work force. Across the districts, it ranges from 2.34 per cent to 7.34 per cent. The southern parts of the state have a rate of 9.76 per cent of child labour. According to 2001 Census, the state has 36.45 lakh of child labourers across the state of whom 3.34 lakh are in the state capital Bangalore City only. *Bangalore, Mysore, Kolar, Gulberga, Davanagery, Chithradurga* are some of the districts where child labourers are concentrated in considerable numbers. In terms of numbers of children employed, the hotels, auto garages and construction works occupy the highest order of employment of the children and an estimated 1.34, 2.21, 1.56 lakhs of children respectively are engaged in such works in the whole of Bangalore District.

As per the recent survey conducted during 2003 the child labour is densely more prevalent in the following sectors in Karnataka :

Sericulture
Auto garage
Agarabathi
Construction
Hotels
Zari embroidery
Rag picking
Domestic works
Stone quarres
Confectionery and
Shops and commercial sectors

Sericulture

Karnataka is known for its silk production and it is the major State contributing about 60% of the silk production in India. The silk processing is done mainly in the decentralized small-scale sector employing about 8-12 workers in each unit. It is also being run as a house holds cottage industry. The location of the industry is in towns and in big villages. It also provides a lot of employment opportunities. The hand charka also is in use apart from the mechanical process. Many children are working in this sector in Bangalore City. Government of India has notified the sericulture processing as hazardous industry under the Child Labour (Prohibition and Regulation) Act, 1996.

2. Garages-Auto Workshops

In these activities, the children are employed on the pretext of teaching them occupational skills. However this is also classified as hazardous activity which prohibits employment of children. Most of the children working in this activity are belongs to the low-income groups from weaker sections and minorities. These garages/ workshops are also small units in decentralized private sector employing 5-10 workers mainly child labourers in each unit. These are all located in towns including Bangalore City. The works undertaken are repairs of vehicles and other activities like welding, cutting, polishing and painting. Though, the employment can be viewed, as a learning process for future employment, special efforts has to be made to regulate child labour in these activities.

Beedi Rolling

It has been estimated that, in Karnataka 3.6 lakhs of workers are working in beedi making industry, The beedi rolling is a household industry where the contractors supply the raw materials and rolled beedies are given back to the contractors. The workers who receive the raw material from the contractors roll the beedies in their dwelling houses. Here, the whole family members including the children are engaged in beedi rolling. Since the children do come in contact with tobacco, it is health hazard and has been declared as a hazardous industry under 1986 Act. However, children working in their dwelling places family members is not covered under the child labour prohibition act. Therefore, it is not possible to enforce in such cases. For elimination of children working in industries various strategies have to be adopted.

Agarabathi/Incenses

This industry is similar to beedi industry. Agarabathi sticks are rolled sitting in the dwelling houses and the raw bathies (semi finished goods) are scented and packed in industrial premises. The primary activity of rolling agarabathi is mainly done in dwelling houses wherein the whole family including the children is engaged. The Child Labour Act is not applicable to the children working in the dwelling places along with their families. This is also classified as hazardous industry. Primarily this industry is situated in Bangalore City, Kolar and Mysore districts.

Building and Construction:

Building and construction activities are widely seen throughout Karnataka. But, it is concentrated more in urban areas including Bangalore City. In this industry, the workmen are mostly migrant labourers coming from other districts of the State and also from neighbouring States. The entire family normally migrates to the place of work. The children are also engaged and they do help their parents in construction activities. The construction activities involve heavy manual labour and are also hazardous for the growing children. This also has been classified as a hazardous industry under the Child Labour (Prohibition and Regulation) Act, 1986.

Hotel Industry

Hotels and restaurants small or big are found in every nook and corner of Karnataka and predominantly in urban areas including Bangalore City. Normally the cooks and suppliers are adults, but the cleaners are children. The existence of child labour is prevalent more in small hotels rather than the bigger ones. In a hotel, there will be an average of 10-12 workers and among them there used to be working out of which 5-6 children will be working as cleaners. Though, hotel industry is not classified as a hazardous industry under the, existing act, it does create bad effects on the physical and mental growth of the children. Though, the children get food and shelter in a hotel, he is influenced by adverse environment and usually picks up habits like smoking, drinking and drug abuse etc. Heavy workloads, long working hours deplete the children of their energy, The employment of children in these establishments is strictly prohibited under Karnataka Shops and Commercial Establishment Act. Even then, it is not possible to control the involvement of the children.

Rag Picking

In rag picking mostly boys in the age group of 8-14 years are engaged with. Some of the rag pickers are self-employed children who pick up rags from the streets and segregate them and sell the same to the dealers who deal with such goods. Some of the rag pickers are employed by shop owners who deal with plastic goods, tin products etc. This is one of a most dangerous and hazardous occupation. The rag picker comes in contact with toxic materials, hospital wastes, glass pieces and plastic wastes, which cause infections to the children. The rag pickers are prone to several diseases. The Govt. India has issued a draft notification to declare rag picking as a hazardous activity.

Biscuit and Confectionery Units

It is found that migrant children especially from rural areas are generally engaged in the confectionery units where sweets and condiments are prepared. Heating processes involved in making these items can be viewed as health hazardous for children. These units are mainly concentrated in certain pockets of Bangalore City and the extension areas. Though, the magnitudes of the problems are not fully known, this sector requires some attention.

Domestic Sector

It is generally found in almost all-urban center of the state. Female children are predominately found in this occupation. Also it is not uncommon that boys are also engaged in this sector. This occupation may include cooking, washing cloths and taking care of the children of their masters. Girl child abuse is most common in this job. Even though this sector does not come under any law still some certain regulatory have to be conditions are imposed for employing children is such activities.

Apart from the above-discussed works in Karnataka children are found to b employed in carpet weaving. Zari embroidery, glass, work in trade centers

So, keeping in mind the future of the children who have been denied their basic rights atleast as human being, the Government agencies have to be put forth enact and enforce such laws which can secure the future of the children.

Economic Significance of Child Labour with reference to India

Child labour plays a significant role in the economic aspect of the country. As for as India is concerned, Child labour has occupied an important place in economy of the country. There is at east one child labourer in every third family in India. (Pandey). A recent survey shows that, the fact is that about 20 per cent of GNP of the country is contributed by the child labourers which are as much as 8 per cent of the total labour force of the country. ghgh Ministry of labour has admitted that the earnings of 1.7 of crores children constitute one-fourth of the income of their families. Children contribute about 23 per cent of the family income of 52 per cent of the families. According to Iftikhar Ahmed, (1999) say the share of agriculture in GDP, school enrollment rates, GNP, per capita and demographic factors are the most powerful determinants of child labour as for as India is concerned. The study also has been revealed that poverty is the powerful determinants when empirically tested for the influence on the incidences of child labour. (Awasthi, P K).

Child Labour: A Global View

The problem of child labour is a universal phenomenon. Since it is inextricably associated with socio economic plight of the people. Children in every society have assisted in the activities, characteristics of their social group. Developed nations have got some control over the social problems, since developed countries have control over poverty and population. Economic development is of very high standard in those countries. Still, one can observe considerable amount of child labour even in the developed nations of the world. But, the developing and underdeveloped nations are facing it very seriously. Because, in these countries usually poverty and population explosion are beyond control. The child labour is a measuring rod for the economy of a country and a black spot on the face value of the so-called modern and civilized society.

The latest International Labour Organisation (ILO) report on the magnitude of child labour has revealed that around 250 million of children are engaged in one or other kinds of works of whom 120 million are working full time workers and 130 million are part time workers. The report says, Asia accounts for 153 million working children, Africa about 80 million and Latin America 17.5 million working children. According to the recent ILO survey, in selected countries like India, Ghana, Indonesia and Senegal 15 per cent children are workers in the total work force. The percentages is as much as 40 per cent in Senegal if seasonal labourers are taken into account. In Ghana more than 75 per cent of working children aged between 10-14 years are girl children and 73 million children in the age group of 10-14 years are workers. There are estimated 250 million child labourers in the age group of 5-14 years in the word, apart from those who work with their families mainly in domestic activities.

Child labour, a form of child exploitation is a worldwide phenomenon. The consideration of age for being child labour is different in different nations and nature of works. In India children below 14 years gainfully engaged physically and or mentally in any occupation either in agriculture or in industry, are called child labourers. The minimum age considered for child labour is 12 years in Egypt, 14 years in Philippines and Hong Kong 13 years percent in Malaysia. In Peru, this age is 14 years for agriculture sector, 15 years for industry, 16 years for ocean fishing and 18 years for working in ports. ILO in its 'Minimum Age (Industrial) Conference (1919)' has determined 12 to 13 years for light works and 18 years for hard and dangerous works. Although the minimum working age determined by ILO is 15 years (as a child is expected to complete his or her primary education). Engaging the children anywhere below this age will be considered as child labour (Murthy)

The problem of child labour is not particularly specific to any culture or geographical areas. It is a world wide problem since a long time. It is prevalent more or less in all the countries of the world. But it is found that Asia has the largest child labourers in the world. Some recent studies shows that even the developed European countries are not exempted from this. Some of the richest countries also have this problem. However, the intensity may be less when compared to other developing countries.

Of the 10-14 years old children the working children are 41.3 per cent in Kenya, 31.4 per cent in Chile 30.1 per cent in Bangladesh, 25.8 per cent in Nigeria, 24 per cent in Turkey, 20.5 percent in Ivory Cost, 17,7 percent in Pakistan, 16.1 per cent in Brazil, 14.4 per cent in India, 11.5 per cent in Chine, 11.3 percent in Egypt, 6.7 per cent in Mexico, 4.5 per cent in Argentina, 1.8 per cent in Portugal and 0.4 per cent in Italy. In some countries of Eastern Europe the difficulties connected with family income had led to a substantial increase in child labour. (Thakur, R N) It shows child labour has been spread from east to west and south to north without fail. All developed, developing and under developed countries are exhibiting with this problem. But in western countries, children are working more in secondary sectors unlike India.

Child Labour Across the Globe

Countries/Continents	*Number of children('000s)*		*Work ratio*	
	5-9	*10-14*	*5-9*	*10-14*
Developed economies	800	1,700	1.4	2.8
Transition economics	900	1,500	3.1	4.2
Asia and the Pacific	40,000	87,300	12.3	26.5
Latin America & Caribbean	5,800	11,600	10.6	21.5
Sub-Saharan Africa	20,900	27,100	23.6	34.7
Middle East and North Africa	4,800	4,800	10.8	19.6

Lieten

USA is considered to be a richest country of the world today. It is true that child labour is banned 60 years ago in USA.. Still, a survey conducted has revealed that about 3 lakh children in the age group of 5-15 yeas of age work in various occupations even in the hazardous sectors. They are paid less and exploited more. In this country children of any age may be employed by their parents or persons standing in place of their parents at any time and in any occupation on in farm owned or operated by their parents or persons standing in place of their parents, with the implication that these children may engage, in activities that they would not be allowed to undertake in other circumstances. It is an irony that the country which is so vocal for abolition of child labour in India and other under developed countries, often threatening to ban imports of goods manufactured using child labourers itself is infected with this kind of disease.

England is the first country, which imposed ban on child labour. According to the latest ILO report more than 3.5-lakh children are working in different part of the United Kingdom. Mainly children belonging to the migrant families are working for few Pounds. A recent study has shown that more then 3.5 per cent of educated couples have agreed with the concept of socialization of the children through work (Grant). The same study has revealed that people unanimously agreed that parents should provide happy and best childhood to children at any cost. But still the rights of the children are not yet effectively implemented through out the country. Many children are working in rural areas as field workers. More than that, children below the age of 16 years of are working in many hazardous industries.

With the transformation to market economy, new kinds of pressures have emerged on children, especially among the poors, to contribute to family income or to provide for themselves. Countries of the former USSR and those in Central and Eastern Europe have witnessed in varying degrees the increase of poverty, family disintegration, migration and population displacement, erosion of social safety nets, deterioration in health and education services and increases in delinquency and drug use among young people. At the same time, opportunities for children to participate in the largely unregulated labour market have rapidly multiplied, especially in expanding informal (and often illegal) economy. With limited experiences in dealing with child labour, government institutions are ill equipped to devise responses. Greater proportional losses by the poor in times of economic crisis have occurred in other regions as well. In countries like Brazil, Chile and Ecuador, for example, poor children are pulled out of schools. But, it is noted that effects are not uniform across countries or socio-economic groups (Bhargav, 2003). But in Asia, household coping strategies appear to be heavily influenced by government policy, especially as regards to social welfare and education pointing to the specific importances of social protection for the poor.

It is reported that more than 250.00 children are working in domestic sector around the globe. In Brazil, Colombia and Ecuador more then 20 per cent of girls in the age group of 10-14 are working in domestic, cocoa, rubber and coffee plantations. In El Salvador, children work in small-scale family based cottage industries for money in which children harvest shellfish and girls also markets the products. This work begins at the age of 10 years. A substantial portion of children is working in fishing and tanning industry in Peru, Mexico etc. It has been observed that many children are working in *ganja* and *hashish* fields in Afghanistan.

In Philippines enrolment of children in schools especially at secondary level declined. At the same time, youth unemployment is increasing. So children are thus more vulnerable to informal, illegal and hazardous economic sectors. Here many of the children are working as swimmers and divers to catch reef fish for marketing. In case of Thailand, the crisis has limited impact on the overall rate of children in schools, but youth unemployment is gradually increasing. In South Thailand, children are working as fish sorters and crews on fishing boats. In Central Java and Sumatra, children are working in fishing industry as divers, draining boats. However, in rural areas school dropout rates are increasing possibly indicating a shift into urban child labour in many parts Southeast Asia. (ILO, 2001)

Child labour is not just ideologically unacceptable, it had no real place in centrally planned economies operated by controlling labour mobility and by strictly regulated job market. Officially, children could perform works only if they prepare it from the point of view of future employment within the framework of education. To this day, Cuba and China claims that child labour does not exist in their countries. Nonetheless, even in pre-reform socialist countries, child labour existed to some extent.

In most of the African countries, the rate of child labour is considerably high because they are under developed countries. Moreover many countries have recently escaped from the clutches of the coloniesm. The economic and other resources exploited by other countries have caused much damage to them. Even though, they have got enough natural resources, they could not succeed in over throwing poverty. Some of the African countries like Kenya, Egypt, Zambia and Nigeria etc where rich natural and human resources could play a role in eradicating poverty, three fourth per cent of total population are living still under the acute poverty line. Not only these countries are facing poverty problem, but also population explosition that has pushed them back to dark. Further, many of the African countries are facing acute internal conflicts and civil wars. Many of the children have become child soldiers for food and money. One of the study has shown that "traditional and superstitious believes have blocked their ways to social and economic development" (Verma). Basically, children are found employed largely in agricultural sectors in many African countries. Also a substantial portions among them are in mining and quarries. Bonded labour system is still prevalent in many African countries. Basically, a notable number of children are working in commercial agricultural forms. In Kenya, Rwanda and West Africa children under the age of 15 years form 27-30 per cent of total workforce in agriculture and selling crafts (Bhargav). In central Africa a large number of children are working in plantations. In Madagascar, more than 53 per cent children are working in small-scale mines. In Dominican Republic basically people are living on sugar cane. It is reported that many children under the age group of 15 are working in sugar plantations and largely children are migrated from Haiti. In Tanzania, children work along with their parents in blue metal industry. In South Africa, children are working in diamond mining.

A recent study has proved that countries with relatively high per capita income could succeed in reducing illiteracy rates and poverty ratio. It is important to note that in some of the countries like Korea, Japan, Kuwait and Saudi Arabia, both poverty ratio and incidence of child Labour have declined to zero per cent. It shows positive correlation between poverty ratio and incidences of child labour. In some countries like Sri Lanka, Thailand and Vietnam despite of significant reduction in rats of illiteracy rate the child labour still persists.

Girls working as domestic servants away from their homes are frequent victims of physical, mental and sexual abuses, which can have devastating consequences of their health. ILO reports on child labour has mentioned categorically about forced prostitution's or forced sex workers in which girl children are subjected to. 'The AIDS' epidemic is a contributing factor to this trend, as adults see the use of children for sexual purposes as the best means of preventing infection. The full extent of the problem is unknown, but in Thailand an estimated 55,000 to 80,000 under aged children are involved in the sex trade. The large number of 'travelers' from industrial countries and other developing countries come to India every year in search of child prostitutes as there is less risk and fear of being defamed and imprisonment. According to the report of "Girls and child prostitutes in Asian Tourism," there are three lakhs of such child prostitutes (girls) in India, one Lakh in Thailand, one lakh in Taiwan, one lakh in Philippines. 40,000 in Vietnam, 30,000 in Sri Lanka and about more than 20,000 in China. Germany, Norway and Sweden have enacted acts to deal with the sex-criminals especially in the tourism industry. Recently Australia, France and New zeland are trying to make such laws (Rajwat, 2004)

It is said to be around 2.89 million child labourers are in Nepal. Many of them are under the age group of 14 years and one fourth of the children are below the age of 10 years. Beside domestic sectors children are found employed largely in agriculture and export industries. Carpet industries are well established in Nepal. According to one of the local NGOs working condition of the children are inhuman, under waged and unhygienic. Many children working in carpet and gem industries are facing acute occupational hazardous health problems.

Not only Nepal, the poor country Bangladesh also is facing acute child labour problem. More than 60 million children are working in many sectors. Since this country is commonly called as a bowl of jute half of the total child labour force are working in garment industry. Most of the children are in between 8-14 years of age. Working condition is below the fused standard. Poor ventilation, and long hours of work are some of the problems faced by the children. One of the studies (ILO,1990) has shown that children are facing a lot of health problems due to cotton dust constant, clatter of machines and very short breakage for lunch and for bathrooms. A lot of children are working in most of the hazardous sectors even without having any minimum protective measurement. Even the Government does not pay much attention to this as 12 per cent of GDP comes from the sector where children are largely found employed.

Basically agriculture is a prime sector in Pakistan like India. So, as usual many million children are working in different segments of the agriculture sector in this country. Also children are working in leather, surgical instruments and manufacturing sporting goods. Most of the children employed are below the age of 12 years. More than that, one fourth of the total child labourers are bonded labourers. It is so common in brick industries, fisheries stone crushing shoe making, powers looms (Bhargava,1999). Since, carpet industry is basically a cottage industry, many children are working in their family units. Those children who are working out side their family units earn not less than 40 Rs per day and they have to work for about 9-10 hours per day. According to the AMNESTY International 13 to 20 per cent of the children are working in sports goods industries. In rural areas it has become a cottage level family units. Here children work for about 10 hours and the wage is Rs 1000 per month. Manufacture of surgical instruments is a well-established industry in Pakistan. Recent study shows that thousand children are working in this industry and all of them are below the age of 17 years. These children are working with out any protective measurements. Recently many western countries have imposed ban on the import of these surgical instruments from Pakistan. Since, Pakistan is more or less an agricultural oriented country one fourth of the total child force is working in the agricultural field (Hansraj, 2001)

Number of Working Children Less than 15 Years old across the globe

Area	*Total(Million)*	*Unpaid Family Worker*	
		Million	*Percentage of Total*
World	52.0	41.2	80
South-East Assia	29.0	23.2	80
East Asia	9.1	6.4	70
Africa	9.7	9.3	96
Latin America	3.1	2.0	65
Europe	0.7	0.4	50
USSR	----	----	--
North America	0.3	----	10
Oceania	0.1	0.1	85

Source : ILO.

Child Labour in India: A Retrospective

Inspite of significant achievements in most of the sectors after independence, India is still facing several social hurdles in the way of national development. Child labour is one such problem. It is not a new phenomenon as for as India is concerned. It has been linked with the socio economic development of every society since time immemorial and became more significant after economic revolution in the mid 20th century. The problem of child labour in India has of late assumed the proportion of a social menace threatening the very fabric of the social milieu. Child labour has become a well explained popular issue ever since many western countries, under the fabric of labour welfare, took it up, targeting developing countries like India and China as the two countries having has very poor record in the sphere of child labour. Despite progressive laws and policies, child labour issue in India is growing more and more. It has remained both an economic and a social problem for a long time. According to the latest report more than 100 million children are toiling in different corners of India. Every one fourth of working child in the world is an Indian. Inspite of industrialization, urbanization, privatization and its various achievements, India ranks first in the world for having the highest number of child workers. Experts assume economic compulsion of the family, adult unemployment and growing trend of employers of hiring children to save the production cost are some of the vital reasons behind child labour in India.

Child labour was prevalent even in the ancient time in different forms in India. But it was not of so exploitative as of now. Effective socialization was the main motive and concern among the parents and teachers in those days (Rao, 2003). Their work was favorably related to the overall development of children. Later on the entire situation has changed. During 1860-1870 there was an enormous growth of coffee, tea, indigo and jute industries in northern and central part of India. These industries belonged to many European countries the colonel rulers. During 1940, children accounted for 17 per cent of the labour force in many agricultural and plantation work. After independence, Mukherjee,1951) writes "it was so common in many parts of India that children were found in the coal mines to help the parents in cart pushing or loading. In mica mines also children were found employed" Lieten (2005) writes "the very precise figures that we find in the official accounts of many industries- tea gardens, coal mines, mica industries, bidi industries and the regulated and non regulated factories have been carefully shifted and convey a picture of the reality in those days"

It is a well-known fact that children were found employed in many household works since ancient time. The main intention was that after the elder's life period, the children were supposed to continue the family occupation. These kinds of activities were so common during the medieval period also in rural India because a predominantly rural society was inevitably characterised by small and marginal economic units. Gradually children become an integral part of the household economy. They were trained while still young and gradually start contributing individually to the family's income .As a result, the children were in a situation where they had to earn for themselves as well as for the families. Experts say even in family run units, where the child is generally better looked after by is parents and may not suffer from any physical hardship, he goes through mental strain because of problems and anxieties regarding the undertaking which he shares with his parents

An important issue in human resources development is the prevalence of child labour. Basically child labour can be defined as the engagement of children between the years of 6-14 years (as per Indian context) working in economically gain full works. Even though, child labour is more or less common in many countries, it is most prevalent among the developing countries. India has the largest population of child labourers who contributes nearly 7 per cent of the work force contributing considerable amount to the GDP (Kumar,2001). Estimates supplied by various agencies regarding the population of child labour in India don't depict a uniform picture. According to ILO, India has the dubious distinction of having perhaps the largest child labour force in the world. Approximately 45 million children are found employed in both organised and unorganised sectors in different corners of India. Among these working children around 24 per cent in urban centers and rest in rural areas. Government statistics in 1986 had shown that that there were 18.4 million children below the age of the 15 in the labour force, constituting 7.8 per cent of rural child labour force and 2.9 per cent of urban labour force. Recent World Bank report says that there are 78.5 million working children in India that is the largest in terms of any country include 27 million bonded working children (World Bank Report, 2001). India alone accounts for about 100 million child labourers. If we go for multiplicity of the concept of child labourers it will be around 140 million. Thus, the magnitude of child labour in India varies from sources to sources.

Bonded Child Labour

Bonded labour takes place when a family receives an advance payment (sometimes as little as U.S. $15) to hand a child-boy or girl-over to an employer. In most cases the child cannot work off the debt, nor can the family raise enough money to buy the child back. The workplace is often structured so that "expenses" and/or "interest" are deducted from a child's earnings in such amounts that it is almost impossible for a child to repay the debt. In some cases, the labour is generational-that is, a child's grandfather or great-grandfather was promised to an employer many years earlier, with the understanding that each generation would provide the employer with a new worker-often with no pay at all.

Bonded labour is outlawed by the 1956 U.N. Supplementary Convention on the Abolition of Slavery, the Slave Trade, and Institutions and Practices Similar to Slavery. Millions of children work as bonded child labourers in countries around the world; the full extent of the problem has yet to be shown. **(see also in the 6th chapter of this book)**

Areas of concentration

The typical nature of child labour in India is more prevalent in rural areas. As we know, three fourth of the national income comes from agricultural sector and more than 75 per cent of the people are depended on agriculture for their subsistence. According to the 1991 Census, 85 per cent of children are employed in different sectors of the agricultural and allied activities. Rural economy, which is characterized by relatively a higher level of poverty, unemployment and illiteracy when compared to urban economy supports 90 per cent of the total number of child labourers in India.

A considerable number of children are engaged in their respective traditional occupations. Many children are helping their family members in the field. Some work as part of contract family labour whereas others work as part of contract family labour where men, women and children all work together. Many of them employed in plantation. Rodgers and Standing (1979) have classified the pattern of child labour found in rural areas as of domestic, non domestic, bonded and wage labourers. The domestic work includes maidservants or domestic servants, where female children have to bear the burden. Non-domestic works include grazing of animals, working in the field's etc. Gender based economic significance's of male child is further enhanced in countries where social and cultural taboos restrict women from participating in paid work of family, occupational work (Narayana). In rural areas, girl child workers are readily available for work and it is found very common for school aged children to be involved in agricultural works as part of family labour. Girls are mostly engaged in domestic sectors than boys, because these children come largely from land less, small and marginal landholders (Murthy, 2001).

Secondary sectors play a predominant role in case of urban child labourers in India. More than one third of the urban workers are children and more than one fourth of them belong to the non-household industries and construction. Children are found employed in many other sectors like hotel, firework, glass, carpet weaving, automobile etc. In urban areas considerable number of girl children are found to be employed in household works, cottage industries etc. Further children are engaged in many unorganised sectors like shops, pavement selling, dhabas, venders, and porters, scavenging etc (Joseph,1999).

Estimated Number of Children involved in the Unconditional Worst Forms of Child Labour in India.

Type of worst form of child labour	*Number of Children (in millions)*
Forced and bonded labour	4.7
Forced recruitment into armed conflict	0.3
Prostitution and pornography	1.8
Other illicit activities	0.6
Trafficked children	(1.2)
Total	7.4

Bargava,1999

Age-specific Work Participation Rates in Indian (1983-2000)

	Age 5-9				*Age 10-14*			
	1983	*1987*	*1993*	*2000*	*1983*	*1987*	*1993*	*2000*
Rural boys	2.5	2.4	1.1	0.6	25.3	19.0	13.9	9.1
Rural girls	2.6	2.3	1.4	0.7	24.0	18.0	14.2	9.6
Urban boys	0.8	0.5	0.5	0.3	11.3	8.5	6.6	4.9
Urban girls	0.7	0.5	0.5	0.2	7.0	6.5	4.5	3.6

Sources: The Indian journal of labour economic, Vol.48, No1, 2005- (Lieten G.K.)

The sector specific distribution of child workers In India, as per the 1991 Governament census reveals that a majority of the children are working in agricultural and its allied activities. The predominance of agriculture is even more pronounced in the case of child workers. More than 80 per cent of the children are working in the major economic sector i. e. agriculture. Agricultural sector can be divided into of cultivators and agricultural labourers. Cultivators constitute 36 per cent and agricultural labourers constitute 45 per cent of total rural child labour force. The table shows more than 3.86 children are working in agricultural activities like live stock, plantation etc. The higher percentage of their employment in cultivation appears to be due to the respondents' bias arising out of higher prestige attached to cultivator category as compared to labourers. The Agricultural Enquiring Committee say "their composition as earners and helpers in the ratio of 11:9. It indicates that majority of child labour working in agriculture, worked for wage and smaller proportion possibly worked as family members and helpers" (Behor, 1990).

Distribution in Different Sectors:

Percentage distribution of total working children in different sectors in India, 1991. Percentage distribution, according to the different sectors. (Source: Census Report, 1991).

	Industrial Category	*Percentage distribution of total working children*		
		Male	*Female*	*Total*
1.	Cultivators	38.14	31.10	35.49
2.	Agricultural labourers	39.73	52.27	44.45
	Total	77.87	85.37	79.94
3.	Livestock, forestry, fishing, hunting, plantation, orchard and allied activities	4.55	2.72	3.86
4.	Mining and Quarrying	0.28	0.31	0.29
5.	Household Industry	2.18	4.68	3.12
	Others	6.19	4.65	5.61
	Total	8.37	9.33	8.73
6.	Construction	0.98	0.44	0.78
7.	Trade & Commerce	3.91	0.59	2.66
8.	Transport Storage, etc.	0.52	0.05	0.34
	Other service	3.52	3.19	3.40
	Grand total	100.0	100.0	100.0
	Number in Million	5.66	3.42	9.08

Manufacture and processing units are the third important sector ofter agriculture where a large number of children are found to be employed. Household and other related works accounts for 5.61 per cent of child labourers. Household works are more visible in rural areas than urban and semiurban areas. The major reason is that household work does not come under any specific laws and acts. One-study reports that more than 0.78 percent children are working in construction cite. It is observed that many children start this work during their early age of the life phase. So, that they can learn all essential skills to become an expert mason. In the future. Considerable amount of children are working in transport and storage field. This includes shops and commercial establishments.

It is known that children are found employed in all three sectors of Indian economy. And it has been established that primary sector has highest concentration of child labourers, both in absolute and relative terms. This table shows that less number of children are in tertiary sectors, probably this sectors requires more skilled adults.

Child Workers in Different Sectors in India

Sectors	*All works*	*Child workers*
Primary	71.12	86.64
Secondary	12.39	8.57
Territory	16.49	4.56
Others	1.56	2.45

Sources: Census Report, 1981.

Location Specific Occupations

One of the unique features of child labour system in India is the location specific nature of the jobs. Even though, child labourers are spread all through the length and breadth of the country, some specific kind of occupations is observed in some areas only. But, however no one should think (From the table) those lists of occupations found only in those areas only. This table shows some specific occupations found more in those areas as than any other places in India. This table includes only widely known occupations where large number of children is found employed. Carpet industry is more common in J and K, West bangal and U P. Working in the construction cites found in every patches of the country. Glass industry predominately found in U P. Like that concentration of large power loom industry can be seen in both Tamil Nadu and Maharashtra state because of availability of enough raw materials and chief labour. Large numbers of girl worker are found in garment industry in Delhi. Children working in fishing industry are common in all along the costal areas of the country. Garage work and street children are found in many parts of the country. Andra pradesh has the highest number of child labourers. Rural child labour is highest in Karnataka. Rate of child employment is very less in Kerala State.

Geographical Concentration

1. Glass & Bangles – Firozabad (Utter Pradesh)
2. Handloom—Tamil Nadu and Maharastra
3. Powerloom –Bhiwandi in Maharashtra.
4. Carpet weaving –Jammu & Kashmir, Utter Pradesh and Rajasthan.
5 Zari and Embroidery –Lucknow (U.P.).
6. Gem cutting and polishing – Jaipur (Rajasthan)
7. Diamond cutting and polishing—Surat (Gujarat).
8. Match & fire works—Sivakasi (Tamil Nadu).
9. Garages and petrol pumps—Through out India
10 Cashew processing and manufacture of coir products- (Kerala.)
11. Helpers in Hotels, Restaurants, Canteens, Tea Stalls, Shops-Through out India
12. Rag picking- Predominately in Megacites of the county
13. Construction-Throughout India
14. Fishing—Kerala, Tamil Nadu, Gujarat
15. Pottery Units—Khuraja (U.P.).
16. Hawkers, Vendors, Newspaper sellers-through out India
17. Coolies—Throughout India
18. Lock Industry—Aligarh.(UP)
19. Bonded Labour- Several patches in India
20. Slate Industry—Mandsaur (M.P.).

Sources: T. M. Dak (2003) 'Child labour in India.'

Child Labour in Selected Sectors

MINES

Children formed a large part of the mining labour force in the early years of the century. According to a report during 1901, there were as a many as few thousand children below the age of 12 years who constituted 4.8 per cent of the total labour force engaged in mines. Administration brought many acts to ban child labour in mines like *The Mines act-1901 and The Indian Mines Act 1921.* In the report of labour conditions in the iron and ore industry, the committee observed that "in particular mines employment of children under 15 years in contravention of the law is frequent." Recently an NGO has observed hat large number of tribal children are found employed in many mines in Utter Pradesh, Madhya Pradesh and Bihar. Children engaged in this work usually suffer with harmful dusts, gases, fumes fatigue and endangered by mercury poisoning. It is most common in UP, MP and Bihar.

Plantations

Quite a large number of children are employed in plantations is between the age of 12-14. According to one findings of the *Ad-hoc* enquiry conducted in Assam in 1976, roughly 57 per cent of the children employed in European owned estates and 63 per cent of those employed in Indian owned estates were between the ages of 12 and 14 years. At present the children in the tea plantations earn about 40 Rs. per day. Here regular employment will no be available unlike factories and mines. Children employed in tea plantations are so common in Tamil Nadu, Orissa, and W. Bengal, Assam Karnataka State. , etc.

Ceramic and Glass work

The children in these works are common. Children must carry molten loads of glass dragged from the tank furnace at a temperature of 1500-1800 degree centigrade. Some times young children of 8-9 years of age carry weight upto 20 kg with their bodies bent and frames trembling with the effort. (Joseph). Some time children have to work with exposed electric wires and sound as high as 100 decibels. Here many children are working like urban bonded labourers. Children get around 35 Rs. per day. Poor eyesight, toxic fumes, injures from the flying glass are common health affected problems that children are facing in this sector. It is found very common among Utter Pradesh, Madhya Pradesh, Rajasthan, Karnataka states.

Construction

Owing to a rapid growth of wealth and an ever-expanding need for housing, construction work is undertaken on large scale under private, cooperative and government auspices. This is the only sector in which without any prior conditions one can enter into the work. Large number of rural migrant families is engaged in this sector. When the head of the family is recruited, he moves to the city with his entire family. The construction sites change, the family is constantly on the move and the child cannot take advantage of the existing schooling facilities. Basically children starts as a helper and after some years of experience, one can become a skilled mason and he gets around 175 Rs per day. Children usually get around 45 Rs per day. One can say among all the jobs where children are engaged, construction work is the hardest and most tiresome. Carrying of heavy loads, mixed cements and bricks etc causes a lot health related problem to the children.

Brassware industry

Brassware industries are most common in many parts of central India like Utter Pradesh, Madhya Pradesh and Bihar. The subcontractors who are responsible for he jobs of molding, polishing and electroplating mostly child labourers. Children are also engaged in welding and scraping. The other process in which many children work is polishing the semi-finished products. Children are also observed working in electroplating and polishing. They have to work with poison's chemicals and molding hot temperature that naturally may cause unimaginable health hazardous to the children. Main reason for the employment of children is low wages that reduces production cost.

Carpet Industry

Uttar Pradesh is commonly known as carpet belt of the country. It has been estimated that more than 4 lakh children are working in carpet industry in Utter Pradesh, Karnataka, Jammu and Kashmir states. Children's nimble fingers play a vital role in carpet weaving. Here wage depends on number of carpet they can weave in a day. Further children work in sorting. Dying and knotting sections. It is found that 8 per cent of the total work force in the hand-knotted carpet industry is child labourers.

Gem Polishing

Gem polishing industry is popular in Gujarat, Rajasthan and Madhya Pradesh State.95 per cent of all colured gemstones in India are polished in these states only. The gem industry caters o he international market because of the easy availability of child labour. Mostly boys between 12-13 years old, polish diamonds for an average of seven to nine hours in a day including cutting washing and polishing diamond chips. In addition, children also polish emeralds, corals, rubi, and topaz. According to a report more than 15.000 thousand children (22 per cent of total work force) are working in this field in Rajasthan. They have to work for about 10 hours for 30 Rs per day. Wages is based on the number of diamonds that they polish. Some time children do not get paid wags for several years in the gem polishing industry because thay are considered as to be learning the craft. People in the industry believe that education is of paramount impordence in the gem industry because they have to deal with dealers and foreign market.

Lock Industry

Aligarh is famous for lock industry. It is estimated that 85 per cent of the locks are made in Aligarh District only. It comes under small-scale cottage industry. More than 15000 children below the age of 12 years are working 12-bhours a day. Family based units are very common in this field. The practice of employing children as part of family labour is very common. Children are engaged in hand press, buffing machines, electroplating, painting- etc, which are very dangerous to health. Lack of attention may cause of accidents and often child may loose the tips of the fingers while working with the machine. Usually children will get 900 Rs per month

Silk

It has been reported that more than 7.000 thousand children are employed in southern parts of Bangalore-Karnataka. Children found employed in this job usually between the age of 6-12 years. It is because the pretences of nimble fingers are very important for silk weaving. They will work for about 10 hours per day. Girl child labourers found more in this sector. Many children are working as bonded labourers. Children commonly prepare yarns on beams and weave the silk. Majority of the children is from poor Muslim families. Children have to work in all activities like weaving, dying, and rolling and washing etc. Since it comes under house holds industry, employers have narrow chance to escape from the clutches of the law.

Auto Garage

With the emergence of private car and taxi or two/three wheeler vehicles, automobiles repair shops have sprung up in almost all parts of the metropolis. It is the most popular sector for child laboures. More than 12 per cent of the total child labourers are working in this sector. Most of the all parents think children should start this work in the early ages so that he can become a good skilled mechanic. Usually children do their jobs without having any protective measures. Depending upon their knowing to undertake repair works, children get their wages. During apprenticeship, children are not paid any money. Tightening of nuts and bolts, cleaning, oiling, washing is the different kind of this works entrusted them. Some risks are definitely involved in this job. Basically children work as helpers to the adult mechanics that undertakes the main repair work and thay are supposed to be the guide to the children. Apart from the physical hazards involved and its unclean nature, the job also entails elements of exploitation. The master generally has a tendency to protract the period of the so-called training so as to impress on the child that he is only learning and not working and hence is not entitled to any wages or remuneration.

Industry wise Distribution of Child Labourers in India

Industry	*Locations (states)*	*Total*
Match and Fireworks processing	Sivakasi	50.000
Stone Quarries	Kerala	20.000
Lead Mines	Meghalaya	28.000
Fish freezing and processing	Kerala	20.000
Handloom Industry.	Kerala, Tripura and Maharashtra	33.000
Bidi Industry	Karnataka,TN, Kerala	25.000
Lock industry	Uttar Pradesh	23.000
Handicraft	Jammu and Kashmir	27.000
Carpet weaving	Kashmir, UP and Rajasthan	2,20,000
Glass Industry	Firozbad (UP)	50,000
Glass Industry	Rajasthan Kerala	34,000
Coir	Kerala	80,000
Pottery	UP	10,000
Brassware	UP Bihar	27,000

Source: Rehabilitation of Child Labour in India-R.N Patil.

Reasons for Child Labour in India

Child labour is a universal problem, which is more common among developing countries. Social factors, poverty, illiteracy, rural migration, family disintegration, inadequate measures of social security, lack of avenues for education, social choices, social polices and shortcomings in institutional arrangements, and resource constraints are the main reasons for this problem. On other hand, due to technological backwardness and labour intensive technology in these countries, there is a search for cheap labour which is compensated out of child labour. An ILO study shows that:

- about 85 per cent of the total child labourers in India are forced work to supplement the income of their families.
- about 75 per cent of parents allow their children to work from the economic point of view.
- about 50 per cent of parents feel that the income earned by their children is essential for the maintenance of their families.
- about 44 per cent of the families have their own cultural and traditional beliefs in maintaining and continuing their family occupations.
- about 70 per cent of child labourers want to continue their present job even if they are given the option to leave them (Pandey, S.2001).

(The Economic Times, Calcutta, Dak (Ed.)1996)

By and large it observed that social factors, poverty, population explosion, and urbanisation are the real factors behind this child labour problem.

Social and Cultural Factors.

A social and cultural concept on child labour has become a more debatable issue of recent time. Culture has its own definition on the term *child* and child labour and it differs greatly across the society. Culture has fixed some functions, which has to be performed by the children in their early ages for the effective socialization. This process of socialization and the cultural objectives to which they are supposed to respond are clearly interdependent with the structural economic system within which the process of socialization occurs. In a culturally bounded society like India, culture plays a vital role on both family structure and sex roles of the every child. Child labour can be seen more among low class people or weaker sections of the society. Due to the unequal distribution of wealth and neglect towards the traditional beliefs among the upper caste people has made domination on low caste group. Hence, child labour can be seen more among low class people or weaker section of the society. In a society like ours sending children to school largely depends on cultural context of the family and basically that decisions will be taken at household level. However, such decisions are not separated from other crucial aspects of household decision making nor are they purely household based. They reflect the norms and values of the wider community within which the household is located and the social and economic possibilities which local contexts offer to different categories of households (Subramaniyan). Some explanation of poverty has focussed on the level of economic development within a given society as the prime cause of poverty. Others have focused on the presumed inferior personnel or cultural traits of the poor. Still others have interpreted poverty as the result of societal conditions that permit or encourage economic deprivation for some societal members.

Poverty

The poverty has two aspects: absolute poverty and relative poverty. In case of absolute poverty the level of the income of people of a country is too low that they cannot meet even their basic minimum requirements, it is called the absolute type of poverty. On the basis of this definition, nearby 27 crores of people which constitutes about 29 per cent of total population fall below this line. Relative poverty means, When we compare incomes of different people we find that some people are poorer than others. This is called Relative poverty. A recent survey on poverty show that, 37 crores of people are living below poverty line. It is most visible, speculative and prime reason for the existence of the problem like child labour. In India basically poor people forces their children to go to the work because augmentation of their income is essential for the survival of the family. The urban poor and rural marginalised and landless poor people send their children for wage earning.

Rapid Growth of Population:

For the most of its 4.000-year history, India has been a rural nation. By 1901, only 27 million people were residing in present day territory, In 2001, 100 crores people are living in India. This represents almost a tenfold increase in less than a century. Now the population of India is increasing rapidly. It is one of the most important causes among others for creating child labour problem Population pressure in India have created widespread misery and suffering for their members and have seriously handicapped their chances to complete economic development. Rapid growth of population in India is a pivotal issue with numerous and far reaching implications on the quality of life economic inequalities and the rate of economic growth. Rapid population growth in India has created gigantic problems, which directly affects on social political and economic aspects of our country. The poor people having low income and who constitute the major portion of the society generally become the victim's of all these phenomena's. For certain extent population growth can be considered as a favourable development. But after crossing the transition point it is a hindrance to economic development of the country and population decreases the per captia income of the nation also constrain the limited resources. Continuous increase in population may lead to excess labour supply and adult unemployment. This high fertility may exert enormous pressure on the parents to save and invest a lot of money on education and health of their respective children.

Urbanisation

Less opportunities, unemployment, drought and unfinished rural development programmes are the main reasons behind rural migration to urban areas. By 1901, 11 percent of total population were lived in cites (Nagpaul, 1988). In 1993, it was 26 percent. However, as incredible as India's urban development has been to date, growth projections for the end of first quarter of the 21st are nothing short of mind boggling. By the 2020, approximately one-half of the country's projected 1,370,000,000 people will be in urban residents (Dogan & Kasarda, 1988). 75 million people will likely to live in India's biggest and Mega cites by the year 2010. India's population is growing at a rate of 2.1

per cent per year, and the cites has been growing at the rate of 3.8 per cent per year, with many urban centers increasing between 4 and 7 percent annually. This rapid urban growth causes many more problems, which led to the existence of childlabour in urban centers. Flow of labour forces in to the urban center leads to the excess availability of labourers for fewer wages to the employers.

These aspects affects in many different ways 1. trance acculturation 2. rising of urban unemployment 3. decrease in living index 4. social disintegration. Some times semi urban areas that very near to border of any villages may emerged as the most important business centers for meeting day-to day requirements of the migrant and slum labourers. The rural migrants working in urban centers and other villagers who visit to semi urban areas would take numerous urban-industrial characteristic with them when they go back to their mother village (Jha, 1998). This greatly affects the homogeneous rural society mainly to customs, tradition and to beliefs. More or less we can say original rural culture will be under heavy influence of another culture. This change may provoke the parent's either to migrate to the so-called urban centers or send their children to such centers to earn more extra money. This finally leads to the social disintegration.

In recent years there has been a decline in the proportion of child labour in organised sector but it is spreading in many more unorganised sectors like loading and unloading, pavement selling, rag-picking, child prostitution, hawking goods, and daily labourers. This is all due to the uncontrolled and unlimited growth of urban centers in India (Murthy, 2001).

Child labour in Karnataka

Children working in different works of economic activities are observed in almost all the states of the country. Recent survey study shows that Karnataka State has a high incidence of child labour after Andra pradesh. In Karnataka child workers form about 6.25 per cent of the total work force. Across the districts, it ranges from 2.34 per cent to 7.34 per cent. The southern parts of the state have a rate of 9.76 per cent of child labour. According to 2001 Census, the state has 36.45 lakh of child labourers across the state of whom 3.34 lakh are in the state capital Bangalore City only. *Bangalore, Mysore, Kolar, Gulberga, Davanagery, Chithradurga* are some of the districts where child labourers are concentrated in considerable numbers. In terms of numbers of children employed, the hotels, auto garages and construction works occupy the highest order of employment of the children and an estimated 1.34, 2.21, 1.56 lakhs of children respectively are engaged in such works in the whole of Bangalore District.

As per the recent survey conducted during 2003 child labour is densely more prevalent in the following sectors in Karnataka

Sericulture
Auto garage
Agarabathi
Construction
Hotels
Zari embroidery
Rag picking
Domestic works
Stone quaries
Confectionery and
Shops and commercial sectors

Sericulture

Karnataka is known for its silk production and it is the major State contributing about 60% of the silk production in India. The silk processing is done mainly in the decentralized small-scale sector employing about 8-12 workers in each unit. It is also being run as a house hold cottage industry. The location of the industry is in towns and in big villages. It also provides a lot of employment opportunities. The hand charka also is in use apart from the mechanical process.. Many children are working in this sector in Bangalore City. Government of India has notified the sericulture processing as hazardous industry under the Child Labour (Prohibition and Regulation) Act, 1996.

2. Garages-Auto Workshops

In these activities, the children are employed on the pretext of teaching them occupational skills. However this is also classified as hazardous activity which prohibits employment of children. Most of the children working in this activity are belongs to the low-income groups from weaker sections and minorities. These garages/ workshops are also small units in decentralized private sector employing 5-10 workers mainly child labourers in each unit. These are all located in towns including Bangalore City. The works undertaken are repairs of vehicles and other activities like welding, cutting, polishing and painting. Though, the employment can be viewed, as a learning process for future employment, special efforts has to be made to regulate child labour in these activities.

Beedi Rolling

It has been estimated that, in Karnataka 3.6 lakhs of workers are working in beedi making industry, The beedi rolling is a household industry where the contractors supply the raw materials and rolled beedies are given back to the contractors. The workers who receive the raw material from the contractors roll the beedies in their dwelling houses. Here, the whole family members including the children are engaged in beedi rolling. Since the children do come in contact with tobacco, it is health hazard and has been declared as a hazardous industry under 1986 Act. However, children working in their dwelling places family members is not covered under the child labour prohibition act. Therefore, it is not possible to enforce in such cases. For elimination of children working in industries various strategies have to be adopted.

Agarabathi/Incenses

This industry is similar to beedi industry. Agarabathi sticks are rolled sitting in the dwelling houses and the raw bathies (semi finished goods) are scented and packed in industrial premises. The primary activity of rolling agarabathi is mainly done in dwelling houses wherein the whole family including the children is engaged. The Child Labour Act is not applicable to the children working in the dwelling places along with their families. This is also classified as hazardous industry. Primarily this industry is situated in Bangalore City, Kolar and Mysore districts.

Building and Construction

Building and construction activities are widely seen throughout Karnataka. But, it is concentrated more in urban areas including Bangalore City. In this industry, the workmen are mostly migrant labourers coming from other districts of the State and also from neighbouring States. The entire family normally migrates to the place of work. The children are also engaged and they do help their parents in construction activities. The construction activities involve heavy manual labour and are also hazardous for the growing children. This also has been classified as an hazardous industry under the Child Labour (Prohibition and Regulation) Act, 1986.

Hotel Industry

Hotels and restaurants small or big are found in every nook and corner of Karnataka and predominantly in urban areas including Bangalore City. Normally the cooks and suppliers are adults, but the cleaners are children. The existence of child labour is prevalent more in small hotels rather than the bigger ones. In a hotel, there will be an average of 10-12 workers and among them there used to be working out of which 5-6 children will be working as cleaners. Though, hotel industry is not classified as a hazardous industry under the, existing act, it does create bad effects on the physical and mental growth of the children. Though, the children get food and shelter in a hotel, he is influenced by adverse environment and usually picks up habits like smoking, drinking and drug abuse etc. Heavy work loads, long working hours deplete the children of their energy. The employment of children in these establishments is strictly prohibited under Karnataka Shops and Commercial Establishment Act. Even then, it is not possible to control the involvement of the children.

Rag Picking

In rag picking mostly boys in the age group of 8-14 years are engaged with. Some of the rag pickers are self-employed children who pick up rags from the streets and segregate them and sell the same to the dealers who deal with such goods. Some of the rag pickers are employed by shop owners who deal with plastic goods, tin products etc. This is one of a most dangerous and hazardous occupation. The rag picker comes in contact with toxic materials, hospital wastes, glass pieces and plastic wastes, which causes infections to the children. The rag pickers are prone to several diseases. The Govt. India has issued a draft notification to declare rag picking as a hazardous activity.

Biscuit and Confectionery units

It is found that migrant children especially from rural areas are generally engaged in the confectionery units where sweets and condiments are prepared. Heating processes involved in making these items can be viewed as health hazardous for children. These units are mainly concentrated in certain pockets of Bangalore City and the extension areas. Though, the magnitudes of the problems are not fully known, this sector requires some attention.

Domestic Sector

It is generally found in almost all-urban center of the state. Female children are predominately found in this occupation. Also it is not uncommon that boys are also engaged in this sector. This occupation may include cooking, washing cloths and taking care of the children of their masters. Girl child abuse is most common in this job. Even though this sector does not come under any law still some certain regulatory have to be conditions are imposed for employing children is such activities.

Apart from the above-discussed works in Karnataka children are found to b employed in carpet weaving. Zari embroidery, glass, work in trade centers

Economic Significance of Child Labour with Reference to India

Child labour plays a significant role in the economic aspect of the country. As for as India is concerned, Child labour has occupied an important place in economy of the country. There is at east one child labourer in every third family in India. (Pandey). A recent survey shows that, the fact is that about 20 per cent of GNP of the country is contributed by the child labourers which are as much as 8 per cent of the total labour force of the country. ghgh Ministry of labour has admitted that the earnings of 1.7 of crores children constitute one-fourth of the income of their families. Children contribute about 23 per cent of the family income of 52 per cent of the families. According to Iftikhar Ahmed, (1999) say the share of agriculture in GDP, school enrollment rates, GNP, per capita and demographic factors are the most powerful determinants of child labour as for as India is concerned. The study also has been revealed that poverty is the powerful determinants when empirically tested for the influence on the incidences of child labour. (Awasthi, P K)

3

Street and Bonded Children in India

This Chapter is Completely Based on the Official Report of Human Right Water (International NGO). It has been downloded from their website to give wide Publicity under Common Creative Licence agreement. Copy Right with "*Human Right Water Only*".

India has the largest population of street children in the world. At least eighteen million children live or work on the streets of urban India, labouring as porters at bus or railway terminals; as mechanics in informal auto-repair shops; as vendors of food, tea, or handmade articles; as street tailors; or as ragpickers, picking through garbage and selling usable materials to local buyers.

Indian street children are routinely detained illegally, beaten and tortured and sometimes killed by police. Several factors contribute to this phenomenon: police perceptions of street children, widespread corruption and a culture of police violence, the inadequacy and non-implementation of legal safeguards, and the level of impunity that law enforcement officials enjoy. The police generally view street children as vagrants and criminals. While it is true that street children are sometimes involved in petty theft, drug-trafficking, prostitution and other criminal activities, the police tend to assume that whenever a crime is committed on the street, street children are either involved themselves or know the culprit. Their proximity to a crime is considered reason enough to detain them. This abuse violates both Indian domestic law and international human rights standards.

Police have financial incentives to resort to violence against children. Many children report that they were beaten on the street because the police wanted their money. The prospect of being sent to a remand home, the police station or jail, coupled with the threat of brutal treatment, creates a level of fear and intimidation that forces children or in some cases, their families, to pay the police or suffer the consequences.

Indian law contributes to the problem. Under the Indian Penal Code, anyone over the age of twelve is considered an adult, and ambiguities in the code concerning the ability of the child to be cognizant of a crime have made it possible for children as young as seven to be treated as adults under the law. There are no provisions in the code that prohibit the detention of juveniles in police stations or jails. The Juvenile Justice Act, which applies to all the states and Union Territories in India except Jammu and Kashmir, does prohibit the detention of "neglected" or "delinquent" juveniles in police lock-ups or jails, but these provisions are routinely ignored by police. Moreover, at the remand stage, the law makes no distinction between neglected and delinquent children, so that a six-year-old orphan on the street and a fifteen-year-old child who has committed murder are likely to be treated the same way under the law, an issue analyzed further below.

OVERVIEW

Child is a man in miniature. The same human tendency exists in every one and an individual with a criminal propensity becomes an anti-social element and a menace to the law-abiding society.

Police abuse of street children is symptomatic of three problems: the increasing population of street children, the perception of street children as criminals, and the lawlessness of police. In the four cities Human Rights Watch visited, UNICEF estimated that the population of street children totaled 295,000. All observers we spoke to agreed that this population was increasing. The rising number of street children is linked to India's burgeoning population growth: eighteen million children are added to the population every year, a rate that will result in India's mid-1993 population of approximately 902 million people doubling to 1.8 billion by about 2043. Rapid urbanization has also contributed to the problem. The Indian government's five-year plan for 1992-1997 reported: There has been a marked acceleration in urbanisation over the past two decades. If the present trends continue, urban population may account for about one-third of the total population by the turn of the century.

Urban population statistics for India reflect this observation. According to the United Nations Development Programme (UNDP), in 1960, 18 percent of India's population lived in cities. In 1992, this number had risen to 26 percent of the population. The UNDP estimates that by 2000, 29 percent of India's population will be urban-more than 261 million people. A major factor that contributes to rapid urbanization is the increased migration from rural areas to

India's urban areas. Many of these migrants are landless agricultural labourers whose traditional occupations no longer exist or do not provide sufficient income, and who have come to the cities in search of employment. In Bangalore, many are migrant construction workers who were promised work by agents and subcontractors for construction companies, but who were abandoned by the construction companies and their agents once the work was completed. In general, rural-to-urban migration can be explained by India's policy of development, which has favored urban, industrial development over rural development. While this policy did create greater industrialization and less reliance on agriculture as the engine of economic development, it did not alleviate rural poverty. According to the UNDP, 49 percent of India's rural population live at or below the poverty line. Some of these unemployed or underemployed people are forced to go to cities in search of economic opportunities. Cities provide a slightly better opportunity for these people. However, since the UNDP estimates that 38 percent of India's urban population is at or below the poverty line, this accounts for morethan eighty-nine million people. A 1992 UNICEF study of street children in Bombay observed that the large-scale migration of families from rural to urban areas... has resulted in severe overcrowding, degrading work conditions, homelessness, deprivation of basic services and appalling living conditions in the city. Yet, to return to the village means starvation: to remain in the city means possible survival at least physically.

Within this population are children, who may become street children when they arrive in the cities. This process was described in a 1992 UNICEF study of street children in Calcutta;

To a great extent the issue of street children is closely associated with the process of fast urbanization that has been taking place in the major cities of India since the sixties... They [the children] come to the city with high expectations and full of hopes that they would easily get jobs there and be able to live comfortably with their families. But except for the fortunate ones the dream is shattered in the case of many. Finding it very hard to make both ends meet they are driven to a life of precarious survival. No place to live, no job to support their family with, they are forced to take to streets as their homes and live on the meagre earnings that they somehow manage by doing various odd jobs. The railway stations and their surroundings, under flyovers [highway overpasses] and overbridges, and in unoccupied spaces they live in large clusters constructing tiny little shanties with bamboo poles and plastic sheets or torn cloths.

Some of these children have been displaced as a result of development projects, like the Subarnarekha Irrigation Project which began in 1982 with a

World Bank loan of $127 million. The goal of the project was to create irrigation for agriculture, industry, and cities, and hydroelectric power for the states of West Bengal, Orissa, and Bihar through the construction of two dams, two barrages, and seven canals. The World Bank estimated that 60,000 people would be displaced by the project, while NGOs estimated that the number of people displaced would be closer to 120,000.

As an increasing number of children face severe economic hardship, more and more children become child labourers in whatever occupations are available, including a practice that the Indian government described as, "decadent social practices like scavenging..." in the form of ragpicking, and increasingly, criminal activity.

According to NGOs, lawyers, and human rights activists working with street children, juvenile crime has been increasing, largely due to an increasing population of children and worsening economic conditions. The Swedish childrens' aid agency, Rädda Barnen, a member of a coalition of agencies affiliated with Save the Children, wrote in October 1995 that;

Limited data reveals that, in 1991, 29,591 juveniles were apprehended for various crimes. Most of them were charged with theft, burglary and riot. Of those, 20% were children aged between 7 and 12 and 64% were between 12 to 16. Over 60% were from families earning less than Rs. 500 [$14.29] a month. Girls formed 27% of juvenile offenders (an uncommonly high percentage). Very little information is available on what happens to these children. Legal representation is rare and there are few facilities existing for the detention of children separately from adults. Little is known about the effectiveness of any rehabilitation centres that may exist. Again, in India, juvenile crime rates are exploding.

Very little information is available because very little information formally recorded and what information is available is not reliable. For example, the National Crime Records Bureau (NCRB) reported that in 1992 there were 1,102 juvenile arrests in India's five largest cities (Bangalore, Bombay, Calcutta, Delhi, Madras). The same year, the United Nations estimated that the population of children in these five cities was 8,919,474, which would mean there was one arrest for every 10,746 children. The figures show that juvenile crime was extremely low in these cities, but the figures are questionable. As author Srikanta Ghosh wrote in 1993:

Illegal Detention

A new procedure is being increasingly adopted by the police where a suspect is being picked up and detained for many days. No permission is sought from the court and no information is given to the relatives regarding the whereabouts of the detainee. Even if the detainee dies, the police do not own responsibility as there is no evidence to show that he died in police custody.

Although prohibited under Indian and international law, the illegal detention of street children is common in every part of India. Arbitrary detention is illegal under Articles 21 and 22 of India's constitution. Sections 50, 56, and 57 of the Code of Criminal Procedure mandate that no person can be detained in custody without knowing the grounds for arrest, and that a detainee must be presented before a magistrate within twenty-four hours of arrest. Section 160 of the code prohibits the detention of males under the age of fifteen or females of any age for the purposes of investigation or questioning by the police. Article 9 of the International Covenant on Civil and Political Rights, and Article 37 of the U.N. Convention on the Rights of the Child prohibit arbitrary detention. India has ratified both. The United Nations Minimum Rules for the Administration of Juvenile Justice, called the "Beijing Rules" because they were drafted in Beijing, state that all juveniles arrested have the right to counsel, notification of charges and the right to have a parent or guardian present at the time of arrest. Both the "Beijing Rules" and the U.N. Rules for Juveniles Deprived of their Liberty state that the human rights of juveniles should be protected and respected while in custody. Moreover, India's Juvenile Justice Act prohibits the detention of juveniles in either police stations or jails.

Many observers have documented the tendency of police to arrest and detain children without good reason. A 1992 study sponsored by the Indian Ministry of Labour and UNICEF on the plight of street children in Bombay noted;

The most common complaint of street children without families was that they are rounded up and locked up by the police for two or three days merely on suspicion. This, they explained, was done to fill the "quota" which police are expected to do. Younger children are generally not caught; it is the older children the police have their eye on.

An NGO representative and human rights activist in New Delhi had a similar comment;

For their reports and to make money, the police lock up a few children and majors [adults] everyday, only to release them later after having taken their money and/or beaten them up. A few are also presented to the magistrate to show proof that the police are performing their "duties."

The Juvenile Justice Act

The Juvenile Justice Act, 1986, was enacted in an attempt to address the plight of children within the justice system. It was based on the United

Nations Standard Minimum Rules for the Administration of Juvenile Justice (the Beijing Rules). Generally, this law, like constitutional rights and other legislation intended to protect children's rights, is ignored.

The Juvenile Justice Act prohibits the detention of juveniles in police station or jails for periods longer than twenty-four hours. It also requires the registration of "neglected" and "delinquent juveniles" and requires that juveniles be sent back to their parents or guardians or to a remand home immediately following either their identification as a "neglected juvenile" or their arrest as a "delinquent juvenile." But, the act also makes the police responsible for identifying neglected juveniles and arresting delinquent juveniles. The police actively abuse this authority, resulting in a pattern of arbitrary arrest, detention, extortion, and beatings of street children, and a practice known as the "round-up," in which children are detained in large groups and either sent to remand homes or disciplined in the police station. There are several reasons for the round-up. The act views children working in railway stations as "delinquent juveniles;" such children are frequently victims of the round-up. In other cases, juvenile boards, the authority designated by the act to handle cases of neglected children and send them to the remand homes, pressure the police to fill vacant remand homes. NGO representatives and lawyers that Human Rights Watch spoke to said that because the shelters were ostensibly designed to care for both neglected and delinquent juveniles, officials fear that an empty home might invite criticism that the juvenile boards, the courts, and the police were not doing their duty. The round-up is also used as an expedient method of detaining possible suspects. Because police generally view street children as criminals, a round-up is an easy way to catch and interrogate them. The 1992 UNICEF study of street children in Bombay described the practice:

When some property (e.g. a bag) belonging to the public is lost/stolen at the station, these children are rounded up and some even framed. To prove that they are not guilty, the children have to do their best to find the culprit and save their skin.

The Juvenile Justice Act, 1986, introduces itself as one meant "to provide for the care, protection, treatment, development and rehabilitation of neglected or deliquent juveniles and for the adjudication of certain matters relating to, and disposition of, delinquent juveniles." This well-meaning statement, in reality, reads, "Letting a child know in no uncertain terms that he is a criminal, therefore cannot live with his parents but with other little criminals, must work while other children play, is 'asking for it' if sexually-molested or raped, is liable to be rounded up fiercely by the police on the slightest murmur of a crime taking place in any locality where he may be, is watched over by people who hate their jobs and couldn't be bothered about probing the child's mind to ensure that he never has to come back there again."

Observation, Remand, Special, and Juvenile Homes

From police custody, the children may be sent before a juvenile board, or a juvenile court, headed by a magistrate with jurisdiction over juveniles who have been arrested on a criminal charge. Both the court and the juvenile board have the authority to send children to institutions known variously as observation, remand, special, or juvenile homes. Thus, regardless of their status as juvenile offenders, abandoned or orphaned children, or children awaiting trial, all children are remanded to the same institutions. This situation was described by the additional commissioner of the Delhi police (ACP), Amod Kanth, who also runs a shelter for street children in Delhi:

Rather than providing custodial care like parents provide, juvenile homes have degenerated into jail-like custodial centres. The JJ Board [Juvenile Justice Board], despite its authority, has remained a mute spectator to the pitiable conditions of the homes. The Juvenile Justice Act strongly advocates that children should not be kept in lock-ups as juvenile justice is distinguished from criminal justice. Most children arrested are non-offenders but the two categories-neglected children and juvenile delinquents are wrongly clubbed together.

The arbitrary nature of detention in observation homes has been documented in studies on street children. The joint reports on street children by the government of India's Ministry of Labour and UNICEF list some of the reasons children had been sent to remand homes:

In Bangalore, the bulk (81.5 percent) of children were sent to remand homes on charges of theft, the second largest group were sent on "doubt" (11.3 percent). This means that 11.3 percent of children were sent to remand homes without having been informed of the reasons.

The Bombay study reported that the majority of children (74.6 percent) were sent to remand homes on charges of vagrancy or suspicion. In other words, they were arrested because the police considered them vagrants or suspected they might commit crimes or may have committed a crime. But these children were never formally charged with any offense. The Madras study found that 87.2 percent of children were sent to remand homes on "petty cases" or other charges not including drug peddling, loitering, theft, or robbery. The study commented.

Torture

The criminal justice system in our country should be reviewed for making it more purposeful and effective. The criminal is happy with the court proceedings, with the law of the land, with the punishments imposed by the courts and with the easy life and comforts in the jails and is unhappy only with the police investigation and their preventative measures involving torture and harassment. It is therefore reasonable to believe that a certain complacence arising from authority derived from law motivates some *policemen* to resort to violence against those held in their custody, lawful or otherwise.

Torture, usually in the form of severe beatings with fists, lathis, or other instruments, and kicking is a common feature of police treatment of street children. Beatings themselves are used extensively as a means of investigation, punishment, and retribution. As an NGO representative in Madras told us:

Regardless of the situation the police beat the children. I have seen broken bones, broken teeth, bruises, etc... The older a child is, the more horrible the treatment. They will tie boys down in a spread-eagled position and beat them, use knives or needles, they will hang them up by the arms and beat them brutally.

The brutality of police in the course of investigating crime, especially in investigations of crimes against property, and as a form of retribution or punishment are acknowledged characteristics of police behaviour. A senior state police officer, Inspector-General I. Ravi Arumugam, himself described this behavior in a paper he presented in 1994. An excerpt of his extraordinary statement, including the two charts which he used to describe illegal detention, torture and punishment, follows; various fences of stolen property takes time: for the normal police officer it is faster to catch the servant in the house, hammer him and if it works and, at his instance, some stolen property is recovered well and good, otherwise tough luck for the complainant; the case goes undetected. Of course, in India, the most superior short-cut is not to register the burglary at all; harass any one who comes to the police station so that an ordinary citizen would think several times before coming to report an offense. Brutality works even better in handling a law and order situation. And, sadly enough, under pressure it seems to be the natural response of police, regardless of country. Yet the desired change in police behaviour is not an impossible undertaking. The general awakening of society against police brutality is a good sign.

The Laws of India

Articles 21 and 22 of the Indian Constitution mandate that no one may be arbitrarily detained or arrested. Article 22 of the Indian Constitution and Sections 50, 56, 57, and 70 of the Code of Criminal Procedure specify that an arrested person must be told of the reason for his or her arrest, and must be presented before a magistrate within twenty-four hours, otherwise the detention is illegal. To detain a person for a period greater than twenty-four hours, the police must obtain permission from a magistrate. In addition to these laws, Section 160 of the Code of Criminal Procedure states that neither males under the age of fifteen nor any women may be brought to a police station for questioning when a crime is investigated.

The Juvenile Justice Act was enacted in 1986 to address the treatment of juveniles by law enforcement officials. Sections 13 and 18 of the Juvenile Justice Act mandate that juveniles cannot be kept in a police station for more than twenty-four hours, and upon identification as a "neglected juvenile" or upon arrest (where the child is not released on bail) as a "delinquent juvenile," may not be remanded to a jail or police station, but must immediately be sent to an observation home or remand center. Juveniles charged with criminal offenses must be tried injuvenile courts and cannot be tried with adults. The act also mandates that arrested juveniles have the right to be informed of the charges against them, the right to remain silent, and the right to an attorney.

The Supreme Court has ruled in five decisions that Article 21 of the Indian constitution forbid torture, although the constitutional prohibition is not explicit. Section 24 of the Indian Evidence Act makes confessions made through "inducement, threat, or promise" inadmissible as evidence and sections 25 and 26 of the Indian Evidence Act make any confession to a police officer inadmissible unless it takes place in the presence of a magistrate. However, under section 27 of the Indian Evidence Act, any evidence obtained by a police officer while a suspect is in custody is admissible in court. Torture by police is subject to criminal charges under the Indian Penal Code.

The Prevention of Corruption Act was enacted in 1988. Sections 7 and 11 forbid public servants to take money or property in discharge of official duties, outside of their normal remuneration. Section 13 of the Act considers any public servant habitually involved in corrupt practices to be guilty of "criminal misconduct." Corruption is a criminal offense in the Indian Penal Code. A beating used to propagate corruption constitutes a criminal offense under Section 329 of the code and calls for a prison term of up to ten years.

The detention, ill-treatment, and torture of street children by police in India has reached epidemic proportions. Torture has long been a routine part of police investigations, and despite widespread recognition of the problem, little has been done to address it. The victims typically represent the most vulnerable sectors of society: they are poor, members of low-caste groups or minorities, and have no political standing that would afford them protection from the lawlessness of the police. Street children, in addition, generally have no family members to intervene on their behalf.

Changing a police culture that not only tolerates but endorses torture is not easy. As a first step toward ending the abuse, the Indian government should implement all of the reforms of the National Police Commission, a step that is now at least fifteen years overdue. The recommendations of the commission include making judicial inquiries into cases of alleged rape, death, or grievous injury in police custody mandatory, and establishing investigative bodies whose members would include civilians as well as police and judicial authorities. Provisions prohibiting the detention of juveniles in police lock-ups should be strictly enforced, and a civilian review board comprised of former police, NGO representatives, judges, and lawyers should be established to monitor police stations.

These reforms will only work, however, if the state governments, for their part, agree to work with local NGOs and citizens' groups to monitor police behavior and enforce the law, and if the central government monitors the state governments' performance. No single agency can bring an end to police abuse. Most importantly, better police training and closer monitoring of police behaviour must be linked to greater accountability, for as long as police feel assured of impunity, custodial violence will not end.

India must also change the laws that contribute to the problem. The Code of Criminal Procedure should be amended to require mandatory medical examinations and age verification at the time of detention. All laws relating to child labour as well as the Juvenile Justice Act should be revised to ensure that the implementation of both laws does not result in criminalizing children who are forced to work.

At the international level, the government of India should ratify the Convention Against Torture and Other Forms of Cruel, Inhuman and Degrading Treatment or Punishment, a pledge made by the current government of India in their platform. It should also invite the United Nations Special Rapporteur on Torture to India to investigate, and the U.N. Working Group on Arbitrary Detention to investigate, respectively, the torture and arbitrary detention of street children by police.

The Juvenile Justice Act, 1986

Introduction

The problem of juvenile justice is, no doubt, one of tragic human interest so much so in fact that it is not only confined to this country alone but cuts across national boundaries. Juvenile delinquency laws are characterised by the feature that they prescribe many acts which are regarded as non-criminal if indulged by elder persons like drinking, smoking, viewing adult films or reading adult literature, *etc.* The extension of the concept of juvenile delinquency to wider limits has drawn adverse criticism on the ground that it is neither necessary nor desirable to use police and courts in private matters which can well be tackled by the family themselves.

The first legislation concerning children which came in 1850 was the Apprentice Act which provided that children in the age groups of ten to eighteen convicted by courts were intended to be provided with some vocational training which might help their rehabilitation. It was followed by the Reformatory Schools Act, 1897. The Indian Jail Committee (1919-1920) brought to the fore the vital need for fair trial and treatment for young offenders. Its recommendations prompted the enactment of the Children Act in Madras in 1920. This was followed by the Bengal and Bombay Acts in 1922 and 1924 respectively. The three pioneer statutes, (i.e., Acts concerning Madras, Bengal and Bombay) were extensively amended between 1948 and 1959.

In 1960 at the second United Nations Congress on the Prevention of Crime and Treatment of Offenders at London, this issue was discussed and some therapeutic recommendations were adopted.

The Central enactment, the Children Act, 1960 was passed to cater to the heads of the Union Territories. To remove the same inherent lacunae of the above mentioned Act, the Children (Amendment) Act was passed in 1978. But the need of a uniform legislation regarding juvenile justice for the whole of the country had been expressed in various fora, including Parliament, but it could not be enacted on the ground that the subject matter of such legislation fell in the State List of the Constitution. To bring the operations of the juvenile justice system in the country in conformity with the UN Standard Minimum Rules for the Administration of Juvenile Justice, Parliament seems to have exercised its power under Article 253 of the Constitution read with Entry 14 of the Union List to make law for the whole of India to fulfill international obligations. On 22nd August, 1986, the Juvenile Justice Bill, 1986 was introduced in the Lok Sabha.

Statement of Objects and Reasons

A review of the working of the existing Children Acts would indicate that much greater attention is required to be given to children who may be found in situations of social maladjustment, delinquency or neglect. The justice system as available for adults is not considered suitable for being applied to juveniles. It is also necessary that a uniform juvenile justice system should be available throughout the country which should make adequate provision for dealing with all aspects in the changing social, cultural and economic situation in the country. There is also a need for larger involvement of informal systems and community based welfare agencies in the care, protection, treatment, development and rehabilitation of such juveniles.

In this context, the proposed legislation aims at achieving the following objectives:-

(i) to lay down a uniform legal framework for juvenile justice in the country so as to ensure that no child under any circumstances is lodged in a jail or a police lock-up. This is being ensured by establishing Juvenile Welfare Boards and Juvenile Courts;

(ii) to provide for a specialised approach towards the prevention and treatment of juvenile delinquency in its full range in keeping with the developmental needs of the child as found in any situation of social maladjustment;

(iii) to spell out the machinery and infrastructure required for the care, protection, treatment, development and rehabilitation of various categories of children coming within the purview of the juvenile justice system. This is proposed to be achieved by establishing observation homes, juvenile homes for neglected juveniles and special homes for delinquent juveniles;

(iv) to establish norms and standards for the administration of juvenile justice in terms of investigation and prosecution, adjudication and disposition and care, treatment and rehabilitation;

(v) to develop appropriate linkages and coordination between the formal system of juvenile justice and voluntary agencies engaged in the welfare of neglected or societally maladjusted children and to specifically define the areas of their responsibilities and roles;

(vi) to constitute special offences in relation to juveniles and provide for punishments therefore;

(vii) to bring the operation of the juvenile justice system in the country in conformity with the United Nations Standard Minimum Rules for the Administration of Juvenile Justice.

As its various provisions come into force in different parts of the country they would replace the corresponding laws on the subject, such as the Children Act, 1960 and other State enactments on the subject.

The Bill seeks to achieve the above objects.

ACT 53 OF 1986

The Juvenile Justice Bill, 1986 was passed by both the Houses of Parliament. After receiving the assent of the President it came on the Statute Book as the Juvenile Justice Act, 1986 (53 of 1986).

THE JUVENILE JUSTICE ACT, 1986

(53 of 1986)

[1st December, 1986]

An Act to provide for the care, protection, treatment, development and rehabilitation of neglected or delinquent juveniles and for the adjudication of certain matters relating to and disposition of, delinquent juveniles.

CHAPTER I

Preliminary

1. Short title, extent and commencement.-(1) This Act may be called the Juvenile Justice Act, 1986.

(2) It extends to the whole of India except the State of Jammu and Kashmir.

(3) It shall come into force on such date as the Central Government may, by notification in the Official Gazette, appoint, and different dates may be appointed for different provisions of this Act and for different States.

2. Definitions.-In this Act, unless the context otherwise requires,-

(a) "begging" means-

(i) soliciting or receiving alms in a public place or entering into any private premises for the purposes of soliciting or receiving alms, whether under the pretense of singing, dancing, fortune-telling, performing tricks or selling articles or otherwise;

(ii) exposing or exhibiting, with the object of obtaining or extorting alms, any sore, wound, injury, deformity or disease, whether of himself or of any other person or of an animal;

(iii) allowing oneself to be used as an exhibit for the purpose of soliciting or receiving alms;

(b) "Board" means a Juvenile Welfare Board constituted under section 4;

(c) "brothel", "prostitute", "prostitution" and "public place" shall have the meanings respectively assigned to them in the Suppression of Immoral Traffic in Women and Girls Act, 1956 (104 of 1956);

(d) "competent authority" means, in relation to neglected Juveniles, a Board and, in relation to delinquent Juveniles, a Juvenile Court and where no such Board or Juvenile Court has been constituted, includes any court empowered under sub-section (2) of section 7 to exercise the powers conferred on a Board or Juvenile Court;

(e) "delinquent juvenile" means a juvenile who has been found to have committed an offence;

(f) "fit person" or "fit institution" means any person or institution (not being a police station or jail) found fit by the competent authority to receive and take care of a juvenile entrusted to his or its care and protection on the terms and conditions specified by the competent authority;

(g) "guardian" in relation to a juvenile, includes, any person who, in the opinion of the competent authority, having cognizance of any proceeding in relation to a juvenile, has, for the time being, the actual charge of, or control over, that juvenile;

(h) "juvenile" means a boy who has not attained the age of sixteen years or a girl who has not attained the age of eighteen years;

(i) "Juvenile Court" means a court constituted under section 5;

(j) "Juvenile home" means an institution established or certified by the State Government under section 9 as a juvenile home;

(k) "narcotic drug" and "psychotropic substance" shall have the meanings respectively assigned to them in the Narcotic Drugs and Psychotropic Substances Act, 1985 (61 of 1985);

(l) "neglected juvenile" means a juvenile who-

  (i) is found begging; or

  (ii) is found without having any home or settled place of abode and without any ostensible means of subsistence and is destitute; or

  (iii) has a parent or guardian who is unfit or incapacitated to exercise control over the juvenile; or

  (iv) lives in a brothel or with a prostitute or frequently goes to any place used for the purpose of prostitution, or is found to associate with any prostitute or any other person who leads an immoral, drunken or depraved life; or

  (v) who is being or is likely to be abused or exploited for immoral or illegal purposes or unconscionable gain;

(m) "observation home" means any institution or place established or recognised by the State Government under section 11 as an observation home;

(n) "offence" means an offence punishable under any law for the time being in force;

(o) "place of safety" means any place or institution (not being a police station or jail), the person in charge of which is willing temporarily to receive and take care of a juvenile and which, in the opinion of the competent authority may be a place of safety for the juvenile;

(p) "prescribed" means prescribed by rules made under this Act;

(q) "probation officer" means an officer appointed as a probation officer under this Act or under the Probation of Offenders Act, 1958 (20 of 1958);

(r) "special home" means an institution established or certified by the State Government under section 10;

(s) "supervision", in relation to a juvenile placed under the care of any parent, guardian, or other fit person or fit institution under this Act, means the supervision of that juvenile by a probation officer for the purpose of ensuring that the juvenile is properly looked after and that the conditions imposed by the competent authority are complied with;

(t) all words and expressions used but not defined in this Act and defined in the Code of Criminal Procedure, 1973 (2 of 1974), shall have the meanings respectively assigned to them in that Code.

3. Continuation of inquiry in respect of juvenile who has ceased to be a juvenile.-Where an inquiry has been initiated against a juvenile and during the course of such inquiry the juvenile ceases to be such, then, not withstanding anything contained in this Act or in any other law for the time being in force, the inquiry may be continued and orders may be made in respect of such person if such person had continued to be a juvenile.

CHAPTER II

Competent Authorities and Institutions for Juveniles

4. Juvenile Welfare Boards.-(1) The State Government may, by notification in the Official Gazette, constitute for any area specified in the notification, one or more Juvenile Welfare Boards for exercising the powers and discharging the duties conferred or imposed on such Board in relation to neglected juveniles under this Act.

(2) A Board shall consist of a Chairman and such other members as the State Government thinks fit to appoint, of whom not less than one shall be a woman; and every such member shall be vested with the powers of a Magistrate under the Code of Criminal Procedure, 1973 (2 of 1974).

(3) The Board shall function as a Bench of Magistrates and shall have the powers conferred by the Code of Criminal Procedure, 1973 (2 of 1974), on a Metropolitan Magistrate or, as the case may be, a Judicial Magistrate of the first class.

5. Juvenile Courts.-(1) Notwithstanding anything contained in the Code of Criminal Procedure, 1973 (2 of 1974), the State Government may, by notification in the Official Gazette, constitute for any area specified in the notification, one or more Juvenile Courts for exercising the powers and discharging the duties conferred or imposed on such court in relation to delinquent juveniles under this Act.

(2) A Juvenile Court shall consist of such number of Metropolitan Magistrates or Judicial Magistrates of the first class, as the case may be, forming a Bench as the State Government thinks fit to appoint, of whom one shall be designated as the Principal Magistrate; and every such Bench shall have the powersconferred by the Code of Criminal Procedure, 1973 (2 of 1974), on a Metropolitan Magistrate or, as the case may be, a Judicial Magistrate of the first class.

(3) Every Juvenile Court shall be assisted by a panel of two honorary social workers possessing such qualifications as may be prescribed, of whom at least one shall be a woman, and such panel shall be appointed by the State Government.

6. Procedure, *etc.* in relation to Boards and Juvenile Courts.-(1) In the event of any difference of opinion among the members of a Board or among the Magistrates of a Juvenile Court, the opinion of the majority shall prevail, but where there is no such majority, the opinion of the Chairman or of the Principal Magistrate, as the case may be, shall prevail.

(2) A Board or Juvenile Court may act notwithstanding the absence of any member of the Board or, as the case may be, any Magistrate of the Juvenile Court, and no order made by the Board or Juvenile Court shall be invalid by reason only of the absence of any member or Magistrate, as the case may be, during any stage of the proceeding.

(3) No person shall be appointed as a member of the Board or as a Magistrate in the Juvenile Court unless he has, in the opinion of the State Government, special knowledge of child psychology and child welfare.

7. Powers of the Board and Juvenile Court.-(1) Where a Board or a Juvenile Court has been constituted for any area, such Board or Court, shall, notwithstanding anything contained in any other law for the time being in force but save as otherwise expressly provided in this Act have power to deal exclusively with all proceedings under this Act relating to neglected juveniles or delinquent juveniles, as the case may be:

Provided that a Board or a Juvenile Court may, if it is of opinion that it is necessary so to do having regard to the circumstances of the case, transfer any proceedings to any Juvenile Court or Board, as the case may be:

Provided further that where there is any difference of opinion between a Board and a Juvenile Court regarding the transfer of any proceedings under the first proviso, it shall be referred to the Chief Metropolitan Magistrate or, as the case may be, the Chief Judicial Magistrate for decision, and in a case where the District Magistrate is functioning as a Board or a Juvenile Court, such difference of opinion shall be referred to the Court of

Session, and the decision of the Chief Metropolitan Magistrate or Chief Judicial Magistrate or, as the case may be, the Court of Session on such reference shall be final.

(2) Where no Board or Juvenile Court has been constituted for any area, the powers conferred on the Board or the Juvenile Court by or under this Act shall be exercised in that area, only by the following, namely:-

(a) the District Magistrate; or

(b) the Sub-Divisional Magistrate; or

(c) any Metropolitan Magistrate or Judicial Magistrate of the first class, as the case may be.

(3) The powers conferred on the Board or Juvenile Court by or under this Act may also be exercised by the High Court and the Court of Session, when the proceeding comes before them in appeal, revision or otherwise.

8. Procedure to be followed by a Magistrate not empowered under the Act.-(1) When any Magistrate not empowered to exercise the powers of a Board or a Juvenile Court under this Act is of opinion that a person brought before him under any of the provisions of this Act (otherwise than for the purpose of giving evidence) is a juvenile, he shall record such opinion and forward the juvenile and the record of the proceeding to the competent authority having jurisdiction over the proceeding.

(2) The competent authority to which the proceeding is forwarded under sub-section (1) shall hold the inquiry as if the juvenile had originally been brought before it.

9. Juvenile homes.-(1) The State Government may establish and maintain as many juvenile homes as may be necessary for the reception of neglected juveniles under this Act.

(2) Where the State Government is of opinion that any institution other than a home maintained under sub-section (1) is fit for the reception of the neglected juvenile to be sent there under this Act, it may certify such institution as a juvenile home for the purpose of this Act.

(3) Every juvenile home to which a neglected juvenile is sent under this Act shall not only provide the juvenile with accommodation, maintenance and facilities for education, vocational training and rehabilitation, but also provide him with facilities for the development of his character and abilities and give him necessary training for protecting himself against moral danger or exploitation and shall also perform such other functions as may be prescribed to ensure all round growth and development of his personality.

(4) The State Government may, by rules made under this Act, provide for the management of juvenile homes, including the standards and the nature of services to be maintained by them and the circumstances under which, and the manner in which, the certification of a juvenile home is granted or withdrawn.

10. Special homes.-(1) The State Government may establish and maintain as many special homes as may be necessary for the reception of delinquent juveniles under this Act.

(2) Where the State Government is of the opinion that any institution other than a home established or maintained under sub-section (1) is fit for the reception of the delinquent juveniles to be sent there under this Act, it may certify such institution as a special home for the purposes of this Act.

(3) Every special home to which a delinquent juvenile is sent under this Act shall not only provide the juvenile with accommodation, maintenance and facilities for education, vocational training and rehabilitation, but also provide him with facilities for the development of his character and abilities and give him necessary training for his reformation and shall also perform such other functions as may be prescribed to ensure all round growth and development of his personality.

(4) The State Government may, by rules made under this Act, provide for the management of special homes, including the standards and the nature of services to be maintained by them, and the circumstances under which, and the manner in which, the certification of a special home may be granted or withdrawn.

(5) The rules made under sub-section (4) may also provide for the classification and separation of delinquent juveniles on the basis of age and nature of offences committed by them.

11. Observation homes.-(1) The State Government may establish and maintain as many observation homes as may be necessary for the temporary reception of juveniles during the pendency of any inquiry regarding them under this Act.

(2) Where the State Government is of opinion that any institution other than a home established or maintained under sub-section (1) is fit for the temporary reception of juveniles during the pendency of any inquiry regarding them under this Act, it may recognise such institution as an observation home for the purposes of this Act.

(3) Every observation home to which a juvenile is sent under this Act shall not only provide the juvenile with accommodation, maintenance and facilities for medical examination and treatment but also provide him with facilities for useful occupation.

(4) The State Government may, by rules made under this Act, provide for the management of observation homes, including the standards and the nature of services to be maintained by them, and the circumstances under which, and the manner in which, an institution may be recognised as an observation home or the recognition may be withdrawn.

12. After-care organisations.-The State Government may, by rules made under this Act, provide-

(a) for the establishment or recognition of after-care organisations and the powers that may be exercised by them for effectively carrying out their functions under this Act;

(b) for a scheme of after-care programme to be followed by such after-care organisations for the purpose of taking care of juveniles after they leave juvenile homes or special homes and for the purpose of enabling them to lead an honest, industrious and useful life;

(c) for the preparation or submission of a report by the probation officer in respect of each juvenile prior to his discharge from a juvenile home or special home, as the case may be, regarding the necessity and nature of after-care of such juvenile, the period of such after-care, supervision there of and for the submission of a report by the probation officer on the progress of each such juvenile;

(d) for the standards and the nature of services to be maintained by such after-care organisations;

(e) for such other matters as may be necessary for the purpose of effectively carrying out the scheme of after-care programme of juveniles.

CHAPTER III

Neglected Juveniles

13. Production of neglected juveniles before Boards.-(1) If any police officer or any other person or organisation authorised by the State Government in this behalf, by general or special order, is of opinion that a person is apparently a neglected juvenile, such police officer or other person or organisation may take charge of that person for bringing him before a Board.

(2) When information is given to an officer-in-charge of a police station about any neglected juvenile found within the limits of such station, he shall enter in a book to be kept for the purpose the substance of such information and take such action thereon as he deems fit and if such officer does not propose to take charge of the juvenile, he shall forward a copy of the entry made to the Board.

(3) Every juvenile taken charge of under sub-section (1) shall be brought before the Board without any loss of time but within a period of twenty-four hours of such charge taken excluding the time necessary for the journey from the place where the juvenile had been taken charge of to the Board.

(4) Every juvenile taken charge of under sub-section (1) shall, unless he is kept with his parent or guardian, be sent to an observation home (but not to a police station or jail) until he can be brought before a Board.

14. Special procedure to be followed when neglected juvenile has parents.-(1) If a person, who in the opinion of the police officer or the authorised person or organisation is a neglected juvenile, has a parent or guardian who has the actual charge of, or control over, the juvenile, the police officer or the authorised person or the organisation may, instead of taking charge of the juvenile, make a report to the board for initiating an inquiry regarding that juvenile.

(2) On receipt of a report under sub-section (1), the Board may call upon the parent or guardian to produce the juvenile before it and to show cause why the juvenile should not be dealt with as a neglected juvenile under the provisions of this Act and if it appears to the Board that the juvenile is likely to be removed from its jurisdiction or to be concealed, it may immediately order his removal (if necessary by issuing a search warrant for the immediate production of the juvenile) to an observation home or a place of safety.

15. Inquiry by Board regarding neglected juveniles.-(1) When a person alleged to be a neglected juvenile is produced before a Board, it shall examine the police officer or the authorised person or the organisation who brought the juvenile or made the report and record the substance of such examination and hold the inquiry in the prescribed manner and may make such orders in relation to the juvenile as it may deem fit.

(2) Where a Board is satisfied on inquiry that a juvenile is a neglected juvenile and that it is expedient so to deal with him, the Board may make an order directing the juvenile to be sent to a juvenile home for the period until he ceases to be a juvenile:

Provided that the Board may, if it is satisfied that having regard to the circumstances of the case it is expedient so to do, for reasons to be recorded, reduce the period of stay to such period as it thinks fit.

Provided further that the Board may, if it is satisfied that having regard to the circumstances of the case it is expedient so to do, for reasons to be recorded, reduce the period of stay to such period as it thinks fit.

(3) During the pendency of any inquiry regarding a juvenile, the juvenile shall, unless he is kept with his parent or guardian, be sent to an observation home or a place of safety for such period as may be specified in the order of the Board:

Provided that no juvenile shall be kept with his parent or guardian if, in the opinion of the Board, such parent or guardian is unfit or unable to exercise or does not exercise proper care and control over the juvenile.

16. Power to commit neglected juvenile to suitable custody.-(1) If the Board so thinks fit, it may, instead of making an order under sub-section (2) of section 15, for sending the juvenile to a juvenile home, make an order placing the juvenile under the care of a parent, guardian or other fit person, on such parent, guardian or fit person executing a bond with or without surety to be responsible for the good behaviour and well-being of the juvenile and for the observance of such conditions as the Board may think fit to impose.

(2) At the time of making an order under sub-section (1) or at any time subsequently, the Board may, in addition, make an order that the juvenile be placed under supervision for any period not exceeding three years in the first instance.

(3) Notwithstanding anything contained in sub-section (1) or sub-section (2), if at any time it appears to the Board, on receiving a report from the probation officer or otherwise, that there has been a breach of any of the conditions imposed by it in respect of the juvenile, it may, after making such inquiry as it deems fit, order the juvenile to be sent to a juvenile home.

17. Uncontrollable juveniles.-Where a parent or guardian of a juvenile complains to the Board that he is not able to exercise proper care and control over the juvenile and the Board is satisfied on inquiry that proceedings under this Act should be initiated regarding the juvenile, it may send the juvenile to an observation home or a place of safety and make such further inquiry as is may deem fit and the provisions of section 15 and section 16 shall, as far as may be, apply to such proceedings.

CHAPTERIV

Delinquent Juveniles

18. Bail and custody of juveniles.-(1) When any person accused of a bailable or non-bailable offence and apparently a juvenile is arrested or detained or appears or is brought before a Juvenile Court, such person shall, notwithstanding anything contained in the Code of Criminal Procedure, 1973 (2 of 1974), or in any other law for the time being in force, be released on bail with or without surety but he shall not be so released if there appear reasonable grounds for believing that the release is likely to bring him into association with any known criminal or expose him to moral danger or that his release would defeat the ends of justice.

(2) When such person having been arrested is not released on bail under sub-section (1) by the officer-in-charge of the police station, such officer shall cause him to be kept in an observation home or place of safety in the prescribed manner (but not in a police station or jail) until he can be brought before a Juvenile Court.

(3) When such person is not released on bail under sub-section (1) by the Juvenile Court it shall, instead of committing him to prison, make an order sending him to an observation home or a place of safety for such period

during the pendency of the inquiry regarding him as may be specified in the order.

19. Information to parent or guardian or probation officer.-Where a juvenile is arrested, the officer-in-charge of the police station to which the juvenile is brought shall, as soon as may be after the arrest, inform-

(a) the parent or guardian of the juvenile, if he can be found, of such arrest and direct him to be present at the Juvenile Court before which the juvenile will appear; and

(b) the probation officer of such arrest in order to enable him to obtain information regarding the antecedents and family history of the juvenile and other material circumstances likely to be of assistance of the Juvenile Court for making the inquiry.

20. Inquiry by Juvenile Court regarding delinquent juveniles.-Where a juvenile having been charged with an offence appears or is produced before a Juvenile Court, the Juvenile Court shall hold the inquiry in accordance with the provisions of section 39 and may, subject to the provisions of this Act, make such order in relation to the juvenile as it deems fit.

21. Orders that may be passed regarding delinquent juveniles.-(1) Where a Juvenile Court is satisfied on inquiry that a juvenile has committed an offence, then, notwithstanding anything to the contrary contained in any other law for the time being in force, the Juvenile Court may, if it so thinks fit,-

(a) allow the juvenile to go home after advice or admonition;

(b) direct the juvenile to be released on probation of good conduct and placed under the care of any parent, guardian or other fit person, on such parent, guardian or other fit person executing a bond, with or without surety as that court may require, for the good behaviour and well-being of the juvenile for any period not exceeding three years;

(c) direct the juvenile to be released on probation of good conduct and placed under the care of any fit institution for the good behaviour and well-being of the juvenile for any period not exceeding three years;

(d) make an order directing the juvenile to be sent to a special home,-

 (i) in the case of a boy over fourteen years of age or of a girl over sixteen years of age, for a period of not less than three years;

 (ii) in the case of an other juvenile, for the period until he ceases to be a juvenile:

Provided that the Juvenile Court may, if it satisfied that having regard to the nature of the offence and the circumstances of the case it is expedient so to do, for reasons to be recorded, reduce the period of stay to such period as it thinks fit:

Provided further that the Juvenile Court may, for reasons to be recorded, extend the period of such stay, but in no case the period of stay shall extend beyond the time when the juvenile attains the age of eighteen years, in the case of a boy, or twenty years, in the case of a girl;

(e) order the juvenile to pay a fine if he is over fourteen years of age and earns money.

(2) Where an order under clause (b), clause (c) or clause (e) of sub-section (1) is made, the Juvenile Court may, if it is of opinion that in the interests of the juvenile and of the public it is expedient so to do, in addition make an order that the delinquent juvenile shall remain under the supervision of a probation officer named in the order during such period, not exceeding three years, as may be specified therein, and may in such supervision order impose such conditions as it deems necessary for the due supervision of the delinquent juvenile:

Provided that if at any time afterwards it appears to the Juvenile Court on receiving a report from the probation officer or otherwise, that the delinquent juvenile has not been of good behaviour during the period of supervision or that the fit institution under whose care the juvenile was placed is no longer able or willing to ensure the good behaviour and well being of the juvenile it may after making such inquiry as it deems fit, order the delinquent juvenile to be sent to a special home.

(3) The Juvenile Court making a supervision order under sub-section (2), shall explain to the juvenile and the parent, guardian or other fit person or fit institution, as the case may be, under whose care the juvenile has been placed the terms and conditions of the order and shall forthwith furnish one copy of the supervision order to the juvenile, the parent, guardian or other fit person or fit institution, as the case may be, the sureties if any, and the probation officer.

(4) In determining the special home, or any person or institution to whose custody a juvenile is to be committed or entrusted under this Act, the court shall pay due regard to the religious denomination of the juvenile to ensure that religious instruction contrary to the religious persuasion of the juvenile is not imparted to him.

22. Orders that may not be passed against the delinquent juvenile.-(1) Notwithstanding anything to the contrary contained in any other law for the time being in force, no delinquent juvenile shall be sentenced to death or imprisonment, or committed to prison in default of payment of fine in default of furnishing security:

Provided that where a juvenile who has attained the age of fourteen years has committed an offence and the Juvenile Court is satisfied that the offence committed is of so serious a nature or that his conduct and behaviour have been such that it would not be in his interest or in the interest of other juveniles in a special home to send him to such special home and that none of the other measures provided under this Act is suitable or sufficient, the Juvenile Court, may order the delinquent juvenile to be kept in safe custody in such place and manner as it thinks fit and shall report the case for the orders of the State Government.

(2) On receipt of a report from a Juvenile Court under sub-section (1), the State Government may make such arrangement in respect of the juvenile as it deems proper and may order such delinquent juvenile to be detained at such place and on such conditions as it thinks fit:

Provided that the period of detention so ordered shall not exceed the maximum period of imprisonment to which the juvenile could have been sentenced for the offence committed.

23. Proceeding under Chapter VIII of the Code of Criminal Procedure not competent against juvenile.-Notwithstanding anything to the contrary contained in the Code of Criminal Procedure, 1973 (2 of 1974), no proceeding shall be instituted and no order shall be passed against a juvenile under Chapter VIII of the said Code.

24. No joint trial of juvenile and person not a juvenile.-(1) Notwithstanding anything contained in section 223 of the Code of Criminal Procedure, 1973 (2 of 1974), or in any other law for the time being in force, no juvenile shall be charged with or tried for, any offence together with a person who is not a juvenile.

(2) If a juvenile is accused of an offence for which under section 223 of Code of Criminal Procedure, 1973 (2 of 1974), or any other law for the time being in force, such juvenile and any person who is not a juvenile would, but for the prohibition contained in sub-section (1), have been charged and tried together, the court taking cognizance of that offence shall direct separate trials of the juvenile and the other person.

25. Removal of disqualification attaching to conviction.-Notwithstanding anything contained in any other law, a juvenile who has committed an offence and has been dealt with under the provisions of this Act shall not suffer disqualification, if any, attaching to a conviction of an offence under such law.

26. Special provision in respect of pending cases.-Notwithstanding anything contained in this Act, all proceedings in respect of a juvenile pending in any court in any area on the date on which this Act comes into force in that area, shall be continued in that court as if this Act had not been passed and if the court finds that the juvenile has committed an offence, it shall record such finding and instead of passing any sentence in respect of the juvenile, forward the juvenile to the Juvenile Court which shall pass orders in respect of that juvenile in accordance with the provisions of this Act as if it had been satisfied on inquiry under this Act that the juvenile has committed the offence.

CHAPTER V

Procedure of Competent Authorities Generally and Appeals and Revision from Orders of Such Authorities

27. Sittings, *etc.* of Boards and Juvenile Courts.-(1) A Board or a Juvenile Court shall hold its sittings at such place, on such day and in such manner, as may be prescribed.

(2) A Board or, as the case may be, a Juvenile Court under sub-section (2) of section 7 shall, while holding any inquiry regarding a juvenile under this Act, as far as practicable, sit in a building or room different from that in which the ordinary sittings of Civil and Criminal Courts are held, or on different days or at times different from those at which the ordinary sittings of such courts are held.

(3) An inquiry regarding a juvenile under this Act shall be held expeditiously and shall ordinarily be completed within a period of three months from the date of its commencement, unless, for special reasons to be recorded in writing, the competent authority otherwise directs.

28. Persons who may be present before competent authority.-(1) Save as provided in this Act, no person shall be present at any sitting of a competent authority, except-

(a) any officer of the competent authority, or

(b) the parties to the inquiry before the competent authority, the parent or guardian of the juvenile and other persons directly concerned in the inquiry including police officers and legal practitioners, or

(c) such other persons as the competent authority may permit to be present.

(2) Not withstanding anything contained in sub-section (1), if at any stage during an inquiry a competent authority considers it to be expedient in the interest of the juvenile or on grounds of decency or morality that any person including the police officers, legal practitioners, the parent, guardian or the juvenile himself should withdraw, the competent authority may give such direction, and if anyperson refuses to comply with such direction, the competent authority may have him removed and may, for this purpose, cause to be used such force as may be necessary.

(3) No legal practitioner shall be entitled to appear before a Board in any case or proceeding before it, except with the special permission of that Board.

29. Attendance of parent or guardian of juvenile.-Any competent authority before which a juvenile is brought under any of the provisions of this Act may, whenever it so thinks fit, require any parent or guardian having the actual charge of, or control over, the juvenile to be present at any proceeding in respect of the juvenile.

30. Dispensing with attendance of juvenile.-If, at any stage during the course of an inquiry, a competent authority is satisfied that the attendance of the juvenile is not essential for the purpose of the inquiry, the competent authority may dispense with his attendance and proceed with the inquiry in the absence of the juvenile.

31. Committal to approved place of juvenile suffering from dangerous disease and his future disposal.-(1) When a juvenile who has been brought before a competent authority under this Act is found to be suffering from a disease requiring prolonged medical treatment or physical or mental complaint that will respond to treatment, the competent authority may send the juvenile to any place recognised to be an approved place in accordance with the rules made under this Act for such period as it may think necessary for the required treatment.

(2) Where a juvenile is found to be suffering from leprosy or is of unsound mind, he shall be dealt with under the provisions of the Lepers Act, 1898 (3 of 1898), or the Indian Lunacy Act, 1912 (4 of 1912), as the case may be.

32. Presumption and determination of age.-(1) Where it appears to a competent authority that a person brought before it under any of the provisions of this Act (otherwise than for the purpose of giving evidence) is a juvenile, the competent authority shall make due inquiry as to the age of that person and for that purpose shall take such evidence as may be necessary and shall record a finding whether the person is a juvenile or not, stating his age as nearly as may be.

(2) No order of a competent authority shall be deemed to have become invalid merely by any subsequent proof that the person in respect of whom the order has been made is not a juvenile, and the age recorded by the competent authority to be the age of the person so brought before it shall, for the purposes of this Act, be deemed to be the true age of that person.

33. Circumstances to be taken into consideration in making orders under the Act.-In making any order in respect of a juvenile under this Act, a competent authority shall take into consideration the following circumstances, namely:-

(a) the age of the juvenile;

(b) the state of physical and mental health of the juvenile;

(c) the circumstances in which the juvenile was and is living;

(d) the reports made by the probation officer;

(e) the religious persuasion of the juvenile;

(f) such other circumstances as may, in the opinion of the competent authority, require to be taken into consideration in the interest of the welfare of the juvenile:

Provided that in the case of a delinquent juvenile, the above circumstances shall be taken into consideration after the Juvenile Court has recorded a finding against the juvenile that he has committed the offence:

Provided further that if no report of the probation officer is received within ten weeks of his being informed under section 19, it shall be open to the Juvenile Court to proceed without it.

34. Sending a juvenile outside jurisdiction.-In the case of a neglected or delinquent juvenile whose ordinary place of residence lies outside the jurisdiction of the competent authority before which he is brought, the competent authority may, if satisfied after due inquiry that it is expedient so to do, send the juvenile back to a relative or other person who is fit and willing to receive him at his ordinary place of residence and exercise proper care and control over him, notwithstanding that such place of residence is outside the jurisdiction of the competent authority; and the competent authority exercising jurisdiction over the place to which the juvenile is sent shall in respect of any matter arising subsequently have the same powers in relation to the juvenile as if the original order had been passed by itself.

35. Reports to be treated as confidential.-The report of the probation officer or any circumstance considered by the competent authority under section 33 shall be treated as confidential:

Provided that the competent authority may, if it so thinks fit, communicate the substance thereof to the juvenile or his parent or guardian and may give such juvenile, parent or guardian an opportunity of producing such evidence as may be relevant to the matter stated in the report.

36. Prohibition of publication of names, *etc.* of juveniles involved in any proceeding under the Act.-(1) No report in any newspaper, magazine or news-sheet of any inquiry regarding a juvenile under this Act shall disclose the name, address or school or any other particulars calculated to lead to the identification of the juvenile nor shall any picture of any such juvenile be published:

Provided that for reasons to be recorded in writing, the authority holding the inquiry may permit such disclosure, if in its opinion such disclosure is in the interest of the juvenile.

(2) Any person contravening the provisions of sub-section (1) shall be punishable with fine which may extend to one thousand rupees.

37. Appeals.-(1) Subject to the provisions of this section, any person aggrieved by an order made by a competent authority under this Act may, within thirty days from the date of such order, prefer an appeal to the Court of Session:

Provided that the Court of Session may entertain the appeal after the expiry of the said period of thirty days if it is satisfied that the appellant was prevented by sufficient cause from filing the appeal in time.

(2) No appeal shall lie from-

(a) any order of acquittal made by the Juvenile Court in respect of a juvenile alleged to have committed an offence; or

(b) any order made by a Board in respect of a finding that a person is not a neglected juvenile.

(3) No second appeal shall lie from any order of the Court of Session passed in appeal under this section.

38. Revision.-The High Court may, at any time, either of its own motion or on an application received in this behalf, call for the record of any proceeding in which any competent authority or Court of Session has passed an order for the purpose of satisfying itself as to the legality or propriety of any such order and may pass such order in relation thereto as it thinks fit:

Provided that the High Court shall not pass an order under this section prejudicial to any person without giving him a reasonable opportunity of being heard.

39. Procedure in inquiries, appeals and revision proceeding.-(1) Save as otherwise expressly provided by this Act, a competent authority while holding any inquiry under any of the provisions of this Act, shall follow such procedure as may be prescribed and subject thereto, shall follow, as far as may be, the procedure laid down in the Code of Criminal Procedure, 1973 (2 of 1974), for trials in summons cases.

(2) Save as otherwise expressly provided by or under this Act, the procedure to be followed in hearing appeals or revision proceedings under this Act shall be, as far as practicable, in accordance with the provisions of the Code of Criminal Procedure, 1973 (2 of 1974).

40. Power to amend orders.-(1) Without prejudice to the provisions for appeal and revision under this Act, any competent authority may, either on its own motion or on an application received in this behalf, amend any order as to theinstitution to which a juvenile is to be sent or as to the person under whose care or supervision a juvenile is to be placed under this Act.

(2) Clerical mistakes in orders passed by a competent authority or errors arising therein from any accidental slip or omission may, at any time, be corrected by the competent authority either on its own motion or on application received in this behalf.

CHAPTER VI

Special Offences in Respect of Juveniles

41. Punishment for cruelty to juvenile.-(1) Whoever, having the actual charge of, or control over, a juvenile, assaults, abandons, exposes or wilfully neglects the juvenile or causes or procures him to be assaulted, abandoned, exposed or neglected in a manner likely to cause such juvenile unnecessary mental or physical suffering shall be punishable with imprisonment for a term which may extend to six months, or with fine, or with both.

(2) No court shall take cognizance of an offence punishable under sub-section (1) unless the complaint is filed with the previous sanction of the State Government or an officer authorised by it in this behalf.

42. Employment of juveniles for begging.-(1) Whoever employs or uses any juvenile for the purposes of begging or causes any juvenile to beg shall be punishable with imprisonment for a term which may extend to three years and shall also be liable to fine.

(2) Whoever, having the actual charge of, or control over, a juvenile abets the commission of the offence punishable under sub-section (1), shall be punishable with imprisonment for a term which may extend to one year and shall also be liable to fine.

(3) The offence punishable under the section shall be cognizable.

43. Penalty for giving intoxicating liquor or narcotic drug or psychotropic substance to a juvenile.-Whoever gives, or causes to be given, to any juvenile any intoxicating liquor in a public place or any narcotic drug or psychotropic substance except upon the order of a duly qualified medical practitioner or in case of sickness shall be punishable with imprisonment for a term which may extend to three years and shall also be liable to fine.

44. Explanation of juvenile employees.-Who ever ostensibly procures a juvenile for the purpose of any employment and withholds the earnings of the juvenile or uses such earnings for his own purposes shall be punishable with imprisonment for a term which may extend to three years and shall also be liable to fine.

45. Alternative punishments.-Where an act or omission constitutes an offence punishable under this Act and also any other Central or State Act, then, notwithstanding anything contained in any law for the time being in force, the offender found guilty of such offence shall be liable to punishment only under such Act as provides for punishment which is greater in degree.

CHAPTER VII

Miscellaneous

46. Power of State Government to discharge and transfer juveniles.-(1) The State Government may, notwithstanding anything contained in this

Act, at any time, order a neglected or delinquent juvenile to be discharged from the juvenile home or special home, either absolutely or on such conditions as it may think fit to impose.

(2) The State Government may, notwithstanding anything contained in this Act, order-

(a) a neglected juvenile to be transferred from one juvenile home to another;

(b) a delinquent juvenile to be transferred from one special home to another or from a special home to a borstal school where such school exists or from a special home to a juvenile home;

(c) a neglected juvenile or a delinquent juvenile to be transferred from a juvenile home or a special home to a fit person or a fit institution;

(d) a juvenile who has been released on licence which has been revoked or forfeited, to be sent to the special home or juvenile home from which he was released or to any other juvenile home or special home or borstal school:

Provided that the total period of the stay of the juvenile in a juvenile home or a special home or fit institution or under a fit person shall not be increased by such transfer.

(3) The State Government may, notwithstanding anything contained in this Act, at any time, discharge a juvenile from the care of any person under whom he was placed under this Act either absolutely or on such conditions as may think fit to impose.

47. Transfers between juvenile homes, *etc.* under the Act, and juvenile homes, *etc.* of like nature in different part of India.-(1) The Government of a State may direct any neglected juvenile or delinquent juvenile to be transferred from any juvenile home or special home within the State to any other juvenile home, special home, or institution of a like nature in any other State with the consent of the Government of that State.

(2) The Government of a State may, by general or special order, provide for the reception in a juvenile home or special home with the State of a neglected juvenile or delinquent juvenile detained in a juvenile home or special home or institution of a like nature in any other State where the Government of that State makes an order for such transfer, and upon such transfer the provisions of this Act shall apply to such juvenile as if he had been originally ordered to be sent to such juvenile home or special home under this Act.

48. Transfer of juveniles of unsound mind or suffering from leprosy or addicted to drugs.-(1) Where it appears to the State Government that any juvenile kept in a special home or juvenile home or institution in pursuance of this Act is suffering from leprosy or is of unsound mind, or is addicted to any narcotic drug or psychotropic substance, the State Government may order his removal to a leper asylum or mental hospital or treatment centre for drug addicts or other place of safe custody for being kept there for such period not exceeding the period for which he is required to be kept in custody under the orders of the competent authority or for such further period as may be certified by the medical officer to be necessary for the proper treatment of the juvenile.

(2) Where it appears to the State Government that the juvenile is cured of leprosy or of unsoundness of mind or drug addiction it may, if the juvenile is still liable to be kept in custody, order the person having charge of the juvenile to send him to the special home or juvenile home or institution from which he was removed or, if the juvenile is no longer liable to be kept in custody order him to be discharged.

49. Placing out on licence.-(1) When a juvenile is kept in a juvenile home or special home, the State Government may, if it so thinks fit, release the juvenile from the juvenile home or special home and grant him a written licence for such period and on such conditions as may be specified in the licence permitting him to live with, or under the supervision of, any responsible person named in the licence willing to receive and take charge of him with a view to educate him and train him for some useful trade or calling.

(2) Any licence so granted under sub-section (1) shall be in force for the period specified in the licence or until revoked or forfeited by the breach of any of the conditions on which it was granted.

(3) The State Government may, at any time, by order in writing, revoke any such licence and order the juvenile to return to the juvenile home or special home from which he was released or to any other juvenile home or special home, and shall do so at the desire of the person with whom or under whose supervision the juvenile has been permitted to live in accordance with a licence granted under sub-section (1).

(4) When a licence has been revoked or forfeited and the juvenile refuses or fails to return to the special home or juvenile home to which he was directed so to return, the State Government may, if necessary, cause him to be taken charge of and to be taken back to the special home or juvenile home.

(5) The time during which a juvenile is absent from a special home or juvenile home in pursuance of a licence granted under this section shall be deemed to be part of the time for which he is liable to be kept in custody in the special home or juvenile home:

Provided that when a juvenile has failed to return to the special home or juvenile home on the licence being revoked or forfeited, the time which elapses after his failure so to return shall be excluded in computing the time during which he is liable to be kept in custody.

50. Provision in respect of escaped juveniles.-Notwithstanding anything to the contrary contained in any other law for the time being in force, any police officer may take charge without warrant of a juvenile who has escaped from a special home or a juvenile home or from the care of a person under whom he was placed under this Act and shall send the juvenile back to the special home or the juvenile home or that person, as the case may be; and no proceeding shall be instituted in respect of the juvenile by reason of such escape but the special home, juvenile home or the person may, after giving the information to the competent authority which passed the order in respect of the juvenile, take such steps against the juvenile as may be deemed necessary.

51. Contribution by parents.-(1) The competent authority which makes an order for sending a neglected juvenile or a delinquent juvenile to a juvenile home or a special home or placing the juvenile under the care of a fit person or fit institution may make an order requiring the parent or other person liable to maintain the juvenile to contribute to his maintenance, if able to do so, in the prescribed manner.

(2) The competent authority before making any order under sub-section (1) shall inquire into the circumstances of the parent or other person liable to maintain the juvenile and shall record evidence, if any, in the presence of the parent or such other person, as the case may be.

(3) The person liable to maintain a juvenile shall, for the purposes of sub-section (1), include in the case of illegitimacy, his putative father:

Provided that where the juvenile is illegitimate and an order for his maintenance has been made under section 125 of the Code of Criminal Procedure, 1973 (2 of 1974), the competent authority shall not ordinarily make an order for contribution against the putative father, but may order the whole or any part of the sums accruing due under the said order for maintenance to be paid to such personas may be named by the competent authority and such sum shall be paid by him towards the maintenance of the juvenile.

(4) Any order made under this section may be enforced in the same manner as an order under section 125 of the Code of Criminal Procedure, 1973 (2 of 1974).

52. Fund.-(1) The State Government may create a Fund under such name as it thinks fit for the welfare and rehabilitation of the juveniles dealt with under this Act.

(2) There shall be credited to the Fund such voluntary donations, contributions or subscriptions as may be made by any individual or organisation.

(3) The fund created under sub-section (1) shall be administered by such officers or authority in such manner and for such purposes as may be prescribed.

53. Advisory Board.-(1) The State Government may constitute an Advisory Board to advise it on matters relating to the establishment and maintenance of homes, mobilisation of resources, provision of facilities for education, training and rehabilitation of neglected and delinquent juveniles and co-ordination among the various official and non-official agencies concerned.

(2) The Advisory Board shall consist of such number of officers and other persons as the State Government thinks fit and may also include experts and the representatives of voluntary organisations engaged in the relevant areas.

54. Visitors.-(1) The State Government may nominate not more than three non-officials to be Visitors for each of the homes established under this Act.

(2) A Visitor nominated for a home under sub-section (1) shall periodically visit such home and make a report to the State Government.

55. Control of custodian over juvenile.-Any person in whose custody a juvenile is placed in pursuance of this Act shall, while the order is in force, have the like control over the juvenile as he would have if he were his parent, and shall be responsible for his maintenance, and the juvenile shall continue in his custody for the period stated by the competent authority, notwithstanding that he is claimed by his parent or any other person:

Provided that no juvenile while in such custody shall be carried except with the permission of the competent authority.

56. Delinquent juvenile undergoing sentence at commencement of the Act.-In any area in which this Act is brought into force, the State Government may direct that a delinquent juvenile who is undergoing any sentence of imprisonment at the commencement of this Act shall, in lieu of undergoing such sentence, be sent to a special home or be kept in safe custody in such place and manner as the State Government thinks fit for the remainder of the period of the sentence; and the provisions of this Act shall apply to the juvenile as if he had beenordered by a Juvenile Court to be sent to such special home or, as the case may be, ordered to be detained under sub-section (2) of section 22.

57. Appointment of officers.-(1) The State Government may appoint as many probation officers, officers for the inspection of special homes, juvenile homes, observation homes or after care organisations and such other officers as it may deem necessary for carrying out the purposes of this Act.

(2) It shall be the duty of the probation officer-

(a) to inquire, in accordance with the direction of a competent authority, into the antecedents and family history of any juvenile accused of an offence, with a view to assist the authority in making the inquiry;

(b) to visit neglected and delinquent juveniles at such intervals as the probation officer may think fit;

(c) to report to the competent authority as to the behaviour of any neglected or delinquent juvenile;

(d) to advise and assist neglected and delinquent juveniles and, if necessary, endeavour to find them suitable employment;

(e) where a neglected or delinquent juvenile is placed under the care of any person or institution on certain conditions to see whether such conditions are being complied with; and

(f) to perform such other duties as may be prescribed.

(3) Any officer empowered in this behalf by the State Government may enter any special home, juvenile home, observation home or after-care organisation and make a complete inspection thereof in all its departments and of all papers, registers and accounts relating thereto and shall submit the report of such inspection to the State Government.

58. Officers appointed under the Act to be public servants. Probation officers and other officers appointed in pursuance of this Act shall be deemed to be public servants within the meaning of section 21 of the Indian Penal Code, 1860 (45 of 1860).

59. Procedure in respect of bonds.-The provisions of Chapter XXXIII of the Code of Criminal Procedure, 1973 (2 of 1974), shall, as far as may be, apply to bonds taken under this Act.

60. Delegation of powers.-The State Government may, by general or special order, direct that any power exercisable by it under this Act shall, in such circumstances and under such conditions, if any, as may be specified in the order, be exercisable also by an officer subordinate to that Government.

61. Protection of action taken in good faith.-No suit or other legal proceeding shall lie against the State Government or any probation officer or other officer appointed under this Act in respect of anything which is in good faith doneor intended to be done in pursuance of this Act or of any rules or orders made there under.

62. Power to make rules.-(1) The State Government may, by notification in the Official Gazette, make rules to carry out the purposes of this Act.

(2) In particular and without prejudice to the generality of the foregoing power, such rules may provide for all or any of the following matters, namely:-

(a) the places at which, the days on which, the time at which, and the manner in which, a competent authority may hold its sittings;

(b) the procedure to be followed by a competent authority in holding inquiries under this Act, and the mode of dealing with juveniles suffering from dangerous diseases or mental complaints;

(c) the circumstances in which, and the conditions subject to which, an institution may be certified as a special home or a juvenile's home or recognised as an observation home, and the certification or recognition withdrawn;

(d) the internal management of special homes, juvenile homes and observation homes and the standards and the nature of services to be maintained by them;

(e) the functions and responsibilities of special homes, juvenile homes and observation homes;

(f) the inspection of special homes, juvenile homes, observation homes and after-care organisations;

(g) the establishment, management and functions of after-care organisations; the circumstances in which, and the conditions subject to which an institution may be recognised as an after-care organisation and such other matters as are referred to in section 12;

(h) the qualifications and duties of probation officers;

(i) the recruitment and training of persons appointed to carry out the purposes of this Act and the terms and conditions of their services;

(j) the conditions subject to which a girl who is neglected or delinquent juvenile may be escorted from one place to another, and the manner in which a juvenile may be sent outside the jurisdiction of a competent authority;

(k) the manner in which a contribution for the maintenance of a juvenile may be ordered to be paid by a parent or guardian;

(l) the officers or authorities by whom, the manner in which and the purpose for which the Fund created under section 52 shall be administered;

(m) the conditions under which a juvenile may be placed out on licence and the form and conditions of such licence;

(n) the conditions subject to which juveniles may be placed under the care of any parent, guardian or other fit person or fit institution under this Act and the obligations of such persons or institutions towards the juveniles so placed;

(o) any other matter which has to be, or may be, prescribed.

(3) Every rule made by a State Government under this Act shall be laid, as soon as may be after it is made, before the legislature of that State.

63. Repeal and savings.-If, immediately before the date on which this Act comes into force in any State, there is in force in that State, any law corresponding to this Act, that law shall stand repealed on the said date:

Provided that the repeal shall not affect-

(a) the previous operation of any law so repealed or anything duly done or suffered thereunder; or

(b) any right, privilege, obligation or liability acquired, accrued or incurred under any law so repealed; or

(c) any penalty, forfeiture or punishment incurred in respect of any offence committed against any law so repealed; or

(d) any investigation, legal proceeding or remedy in respect of any such right, privilege, obligation, liability, penalty, forfeiture or punishment as aforesaid,

and any such investigation, legal proceeding or remedy may be instituted, continued or enforced and any such penalty, forfeiture or punishment may be imposed, as if this Act had not been passed.

The United Nations Minimum Rules for the Administration of Juvenile Justice (The Beijing Rules)

United Nations Standard Minimum Rules for the Administration of Juvenile Justice ("The Beijing Rules"), G.A. res. 40/33, annex, 40 U.N. GAOR Supp. (No. 53) at 207, U.N. Doc. A/40/53 (1985).

PART ONE

GENERAL PRINCIPLES

1. Fundamental perspectives

   1.1 Member States shall seek, in conformity with their respective general interests, to further the well-being of the juvenile and her or his family.

   1.2 Member States shall endeavor to develop conditions that will ensure for the juvenile a meaningful life in the community, which, during that period in life when she or he is most susceptible to deviant behaviour, will foster a process of personal development and education that is as free from crime and delinquency as possible.

   1.3 Sufficient attention shall be given to positive measures that involve the full mobilization of all possible resources, including the family, volunteers and other community groups, as well as schools and other community institutions, for the purpose of promoting the well-being of the juvenile, with a view to reducing the need for intervention under the law, and of effectively, fairly and humanely dealing with the juvenile in conflict with the law.

1.4 Juvenile justice shall be conceived as an integral part of the national development process of each country, within a comprehensive framework of social justice for all juveniles, thus, at the same time, contributing to the protection of the young and the maintenance of a peaceful order in society.

1.5 These Rules shall be implemented in the context of economic, social and cultural conditions prevailing in each Member State.

1.6 Juvenile justice services shall be systematically developed and coordinated with a view to improving and sustaining the competence of personnel involved in the services, including their methods, approaches and attitudes.

2. Scope of the Rules and definitions used

2.1 The following Standard Minimum Rules shall be applied to juvenile offenders impartially, without distinction of any kind, for example as to race, color, sex, language, religion, political or other opinions, national or social origin, property, birth or other status.

2.2 For purposes of these Rules, the following definitions shall be applied by Member States in a manner which is compatible with their respective legal systems and concepts:

(a) A juvenile is a child or young person who, under the respective legal systems, may be dealt with for an offense in a manner which is different from an adult;

(b) An offense is any behaviour (act or omission) that is punishable by law under the respective legal system;

(c) A juvenile offender is a child or young person who is alleged to have committed or who has been found to have committed an offense.

2.3 Efforts shall be made to establish, in each national jurisdiction, a set of laws, rules and provisions specifically applicable to juvenile offenders and institutions and bodies entrusted with the functions of the administration of juvenile justice and designed:

(a) To meet the varying needs of juvenile offenders, while protecting their basic rights;

(b) To meet the needs of society;

(c) To implement the following rules throughly and fairly.

3. Extension of the Rules

3.1 The relevant provisions of the Rules shall be applied not only to juvenile offenders but also to juveniles who may be proceeded against for any specific behavior that would not be punishable if committed by an adult.

3.2 Efforts shall be made to extend the principles embodied in the Rules to all juveniles who are dealt with in welfare and care proceedings.

3.3 Efforts shall also be made to extend the principles embodied in the Rules to young adult offenders.

4. Age of criminal responsibility

4.1 In those legal systems recognizing the concept of the age of criminal responsibility for juveniles, the beginning of that age shall not be fixed at too low an age level, bearing in mind the facts of emotional, mental and intellectual maturity.

5. Aims of juvenile justice

5.1 The juvenile justice system shall emphasize the well-being of the juvenile and shall ensure that any reaction to juvenile offenders shall always be in proportion to the circumstances of both the offenders and the offense.

6. Scope of discretion

6.1 In view of the varying special needs of juveniles as well as the variety of measures available, appropriate scope for discretion shall be allowed at all stages of proceedings and at the different levels of juvenile justice administration, including investigation, prosecution, adjudication and the follow-up of dispositions.

6.2 Efforts shall be made, however, to ensure sufficient accountability at all stages and levels in the exercise of any such discretion.

6.3 Those who exercise discretion shall be specially qualified or trained to exercise it judiciously and in accordance with their functions and mandates.

7. Rights of juveniles

7.1 Basic procedural safeguards such as the presumption of innocence, the right to be notified of the charges, the right to remain silent, the right to counsel, the right to the presence of a parent or guardian, the right to confront and cross-examine witnesses and the right to appeal to a higher authority shall be guaranteed at all stages of proceedings.

8. Protection of privacy

8.1 The juvenile's right to privacy shall be respected at all stages in order to avoid harm being caused to her or him by undue publicity or by the process of labelling.

8.2 In principle, no information that may lead to the identification of a juvenile offender shall be published.

9. Saving clause

9.1 Nothing in these Rules shall be interpreted as precluding the application of the Standard Minimum Rules for the Treatment of Prisoners adopted by the United Nations and other human rights instruments and standards recognized by the international community that relate to the care and protection of the young.

PART TWO

INVESTIGATION AND PROSECUTION

10. Initial contact

10.1 Upon the apprehension of a juvenile, her or his parents or guardian shall be immediately notified of such apprehension, and, where such immediate notification is not possible, the parents or guardian shall be notified within the shortest possible time thereafter.

10.2 A judge or other competent official or body shall, without delay, consider the issue of release.

10.3 Contacts between the law enforcement agencies and a juvenile offender shall be managed in such a way as to respect the legal status of the juvenile, promote the well-being of the juvenile and avoid harm to her or hi m, with due regard to the circumstances of the case.

11. Diversion

11.1 Consideration shall be given, wherever appropriate, to dealing with juvenile offenders without resorting to formal trial by the competent authority, referred to in rule 14.1 below.

11.2 The police, the prosecution or other agencies dealing with juvenile cases shall be empowered to dispose of such cases, at their discretion, without recourse to formal hearings, in accordance with the criteria laid down for that purpose in the respective legal system and also in accordance with the principles contained in these Rules.

11.3 Any diversion involving referral to appropriate community or other services shall require the consent of the juvenile, or her or his parents or guardian, provided that such decision to refer a case shall be subject to review by a competent authority, upon application.

11.4 In order to facilitate the discretionary disposition of juvenile cases, efforts shall be made to provide for community programmes, such as temporary supervision and guidance, restitution, and compensation of victims.

12. Specialization within the police

12.1 In order to best fulfil their functions, police officers who frequently or exclusively deal with juveniles or who are primarily engaged in the prevention ofjuvenile crime shall be specially instructed and trained. In large cities, special police units should be established for that purpose.

13. Detention pending trial

13.1 Detention pending trial shall be used only as a measure of last resort and for the shortest possible period of time.

13.2 Whenever possible, detention pending trial shall be replaced by alternative measures, such as close supervision, intensive care or placement with a family or in an educational setting or home.

13.3 Juveniles under detention pending trial shall be entitled to all rights and guarantees of the Standard Minimum Rules for the Treatment of Prisoners adopted by the United Nations.

13.4 Juveniles under detention pending trial shall be kept separate from adults and shall be detained in a separate institution or in a separate part of an institution also holding adults.

13.5 While in custody, juveniles shall receive care, protection and all necessary individual assistance-social, educational, vocational, psychological, medical and physical-that they may require in view of their age, sex and personality.

PART THREE

ADJUDICATION AND DISPOSITION

14. Competent authority to adjudicate

14.1 Where the case of a juvenile offender has not been diverted (under rule 11), she or he shall be dealt with by the competent authority (court, tribunal, board, council, etc.) according to the principles of a fair and just trial.

14.2 The proceedings shall be conducive to the best interests of the juvenile and shall be conducted in an atmosphere of understanding, which shall allow the juvenile to participate therein and to express herself or himself freely.

15. Legal counsel, parents and guardians

15.1 Throughout the proceedings the juvenile shall have the right to be represented by a legal adviser or to apply for free legal aid where there is provision for such aid in the country.

15.2 The parents or the guardian shall be entitled to participate in the proceedings and may be required by the competent authority to attend them in the interest of the juvenile. They may, however, be denied participation by the competent authority if there are reasons to assume that such exclusion is necessary in the interest of the juvenile.

16. Social inquiry reports

16.1 In all cases except those involving minor offenses, before the competent authority renders a final disposition prior to sentencing, the background and circumstances in which the juvenile is living or the conditions under which the offense has been committed shall be properly investigated so as to facilitate judicious adjudication of the case by the competent authority.

17. Guiding principles in adjudication and disposition

17.1 The disposition of the competent authority shall be guided by the following principles:

(a) The reaction taken shall always be in proportion not only to the circumstances and the gravity of the offense but also to the circumstances and the needs of the juvenile as well as to the needs of the society;

(b) Restrictions on the personal liberty of the juvenile shall be imposed only after careful consideration and shall be limited to the possible minimum;

(c) Deprivation of personal liberty shall not be imposed unless the juvenile is adjudicated of a serious act involving violence against another person or of persistence in committing other serious offenses and unless there is no other appropriate response;

(d) The well-being of the juvenile shall be the guiding factor in the consideration of her or his case.

17.2 Capital punishment shall not be imposed for any crime committed by juveniles.

17.3 Juveniles shall not be subject to corporal punishment.

17.4 The competent authority shall have the power to discontinue the proceedings at any time.

18. Various disposition measures

    18.1 A large variety of disposition measures shall be made available to the competent authority, allowing for flexibility so as to avoid institutionalization to the greatest extent possible. Such measures, some of which may be combined, include:

    (a) Care, guidance and supervision orders;
    (b) Probation;
    (c) Community service orders;
    (d) Financial penalties, compensation and restitution;
    (e) Intermediate treatment and other treatment orders;
    (f) Orders to participate in group counseling and similar activities;
    (g) Orders concerning foster care, living communities or other educational settings;
    (h) Other relevant orders.

    18.2 No juvenile shall be removed from parental supervision, whether partly or entirely, unless the circumstances of her or his case make this necessary.

19. Least possible use of institutionalization

    19.1 The placement of a juvenile in an institution shall always be a disposition of last resort and for the minimum necessary period.

20. Avoidance of unnecessary delay

    20.1 Each case shall from the outset be handled expeditiously, without any unnecessary delay.

21. Records

    21.1 Records of juvenile offenders shall be kept strictly confidential and closed to third parties. Access to such records shall be limited to persons directly concerned with the disposition of the case at hand or other duly authorized persons.

    21.2 Records of juvenile offenders shall not be used in adult proceedings in subsequent cases involving the same offender.

22. Need for professionalism and training

    22.1 Professional education, in-service training, refresher courses and other appropriate modes of instruction shall be utilized to establish and maintain the necessary professional competence of all personnel dealing with juvenile cases.

    22.2 Juvenile justice personnel shall reflect the diversity of juveniles who come into contact with the juvenile justice system. Efforts shall be made to ensure the fair representation of women and minorities in juvenile justice agencies.

PART FOUR

NON-INSTITUTIONAL TREATMENT

23. Effective implementation of disposition

23.1 Appropriate provisions shall be made for the implementation of orders of the competent authority, as referred to in rule 14.1 above, by that authority itself or by some other authority as circumstances may require.

23.2 Such provisions shall include the power to modify the orders as the competent authority may deem necessary from time to time, provided that such modification shall be determined in accordance with the principles contained in these Rules.

24. Provision of needed assistance

24.1 Efforts shall be made to provide juveniles, at all stages of the proceedings, with necessary assistance such as lodging, education or vocational training, employment or any other assistance, helpful and practical, in order to facilitate the rehabilitative process.

25. Mobilization of volunteers and other community services

25.1 Volunteers, voluntary organizations, local institutions and other community resources shall be called upon to contribute effectively to the rehabilitation of the juvenile in a community setting and, as far as possible, within the family unit.

PART FIVE

INSTITUTIONAL TREATMENT

26. Objectives of institutional treatment

26.1 The objective of training and treatment of juveniles placed in institutions is to provide care, protection, education and vocational skills, with a view to assisting them to assume socially constructive and productive roles in society.

26.2 Juveniles in institutions shall receive care, protection and all necessary assistance-social, educational, vocational, psychological, medical and physical-that they may require because of their age, sex, and personality and in the interest of their wholesome development .

26.3 Juveniles in institutions shall be kept separate from adults and shall be detained in a separate institution or in a separate part of an institution also holding adults.

26.4 Young female offenders placed in an institution deserve special attention as to their personal needs and problems. They shall by no means receive less care, protection, assistance, treatment and training than young male offenders. Their fair treatment shall be ensured.

26.5 In the interest and well-being of the institutionalized juvenile, the parents or guardians shall have a right of access.

26.6 Inter-ministerial and inter-departmental co-operation shall be fostered for the purpose of providing adequate academic or, as appropriate, vocational training to institutionalized juveniles, with a view to ensuring that they do no leave the institution at an educational disadvantage.

27. Application of the Standard Minimum Rules for the Treatment of Prisoners adopted by the United Nations

27.1 The Standard Minimum Rules for the Treatment of Prisoners and related recommendations shall be applicable as far as relevant to the treatment of juvenile offenders in institutions, including those in detention pending adjudication.

27.2 Efforts shall be made to implement the relevant principles laid down in the Standard Minimum Rules for the treatment of Prisoners to the largest possible extent so as to meet the varying needs of juveniles specific to their age, sex and personality.

28. Frequent and early recourse to conditional release

28.1 Conditional release from an institution shall be used by the appropriate authority to the greatest possible extent, and shall be granted at the earliest possible time.

28.2 Juveniles released conditionally from an institution shall be assisted and supervised by an appropriate authority and shall receive full support by the community.

29. Semi-institutional arrangements

29.1 Efforts shall be made to provide semi-institutional arrangements, such as half-way houses, educational homes, day-time training centers and other such appropriate arrangements that may assist juveniles in their proper reintegration into society.

PART SIX

RESEARCH, PLANNING, POLICY FORMULATION AND EVALUATION

30. Research as a basis for planning, policy formulation and evaluation

30.1 Efforts shall be made to organize and promote necessary research as a basis for effective planning and policy formulation.

30.2 Efforts shall be made to review and appraise periodically the trends, problems and causes of juvenile delinquency and crime as well as the varying particular needs of juveniles in custody.

30.3 Efforts shall be made to establish a regular evaluative research mechanism built into the system of juvenile justice administration and to collect and analyze relevant data and information for appropriate assessment and future improvement and reform of the administration.

30.4 The delivery of services in juvenile justice administration shall be systematically planned and implemented as an integral part of national development efforts.

RECOMMENDATIONS

To the government of India

* Implement the recommendations made by the National Police Commission in 1980, specifically those that call for a mandatory judicial inquiry in cases of alleged rape, death, or grievous injury of people in police custody and the establishment of investigative bodies whose members would include civilians as well as police and judicial authorities.
* Implement the Juvenile Justice Act in all states and Union Territories and amend the Juvenile Justice Act to provide for a complaints and prosecution mechanisms for cases of custodial abuse of children. These mechanisms should be constituted along the lines described in the National Police Commission's recommendations for the creation of civilian, judicial, and police complaints bodies for cases of police abuse.
* Implement the recommended amendments to the Code of Criminal Procedure made by the Parliamentary Committee on Home on March 4, 1996. These recommendations include a mandatory judicial inquiry in cases of custodial death or rape and compensation to families of people who have died in custody.
* Amend Sections 53 and 54 of the Code of Criminal Procedure so that medical examination (including age verification) is mandatory at the time of detention, in order to provide a medical record of the condition of the detainee. Subsequent examinations should be carried out at regularly scheduled intervals. This procedure would circumvent attempts by police officers to intimidate detainees not to complain of torture, and would also protect police from frivolous claims of torture because a complete medical record would exist for the duration of the detention. The order for a medical examination would be independent of the detainee and the police. The initial and final examinations should be done by different people to further ensure their validity.

* Amend Section 197, specifically Sections 3, 3A, and 3B of the Code of Criminal Procedure to delete the provision that requires government approval for prosecution of law enforcement officials when complaints of custodial abuse or illegal detention are alleged.
* Amend Section 43 of the Police Act, so that police cannot claim immunity for actions while executing a warrant in cases of illegal detention or custodial abuse.
* Amend the Trade Union Act to allow children to form and participate in trade unions. The Convention on the Rights of the Child, which India has ratified, guarantees children the right of freedom of association.
* Review all laws relating to child labour and the Juvenile Justice Act to ensure that the implementation of these laws does not result in criminalizing children who are forced to work.
* Establish a civilian review board comprised of NGO representatives, judges, and lawyers to monitor police stations. Members of the review boards should be adequately trained and provided access to lock-ups and detention registers.
* Establish a high-level commission to investigate allegations of custodial abuse and killings of children.
* Complaints against law enforcement personnel should be promptly and thoroughly investigated by an independent agency with subpoena power and an adequately trained investigatory staff. This agency should be directly accessible to street children.
* Investigate all complaints of illegal detention, physical abuse, and killings of children by law enforcement officers, and prosecute to the full extent of the law those found responsible.
* Investigate all complaints of extortion and bribes from children, their families, or NGO representatives working with street children and prosecute to the full extent of the law those found responsible.
* Require the registration of each child taken to a police station, including the time, date, and reason for detention. The registers should be subject to frequent mandatory review by a judicial magistrate.
* Enforce payment of compensation for people who have been victims of custodial abuse, as per the Supreme Court decision in *Nilabati Behara v.State of Orissa (1993)* which ordered compensation in case of custodial death under Article 32 of the Constitution of India.
* Conduct a census of street children through city-wide surveys with the assistance of nongovernmental organizations (NGOs). Without an accurate estimate of the population of street children, it is difficult to plan and implement programs for their benefit.

* Promptly submit the report on India's compliance with the United Nations Convention on the Rights of the Child to the Committee on the Rights of the Child.
* Ratify the United Nations 1984 Convention Against Torture and Other Forms of Cruel, Inhuman, or Degrading Treatment or Punishment.
* Invite the United Nations Special Rapporteur on Torture and Other Forms of Cruel, Inhuman or Degrading Treatment or Punishment and the Working Group on Arbitrary Detention to India to investigate allegations of illegal detention, abuse and deaths of children in police custody.

To the United Nations

* The United Nations Special Rapporteur on Torture and Other Forms of Cruel, Inhuman or Degrading Treatment or Punishment and the Working Group on Arbitrary Detention should visit India and investigate police abuse of street children.
* The United Nations Committee on the Rights of the Child should investigate the abuse and killings of street children by police in India.
* The United Nations Committee on the Rights of the Child should devote one of its theme days to police violence against street children.

To Non-governmental Organizations Working With Street Children

Maintain detailed records of incidents of violence between police and children in order to monitor and document abuses by police. Submit these records to the National Human Rights Commission on a regular basis.

Bonded Labour**

"Bonded child labour" refers to the phenomenon of children working in conditions of servitude in order to pay off a debt. The debt that binds them to their employer is incurred not by the children themselves, but by their relatives or guardians-usually by a parent. In India, these debts tend to be relatively modest, ranging on average from 500 rupees to 7,500 rupees, depending on the industry and the age and skill of the child. The creditors-cum-employers offer these "loans" to destitute parents in an effort to secure the labour of a child, which is always cheap, but even cheaper under a situation of bondage. The parents, for their part, accept the loans. Bondage is a traditional worker-employer relationship in India, and the parents need the money-perhaps to pay for the costs of an illness, perhaps to provide a dowry to a marrying child, or perhaps-as is often the case-to help put food on the table.

The children who are sold to these bond masters work long hours over many years in an attempt to pay off these debts. Due to the astronomically

** Copy Right with Human Rights Water only.

high rates of interest charged and the abysmally low wages paid, they are usually unsuccessful. As they reach maturity, some of them may be released by the employer in favor of a newly-indebted and younger child. Many others will pass the debt on, intact or even higher, to a younger sibling, back to a parent, or on to their own children.

The past few years have seen increasing public awareness-in India itself, but particularly in the international arena-of the high incidence of child servitude in the carpet industry of South Asia. As a consequence, the international public has come to associate "child servitude" with the image of small children chained to carpet looms, slaving away over the thousands of tiny wool knots that will eventually become expensive carpets in the homes of the wealthy. International concern for the carpet weavers reached a peak in April 1995, when children's rights activist Iqbal Masih, a twelve-year-old ex-carpet weaver in Pakistan, was murdered.

This attention and the outrage it has provoked are entirely warranted-the use of bonded child labour in the production of carpets for export is extensive, and conditions in that industry are horrendous. But it is vital that the public's concern for children in servitude not begin and end with carpets. More than 300,000 children are estimated to be working in the carpet industry, the majority of them in bondage. This is a large number, but it represents only about 2 percent of the bonded child labourers of India.

The great majority of the carpet weavers' bonded brothers and sisters are working in the agricultural sector, tending cattle and goats, picking tea leaves on vast plantations, and working fields of sugar cane and basic crops all across the country. Apart from agriculture, which accounts for 64 percent of all labour in India, bonded child labourers form a significant part of the work force in a multitude of domestic and export industries. These include, but are not limited to, the production of silk and silk saris, beedi (hand-rolled cigarettes), silver jewelry, synthetic gemstones, leather products (including footwear and sporting goods), hand woven wool carpets, and precious gemstones and diamonds. Services where bonded child labour is prevalent include prostitution, small restaurants, truck stops and tea shop services, and domestic servitude.

The practice of child debt servitude has been illegal in India since 1933, when the Children (Pledging of Labour) Act was enacted under British rule. Since independence, a plethora of additional protective legislation has been put in place. There are distinct laws governing child labour in factories, in commercial establishments, on plantations, and in apprenticeships. There are laws governing the use of migrant labour and contract labour. A relatively recent law-the Child Labour (Prohibition and Regulation) Act of 1986-designates a child as "a person who has not completed their fourteenth year of age." It purports to regulate the hours and conditions of some child workers and to prohibit the use of child labour in certain enumerated hazardous industries. (There is no blanket prohibition on the use of child labour, nor any universal minimum age set for child workers.) Most important of all, for children in servitude, is the Bonded Labour System (Abolition) Act, 1976 which strictly outlaws all forms of debt bondage and forced labour. These extensive legal safeguards mean little, however, without the political will to implement them. In India, this will is sorely lacking. All of the labour laws areroutinely flouted, and with virtually no risk of punishment to the offender. Whether due to corruption or indifference-and both are much in evidence-these laws are simply not enforced. In those rare cases where offenders are prosecuted, sentences are limited to negligible fines.

Why does India-the Indian government, the ruling elite, the business interests, the populace as a whole-tolerate this slavery in its midst? According to a vast and deeply entrenched set of myths, bonded labour and child labour in India are inevitable. They are caused by poverty. They represent the natural order of things, and it is not possible to change them by force; they must evolve slowly toward eradication.

In truth, the Indian government has failed to protect its most vulnerable children. When others have stepped in to try to fill the vacuum and advocate on behalf of those children, India's leaders and much of its media have attributed nearly all "outside" attempts at action to an ulterior commercial motive. The developed world is not concerned with Indian children, this view holds, but rather with maintaining a competitive lead in the global marketplace. Holding to this defensive stance, some officials have threatened to end all foreign funding of child labour-related projects. This nationalist rhetoric has been largely a diversionary tactic. What the government has hoped to hide is the news that, no matter how the data are analyzed, official efforts to end the exploitation of child labourers are woefully deficient.

By focusing primarily on child labour in export industries and the threat of sanctions on exports, the international community has sent the unfortunate message that only child labour in export industries must be addressed. In response, the Indian government has accused its international critics of protectionism and has adopted superficial remedies designed to assuage their concerns while continuing to ignore its legal obligation to identify, release and rehabilitate bonded labourers.

The Context of Bonded Child Labour

It is commonly asserted that poverty is the cause of bonded and other forms of child labour. In fact, poverty is only one of many factors at play in creating and sustaining the conditions that facilitate endemic bondage.

In India, other key elements behind bonded child labour include: an ancient tradition of slavery and debt bondage; the lack of alternative small-scale loans for the rural and urban poor and the lack of a concerted social welfare scheme to safeguard against hunger and illness; a noncompulsory and unequal educational system; the lack of employment opportunities and living wages for adults; corruption and indifference among government officials; and societal apathy. A final element is caste-based discrimination, which is closely inter twined particularly with agricultural debt bondage.

A new economic policy introduced in 1991 is transforming the Indian economy, supporting a burgeoning middle class and a thin layer of the ultra rich. The liberalization package includes lower import duties, access for foreign investors to India's growing industrial sector, privatization of previously state-run industries and services, and increased competition. India's total exports, valued at twenty-six billion U.S. dollars in 1994 (most of this in consumer goods), are expected to triple by the year 2000, pushing India into fourth place among the world's largest economies. (With over 900 million inhabitants, in 1996 India was the second largest country in terms of population.)

Overview of Bonded Child Labour

Approximately fifteen million children work as bonded labourers in India. Most were put into bondage in exchange for comparatively small sums of money: two thousand rupees-equal to about thirty-five U.S. dollars-is the average amount "loaned" in exchange for a child's labour. To India's vast numbers of extremely poor, however, this money can be, literally, a life-saver. With scant alternative sources of credit available-few rural banks, cooperative credit schemes or government loans-the poor are forced to turn to the local moneylender, who extracts the only collateral available: the promise of their labour or the labour of their children.

Two players create the debt bondage arrangement: the creditor-employer, who offers money to an impoverished parent in an attempt to secure the extremely cheap and captive labour of his or her child, and the parent who accepts this money, agreeing to offer the child's labour as surety for the debt. The child is a commodity of exchange. She or he is powerless to affect the agreement or its terms and-whether willing or unwilling to serve the bond master-powerless to refuse.

The arrangements between parents and contracting agents are usually informal and unwritten. The number of years required to pay off such a loan is indeterminate. Many of the children interviewed by Human Rights Watch had already been working for several years, and even among those relatively new to their jobs, none said that they expected to be released prior to maturity.

Some intended to walk away from their bondage when they married, leaving a younger sibling to take over the labour-payment or a parent to somehow extinguish the debt-perhaps by a new loan from a different creditor-employer.

In many industries marked by the use of debt bondage, the child's labour does not function to pay off the original loan at all. Instead, the child's labour serves as both interest on the loan-for the children are paid only a fraction of what their labour would bring them on the open market-and as a surety for the loan's repayment. The original amount loaned to the parent must be repaid in full in a single installment; only then will the child be released from servitude.

The making of beedi cigarettes is one such industry. The average advance in the beedi industry is 1,500 rupees. The average number of beedies a bonded child labourer rolls in a day is 1,500, for an average daily wage of nine rupees. Were the value of the child's labour to be counted as gradual payment of the money advanced-and were it calculated honestly, at the official minimum wage established for beedi rolling (30.9 rupees per thousand beedies)-the agent-employer would recoup in labour value the original debt in about six weeks. But the beedi worker's debt is not set off against the value of the labour, and the labour's value is not compensated honestly. If it were, the child would be earning forty to fifty rupees a day instead of nine, and would be able to save enough to quickly fulfill the lump-sum payment requirement of the original advance. As it is, this requirement, together with the abysmally low "wages" paid, virtually ensure that the bonded child will not escape servitude. Most children work many years for their agents, for which the agents, and particularly the owners of the beedi companies, profit handsomely. It is, simply, a severe form of economic exploitation.

Industries that do allow for gradual repayment of the original debt do not provide an easier escape from bondage. First, employers may increase the principal of the loan by adding on to it miscellaneous costs and expenses-the cost of materials, the loss of "defective" goods, meals given to the children, or medical care, on the rare occasions that it is provided. Second, the low wages paid may spur the child's parent to seek an additional loan from the employer. Finally, and most significantly, the value of the child's labour as against the loan is decided by the employer. The bonded children and their parents have virtually no bargaining power with the bond master, with the result that interest rates of 1,200 percent a year, taken out in labour value, are not uncommon.

Regardless of which of these debt structures the child labours under, the end result is the same: it is very difficult to escape bondage. The underlying reason for this difficulty is the grossly unequal power relationships between the child workers and their parents on the one hand and the creditors-cum-employers on the others. The former are frequently low caste, illiterate, and extremely poor. The latter are usually higher caste, literate, comparatively wealthy, and powerful members of the community. Often, these creditors-employers are the only money lenders in town, and as such are extremely influential. They are also frequently connected, by caste and by the social and political hierarchy of the community, with local officials, including police officers, factory inspectors, and other local authorities who might normally be expected to safeguard the rights of children.

Three of the industries studied in many report-carpet weaving, beedi rolling, and cloth (silk) weaving-have been classified as "hazardous" under India's Child Labour (Prohibition and Regulation) Act of 1986. Employment of children under fourteen years of age is illegal in these industries. Despite this prohibition, children continue to form the backbone of all three industries, which together employ approximately 850,000 children. Not only has the government failed to enforce this protective legislation, but the government itself is guilty of violating it-the central government's Handloom and Handicrafts Export Corporation runs approximately two hundred "training centers" for child labourers in the carpet industry.

Factors Behind Bonded Child Labour:
Poverty and Tradition

Slavery in India dates back at least 1,500 years. Various forms of debt bondage coexisted with formal slavery, and while the British abolished slavery legislatively through the Anti-Slavery Act of 1843, large numbers of former slaves traded their status for that of perpetually bonded servitude. This was in part due to the fact that the British did not abolish debt-bondage; instead they regulated it. The Workman's Breach of Contract Act, 1859 (13 of 1859) enforced the obligation to provide labour in lieu of an advance, and Section 200 of the Civil Procedure Code, also enacted in 1859, allowed landlords and moneylenders to seize the property of bonded labourers and provided for imprisonment of bonded labourers who did not honor their obligations when they received advances. The Workman's Breach of Contract Act was repealed in 1925, and Section 200 of the Civil Procedure Code was amended in 1879 to remove punishments for bonded labourers.

The difference between slavery and debt bondage is often rather small, particularly in the context of agriculture. In both systems workers may be considered to be attached to the land, with ownership of them transferred as part of land sales or exchanges. Both slavery and debt bondage grant significant powers of ownership to the master: the worker cannot seek employment elsewhere, the worker cannot refuse to work, the worker is subject to the master's demands twenty-four hours a day, and the master controls the worker's family. A worker who resists this is subject to severe mistreatment, including beatings and torture. Many grass-roots organizations, including children's advocates and low-caste and tribal groups, oppose the practice of bonded labour and other forms ofcontemporary slavery. Nonetheless, debt bondage is tolerated by large segments of society who accept it as the normal and proper state of affairs.

Those who stand to gain from the abolition of debt bondage, on the other hand, are precisely those who are least likely to be in a position to exert pressure or claim their rights. Bonded labourers are extremely vulnerable to negative repercussions should they attempt to organize or otherwise agitate for enforcement of the law. Even requests for minimal improvements can lead to a violent response from employers. Bonded labourers have been severely beaten after asking for a raise of a few cents a day, or asking the employer to fulfill a promise to give them a few sacks of grain each year, or for other relatively mild "challenges" to the status quo. Scores of children told Human Rights Watch that their master would beat them if they brought up the subject of wages.

More serious challenges to the master's authority may be met with a more violent or even deadly response. During a much-publicized series of events in 1985, in the state of Haryana, protesting quarry workers were beaten by their employers' hired thugs while uniformed police officers looked on. One of the workers was beaten to death and thirty-four others were seriously wounded. Police later took the injured workers from the hospital to the police station, where they were arrested and fingerprinted.

According to a regional activist in the state of Rajasthan, mine owners continue to respond to labour disputes with unchecked brutality. "Murder and mayhem is nothing to these people. If they are challenged, they will kill theworkers and bury the bodies in the quarries." The same activist told Human Rights Watch that most government officials in the region have ties to the industry, making legal remedies out of the question.

Poverty is inextricably linked to bondage and the combination of poverty and the lack of access to credit is another essential factor behind bonded labour. Hundreds of millions of India's people are extremely poor and live hand-to-mouth. When additional financial needs arise-to compensate for seasonal declines in earnings or crops, to pay for medical expenses, or to pay for wedding or funeral ceremonies-there is no store of resources available, and the money must be borrowed.

There are very few borrowing options for a poor rural Indian. Even if a bank or cooperative society is accessible-and for most they are not-the poor labourer cannot qualify for a loan, having no security or collateral to offer. With no institutionalized credit sources to turn to, the labourer is forced to take loans from other sources, namely, the local moneylender or local employers or landlords. Often, the village moneylender and the village employer are the same person.

Moneylenders charge 20 percent monthly interest or more. Bond masters charge a much higher rate, but it is less visible since it is taken out in labour value. Many labourers fall into debt bondage as a direct result of borrowing from moneylenders: they borrow the money, are unable to pay it back because of the accelerated interest rate, then find themselves forced to submit to debt bondage-of themselves or of a child-to obtain enough money to repay the original loan.

"Nimble Fingers," and Other Myths of Child Labour

A number of myths underlie and perpetuate child labour, justifying it on the grounds that the system "benefits" everyone involved: the country, the community, the family, the craft and the child. Children must be trained at the right age or they will never learn a skill; children must be trained in a profession appropriate to their background and class; children are particularly suited for certain kinds of work because of their "nimble" fingers; and child labour is a natural and desirable function of the family unit. These myths have widespread support.

The "nimble fingers" theory is applied to some of the harshest industries employing children, including the carpet, silk, beedi and silver industries. It asserts that children make the best products in these occupations thanks to their nimble fingers which are, according to the myth, better able to tie the tiny knots of wool, unravel thread from boiling silk cocoons, and solder tiny silver flowers to a chain. In this view, child labour is not an evil, but a production necessity. This rationalization is a lie. In fact, children make the cheaper goods; only master weavers make the best quality carpets and saris.

Legal Context

Applicable International Law

The practice of bonded child labour violates the following international human rights conventions; India is a party to all of them, and as such is legally bound to comply with their terms.

Convention on the Suppression of Slave Trade and Slavery, 1926

This convention requires signatories to "prevent and suppress the slave trade" and "to bring about, progressively and as soon as possible, the complete abolition of slavery in all its forms." It also obligates parties to "take all necessary measures to prevent compulsory or forced labour from developing into conditions analogous to slavery."

Supplementary Convention on the Abolition of Slavery, the Slave Trade, and Institutions and Practices Similar to Slavery, 1956

The supplementary convention on slavery offers further clarification of prohibited practices and refers specifically to debt bondage and child servitude as institutions similar to slavery. It requires States Parties to "take all practicable and necessary legislative and other measures to bring about progressively and as soon as possible the complete abolition of... debt bondage... [and] any institution or practice whereby a child or young person under the age of 18 years, is delivered by either or both of his natural parents or by his guardian to another person, whether for reward or not, with a view to the exploitation of the child or young person or of his labour." The convention defines debt bondage as follows:

Debt bondage, that is to say, the status or condition arising from a pledge by a debtor of his personal services or those of a person under his control as security for a debt, if the value of those services as reasonably assessed is not applied towards the liquidation of the debt or the length and nature of those services are not respectively limited and defined.

Forced Labour Convention, 1930

The International Labour Organisation (ILO) Forced Labour Convention requires signatories to "suppress the use of forced or compulsory labour in all its forms in the shortest period possible." In 1957, the ILO explicitly incorporated debt bondage and serfdom within its definition of forced labour.

International Covenant on Civil and Political Rights (ICCPR), 1966

Article 8 of the ICCPR prohibits slavery and the slave trade in all their forms, servitude, and forced or compulsory labour. Article 24 entitles all children to "the right to such measures of protection as are required by his status as a minor, on the part of his family, society and the State."

International Covenant on Economic, Social and Cultural Rights (ICESCR), 1966

Article 7 of the ICESCR provides that States Parties shall "recognize the right of everyone to the enjoyment of just and favourable conditions of work." Article 10 requires Parties to protect "children and young persons... from economic and social exploitation."

Convention on the Rights of the Child, 1989

The following three provisions mandate protections that are particularly relevant for the bonded child labourer:

Article 32: "States Parties recognize the right of the child to be protected from economic exploitation and from performing any work that is likely to be hazardous or... be harmful to the child's health or physical, mental, spiritual, moral or social development." States are directed to implement these protections through appropriate legislative, administrative, social and educational measures. In particular, they are to:

(a) provide for a minimum age or minimum ages for admissions to employment;

(b) provide for appropriate regulation of the hours and conditions of employment; and

(c) provide for appropriate penalties or other sanctions to ensure the effective enforcement of this article.

Article 35: "States Parties shall take all appropriate. . . measures to prevent the abduction, the sale of or traffic in children for any purpose or in any form." A significant portion of the bonded child labourers of India are trafficked from one state to another, and some are sold outright.

Article 36: "States Parties shall protect the child against all other forms of exploitation prejudicial to any aspects of the child's welfare."

Applicable Domestic Law

A plethora of national laws, some dating back to the 1930s, offer protection from exploitation to India's working children. The Bonded Labour System (Abolition) Act of 1976 is, for the purposes of this report, the most significant and far-reaching of these laws-it outlaws all debt bondage, including that of children, and it requires government intervention and rehabilitation of the bonded worker. It is further set apart from the other laws by the fact that it has none of the exemptions from compliance that virtually nullify many of India's other labour laws. Unfortunately, lack of loopholes is no guarantee of enforcement. The Bonded Labour System (Abolition) Act, the Child Labour (Prohibition and Regulation) Act, and the other pieces of protective legislation that apply in varying circumstances to the situation of the bonded child labourer, are betrayed by an extremely low rate of enforcement. This lack of enforcement is discussed in the chapter on the role of the Indian government.

Every industry discussed in this report, and every individual case referred to, violates the Bonded Labour System (Abolition) Act and the constitutional provisions that underlie such an act. These violations represent the most severe and egregious of the many legal failings contributing to the persistence of bonded child labour in India. All of the cases and all of the industries mentioned in this report also violate the Child Labour (Prohibition and Regulation) Act: they all violate its regulatory provisions, and the largest and most significant industries-beedi, carpets, and silk-also violate its prohibitory provisions. In addition to violating these two centerpieces of protective legislation, most industries also violate one or more of the following laws: the Factories Act; the Beedi and Cigar the Workers (Conditions of

Employment) Act; the Contract Labour (Regulation and Abolition) Act; and the Inter-State Migrant Workmen (Regulation of Employment and Conditions of Service) Act. All cases documented in this report also violate the Children (Pledging of Labour) Act, which is similar in its protections to the Bonded Labour System (Abolition) Act.

In addition, under the Indian Penal Code (IPC) rape, extortion, causing grievous hurt, assault, kidnapping, abduction, wrongful confinement, buying or disposing of people as slaves, and unlawful compulsory labour are criminal offences, punishable with up to ten years imprisonment and fines. Under the Juvenile Justice Act, 1986, cruelty to juveniles and withholding the earnings of a juvenile are criminal offences, punishable with up to three years imprisonment and fines.

Bonded Labour System (Abolition) Act, 1976

The Bonded Labour System (Abolition) Act purports to abolish all debt agreements and obligations arising out of India's longstanding bonded labour system. It is the legislative fulfillment of the Indian Constitution's mandate against *begar* and forced labour. It frees all bonded labourers, cancels any outstanding debts against them, prohibits the creation of new bondage agreements, and orders the economic rehabilitation of freed bonded labourers by the state. It also criminalizes all post-act attempts to compel a person to engage in bonded labour, with maximum penalties of three years in prison and a 2,000 rupee fine. The Bonded Labour System (Abolition) Act offers the following definition of the practices being abolished.

Sec. 2(g) "bonded labour system" means the system of forced, or partly forced labour under which a debtor enters...or is presumed to have entered, into an agreement with the creditor to the effect that,-

(i) in consideration of an advance obtained by him or by any of his lineal ascendants or descendants (whether or not such advance is evidenced by any document) and in consideration of the interest, if any, due on such advance, or

(ii) in pursuance of any customary or social obligation, or

(iii) in pursuance of an obligation devolving on him by succession, or

(iv) for any economic consideration received by him or by any of his lineal ascendants or descendants, or

(v) by reason of his birth in any particular caste or community, he would-

(1) render, by himself or through any member of his family... labour or service to the creditor, or for the benefit of the creditor, for a specified period or for an unspecified period, either without wages or for nominal wages, or

(2) forfeit the freedom of employment or other means of livelihood for a specified period or for an unspecified period, or

(3) forfeit the right to move freely throughout the territory of India, or

(4) forfeit the right to appropriate or sell at market value any of his property or product of his labour or the labour of a member of his family or any person dependent on him...

This definition is meant to, and does, cover all of the many permutations of the bonded labour system in modern India. There are differences from one part of the country to the next and from one industry or landlord to another in terms of wages paid, the amount advanced, whether the advance is considered a type of loan or a type of wage, the hours worked per day and days worked per year, and whether the worker has some freedom from the bond master or is kept under constant control. Some bonded labourers receive no wages at all, apart from meager food stipends and a yearly change of clothing; some receive extremely low wages, constituting as little as 10 percent of the mandated minimum wage; some receive a standard wage in theory, but in fact lose 70 or 80 percent of it, sight unseen, back to the employer as "interest" on the advance. Some labourers are working to pay off a 500 rupee loan, others a 15,000 rupee loan. Some inherited their debt from their parents; others have contracted for a ten-month period of servitude. Some work sixteen hours a day, 365 days a year, every year of their lives. Others work ten hours a day, six days a week. Despite these differences, all are bonded labourers within the definition of the act.

It is what they have in common that determines their bonded status: they are working for nominal wages in consideration of an advance, and they are not free to discontinue their work. These three elements-an advance, low wages, and compulsion-are at the core of all bonded labour. The act defines "nominal wages" as those that are less than minimum wages or, where no minimum wage has beenset, less than wages normally paid for the same or similar work in the same locality.

District magistrates-called district collectors, or deputy commissioners, in some states-are responsible for enforcement of the Bonded Labour System (Abolition) Act. The district magistrate, an appointed civil servant, is the top authority at the district level and as such oversees government administration, including the administration of justice. His duties are varied and many, and include overseeing the work of fifty to sixty distinct departments. In addition to these duties, he is required by the Bonded Labour System (Abolition) Act to identify all cases of bonded labour occurring in his district, free the labourers, and initiate prosecution under the act. He is also charged with making sure available credit sources are in place, so that freed labourers will not be forced into bondage again. Finally, the district magistrate is to constitute and participate in the functioning ofa district-level "vigilance committee." The statutory functions of this committee are:

(a) to advise the District Magistrate . . . as to the efforts made, and action taken, to ensure that the provisions of this act... are properly implemented;

(b) to provide for the economic and social rehabilitation of the freed bonded labourers;

(c) to coordinate the functions of rural banks and cooperative societies with a view to canalizing adequate credit to the freed bonded labourers;

(d) to keep an eye on the number of offences of which cognizance has been taken under [the] act;

(e) to make a survey as to whether there is any offence of which cognizance ought to be taken under the act;

(f) to defend any suit instituted against a freed bonded labourer or a member of his family... for the recovery of the whole or part of any bonded debt.

Very few such vigilance committees have been formed, and Human Rights Watch knows of no district in which such a committee is currently operative.

References to rehabilitation of freed bonded labourers occur twice in the Bonded Labour System (Abolition) Act-once in reference to the district magistrate's duty to "secure and protect the economic interests" of the bonded labourer (Sec. 11), and once in stipulating the vigilance committees' duty to provide for the "economic and social rehabilitation" of the bonded labourer (Sec. 14). The act itself, however, does not specify of what this rehabilitation should consist and left implementation of rehabilitation up to the state governments, and largely dependent on the initiative of District Magistrates.

In 1978, the Ministry of Labour launched a scheme that specified a "rehabilitation allowance" in order to assist state governments with rehabilitation. Under this scheme, the central government contributes half of the rehabilitation assistance allowance due to every freed bonded labourer, and the state where the bonded labourer resides pays the other half. The allowance, determined by a Ministry of Labour Planning Commission, was originally set at 4,000 rupees. Ithas been raised once, to 6,250 rupees, in 1986. In 1982, cognizant of the reasons that lead to bondage and possibility of relapse if those released are not rehabilitated, the government expanded this program by adding guidelines for rehabilitation under Ministry of Labour Direct Order No. S.11011/20/82-BL, which stated that:

(i) Psychological rehabilitation must go side by side with physical and economic rehabilitation;

(ii) The physical and economic rehabilitation has fifteen major components namely allotment of house-sites and agricultural land, land development, provision of low cost dwelling units, agriculture, provision of credit, horticulture, animal husbandry, training for acquiring new skills and develop in existing skills, promoting traditional arts and crafts, provision of wages employment and enforcement of minimum wages, collection and processing of minor forest products, health, medical care and sanitation, supply of essential commodities, education of children of bonded labourers and protection of civil rights;

(iii) There is scope for bringing about an integration among the various Central and Centrally Sponsored Schemes and the ongoing schemes of State Government for more qualitative rehabilitation. The essence of such duplication, i.e., pooling resources from different sources for the same purpose. It should be ensured that while funds are not drawn from different sources for the same purpose, [funds] drawn from different sectors [schemes] for different components of the rehabilitation scheme are integrated skillfully; and

(iv) While drawing up any scheme/programme of rehabilitation of freed bonded labour, the latter must necessarily be given the choice between the various alternatives for their rehabilitation and such programme should be finally selected for execution as would need the total requirements of the families of freed bonded labourers to enable them to cross the poverty line on theone hand and to prevent them from sliding back into debt bondage on the other.

In its *1994-95 Annual Report,* the Ministry of Labour stated that funds for rehabilitation assistance would be increased from Rs. 6,250 to Rs.10,000 for each bonded labourer, and that "respective State Governments will undertake further surveys to identify bonded labourers as may still be in existence and report to the Government of India. The State Governments have also agreed to undertake selective follow-up studies to assess whether rehabilitated bonded labourers have relapsed into bondage and to set up Vigilance Committees, wherever they are not in existence."

However, the extent to which bonded labourers have been identified, released, and rehabilitated by government officials has been negligible; this is discussed in the chapter on the role of the government.

Children (Pledging of Labour) Act, 1933

This act predates Independence but remains in force. It is rarely used and rarely mentioned in discussions of bonded labour and child labour, probably because the more recent laws carry penalties that, while lenient themselves, are nonetheless stiffer than those of the **Children (Pledging of Labour) Act.**

The act calls for penalties to be levied against any parent, middleman, or employer involved in making or executing a pledge of a child's labour. Such a pledge is defined as an "agreement, written or oral, express or implied, whereby the parent or guardian of a child, in return for any payment or benefit received or to be received by him, undertakes to cause or allow the services of the child to be utilized in any employment." Lawful labour agreements are limited to those made in consideration of reasonable wages and terminable at seven days' or less notice. The fines for violating this law are fifty rupees against the parent and two hundred rupees against either the middleman or employer.

Types of Bonded Labour

Bonded labour, local bonded labour, and wage earners. The worst conditions and the most severe bondage are inflicted on the migrant children, most of whom are trafficked to the carpet belt from the desperately poor state of Bihar. Some are lured in with agents' promises to their parents that the boys will receive good wages and enjoy a bright future. Others, estimated to number in the tens of thousands, are kidnapped into bondage through force or trickery. Anti-Slavery International, for example, reported that twenty-seven boys between the ages of five and twelve were kidnapped by their local barber, who took them in with the ruse that he was going to take them to the movies, so long as they kept it secretfrom their parents. He then sold them into slavery in a remote village of another state.

The failure of state governments to comply with their legal obligations under the Bonded Labour System (Abolition) Act-particularly the formation and adequate functioning of the district-level vigilance committees-is one of the primary reasons behind the low enforcement rate of the law and the continuing high prevalence of bonded labour. (Indeed, by some accounts, bonded labour is actually increasing during the 1990s.) Another contributing factor, mentioned previously in the context of child labour policy, is the failure of the government to gather and maintain accurate or even plausible statistics.

The statistics problem is as acute in the bonded labour context as it is in the child labour context. According to credible estimates, the number of bonded labourers in India is approximately sixty-five million, representing slightly more than 7 percent of the country's total population. Certain individual states alone are estimated to have bonded labour populations of one to two million people; a report from Tamil Nadu, based on extensive research conducted at the direction ofthe Supreme Court, concluded that there were "well over 10 lakhs" (one million) bonded labourers working in that state.

Other states known to have high rates of bondage include Andhra Pradesh, Karnataka, Madhya Pradesh, Maharashtra, Gujarat, Rajasthan, Uttar Pradesh, Haryana, and Bihar.

In contrast to the figures used by social scientists, the Indian government's figures regarding bonded labour are unconvincingly low. The central Ministry of Labour relies on the state Ministries of Labour-which are charged with enforcing the Bonded Labour System (Abolition) Act-to report the number of bonded labourers identified, released, and rehabilitated. Based on information submitted by the states, the central Ministry of Labour's 1994-1995 Annual Report stated that the nationwide target for 1994-1995 was the rehabilitation of 2,784 bonded labourers-a figure representing less than .005 percent of all estimated bonded labourers. The figure for the total number of bonded labourers identified, when viewed in contrast to the same figures provided in 1989, illustrate the lack of implementation of the Bonded Labour (Abolition) Act. In 1989, the total number of bonded labourers identified was 242,532. By 1995, this number had risen to 251,424. These figures indicate that from 1988 to 1995, only 8,892 bonded labourers had been identified throughout the country, at a time when nongovernmental sources were reporting that there were as many as sixty-five million bonded labourers in India by 1994. Ironically, in the paragraph following the presentation of statistics in the 1994-95 *Annual Report*, the report states that "[t]he [state] Governments are attaching the highest priority to the total eradication of the bonded labour system in the country."

The central government's reliance on and acceptance of state government statistics regarding bonded labour is misplaced and irresponsible. The majority ofstate governments vastly underreport the incidence of bonded labour within their borders. For instance, the government of Tamil Nadu, where an independent commission recently concluded that there existed more than one million bonded labourers, stated in a sworn affidavit to the Supreme Court that "in Tamil Nadu, only stray cases of bonded labour are noticed..." Twelve other state governments made the same assertion to the court, which expressed its disbelief by ordering independent investigations into the matter.

Corruption and neglect are not the only reasons for bad statistics regarding bonded labour. Another is passivity on the part of enforcing officials, who too often take no affirmative steps to discover and root out debt bondage in their districts. Whether this is due to simple apathy or to a misunderstanding on their part of their official duties, the effect is disastrous for bonded labourers, who are left in their state of enslavement indefinitely. In Tamil Nadu, for example, the investigators found that "most District Collectors... had one basis to assume that bonded labour does not exist-No one is coming forward [to report that they are in bondage]."

Obstacles to Enforcement

Apathy

The endemic apathy among government officials charged with enforcing India's labour laws is apparent at all levels: national, state, and district. While undoubtedly there are many committed men and women among their ranks-including, for example, the district collector of North Arcot in Tamil Nadu, whom Human Rights Watch interviewed-such commitment is not the norm. From India's top labour officials all the way down to the local level, where tehsildars (community leaders) use their influence to support the status quo, Human Rights Watch and other researchers have found a profound lack of concern for the plight of bonded and child labourers.

There are many concrete examples of government neglect. The Child Labour (Prohibition and Regulation) Act, signed into law in 1986, requires each state to formulate rules for its implementation. Until this is done, the law cannot be applied in those states. As of July 1996, a full ten years after the act's birth, the majority of states have failed to formulate and implement these necessary rules. It is a sign of the government's disregard of this issue that we are unable to report the exact number of India's twenty-five states that have made rules for the act's application.

Regarding the Bonded Labour System (Abolition) Act, the government's egregious neglect of the law is most evident in the nearly universal failure of districts to form the requisite vigilance committees, much less ensure that the committees function meaningfully. The vigilance committees form the core of act enforcement-if implemented as intended, these committees could contribute dramatically to the eradication of bonded labour. For overburdened district collectors, they would provide resources; for corrupt district collectors, they would provide oversight; and for all district collectors, they would provide essential liaison possibilities to the bonded labourer population, whose interests are usually at odds with the interest and sympathies of their local leaders.

Apathy, or at least a low prioritization of child and bonded labour issues, is also evident in the slow pace at which complaints are adjudicated-enforcement in the courts is very slow. One attorney told us of a case he filed with the Supreme Court under the Bonded Labour System (Abolition) Act in 1984. A fact finding committee was not appointed until 1991 and, although arguments and submissionsbefore the court concluded in 1994, as of 1996 no decision had yet been issued. The time table is not much better for the bonded labour case before the Supreme Court, *People's Union for Civil Liberties v. State of Tamil Nadu, et al.*, which was filed in 1985 and as of 1996 was under consideration by the court.

Delays in prosecuting cases under the Child Labour (Prohibition and Regulation) Act are also not uncommon. One such case, filed in 1986 shortly after the act took effect, was reported to be still pending at the prosecution stage eight years later, in 1994, with the accused continuing to engage in prohibited practices. The delay in processing the complaint, filed against an owner of a glass and bangles factory in Firozabad, is all the more startling in view of the fact that the complaint was filed by then-Labour Minister P. A. Sangma.

Caste and Class Bias

A key element of enforcement is the attitude and the tendency toward a subjective interpretation of the Bonded Labour System (Abolition) Act, 1976 by government officials, including district magistrates, police officers, labour inspectors, and judges. Too often, because of their own backgrounds and the climate in which they work, those officers entrusted with enforcement are more sympathetic to the employers than to the child or bonded labourers. This phenomenon has been noted repeatedly in the context of enforcement of the Bonded Labour System (Abolition) Act.

We had some time back a case before us where pursuant to a direction given by the Collector as a result of an order made by this Court, the Tehsildar went to the villages in question and sitting on a dais with the landlords by his side, he started enquiring of the labourers whether they were bonded or not and when the labourers, obviously inhibited and terrified by the presence of the landlords, said that they were not bonded but they were working freely and voluntarily, he made a report to the Collector that there were no bonded labourers.

In the rare instances where vigilance committees or similar bodies have been formed, according to one researcher, they have been composed of people who themselves, either directly or through their families, employ bonded labour. District collectors and other civil servants assigned to bonded labour enforcement are also more often than not aligned with the property-holding-including the holding of bonded labourers-class. One researcher told Human Rights Watch of working with a team of three Indian Administrative Service officers, who had been assigned by the Supreme Court to investigate a case of bonded labour affecting between 2,500 and 3,000 people. The investigators were urban middle-class men from land-owning families in the region; in private conversations, they made it clear that they considered the use of bonded labour to be an acceptable practice.

Many bond masters are themselves government employees, including teachers, railway workers, and civil administrators. Because of their steady income, these people are more likely to own land-which they need someone to cultivate-and are more likely to have money available for lending purposes. They are also more likely to be local leaders and to have ties to the local and district administration, both factors which tend to inhibit prosecution.

Despite the obvious limitations of relying on high-caste and local landowning officials to attack bonded labour, outreach by the government to affected populations and collabouration with grass-roots social actions groups have not yet been implemented to any significant degree.

Obstruction

It is not uncommon for those accused of violating labour laws to engage in overt obstruction of the legal process. This ranges from intimidation of thecomplaining workers, to bribery of government officials, to physical threats and violence against the bonded labourers and their advocates.

Those who file suit against employers of bonded labour are frequently harassed, according to a New Delhi lawyer who has been engaged in bonded labour cases for more than a decade.

The danger is greatest to those who work in rural areas, where bondage is often the norm and is employed by powerful and ruthless owners. According to another attorney closely related to bonded labour litigation, the advocates and especially the workers who complain about their status are "risking their lives... they are putting their lives on the line, and the state officials have turned a callous eye to it."

Government officials may do more than just turn a "callous eye" toward violence against the bonded labourers and their advocates. Several activists told Human Rights Watch of police collusion with local employers, including returning escaped workers to the employers and intimidating, through force or threat of force, workers who are attempting to organize for improved conditions.

Corruption

As noted in previous chapters, corruption among government officials charged with enforcement of labour laws is notorious and widespread. Labour inspectors, medical officers, local tehsildars (representatives of the district magistrates at the local level), and judges and judicial magistrates are all known to be susceptible to bribery.

Lack of Accountability

Under the Bonded Labour System (Abolition) Act, district magistrates are supposed to report to the state government periodically regarding the number of cases of bonded labourers identified, released, and rehabilitated.

Most districtmagistrates either do not make these reports at all, or make them sporadically. Furthermore, no mechanism is in place whereby the accuracy of the district-level reports can be ascertained, including such important issues as how many of the identified workers have actually been released, and whether any released workers have relapsed into bondage. Often, the district magistrates will simply report that identified bonded labourers, or formerly released bonded labourers, are "unavailable for rehabilitation." That is to say, that their whereabouts are unknown. Hence the central government's figures for 1994-1995, which state that, of 251,424 bonded labourers identified between 1976 and 1995, 17,127 are "not available for rehabilitation."

The rate of return into bondage by previously released bonded labourers is neither studied nor recorded by the government; the effectiveness of the rehabilitation scheme is therefore unknown. Various nongovernmental sources believe the relapse rate to be very high. Part of the reason for return may be the long delays between identification of bonded labourers and dispersal of rehabilitation monies to them. Another factor may be the reportedly widespread corruption among enforcing officials, who are accused of siphoning off funds earmarked for rehabilitation purposes.

RECOMMENDATIONS

Recommendations to the Government of India

The government of India should demonstrate its commitment to the eradication of bonded child labour by implementing the following recommendations at the earliest possible date:

General Recommendations

* Design and implement a multi-pronged effort to end bonded child labour, composed of both persuasive and mandatory means. At a minimum, this effort should include stepped-up enforcement efforts, free, compulsory, and quality public education, and financial support for children to go to school.
* Implement measures designed to bring current practice into compliance with Article 45 of the constitution which mandates free and compulsory education for all children up to fourteen years of age.
* Pressure states and districts to constitute and oversee bonded labour vigilance committees, as required by the Bonded Labour (System) Abolition Act, 1976. Ensure that a sufficient number of investigators can be included in the committee to guarantee implementation of the act. Given the massive numbers of children involved, nongovernmental organization (NGO) representatives, lawyers, social workers, teachers, civil servants, and others with ties to bonded labourers and their families

should be enlisted as investigators. Provide in-depth training to district officials charged with enforcing the act, as directed by the Supreme Court in *Neeraja Chaudhary v. State of Madhya Pradesh*, 1984.

* Establish an independent monitoring agency at the state and national level to oversee the enforcement of the Bonded Labour (System Abolition) Act, 1976. For full implementation of the Act, this body should be statutorily empowered to receive and address complaints of Act violations and complaints of official misconduct. It should also be able to file First Information Reports (FIRs), the first step in prosecution of a criminal charge, when bonded child labourers are identified.
* Establish a similar independent monitoring agency to oversee the enforcement of the Child Labour (Prohibition and Regulation) Act, 1986.
* Ensure the active involvement of the Scheduled Castes and Scheduled Tribes Commission in the process of identifying, releasing, and rehabilitating bonded child labourers.
* Establish and make public a master list or national register of children released from bondage, including how they were rehabilitated (provided with schooling, vocational training, or other alternative measures).
* Establish and make public a master list or national register of people prosecuted under the Bonded Labour (System Abolition) Act, 1976 and the Child Labour (Prohibition and Regulation) Act, 1986 and include information on the nature of sentences given to guilty parties.
* Establish and make public up-to-date and accurate information regarding the incidence and distribution of bonded child labourers, and the industries in which such children work.
* Investigate the abuse and exploitation of children by agents and employers, and prosecute such agents and employers under the relevant domestic law such as Chapter VI of the Juvenile Justice Act, or Chapter XVI of the Indian Penal Code.
* Condition all entitlements, subsidies, special tax allowances, and other concessions currently extended to industries that employ bonded child labour on compliance with the Bonded Labour System (Abolition) Act, 1976 and other relevant laws.
* Condition all new subsidies and incentives on industry compliance with applicable domestic laws banning bonded labour.
* Launch a nationwide public awareness campaign regarding the legal prohibition of bonded child labour. This campaign should explain in simple terms what actions are legally prohibited and what recourses and resources are available to bonded child labourers and their families.
* Amend relevant legislation, including the Child Labour (Prohibition and Regulation) Act, to bring it into compliance with the requirements of the Indian Constitution.

* Add to the Bonded Labour System (Abolition) Act and the Child Labour (Prohibition and Regulation) Act additional punishments for violators, including forfeiture of operating licenses, seizure of manufacturing equipment, and short and long-term closure of plants. Amend the Bonded Labour System (Abolition) Act, 1976 to significantly increase fines and allow the fines to be paid as compensation to the freed bonded labourers. Amend Section 10 to require all employers to have and show on demand proof of age of all children working on their premises. Failure to have adequate proof should constitute a separate violation of the act. In the event of a dispute regarding a child's age, the burden of proof should be on the employer to prove that the child is above the age of fourteen years.
* Amend the Child Labour (Prohibition and Regulation) Act, 1986 so that household enterprises and government schools and training centers are no longer exempted for prohibitions on employing children; rules formulated by the central government will apply until replaced by rules formulated by the states themselves; and coverage under the act should be expanded to include agriculture and informal sectors.
* Amend the Beedi and Cigar Workers Act so that exemptions for household-based production are eliminated.
* Amend the Children (Pledging of Labour) Act so that fines to employers, agents, and creditors are increased, the funds collected are contributed to the compensation and rehabilitation of the children exploited; imprisonment as a sentencing alternative is added; and specify which governmental department is responsible for enforcement of this act.
* Amend the Factories Act to cover all factories or workshops employing child labour, not just those with twenty or more workers, or ten or more workers where power is used.
* Meet International Labour Organisation norms of one Ministry of Labour inspector for every 150 factories and establishments.
* Amend the Trade Union Act to allow children to form and participate in trade unions as an interim measure pending the elimination of bonded child labour. The Convention on the Rights of the Child, which India has ratified guarantees the children the right of freedom of association.
* Promptly submit the Indian government's report on compliance with the Convention on the Rights of the Child to the United Nations Committee on the Rights of the Child, as this has been overdue for more than one year.

  Continue cooperation with international organizations working to abolish bonded child labour, in particular the International Labour Organisation's International Programme to Eliminate Child Labour

Recommendations to United Nations Agencies

* The United Nations Working Group on Contemporary Forms of Slavery should press the United Nations Human Rights Commission to examine the government of India's compliance with international laws and standards outlawing bonded labour, and to censure non-compliance. As a step toward ending bonded labour in India, Human Rights Watch recommends that the working group undertake a fact-finding mission to India and make recommendations designed to eliminate bonded labour.
* The ILO should send a technical mission to India to make recommendations with the understanding that India would develop an action plan for abolishing bonded child labour over a specific time period, either through the International Program to Eliminate Child Labour (IPEC) or other ILO programs.
* UNICEF should make the elimination of bonded child labour a stated priority of its efforts in India and elsewhere. It should formulate a consistent institutional policy regarding bonded child labour, and work with local, state, and national government officials toward the achievement of the stated goals.
* WHO should investigate and publicize the adverse health consequences for children of bonded child labour, and promote measures to eliminate the exposure of children to hazardous conditions and labour practices.
* WHO should formulate a policy on the elimination of bonded child labour, and collabourate with other UN agencies toward this end.

Recommendations to the World Bank and Other International Lending Institutions

* Condition receipt of loans and other subsidies on verified compliance with all domestic legal prohibitions on the use of bonded and child labour.
* Suspend the flow of aid to the sericulture (silk) industry until the government of India has taken concrete steps to identify, eradicate, and rehabilitate children in bondage.
* Prior to approval of projects, investigate the effect of proposed policies and programs on the incidence of child servitude.
* Provide funding for a program with NGOs and the Indian government to effectively implement India's Bonded Labour System (Abolition) Act, and to assist in identifying, releasing, and rehabilitating bonded child labourers, with a priority on industries which have previously

received aid. Establish an institutionalized mechanism for incorporating local NGO ideas and opinions into projects at all stages of the decision making process-before a loan is released, while the project is being implemented, and in the course of any post-project evaluation.

Recommendations to the International Community

* India's international donors should suspend funding for any projects, such as sericulture, that are known to employ bonded child labour unless the project includes specific programs for the elimination of bonded child labour, education and rehabilitation of the affected children, and for improving the social welfare of the children and their families.
* Donors should explore the possibility of funding a program with NGOs and the Indian government to effectively implement India's Bonded Labour (Abolition) Act and accompanying rehabilitation scheme.

  Trade benefits provided under the Generalized System of Preferences in both the United States and in Europe are prohibited to countries where forced labour is tolerated. Accordingly, Human Rights Watch/Asia calls upon the United States Trade Representative and the European Union to initiate an investigation into the use of bonded child labour in India and into the Indian Government's enforcement of the Bonded Labour System (Abolition) Act, 1976. India's trading partners should use the leverage ofGSP trade benefits to encourage the government to eradicate bonded child labour and to provide rehabilitation and education to the children involved.

Recommendations to Retailers, Suppliers, and Indian and International Consumers

* When making purchases from industries known to employ large numbers of children in bonded labour, such as the silk, carpet, beedi, silver, leather and agricultural sectors, consumers in India and abroad should require their retailers to pledge to reject goods from suppliers which employ bonded child labour in the manufacture of these goods and to support a good faith program to phase children out of bondage, offering them financial assistance and access to formal education. Consumers should also require retailers to guarantee that they and their suppliers offer full access to independent monitors to all facilities and supplier facilities to check on the incidence of bonded child labour.
* Corporations should incorporate a monitoring process for bonded child labour into their quality control procedures and in setting standards for selecting suppliers and products.

* Indian consumers should appeal to their members of the legislative assembly (MLA), district magistrates, and district collectors to demand that vigilance committees be established and strengthened, and demand that the government of India identify, release, and rehabilitate all bonded labourers (including children) as required under the Bonded Labour (Abolition) Act, 1976, and accompanying rehabilitation scheme.

  International consumers should appeal to their own governments to press the Government of India to abide by its own law by administering in good faith the Bonded Labour (Abolition) Act, 1976, and accompanying procedures for the identification, release, and rehabilitation of bonded labourers.

********NOTE***: This chapter is not an original work of the author. It is completely based on the various reports and publications of Human Rights Watch (International NGO). Its WEBSITE resources are greatly acknowledged-Author**

4

Policies and Programmes

Child Labour and International Labour Organisation (ILO):

Children are part and parcel of the economic activity of each and every society. In the ancient period, socialization was the main intention behind the child labour. The kind of work assigned to them was so helpful for the overall development of the children. The kind of involvements of the children in their early ages were aimed at in preparing for their adult hood. Moreover those kind of works were free of any harm to the children. But, after industrialization the meaning of child labour went on changing. Children gradually started to work for others in the form of labourer. Slowly, the world community started to discuss about the conditions of working children. Kind of large scale protestations were took place here and there around the globe. The first international effort to fight against child labour has began with the establishment of International Labour Organisation (ILO).

The ILO since 1919 has been much concerned with the general elimination of child labour and the promotion of well being of the children. Improvement of labour standard around the world is the basic aim of the ILO and has given a lot of emphasize to protect the working children in the form of conventions and recommendations. From its inception, it has made child labour one of its central concern. ILO works on the child labour and related issues over the decades has mainly taken its cue from the phrase "protection of children" in its preamble of its constitution (Bhargava). The ILO's prime tool in pursuing the abolition of child labour has always been and has remained to this day, the labour standards that embody the concept of a minimum age to enter into employment. Further the main function of the ILO is to work with various Governments by providing technical and financial assistance for the effective implementations of the anti child labour programmes in the respective countries.

The existing international efforts are of two kinds as Kaushik Basu had explained: (1) extranational and (2) supranational. An extranational effort is a reform and action taken with in the industrialized countries that provoke the underdeveloped countries to raise labour standards. A good example is that of banning on the export of items in which the exporting country intensively involves children in the manufacturing of such goods exported. Supranational effort is execution of rights of the workers, raising the standard of working conditions, aid to curb child labour through international bodies like ILO and UNISEF etc.(Kaushik Basu).

The ILO policy in the field of child labour derives from two related but distinct objectives. The first is the effective abolition of child labour. To attain this objective, the concerned countries are requested to carry out a series of socioeconomic measures. All this countries are supposed to make necessary amendments of their existing constitution to protect their children. Further improvement of living standards, increase in higher economic growth, open avenues for adult employment, universalisation of primary education have to be adapted in order to make child labouer as socially and economically unnecessary and to enhance the moral force and practical application of the existing laws (Prasad, 2000).

ILO since its inception in 1919 has adopted the following conventions with regard to children and adults:-

Medical examination of young persons (Sea) convention, 1921
Minimum Age convention, 1929
Night work of young person convention, 1919
Minimum Age (New Industrial Employment) Convention, 1932
Minimum Age (Sea) Convention (Revised), 1937.
Minimum Age (Non industrial) revised convention 1937
Medical Examination of Young Persons (Revised), 1946
Nightwork of young persons (Non-Industrial Occupation) convention 1946
Night work of young persons (Industry) Convention (Revised), 1948

One of the recent policy to curb this problem is *product labeling,* i.e., pasting of labels on the products with a message such as Guanine: produced without small hands. Some of the export items should have this kind of labelling on their respective products. Now, it is the choice left over to the customer whether he/she has to buy it or not. But now a days, the validity of the labelling is highly questionable.

International Programme on Elimination of Child labour

The issue of childlabour in India attracted public attention and debate for the first time in1985. However, it become the focus of major concern in the aftermath of globalization in 1991,whereby India ushered in a new era of liberalization and privatization. The international community has already expressed through various conventions and declarations its strong opinion that child labour needs to be eliminated. Apart from ILO, other international agencies to eliminate child labour signed a joint declaration in New Delhi in1998, Many international agencies have launched some major projects to eliminate child labourer from hazardous sectors.

The International Programme for the Elimination of Child Labour is a global programme launched by the International Labour Organisation in December 1991. India was the first country to join it in 1992 and it signed a MoU with ILO. The long-term objective of IPEC is for the effective abolition of childlabour.

Its immediate objectives are:-

- Enhancement of the capability of ILO constituents and non-government organizations to design, implement and evaluate programmes with regarded to child labour elimination;
- To identify interventions at community and national levels which could serve as models for replication and
- Creation of awareness and social mobilization for the elimination of child labour.

At the international level International Project for Eliminating Child labour (IPEC) has a Programme Steering Committee consisting of representatives of the ILO, the donors and participating countries. The IPEC Programme Management is guided from the ILO Headquarters. At the national level in India, there is a National Steering Committee of which the Union Labour Secretary is the Chairman. This Committee is tripartite in composition with representations from different NGOs and other organisations

IPEC became operational in the field in early 1993. The period till 1996 saw a focus on NGOs actions in a large number of action programmes covering almost every State of the country. The second phase of during the period 1998-99 marked larger programmes in 6 selected districts in the country in conjunction with the Government of India's National Child Labour Projects which now are the vehicle of ILO's outreach strategy.

During the period 1992-2001 the budget allocation and commitment for India approved by IPEC was US$ 6.9 million. The amount disbursed during this period is of the order of 5.6 million US dollar. Altogether about 165 action programmes were taken up for implementation under IPEC during 1992-2001. 11 projects are currently being under implementation. A proposal for taking up 'New Comprehensive IPEC Projects' in 10 identified industries, in selected areas in 4 states is also on the anvil of Govt. of India). A proposal for taking up

'New Comprehensive IPEC Projects in 10 identified industries in selected areas in 4 states, is also on the anvil (Ministry of Labour, Govt. of India).

In recent times, it has been decided including at the meeting of the IPEC Programme Steering Committee that IPEC activities should be conducted in conjunction with national policies, priorities and programmes of the recipient member states. The concerned member states should fully aware of the activities undertaken under IPEC. All proposals recommended by the National Steering Committee must be processed with expeditiously and sanctions communicated in time backed with timely release of funds. It has also been decided that it is essential to augment funding for IPEC activities in India and that contributions should be towards core funding rather than specific projects.

In 1998 ILO has set-up Statistical Information and Monitoring Programme on Child Labour (SIMPOC) as a part of IPEC. This new programme was formulated IPEC and ILO's Bureau of Statistics jointly. It is designed with the major aim of assisting individual countries in collecting comprehensive qualitative and quantitative date on child labour of the respective countries. Further this programme aim's at to improve the capacity of building statistical offices and train the statisticians.

The ILO Bureau of Employers Activities assists employer organizations in member states with information, advice and assistance regarding child labour issue. Further this organisation conducts various programmes like establishment of child labour cell in every trade unions, action research projects and to involve employers in advocating the elimination of child labour. Not only ILO many other international organisations like UNISEF, DFDI, Wold Bank and IMF also extend their help to the countries where high incidences of child labour. Many structural causes of child labour like poverty, illiteracy, health are the mandates of these different agencies.

Apart from the International Confederation of Free Trade Unions (ICFTU), Southern Asian Developmental Community (SADC), Universal Alliance of Diamond Workers (UADW)and World Confederation of Labour (WCL), are some of the International Organisations working in India to eradicate the child labour problem. In 1999, more than 191 countries have ratified the Convention on the Rights of the Child. This treaties mapout the international legal framework of the fundamental requirements of right for education and to secure free primary education for all children.

For the first time in the history of child labour, USA Government brought out a welfare programme which may be guide rest of the countries in 1996- the Aid to Families with Department Children (AFDC). Through this programme, qualified families can get some special assistance from the federal Governament. AFDC also assured access to other benefits, such as medical aid and food, so that these families could send their children to work up to certain standard. Some of the African countries have implanted some programmes with the help of World Bank. UNO also has instructed its members to take some projects, which could promote gender equality, reduce child mortality and improve mantel health. Many international NGO's are helping to poor African and Asian countries under this programme.

Child Labour and Indian Constitution:

Ever society has its own pattern of life suited to their livelihood. This pattern of life in the old society was regulated through certain social norms. Social norms and values were upheld by an approved machinery of the society to regulate and maintain the social order. In a complex society where the existing social systems are easily broken, it becomes much more difficult to maintain the continuing of the existing the social systems. Hence, in that modern time, formal laws and acts will be of highly useful (Prasad). Constitutions usually reflects the basic laws of the particular soil and society. Basically all laws and provisions in the constitution reveal the background of social and economic situations of the concerned country.

Child is the wealth of the society and future hope of the Nation. Children a supremely important national asset. It is obvious that children need special protection from various exploitations. With a view to protect the children from undue exploitation and ill treatment, various legislative measures had been enacted till today. During the tender age, children need some kind of love and affection that plays a vital role in overall development of the children. In western countries, spending at school at least during childhood period is mandatory by law.

It is estimated that two-fifth of India's population is reported to have been below 14 years and considerable number of children is working in different corners of India. As for as India is considered children are working in all the three sectors of Indian economy. According to ILO in developing countries children in the age group of 12-15 years work in some places or the other and it is a part and parcel of their life and most of them are found employed in most hazardous sectors of the economy.

Many nations are bounded to one or other international conventions on welfare of children. Countries having high incidences of child labour have made some amendments in their respective Constitutions to enforce strict laws on the exploitations of the children. Some of the international bodies like ILO, UNO, UNESCO, UNISEF and WHO are implementing several programmes in some developing countries to help the governments and local NGOs in curbing the problem. These Organisations have also brought UNO convention on the rights of children to which India is also one of the signatory. Further the comprehensive Human Rights Convention has drafted the rights of the child which has a binding effect on all signatories. Being a democratic country, India has also provide protection of children in its constitution against child labour to regulate the minimum age of employment, hours of work and physical conditions at work place. The constitution of India has given protection to children in two ways. Through fundamental rights and directive principal of state police.

The following articles are note writhing to mention

Article 15(3)- provision to enact laws to protect women and child.

Article 21- protection of life and personnel liberty

Article 23- right against exploitations and ban on traffic in human beings and forced labour.

Selected Articles of the Indian Constitution

Article 21. Protection of life and personal liberty-No person shall be deprived of his life or personal liberty except according to procedure established by law.

Article 23. Prohibition of traffic in human beings and forced labour- (1) Traffic in human beings and begar and other similar forms of forced labour are prohibited and any contravention of this prohibition shall be an offence punishable in accordance with law.

(2) Nothing in this article shall prevent the State from imposing compulsory service for public purposes, and in imposing such service the State shall not make any discrimination on grounds only of religion, race, caste or class or any of them.

Article 24. Prohibition of employment of children in factories, prohibition the employment of children in factories etc. This article state "No children below 14 years shall be employed to work in factory or mines or in any other hazardous jobs." Employment of children below a particular age is also prohibited so also injurious work may be prohibited to children taking in to consideration their physical structure. This is the most important and vital article regarding child labour.

Article 39. Certain principles of policy to be followed by the State-The State shall, in particular, direct its policy towards securing-

(a) that the citizens, men and women equally, have the right to an adequate means of livelihood;

(b) that the ownership and control of the material resources of the community are so distributed as best to subserve the common good;

(c) that the operation of the economic system does not result in the concentration of wealth and means of production to the common detriment;

(d) that there is equal pay for equal work for both men and women;

(e) that the health and strength of workers, men and women, and the tender age of children are not abused and that citizens are not forced by economic necessity to enter avocations unsuited to their age or strength;

(f) that children are given opportunities and facilities to develop in a healthy manner and in conditions of freedom and dignity and that childhood and youth are protected against exploitation and against moral and material abandonment.

Article 39A. Equal Justice and free legal aid-The State shall secure that the operation of the legal system promotes justice, on a basis of equal opportunity, and shall, in particular, provide free legal aid, by suitable legislation or schemes or in any other way, to ensure that opportunities for securing justice are not denied to any citizen by reason of economic or other disabilities.

Article 39(e) obligation of the states to safeguard the health of the children. Article 39(b) and (e) states that during the tender age, children should not be abused and that they should not be forced by economic necessity to enter avocations unsuited to their age or strength.

Article 39(f) proclaims that the children are given opportunities and facilities to develop in a healthy manner in conditions of freedom and dignity and that childhood and youth are protected against exploitation and against moral and material abandonment. Article 45 is a supplementary to the Article number 24 on the ground that when the child is not be employed before the age of 14 years he /she should be in educational field. Also this article states, free and compulsory education for children up to 14 years of age.

Article 41. Right to work, to education and to public assistance in certain cases-The State shall, within the limits of its economic capacity and development, make effective provision for securing the right to work, to education and to public assistance in cases of unemployment, old age, sickness and disablement, and in other cases of undeserved want.

Article 42. Provision for just and humane conditions of work and maternity relief-The State shall make provision for securing just and humane conditions of work and for maternity relief.

Article 43. Living wage, etc., for workers-The State shall endeavour to secure, by suitable legislation or economic organisation or in any other way, to all workers, agricultural, industrial or otherwise, work, a living wage, conditions of work ensuring a decent standard of life and full enjoyment of leisure and social and cultural opportunities and, in particular, the State shall endeavour to promote cottage industries on an individual or cooperative basis in rural areas.

Article 43A. Participation of workers in management of industries- The State shall take steps, by suitable legislation or in any other way, to secure the participation of workers in the management of undertakings, establishments or other organizations engaged in any industry.

Article 45. Provision for free and compulsory education for children- The State shall endeavour to provide within a period of ten years from the commencement of this Constitution, for free and compulsory education for all children until they complete the age of fourteen years.

Article 46. Promotion of educational and economic interests of Scheduled Castes, Scheduled Tribes and other weaker sections-The State shall promote with special care the educational and economic interests of the weaker sections of the people, and, in particular, of the Scheduled Castes and the Scheduled Tribes, and shall protect them from social injustice and all forms of exploitation.

APPENDIX B: The Bonded Labour System (Abolition) Act, 1976

An act to provide for the abolition of bonded labour system with a view to preventing the economic and physical exploitation of the weaker sections of the people and for matters connected therewith or incidental thereto

Be it enacted by Parliament in the Twenty-seventh Year of the Republic of India as follows:

Preliminary

1. Short title, extent and commencement.-(1) This act may be called the Bonded Labour System (Abolition) Act, 1976.

(2) It extends to the whole of India.

(3) it shall be deemed to have come into force on the 25th day of October, 1975.

2. Definitions.-(1) In This act, unless the context otherwise requires,-

(a) "advance" means an advance, whether in cash or in kind, or partly in cash or partly in kind, made by one person (hereinafter referred to as the creditor) to another person (hereinafter referred to as the debtor);

(b) "agreement" means an agreement (whether written or oral, or partly written and partly oral) between a debtor and creditor, and includes an agreement providing for forced labour, the existence of which is presumed under any social custom prevailing in the concerned locality;

Explanation.-The existence of an agreement between the debtor and creditor is ordinarily presumed, under the social custom, in relation to the following forms of forced labour, namely:

Adiyamar, Baramasi, Bethu, Bhagela, Cherumar, Garrugalu, Hali, Hari, Harwai, Holya, Jolya, Jeeta, Kamiya, Khundit-Mundit, Kuthia, Lakhari, Munjhi, Mat, Musish system, Nit-Majoor, Paleru, Padiyal, Pannaayilal, Sagri, Sanji, Sanjawal, Sewak,, Sewakis, Seri, Vetti;

(c) "ascendant" or "descendant" in relation to a person belonging to matriarchal society, means the person who corresponds to such expression in accordance with the law of succession in such society;

(d) "bonded debt" means an advance obtained, or presumed to have been obtained, by a bonded labourer, or in pursuance of, the bonded labour system

(e) "bonded labour" means any labour or service rendered under the bonded labour system;

(f) "bonded labourer" means a labourer who incurs, or has, or is presumed to have, incurred, a bonded debt;

(g) "bonded labour system" means the system of forced, or partly forced labour under which a debtor enters, or has, or is presumed to have, entered, into an agreement with the creditor to the effect that,-

(i) In consideration of an advance obtained by him or by any of his lineal ascendants or descendants (whether or not such advance is evidenced by any document) and in consideration of the interest, if any, due on such advance, or

(ii) in pursuance of any customary or social obligation, or

(iii) in pursuance of an obligation devolving on him by succession, or

(iv) for any economic consideration of the interest, if any, due on such advance, or

(v) by reason of his birth in any particular caste or community, he would-

(1) render, by himself or through any member of his family, or any person dependent on him, labour or service to the creditor, or for the benefit of the creditor, for a specified period or for an unspecified period, either without wages or for nominal wages, or

(2) forfeit the freedom of employment or other means of livelihood for a specified period or for an unspecified period, or

(3) forfeit the right to move freely throughout the territory of India, or

(4) forfeit the right to appropriate or sell at market value any of his property or product of his labour or the labour of a member of his family or any person dependent on him and includes the system of forced, or partly forced, labour under which a surety for a debtor or has, or has, or is presumed to have, entered, into an agreement with the creditor to the effect that in the event of the failure of the debtor to repay the debt, he would render the bonded labour on behalf of the debtor;

Explanation.- For the removal of doubts, it is hereby declared that any system of forced, or partly forced labour under which any workman being contract labour as defined in Cl. (b) of subsection (1) or Sec. 2 of the Contract Labour (Regulation and Abolition) Act, 1970 (37 of 1970), or an inter-State migrant workman as defined in Cl. (e) of sub-section (1) of Sec. 2 of the Inter-State Migrant Workmen (Regulation and of Employment and Conditions of Service) Act, 1979 (30 of 1979), is required to render labour or service in circumstances of the nature mentioned in sub-clause (1) of this clause or is subjected to all or any of the disabilities referred to in sub-clauses (2) to (4), is "bonded labour system" within the meaning of this clause.

(h) "family", in relation to a person, includes the ascendant and descendant of such person;

(i) "nominal wages", in relation to any labour, means a wage which is less than,-

(a) the minimum wages fixed by the Government, in relation to the same or similar labour, under any law for the time being in force; and

(b) where no such minimum wage has been fixed in relation to any form of labour, the wages that are normally paid, for the same or similar labour to the labourers working in the same locality;

(j) "prescribed" means prescribed by rules made under this act.

3. Act to have overriding effect.-The provisions of this act shall have effect notwithstanding anything inconsistent therewith contained in any enactment other than this act, or in any instrument having effect by virtue of any enactment other than this act.

Abolition of Bonded Labour System

4. Abolition of bonded labour system.-(1) On the commencement of this act, the bonded labour system shall stand abolished and every bonded labourer shall, on such commencement, stand freed and discharged from any obligation to render any bonded labour.

(2) After the commencement of this act, no person shall-

(a) make any advance under, or in pursuance of the bonded labour system, forced labour, or

(b) Compel any person to render any bonded labour or other form of forced labour.

5. Agreement, custom, etc. to be void.-On the commencement of this act, any custom or tradition or any contract, agreement or other instrument (whether entered into or executed before or after the commencement of this act), by virtue of which any person, or any member of the family or dependent of such person, is required to do any work or render any service as a bonded labourer, shall be void and inoperative.

Extinguishment of liability to repay bonded debt

6. Liability to repay bonded debt to stand extinguished-(1) On the commencement of this act, every obligation of a bonded labourer to repay any bonded debt, or such part of any bonded debt as remains unsatisfied immediately before such commencement, shall be deemed to have been extinguished.

(2) After the commencement of this act, no suit or other proceeding shall lie in any civil Court or before any other authority for the recovery of any bonded debt or any part thereof.

(3) Every decree or order for the recovery of bonded debt, passed before the commencement of this act and not fully satisfied before such commencement, shall be deemed, on such commencement, to have been fully satisfied.

(4) Every attachment made before the commencement of this act, for the recovery of any bonded debt, shall, on such commencement, stand vacated; and where, in pursuance of such attachment, any moveable property of the bonded labourer was seized and removed from his custody and kept in the custody of any Court or other authority pending sale thereof such moveable property shall be restored, as soon as may be practicable after such commencement, to the possession of the bonded labourer.

(5) Where, before the commencement of this act, possession of any property belonging to a bonded labourer or a member of his family or other dependent was forcibly taken over by any creditor for the recovery of any bonded debt, such property shall be restored, as soon as may be practicable after such commencement, to the possession of the person from whom it was seized.

(6) If restoration of the possession of any property referred to in sub-section (4) or sub-section (5) is not made within thirty days from the commencement of this act, the aggrieved person may, within such time as may be prescribed, apply to the prescribed authority for the restoration of the possession of such property and the prescribed authority may, after giving the creditor a reasonable opportunity of being heard, direct the creditor to restore to the applicant the possession of the concerned property within such time as may be specified in the order.

(7) An order made by any prescribed authority, under sub-section (6), shall be deemed to be an order made by a civil Court of the lowest pecuniary jurisdiction within the local limits of whose jurisdiction the creditor voluntarily resides or carries on business or personally works for gain.

(8) For the avoidance of doubts, it is hereby declared, that, where any attached property was sold before the commencement of this act, in execution

of a decree or order for the recovery of a bonded debt, such sale shall not be affected by any provision of this act:

Provided that the bonded labourer, or an agent authorized by him in this behalf, may, at any time within five years rom such commencement, apply to have the sale set aside on his depositing in Court, for payment to the decree-holder, the amount specified in the proclamation of sale, for the recovery of which sale was ordered, less any amount as well as mesne profits, which may, since the date of such proclamation of sale, have been received by the decree-holder.

(9) Where any suit or proceeding, for the enforcement of any obligation under the bonded labour system, including a suit or proceeding for the recovery of any advance made to a bonded labourer, is pending at the commencement of this act, such suit or other proceeding shall, on such commencement, stand dismissed.

(10) On the commencement of this act, every bonded labourer who has been detained in civil prison, whether before or after judgement, shall be released from detention forthwith.

7. Property of bonded labourer to be freed from mortgage, etc.-(1) All property vested in a bonded labourer which was, immediately before the commencement of this act under any mortgage, lien, charge, or other incumbrances in connection with any bonded debt shall, in so far as it is reliable to the bonded debt, stand freed and discharged from such mortgage, charge, lien or other incumbrances in connection with any bonded debt, and where any such property was, immediately before the commencement of this act, in the possession of the mortgagee or the holder of the charge, lien or incumbrance, such property shall (except where it was subject to any other charge), on such commencement, be restored to the possession of the bonded labourer.

(2) If any delay is made in restoring any property, referred to in sub-section (1), to the possession of the bonded labourer, such labourer shall be entitled, on and from the date of such commencement, to recover from the mortgagee or holder of the lien, charge or incumbrance, such mesne profits as may be determined by the Civil Court of the lowest pecuniary jurisdiction within the local limits of whose jurisdiction such property is situated.

8. Freed bonded labourer not to be evicted from homestead, etc.- (1) No person who has been freed and discharged under this act from any obligation to render any bonded labour, shall be evicted from any homestead or other residential premises which he was occupying immediately before the commencement of this act as part of the consideration for the bonded labour.

(2) If, after the commencement of this act, any such person is evicted by the creditor from any homestead or other residential premises, referred to in sub-section (1), the Executive Magistrate in charge of the sub-division within which such homestead or residential premises, is situated shall, as early as practicable, restore the bonded labourer to the possession of such homestead or other residential premises.

9. Creditor not to accept payment against extinguished debt.-(1) No creditor shall accept any payment against any bonded debt which has been extinguished or deemed to have been extinguished or fully satisfied by virtue of the provisions of this act.

(2) whoever contravenes the provisions of sub-section (1), shall be punishable with imprisonment for a term which may extend to three years and also with fine.

(3) The Court, convicting any person under sub-section (2) may, in addition to the penalties which may be imposed under that sub-section, direct the person to deposit, in Court, the amount accepted in contravention of the provisions of sub-section (1), within such period as may be specified in the order for being refunded to the bonded labourer.

Implementing Authorities

10. Authorities who may be specified for implementing the provisions of this act.- The State Governments may confer such powers and impose such duties on a District Magistrate as may be necessary to ensure that the provisions of this act are properly carried out and the District Magistrate may specify the officer, subordinate to him, who shall exercise all or any of the powers, and perform al or any of the duties, so conferred or imposed and the local limits within which such powers or duties shall be carried out by the officers so specified.

11. Duty of District Magistrates and other officers to ensure credit.- The District Magistrate authorized by the State Government under Sec. 10 and the officer specified by the District Magistrate under that section shall, as far as practicable, try to promote the welfare of the freed bonded labourer by securing and protecting the economic interests of such bonded labourer so that he may not have any occasion or reason to contract any further debt.

12. Duty of the District Magistrate and officers authorized by him.-It shall be the duty of every District Magistrate and every officer specified by him under Sec. 10 to inquire whether after the commencement of this act, any bonded labour system or any other form of forced labour is being enforced by, or on behalf of, any person resident within the local limits of his jurisdiction and if, as a result of such inquiry, any person is found to be enforcing the bonded labour system or any other system of forced labour, he shall forthwith take such action as may be necessary to eradicate the enforcement of such forced labour.

Vigilance Committees

13. Vigilance Committees.-(1) Every State Government shall, by notification in the Official Gazette, constitute such number of Vigilance Committees in each district and each sub-division as it may think fit.

(2) Each Vigilance Committee, constituted for a district, shall consist of the following members, namely:

(a) The District Magistrate, or a person nominated by him, who shall be the Chairman;

(b) three persons belonging to the Scheduled Castes or Scheduled Tribes and residing in the district, to be nominated by the District Magistrate;

(c) two social workers, resident in the district, to be nominated by the District Magistrate;

(d) not more than three persons to represent the official or non-official agencies in the district connected with rural development, to be nominated by the State Government;

(e) one person to represent the financial and credit institutions in the district, to be nominated by the District Magistrate.

(3) Each Vigilance Committee, constituted for a sub-division, shall consist of the following members, namely:

(a) The Sub-Divisional Magistrate, or a person nominated by him, who shall be the Chairman;

(b) three persons belonging to the Scheduled Castes or Scheduled Tribes and residing in the sub-division, to be nominated by the Sub-divisional Magistrate;

(c) two social workers, resident in the sub-division, to be nominated by the Sub-divisional Magistrate;

(d) not more than three persons to represent the official or non-official agencies in the sub-division connected with rural development, to be nominated by the State Government;

(e) one person to represent the financial and credit institutions in the sub-division, to be nominated by the Sub-divisional Magistrate.

(f) one officer specified under Sec. 10 and functioning in the sub-division;

(4) Each Vigilance Committee shall regulate its own procedure and secretarial assistance as may be necessary, shall be provided by-

(a) the District Magistrate, in the case of Vigilance Committee constituted for the district;

(b) the Sub-divisional Magistrate, in the case of a Vigilance Committee constituted for the sub-division.

(5) No proceeding of a Vigilance Committee shall be invalid merely by reason of any defect in the constitution, or in the proceedings, of the Vigilance Committee.

14. Functions of Vigilance Committees.-(1) The functions of each Vigilance Committee shall be-

(a) to advise the District Magistrate or any officer authorized by him as to the efforts made, and action taken, to ensure that the provisions of this act or any rule made there under are properly implemented;

(b) to provide for the economic and social rehabilitation of the freed-bonded labourers;

(c) to co-ordinate the functions of rural banks and co-operative societies with a view to canalizing adequate credit to the freed-bonded labourers;

(d) to keep an eye on the number of offences of which cognizance has been taken under this act;

(e) to make a survey as to whether there is any offence of which cognizance ought to be taken under this act;

(f) to defend any suit instituted against a freed-bonded labourer or a member of his family or any other person dependent on him for the recovery of the whole or part of any bonded debt or any other debt which is claimed by such person to be bonded debt.

(2) A Vigilance Committee may authorize one of its members to defend a suit against a freed-bonded labourer and the member so authorized shall be deemed, for the purpose of such suit, to be the authorized agent of the freed-bonded labourer.

15. Burden of proof.- Whenever any debt is claimed by a bonded labourer, or a Vigilance Committee, to be a bonded debt, the burden of proof that such debt, is not a bonded debt shall lie on the creditor.

Offences and Procedure for Trial

16. Punishment for enforcement of bonded labour.-Whoever, after the commencement of this act, compels any person to render any bonded labour shall be punishable with imprisonment for a term which may extend to three years and also with fine which may extend to two thousand rupees.

17. Punishment for advancement of bonded debt.-Whoever advances, after the commencement of this act, any bonded debt shall be punishable with imprisonment for a term which may extend to three years and also with fine which may extend to two thousand rupees.

18. Punishment for extracting bonded labour under the bonded labour system.-Whoever enforces, after the commencement of this act, any custom, tradition, contract, agreement or other instrument, by virtue of which any person or any member of the family of such person or any dependent of such person is required to render any service under the bonded labour system shall be punishable with imprisonment for a term which may extend to three years and also with fine which may extend to two thousand rupees; and out of the fine, ifrecovered, payment shall be made to the bonded labourer at the rate of rupees five for each day for which the bonded labour was extracted from him.

19. Punishment for omission or failure to restore possession of property to bonded labourers.-Whoever, being required by this act to restore any property to the possession of any bonded labourer, omits or fails to do so, within a period of thirty days from the commencement of this act, shall be punishable with imprisonment for a term which may extend to one year, or with fine which may extend to one thousand rupees, or with both; and, out of the fine, if recovered payment shall be made to the bonded labourer at the rate of rupees five for each day during which possession of property was not restored to him.

20. Abetment to be an offence.-Whoever abets any offence punishable under this act shall, whether or not the offence abetted is committed, be punishable with the same punishment as is provided for the offence which has been abetted.

Explanation.-For the purpose of this act, "abetment" has the meaning assigned to it in the Indian Penal Code.

21. Offences to be tried by Executive Magistrates.-(1) The State Government may confer, on an Executive Magistrate the powers of a Judicial Magistrate of the first class or of the second class for the trial of offences under this act; and on such conferment of powers, the Executive Magistrate, on whom the powers are so conferred, shall be deemed, for the purposes of the Code of Criminal Procedure, 1973 (2 of 1974), to be a Judicial Magistrate of the first class, or of the second class, as the case may be.

22. Cognizance of offences.-Every offence under this act shall be cognizable and bailable.

23. Offences by companies.-(1) Where an offence under this act has been committed by a company, every person who, at the time the offence was committed, was in charge of, and was responsible to, the company for the conduct of the business of the company, as well as the company, shall be deemed to be guilty of the offence and shall be liable to be proceeded against and punished accordingly.

(2) Notwithstanding anything contained in sub-section (1), where any offence under this act has been committed by a company and it has been proved that the offence has been committed with the consent or connivance of, or is attributable to, any neglect on the part of, any director, manager, secretary or other officer of the company, such director, manager, secretary or other officer shall be deemed to be guilty of that offence and shall be liable to be proceeded against and punished accordingly.

Explanation.-For the purposes of this section,-

(a) "company" means any body corporate and includes a firm or other association of individuals; and

(b) "director", in relation to a firm, means a partner in the firm.

Miscellaneous

24. Protection of action taken in good faith.-No suit, prosecution or other legal proceeding shall lie against any State Government or any officer of the State Government or any member of the Vigilance Committee for anything which is in good faith done or intended to be done under this act.

25. Jurisdiction of Civil Courts barred.-No Civil Court shall have jurisdiction in respect of any matter to which any provision of this act applies and no injunction shall be granted by any Civil Court in respect of anything which is done or intended to be done by or under this act.

26. Power to make rules.-(1) The Central Government may, by notification in the official Gazette, make rules for carrying out the provisions of this act.

(2) In particular, and without prejudice to the foregoing power, such rules may provide for all or any of the following matters, namely:

(a) the authority to which application for the restoration of possession of property referred to in sub-section (4), or sub-section (5) of Sec. 6 is to be submitted in pursuance of sub-section (6) of that section;

(b) the time within which application for restoration of possession of property is to be made under sub-section (6) of Sec. 6, to the prescribed authority;

(c) steps to be taken by Vigilance Committees under Cl. (a) of sub-section (1) of Sec. 14, to ensure the implementation of the provisions of this act or of any rule made there under;

(d) any other matter which is required to be, or may be prescribed.

(3) Every rule made by the Central Government under this act shall be laid, as soon as may be after it is made, before each House of Parliament while it is in session, for a total period of thirty days which may be comprised in one session or in two or more successive sessions, and if, before the expiry of the

session immediately following the session or successive sessions aforesaid, both Houses agree in making any modification in the rule or both Houses agree that the rule should not be made, the rule shall thereafter have effect only in such modified form or be of no effect, as the case may be; so however, that any such modification or annulment shall be without prejudice to the validity of anything previously done under that rule.

(1) The Bonded Labour System (Abolition) Ordinance, 1975 (17 of 1975), is hereby repealed.

(2) Notwithstanding such repeal, anything or any action taken under the Ordinance (including any notification published, direction of a nomination made, power conferred, duty imposed or officer specified) shall be deemed to have been done or taken under the corresponding provisions of this act.

The Bonded Labour System (Abolition) Rules, 1976

1. Short title and commencement.-(1) These rules may be called the Bonded Labour System (Abolition) Rules, 1976.

(2) They shall come into force on the date of their publication in the official Gazette.

2. Definitions.-In these rules, unless the context otherwise requires,-

(a) "Act" means the Bonded Labour System (Abolition) Act, 1976 (19 of 1976);

(b) "District Vigilance Committee: means a Vigilance Committee constituted for a district under sub-section (1) of Sec. 13;

(c) "section" means a section of the act;

(d) "Sub-divisional Vigilance Committee" means a Vigilance Committee constituted for a sub-division under sub-section (1) of Sec. 13.

3. Term of office, and vacation of seat members of District Vigilance Committees.-(1) Every member of a District Vigilance Committee, nominated under Cls. (b), (c), (d) and (e) of sub-section (2) of Sec. 13 shall hold office for a period of two years from the date on which his nomination is notified in the official Gazette and shall, on the expiry of the said period, continue to hold office until his successor is nominated and shall also be eligible for re-nomination.

(2) Every member referred to in sub-rule (1), -

(a) may, by giving notice in writing of not less than thirty days to authority which nominated him, resign his office and, on such resignation being accepted or on the expiry of the notice period of 30 days, whichever is earlier, shall be deemed to have vacated his office.

(b) shall be deemed to have vacated his office,-

(I) if he fails to attend three consecutive meetings of the District Vigilance Committee without obtaining leave of the Chairman of such absence:

Provided that the authority, which nominated him, may, if he is satisfied that such member was prevented by sufficient cause from attending the three consecutive meetings of the Committee restore him to membership;

(ii) if he becomes subject to any of the following disqualifications, namely:

(1) is adjudged insolvent;

(2) is declared to be of unsound mind by a competent court;

(3) is convicted of an offence which, in the opinion of the authority which nominated him, involves moral turpitude;

(c) may be removed from office, if the authority, which nominated such member is of the opinion that such member has ceased to represent the interest to represent which he was nominated:

Provided that a member shall not be removed from office under this clause unless a reasonable opportunity is given to him for showing cause against such removal.

(3) A member, nominated to fill a casual vacancy shall gold office for the unexpired portion of the term of his predecessor.

4. Term of office, and vacation of seat of members of Sub-divisional Vigilance Committees.-(1) Every member of a Sub-divisional Vigilance Committee, nominated under Cls. (b), (c), (d) and (e) of sub-section (2) of Sec. 13 shall hold office for a period of two years from the date on which his nomination is notified in the official gazette and shall, on the expiry of the said period, continue to hold office until his successor is nominated and shall also be eligible for re-nomination.

(2) Every member referred to in sub-rule (1), -

(a) may, by giving notice in writing of not less than thirty days to authority which nominated him, resign his office and, on such resignation being accepted or on the expiry of the notice period of 30 days, whichever is earlier, shall be deemed to have vacated his office.

(b) shall be deemed to have vacated his office,-

(i) if he fails to attend three consecutive meetings of the Sub-divisional Vigilance Committee without obtaining leave of the Chairman of such absence:

Provided that the authority, which nominated him, may, if he is satisfied that such member was prevented by sufficient cause from attending the three consecutive meetings of the Committee restore him to membership;

(ii) if he becomes subject to any of the following disqualifications, namely:

(1) is adjudged insolvent;

(2) is declared to be of unsound mind by a competent court;

(3) is convicted of an offence which, in the opinion of the authority which nominated him, involves moral turpitude;

(c) may be removed from office, if the authority, which nominated such member is of the opinion that such member has ceased to represent the interest to represent which he was nominated:

Provided that a member shall not be removed from office under this clause unless a reasonable opportunity is given to him for showing cause against such removal.

(3) A member, nominated to fill a casual vacancy shall gold office for the unexpired portion of the term of his predecessor.

5. Prescribed authority under sub-section (6) of Sec.6.-An application under sub-section (6) of Sec. 6 for restoration of possession of any property referred to in sub-section (4) or sub-section (5) of that section shall be made to the Executive Magistrate, on whom the powers of a Judicial Magistrate of the first class or of the second class have been conferred under sub-section (1) of Sec. 21, and within the local limits of whose jurisdiction the said property is, or the applicant has reason to believe is, situated at the time of making the application:

Provided that where there are two Executive Magistrates, on one of whom the powers of a Judicial Magistrate of the first class and on the other the powers of a Judicial Magistrate of the second class have been conferred under sub-section (1) of Sec. 21 having jurisdiction to entertain the application for restoration of possession of property referred to in sub-rule (1), the application shall be made to the Executive Magistrate on whom the powers of a Judicial Magistrate of the second class have been conferred.

6. Time within which an application under sub-section (6) is to be made.-

An application under sub-section (6) of Sec. 6 for restoration of possession of any property referred to in sub-section (4) or sub-section (5) of that section shall be made within a period of ninety days from the date on which these rules come into force.

7. Records to be maintained by District Vigilance Committees to ensure the implementation of the provisions of the act and rules.-In order to ensure the implementation of the act and rules, every District Vigilance Committee shall maintain the following registers in respect of freed-bonded labourer with the local limits of its jurisdiction, namely:

(a) a register containing the name and address of free bonded labourer;

(b) a register containing the statistics relating to the vacation, occupation, and income of every freed-bonded labourer;

(c) a register containing the details of the benefits which the freed-bonded labourers are receiving, including benefits in the form of land, inputs for agriculture, training in handicrafts and allied occupations, loans at differential rates, interest of employment in urban or non-urban areas;

(d) a register containing details of cases under sub-section (6) of Sec. 6, sub-section (2) of Sec. 8, sub-section (2) of Secs. 9, 16, 17, 18, 19, and 20.

The Children (Pedging of Labour) Act, 1933

An act to prohibit the pledging of labour of children

Whereas it is expedient to prohibit the making of agreements to pledge the labour of children and the employment of children whose labour has been pledged;

It is hereby enacted as follows:

1. Short title, extent and commencement.-(1) This act may be called the Children (Pledging of Labour) Act, 1933.

(2) It extends to the whole of India

(3) This section and Secs. 2 and 3 shall come into force at once, and the remaining sections of this act shall come into force on the first day of July, 1933.

2. Definitions.- In this act, unless there is anything repugnant in the subject or context,-

"an agreement to pledge the labour of a child" means in agreement, written or oral, express or implied, whereby the parent or guardian of a child, in return for any payment or benefit received by him, undertakes to cause or allow the services of the child to be utilized by him, undertakes to cause or allow the services of the child to be utilized in any employment:

Provided that an agreement made without detriment to a child , and not made in consideration of any benefit other than reasonable wages to be paid for the child's services, and terminable at not more than a week's notice, is not an agreement within the meaning of this definition;

"child" means a person who is under the age of fifteen years; and "guardian" includes any person having legal custody of or control over a child.

3. Agreement contrary to the act to be void.-An agreement to pledge the labour of a child shall be void.

4. Penalty for parent or guardian making agreement to pledge the labour of a child.-Whoever, being the parent or guardian of a child, makes an agreement to pledge the labour of that child, shall be punished with fine which may extend to fifty rupees.

5. Penalty for making with a parent or guardian agreement to pledge the labour of a child.-Whoever makes with the parent or guardian of a child shall be punished with fine which may extend to two hundred rupees.

6. Penalty for employing a child whose labour has been pledged.-Whoever, knowing or having reason to believe that an agreement has been made to pledge the labour of a child, in furtherance of such agreement employs such child, or permits such child to be employed in any premises or place under his control, shall be punishable with fine which may extend to two hundred rupees.

The Child Labour (Prohibition and Regulation) Act, 1986
Statement of Objects and Reasons

There are a number of acts which prohibit the employment of children below 14 years and 15 years in certain specified employments. However, there is no procedure laid down in any law for deciding in which employments, occupations or processes the employment of children should be banned. There is also no law to regulate the working conditions of children in most of the employments where they are not prohibited from working and are working under exploitative conditions.

2. This Bill intends to-

(i) ban the employment of children, i.e., those who have not completed their fourteenth year, in specified occupations and processes;

(ii) lay down a procedure to decide modifications to the Schedule of banned occupations or processes;

(iii) regulate the conditions of work of children in employments where they are not prohibited from working;

(iv) lay down enhanced penalties for employment of children in violation of the provisions of this act, and other acts which forbid the employment of children;

(v) to obtain uniformity in the definition of "child" in the related laws.

3. The bill seeks to achieve the above objects.

An act to prohibit the engagement of children in certain employments and to regulate the conditions of work of children in certain other employments.

Be it enacted by Parliament in the Thirty-seventh year of the Republic of India as follows:

PART I
PRELIMINARY

1. Short title, extent and commencement.-(1) The act may be called the Child Labour (Prohibition and Regulation) Act, 1986.

(2) It extends to the whole of India.

(3) The provisions of this act, other than part III, shall come into force at once, and part III shall come into force on such date as the Central Government may, by notification in the Official Gazette, appoint, and different dates may be appointed for different states and for different classes of establishments.

2. Definitions.- In this act, unless the context otherwise requires.

(i) "appropriate Government" means, in relation to an establishment under the control of the Central Government or a railway administration or a major port or a mine or oil field, the Central Government, and in all other cases, the State Government;

(ii) "child" means a person who has not completed his fourteenth year of age;

(iii) "day" means a period of twenty-four hours beginning at mid-night;

(iv) "establishment" includes a shop, commercial establishment, workshop, farm, residential hotel, restaurant, eating house, theatre or other place of amusement or public entertainment;

(v) "family" in relation to an occupier, means the individual, the wife or husband, as the case may be, of such individual, and their children, brother or sister of such individual;

(vi) "occupier", in relation to an establishment or a workshop, means the person who has the ultimate control over the affairs of the establishment or workshop;

(vii) "port authority" means any authority administering a port;

(viii) "prescribed" means prescribed by rules made under Section 18;

(ix) "week" means a period of seven days beginning at mid-night on Saturday night or such other night as may be approved in writing for a particular area by the inspector;

(x) "workshop" means any premises (including the precincts thereof) wherein any industrial process is carried on, but does not include any premises to which the provisions of section 67 of the Factories Act, 1946, for the time being, apply.

PART II

PROHIBITION OF EMPLOYMENT OF CHILDREN IN CERTAIN OCCUPATIONS AND PROCESSES

3. Prohibition of employment of children in certain occupations and processes.-No child shall be employed or permitted to work in any of the occupations set forth in Part A of the Schedule or in any workshop wherein any of the processes set forth in Part B of the Schedule is carried on:

Provided that nothing in this section shall apply to any workshop wherein any process is carried on by the occupier with the aid ofhis family or to any school established by, or receiving assistance or recognition from, Government.

4. Power to amend the Schedule.-The Central Government after giving, by notification in the Official Gazette, not less than three months notice of its intention so to do, may, be like notification, add any occupation or process to the Schedule and thereupon the Schedule shall be deemed to have been amended accordingly.

5. Child Labour Technical Advisory Committee.-(1) The Central Government may, by notification in the Official Gazette, constitute an advisory committee to be called the "Child Labour Technical Advisory Committee" (hereafter in this section referred to as the Committee) to advise the Central Government for the purpose of addition of occupations and processes to the Schedule.

(2) The Committee shall consist of a Chairman and such other members not exceeding ten, as may be appointed by the Central Government.

(3) The Committee shall meet as often as it may consider necessary and shall have power to regulate its own procedure.

(4) The Committee may, if it deems necessary so to do, constitute one or more sub-committees, and may appoint any such sub-committee, whether generally or for the consideration of any particular matter, any person who is not a member of the Committee.

(5) The term of office of, the manner of filing casual vacancies in the office of, and the allowances, if any, payable to, the Chairman and other members of the Committee, and the conditions and restrictions subject to which the Committee may appoint any person who is not a member of the Committee as a member of any of its sub-committees shall be such as may be prescribed.

PART III
REGULATION OF CONDITIONS OF WORK OF CHILDREN

6. Application of Part.-The provisions of this Part shall apply to an establishment or a class of establishments in which none of the occupations or processes referred to in section 3 is carried on.

7. Hours and period of work.-(1) No child shall be required or permitted to work in any establishment in excess of such number of hours as may be prescribed for such establishment or class of establishments.

(2) The period of work on each day shall be so fixed that no period shall exceed three hours and that no child shall work for more than three hours before he has had an interval for rest for at least one hour.

(3) The period of work of a child shall be so arranged that inclusive of his interval for rest, under sub-section (2), it shall not be spread over more than six hours, including the time spent in waiting for work on any day.

(4) No child shall be permitted or required to work between 7 p.m. and 8 a.m.

(5) No child shall be required or permitted to work overtime.

8. Weekly holidays.-Every child employed in an establishment shall be allowed in each week, a holiday of one whole day, which day shall be specified by the occupier in a notice permanently exhibited in a conspicuous place in the establishment and the day so specified shall not be altered by the occupier more than once in three months.

9. Notice to Inspector.-(1) Every occupier in relation to an establishment in which a child was employed or permitted to work immediately before the date of commencement of this act in relation to such establishment shall, within a period of thirty days from such commencement, send to the Inspector within whose local limits the establishment is situated, a written notice containing the following particulars, namely:-

(a) the name and situation of the establishment;

(b) the name of the person in actual management of the establishment;

(c) the address to which communications relating to the establishment should be sent; and

(d) the nature of the occupation or process carried on in the establishment.

(2) Every occupier, in relation to an establishment, who employs, or permits to work, any child after the date of commencement of this act in relation t such establishment, shall, within a period of thirty days from the date of such employment, send to the Inspector within whose local limits the establishment is situated, a written notice containing the particulars as are mentioned in sub-section (1).

Explanation.-For the purposes of sub-sections (1) and (2), "date of commencement of this act, in relation to an establishment" means the date of bringing into force of this act in relation to such establishment.

(3) Nothing in sections 7, 8 and 9 shall apply to any establishment wherein any process is carried on by the occupier with the aid of his family or to any school established by, or receiving assistance or recognition from, Government.

10. Disputes as to age.-If any question arises between an Inspector and an occupier as to the age of any child who is employed or is permitted to work byhim in an establishment, the question shall, in the absence of a certificate as to the age of such child granted by the prescribed medical authority, be referred by the inspector for decision to the prescribed medical authority.

11. Maintenance of register.-There shall be maintained by every occupier in respect of children employed or permitted to work in any establishment, a register to be available for inspection by an Inspector at all times during working hours or when work is being carried on in any such establishment, showing-

(a) the name and date of birth of every child so employed or permitted to work;

(b) hours and periods of work of any such child and the intervals of rest to which he is entitled;

(c) the nature of work of any such child; and

(d) such other particulars as may be prescribed.

12. Display of notice containing abstracts of sections 3 and 14.-Every railway administration, every port authority and every occupier shall cause to be displayed in a conspicuous and accessible place at every station on its railway or within the limits of a port or at the place of work, as the case may be, a notice in the local language and in the English language containing an abstract of sections 3 and 14.

13. Health and safety.-(1) The appropriate Government may, by notification in the Official Gazette, make rules for the health and safety of the children employed or permitted to work in any establishment or class of establishments.

(2) Without prejudice to the generality of the foregoing provisions, the said rules may provide for all or any of the following matters, namely:-

(a) cleanliness in the place of work and its freedom from nuisance;

(b) disposal of wastes and effluents;

(c) ventilation and temperature;

(e) artificial humidification;

(f) lighting;

(g) drinking water;

(h) latrine and urinals;

(i) spittoons;

(j) fencing of machinery;

(k) work at or near machinery in motion;

(l) employment of children on dangerous machines;

(m) instructions, training and supervision in relation to employment of children on dangerous machines;

(n) device for cutting off power;

(o) self-acting machines;

(p) easing of new machinery;
(q) floor, stairs and means of access;
(r) pits, sumps, openings in floors, etc.;
(s) excessive weights;
(t) protection of eyes;
(u) explosive or inflammable dust, gas, etc.;
(v) precautions in case of fire;
(w) maintenance of buildings; and
(x) safety of buildings; and machinery.

PART IV

MISCELLANEOUS

14. Penalties.-(1) Whoever employs any child or permits any child to work in contravention of the provisions of section 3 shall be punishable with imprisonment for a term which shall not be less than three months but which may extend to one year or with fine which shall not be less than ten thousand rupees but which may extend to twenty thousand rupees or with both.

(2) Whoever, having been convicted of an offence under section 3, commits a like offence, afterwards, he shall be punishable with imprisonment for a term which shall not be less than six months but which may extend to two years.

(3) Whoever-

(a) fails to give notice as required by section 9; or

(b) fails to maintain a register as required by section 11 or makes any false entry in any such register; or

(c) fails to display a notice containing an abstract of section 3 and this section as required by section 12; or

(d) fails to comply with or contravenes any other provisions of this act or the rules made there under, shall be punishable with simple imprisonment which may extend to one month or with fine which may extend to ten thousand rupees or with both.

15. Modified application of certain laws in relation to penalties.-(1) Where any person is found guilty and convicted of contravention of any of the provisions mentioned in sub-section (2), he shall be liable to penalties as providedin sub-sections (1) and (2) of section 14 of this act and not under the acts in which these provisions are contained.

(2) The provisions referred to in sub-section (1) are the provisions mentioned below:-

(a) section 67 of the Factories Act, 1948 (63 of 1948);

(b) section 40 of the Mines Act, 1952 (35 of 1952);

(c) section 109 of the Merchant Shipping Act, 1958 (44 of 1958); and

(d) section 21 of the Motor Transport Workers Act, 1961 (27 of 1961).

16. Procedure relating to offences.-(1) Any person, police officer or Inspector may file a complaint of the commission of an offence under this act in any court of competent jurisdiction.

(2) Every certificate of as to the age of a child which has been granted by a prescribed medical authority shall, for the purposes of this act, be conclusive evidence as to the age of the child to whom it relates.

(3) No court inferior to that of a Metropolitan Magistrate or a Magistrate of the first class shall try any offence under this act.

17. Appointment of Inspectors.-The appropriate Government may appoint Inspectors for the purposes of securing compliance with the provisions of this act and any Inspector so appointed shall be deemed to be a public servant within the meaning of the Indian Penal Code (45 of 1860).

18. Power to make rules-(1) The appropriate Government may, by notification in the Official Gazette and subject to the condition of previous publication, make rules for carrying into effect the provisions of The act.

(2) In particular and without prejudice to the generality of the foregoing power, such rules may provide for all or any of the following matters, namely:-

(a) the term of office of, the manner of filing casual vacancies of, and the allowances payable to, the Chairman and member of the Child Labour Technical Advisory Committee and the conditions and restrictions subject to which a non-member may be appointed to a sub-committee under sub-section (5) of section 5;

(b) number of hours for which a child may be required or permitted to work under sub-section (1) of section 7;

(c) Grant of certificates of age in respect of young persons in employment or seeking employment, the medical authorities which may issue such certificate, the form of such certificate, thecharges which may be thereunder and the manner in which such certificate may be issued:

Provided that no charge shall be made for the issue of any such certificate if the application is accompanied by evidence of age deemed satisfactory by the authority concerned;

(d) the other particulars which a register maintained under section 11 should contain.

19. Rules and notifications to be laid before Parliament or State legislature.-(1) Every rule made under this act by the Central Government and every notification issued under section 4, shall be laid, as soon as may be after it is made or issued, before each House of Parliament, while it is in session for a total period of thirty days which may be comprised in one session or in two or more successive sessions, and if, before the expiry of the session immediately following the session or the successive sessions aforesaid, both Houses agree that the rule or notification should not be made or issued, the rule or notification shall thereafter have effect only in such modified form or be of no effect, as the case may be; so, however, that any such modification or annulment shall be without prejudice to the validity of anything previously done under that rule or notification.

(2) Every rule made by a State Government under this act shall be laid as soon as may be after it is made, before the legislature of that State.

20. Certain other provisions of law not barred.-Subject to the provisions contained in section 15, the provisions of this act and the rules made thereunder shall be in addition to, and not in derogation of, the provisions of the Factories Act, 1948 (63 of 1948), the Plantations Labour Act, 1951 (69 of 1951), and the Mines Act, 1952 (35 of 1952).

21. Power to remove difficulties.-(1) If any difficulty arises in giving effect to the provisions of this act, the Central Government may, by order published in the Official Gazette, make such provisions not inconsistent with the provisions of this act as appear to it to be necessary or expedient for removal of the difficulty:

Provided that no such order shall be made after the expiry of a period of three years from the date on which this act receives the assent of the President.

(2) Every order made under this section shall, as soon as may be after it is made, be laid before the Houses of Parliament.

22. Repeal and savings.-The Employment of Children, Act, 1938 (26 of 1938) is hereby repealed.

(2) Notwithstanding such repeal, anything done or any action taken or purported to have been done or taken under the act so repealed shall, in so far as it is not inconsistent with the provisions of this act, be deemed to have been done or taken under the corresponding provisions of this act.

Also a number of specific legislation's have been enacted prescribing minimum age and working conditions and to regulate hours of work. More over the children have the rights to enjoy all the fundamental rights, which are guaranteed to the citizens of India under Articles 15,16,19 and 29 of the constitution. Out of all these article only the article 24 is directly related to the child labour problem in India. More unfortunate that this article does not spell out an absolute ban to the employment of children below 14 years of age. Next this article does not say anything about complete prohibition of employment of children altogether. Just it talks about ban of children employed in hazardous sectors. But till today Government could not list out the different sectors which comes under hazardous one.

Interpreting Constitutional Rights for Children.

The Supreme Court has held that when it comes to uphold or guaranteeing the fundamental rights that rights are not be seen in isolation but as a bundle of rights to fulfil the mandate outlined in the Preamble of our Constitution. The Supreme Court time and again has held that paramount among rights is the right to life and that right to life includes the right to livelihood and the right to live in dignity and security. Denial of survival and development, freedom of expression causing harm of neglect and exploitation of children in any form is a violation of the right to live with dignity and the right of protection against exploitation. Employment of children thus violates the essence of Article 21.

The Constitution expressly prohibits employment of children below fourteen years. Children below 14 years as per Article 24 cannot be employed in any factory or mine or any other hazardous works. The Constitution of India has not attempted to outline what is hazardous and what is non-hazardous. What is hazardous for an able bodied adult cannot be the barometer for deciding what is hazardous for the child. It is for this reason that Article 24 did not stop with factories and mines but said "or engaged in any other hazardous employment." According to the Constitution of India therefore, all forms of work by children below the age of 14 years is hazardous. This is now supplemented by the 93rd Constitutional Amendment Act that guarantees free and compulsory education as a fundamental right for all children between 6 to 14 years of the country. Added to this for the first time the constitution by an (amendment to articles 45) of the directive principle recognizes the needed to provide for early childhood care and education for all children 0-6 years. Though many of the other Articles in the constitution related to children special rights an abolition of child labour are part of the Directive Principles, they are fundamental in the governance of our country and as required by Article 37 it is the duty of all the organizations of the State to keep the same in mind when called upon to decide maters of grate public importance. Together with this is a well development of corpus of jurisprudence wherein courts have amplifies the essence of fundamental rights by breathing into them the humanism from the directive principles.

Since children have a fundamental right under Article 45 to have basic education and to be brought up in a healthy manner if the child is denied primary elementary education because of the need to work for survival for social and familial it is a hazard. Article 45 and the Supreme Court judgement clearly explains that every child is not merely expected, but is under a duty, to be educated. Similarly any work under taken by a child that results in exploitation and material abandonment is a hazard. The industrial definition of hazardous in the Factories Act and other labour laws cannot be the basis of deciding what is hazardous for a child. There is no possibility of exploitation not being hazardous and it is against this hazard which the constitution speaks of in Article 24 and related articles. Article 24 must be read and understood along with Article 14, 15 (3), 21, 23, 45, 39 (e) and 39 (f) and the 93rd Constitutional Amendment.

Non-discrimination (among children) is one of the most important guarantees provided in Article 14, wherein the state is bound not to deny to any person equality before the law or equal protection of laws. Since millions of children are being discriminated and exploited, the Constitution makers have revealed Article 14 with Article 24 (Prohibiting Employment) and Article 15 (3), where the state is empowered to make any special law for children. Central to these articles is the article 21 on fundamental rights whereby no person (read also children) shall be deprived of his life or personal liberty. And any form of employment of children amounts to forced labour or bonded labour and bonded labour is a violation of Article 21 and Article 23.

The constitution contains other provisions, guaranteeing that a child must be given an opportunity and facility to be brought up in a healthy manner. Article 39 (e) mandates that the tender age of children is not abused and those citizens are not forced by economic necessity to enter avocations unsuited to their age or strength. Article 39 (f) ensure childhood and all-round development of children. It states that "Children are given opportunities and facilities to develop in a healthy manner and in conditions of freedom and dignity and that childhood and youth are protected against exploitation and against moral and material abondment". Thus, several Articles must be read and understood along with Article have 14. 15(3), 21, 23, 24, 39 (e) and 45 .

Article 41 read with Article 21 and 47 mean that the state and private sector must only employ adults. Article 47 enjoins upon the state to "regard" the raising of the level of nutrition and standard of living of its people and the improvement of public health as among its primary duties. These two articles are very essential for fulfilling the Constitutional mandate of right to life with dignity, security and in freedom. Strictly speaking according to Article 41 means that every adult should be guaranteed the right of work.

Thus Article 41 and 47 is also ment to strengthen Article 24, 25, 45, 39(e), 39(f). If all adults have the right to work 80 million or more child labourers would be in schools and not in the workplace. For the full realization of the holistic development of the child it is important to also guarantee Article 39 (a) and 39 (b) which speaks of the right to adequate means of livelihood and that the ownership and control of the material resources of the community are so distributed as a best to subsets the common good. This is crucial for equality, non-discrimination and the right to life. All these provisions were meant very clearly to guarantee and egalitarian and just social order, which would in turn be the basis of the development of children in a holistic manner. Further a large percentage of child labourers are form SC, ST, OBC communities and minorities. Article 46 seeks the promotion of educational and economic interests of SC, ST and weaker sections and their protection form all forms of exploitation. Thus Article 46 read with all the above provisions means that children form these oppressed communities should not be in employment but be guaranteed education, health care, nutrition, adequate shelter and protection form economic exploitation.

Further article 51 (A) (a) of the Indian Constitution makes it the duty of every citizen of India to abide by the Constitution and respect its deals and institutions. Article 13 (2) codifies that the State shall not make any laws, which take always or abridge the fundamental rights guaranteed by the Constitution. It clarifies that "law" includes among other things any notification having the force of law. Reading the above guarantees of the Constitution together we get a complete picture of the duties of the State towards India's children. Any employment of children defeats the notion of the child's holistic development articulated in the constitution and hence is unconstitutional. Nevertheless, nemours legislation, especially and child labour ACT 1986, Factories Act 1946, The beedi and Cigar Workers (condition of employment) Act 1966, State law for handloom and powerloom workers. The shops and commercial establishment Act 1961 etc. Are in violation of Article 14,21,23 and 24 of the constitution. This legislation removes the protection given by these Articles to children against employment in all hazardous work and against exploitation and injustice by not prescribing a minimum age and prohibit employment of children only in certified occupation an process.

Article 51(C) enjpoins th state to transfer rpect fro internatioal law and trety oblibgations.The UN convetion on the rights of the child goes much further than the constipation in defining a child as anyone upto the age of 18 an categorically in 1992.Having subscribed to its objectives an purposes and its principle of the best interests of the child as primary, India nevertheless expressed a reservation. The reservation placed was on "prescribing minimum wages for each and every area of employment" which impinge on other rights which were unconditionally accepted such as the right to education and right to an adequate standard of living. India must endorse the convention in its entirety The child labour(Protection and Regulation)Act 1986 must be radically altered to fulfill the constitutional obligation and the commitments guaranteed in the Unconventional on the Rights of the Child and the conventions of the ILO ratified by India.

Indian Constitution both in the directive principle of state polices and in the fundamental rights has laid down that state is obligated to frame polices for the welfare of her citizens including the children. A child must be given enough scope to come up in healthy environment in the interest of the nation and dignity and no citizen will be forced by economic necessity to enter avocation unsuitable to their age or strength (Shandilya and Khan). Since child hood plays an important role in shaping the future of that child and there by the development of the concerned country there should be enough provisions in all the constitutional meaures to protect children from various possible exploitations.

Child Labour and Welfare Legislation

Before going in to the welfare legislation's of the government, it is better to analyse the different kind of questions that arises in our mind. Why is the Indian state unable or unwilling to deal with the high and increasing illiteracy, low school enrollment, high drop out rate and rampant child labour? Between official rhetoric and practice, there is a wide gap. Before we solve the puzzle why the Indian Government is unable to do what it says it wants to do, let us see what it has done for the abolition of child labour since the beginning period of colonisum (Reddy, 2001).

In every society, old tradition customary norms and values create difficulty in adopting new changes for development and growth of its members. So, reformation in relating is to change its old system and to meet the needs for their welfare and development. Long ago, child labour was a not a social problem, but with the change in social understanding, child labour needed legislative protection against their exploitations and for their proper growth and development. (Singh,1999).

In India, it is due to the attempts to provide legal protection for children, that the present structure of labour legislation was developed. In 1875 colonial government had appointed a committee to suggest the necessity of legislation. Extended first to women workers, labour legislation now covers all workers and is based on the conviction that it is one of the principal duties of the state to guard and promote the well being of her citizens.

The Factories Act 1881

The Factories Act of India was passed in 1881. It defined a child as a person below the age of 12 years and prohibited the employment of children below the age of 7 years. The act of 1891 raised the minimum age of employment of children from 9 years to 14 and maximum of two-day holiday. The minimum age of employment was raised to 12 years in 1905.

The Children (Pledging of Labour) Act, 1923

This act defines child means a person who is under the age of 15 years. This act prohibits to go in for an agreement to pledge the labour of children and the employment of children whose labour has been pledged.

The Minimum Wage Act-1948

This act makes provision in fixing minimum rates of wages in certain employment which have been specified by appropriate government in the Schedule of the Act.

Employment of Children Act –1938

It regulates the admission of children to certain industrial employments. No child who has not completed his fifteenth year shall be employed or permitted to work in any occupation connected with the transport of passengers, goods or mails by a Railway or connected with a Port authority within the limits of any port, No child who has completed his fifteenth year but has not completed his eighteenth year may be employed on any day, unless the periods of work are so fixed as to allow an interval of rest for at least 12 consecutive hours, seven of which must fall between 10 p.m. and 7 a.m.

The Indian Factories Act-1948

This Act defines an adolescent as a person who has completed his eighteenth year and a child as a person who has not completed his fifteenth year. No person who has not completed his fourteenth year may be allowed to work on any factory. The hours of work of children should be limited to 4 $^{1/2}$ hours per day and must be spread over on shift only of not more than 5 hours' duration. A child may not work in any factory on any day on which he has already been working in another factory. The employer has to maintain a register of child workers and the periods of work have to be notified.

The Plantation Labour Act-1952

This Act applies to all tea, coffee, rubber and cinchona plantations. Children under 12 years of age shall not work in any plantation. No child worker shall be employed except between the hours 6 a.m. and 7 p.m. with due permission of the State government. No child or adolescent may work in a plantation the employer is in possession of a certificate of fitness given certifying surgeon and the worker himself carries a token giving to such certificate.

The Mines Act-1952

Under this Act, no child under 15 years of age may be employed in mines. No child may be allowed to be present underground excavation where mining operations are carried out. He however, be given half an hour's rest after every 4 1/2 hours work An adolescent may be employed in any operation above ground provided that he shall not be required to work more than fixed hours.

The Merchant Shipping Acy-1958

This act prohibits employment of children under 15 years in a ship or sea related activities. This act is not of much impordence today

The Motor Transport Workers Act-1961

This act prohibits employment of persons less than 14 years of age in any capacity in the motor transport undertaking. It covers every motor transport undertakings across the county.

The Apprentices Act-1961

This act lays down that a person shall not be qualified for being engaged as an apprentice to undergo apprenticeship training in any recognized trade unless he is not less then 14 years of age.

The Beedi and Cigar Workers Act-1966

This act prohibits the employment of children below 14 years of age in all industrial premises where in any manufacturing process connected with making of beedi and cigarette.

Shop and Establishment Act.-1948

This act prohibit the employment of children in shops, commercial establishments, restaurants, hotels etc The age of children varies from 12 to 15 years.

In 1958 Central Board for Worker's Education and Child Labour was started. It was entrusted with the effective implementation of the worker's education scheme in India with a view to equip all sections of workers for the participation in social and economic developments of the country. Further this center conducts seminars, workshops, symposiums and training's for all workers, child labourers and human right workers on child labour issues. It works as a resource center on child labour. It is a nation –wide network in all sectors of employment.

Laws and acts enacted and welfare programmes implemented for the sake of child labourer's revealed that the Governament is go on keep doing its best to avoid children from various exploitations. But, the ground situation is really very pathetic. In 1979 the central Governament constituted *Gurupadaswamy* Committee on child labour. Report has emphasized on the distinction between child labour and the exploitation of child labour because they are of different orders. Most interesting fact is that the committee never mentioned about to impose ban on the child labour using any new laws or acts. Instead, this committee has stressed to improve the working condition and protection must be given to the child labours working both in hazardous and non-hazardous sectors.

Further committee has expressed the view that the state should give attention for rectification amelioration and regulation through specific laws and act's. It has felt that the existing laws relating to prohibitions and regulation of employment of children should be consolidated into a simple comprehensive one.

In 1974 The National Policy for Children Resolution was adopted. It was the main avenue to frame new programmes and polices for the betterment of children. This resolution stressed on the free and compulsory education, Nutrition programmes to children, alternative courses for whom formal education is not possible and attention against various exploitation's.

In 1979, Child Labour Cell was set up as an integral part in the Department of Labour. The main function of this cell is responsible for the formulation, coordination and effective implementation of various programmes for the welfare of child labourers. This cell has been empowered with to evaluate the projects and recommend release fund to various NGOs working against child labour across the country.

In 1981 central Government of India constituted Child Labour Advisory Board. The main intention was to review the existing laws and acts, evaluation of the field projects and recommend to the governament and industries where there must be progressive elimination of child labour. The advisory board was reconstituted in 1994 by taking representatives from link ministries, MPs NGOs and representatives from trade unions coming under chairmanship of Union Labour Minster.

In 1986, Governament of India implemented a comprehensive Act, Child Labour (Prohibition and Regulation) Act was implemented which was applicable o entire India. This act draws a clear line between hazardous and non-hazardous sectors. The headline of this law is the total prohibition of employment of children below 14 years of age that aims at to abolish the problem within 10 years after its commencement. This is the first comprehensive

Act that defined the term child labour more precisely for the first time. More over, this act does empower anybody to file a complaint against an offender in any court of competent authority. Further this act empowered the government to revise any existing laws and acts. According to the provision made in this act Government of India set up *Child Labour Technical Advisory Committee* for the purpose of addition of occupations and process to the schedule in 1989.

In 1987, Government adopted the National Child Labour Policy (NCLP) under which several legislative steps have been taken to curb the practice and several development schemes initiated to rehabilitate the child labour. Under the protected action plan, 13 projects are now operating in 79 districts across the India. Adequate non-formal education, vocational training, supplementary nutrition, stipend and health care are also provided to the child labourers.

In 1988, Ministry of Labour implemented National Child Labour Projects (NCLPS), a scheme for the effective rehabilitation of child labour. The major activities undertaken under the NCLP are the establishment of special schools which provide a package of welfare measures, including technical and non-formal education to present and ex-child laboures. Besides the NCLP, the child labour action and support programme (CLASP) with the aid of Government of Germany and an action programme under the International Programme for Elimination Child Labour with the assistance from ILO is going on since 1991. The allocation of funds since 1992, for IPEC programme in India stands at 4.15 million US$ supporting 100 projects in 15 states benefiting 81,000 children. In 1990, a separate child labour cell was established at National Labour Institute. The main function of the cell is publication of related to the child labour issue, documentation, evaluation of government and NGO's field project from time to time and conducting action research projects (Khan, 1991).

In India, International Programme on the Elimination of Child Labour was established in 1992 with an objective to enhance the capability of ILO constituents and NGO's to design, implement and evaluate programmes to create awareness and social mobilization for securing child labour elimination. Besides, IPEC also undertakes district support programmes, sensitizes trade unions and their workers against employment of child labour, conducts research on child labour, and organizes training for labour inspectors and NGO's personnel's on various aspects of child labour. (Patnaik and Bedi, 2003).

The National Authority for Elimination of Child Labour was constituted on 1994. The vital role of this authority is required to implement and monitor the progress of implementation of programmes, projects and schemes for the elimination of child labour, especially in hazardous industries. It ensures convergence of services for the benefit of child labour. The purpose of securing convergence of service is to provide education, health and other inputs to the children forced to leave their studies from schools in a cost-effective manner by pooling the resources of various ministries Further it co-ordinate among different projects running by the various ministries. Apart from this institutional framework Ministry of Labour has implemented many programmes with the collabouration of labour departments of respective states.

The Central Governament in 1995 set-up National Resource Centre on Child labour (NRCCL) involving many NGOs. This centre is intended to activate and supplement all programmes taken up by the ILO under its International Programme on Elimination of child labour and by other foreign agencies. Besides, NRCCL has been entrusted with the task of assisting central and social groups working in the field of child labour. In 1990, one of the task force recommended the Government to set up child labour commission, that all the laws pertaining to child labour be integrated to form an unified child labour code. This task force has insisted the Government to produce a white paper on the present condition of the child labour across the country.

In 1996 few noted NGOs in India, working against child labour decided to form South Asian Coalition Child Servitude (SACCS) vigilance committee on child labour to monitor nation wide implementation of Supreme Court's judgement banning on child labour in all hazardous and non hazardous industries. SACCs emphasized, "child labour is not a necessary consequence of poverty. Rather it is rampant menace of child labour that perpetuates poverty." It is a known factor that poverty is the heart and sole of this problem. The Government of Indian has implemented many polices and programmes to curb poverty especially in urban areas. Despite of all these efforts poverty is still more prevalent among the people just because, these programmes have been framed without involving any poor people.

- Urban Basic service for the poor Programme (UBSPP)
- Prime Minister's Integrated Urban Poverty Eradication Programme (PMIUPEP)
- Self-employment to the Educated Urban youth Programme (SEEYP)
- Financial Assistance for Constructing houses.(FACH)
- Emphasis on vocational education
- Sampoorna Nager rozgar Yojana (PMGY)
- The Millennium development goals-2015.

On 7th April 2003 there was a statement in the Lok Sabha that the "Minimum Wages act 1948 (Revised) provides for fixation of different rates of minimum rate of minimum wages for adults, adolescents, children and apprentices. Since this tends to encourage engagement of child labour, the government is exploring deletion of the relevant section of the Act. In the proposed Integrated Draft Law on Wages based on the recommendations of the Second National Commission on Labour, there is no mention of different rates of minimum wages for children.

Currently the Ministry of Labour Government of India in collabouration with ILO has issued guide lines to all the states that all concerned labour inspectors so notified should be made responsible for securing compliance of the directions of the Supreme Court in the matter of inspecting the work-place for identification of the child labour, collection of Rs. 20,000 per child from the employer and depositing this amount in the Child Labour Rehabilitation-cum-Welfare Fund. Interest amount will goes to the released child family.

A Child Labour Rehabilitation-cum-Welfare Fund should be immediately set up at the district level under the overall control of the Collector/District Magistrate. The State Government may consider constituting an Advisory Board which could be a compact body under the chairmanship of the collector to manage the affairs of the fund including those relating to investment of the fund money with the nationalized banks or other public bodies and disbursement of the corpus income among the families of the children withdrawn from hazardous occupations.

The State government should take necessary steps for conducting survey relating to children working in hazardous occupations as also the details of their family members and in consultation with the concerned departments of the State Government, management of the public sector undertakings and management of the establishments where the children are working, should identify manual jobs which could be offered to the adult members of the family concerned.

As far as possible, the employment to the adult members of the family would be given in an establishment which is nearest to the place of residence of the family. In case it is not possible for the State Government to provide job to adult members of the families whose children are working in hazardous occupations, the State Governments are required to make a deposit of Rs.5,000. per child in the Child Labour Rehabilitation-cum-Welfare Fund, as its contribution/grant. The State governments are, therefore, required to make necessary budget provisions for meeting with such expenditure.

The State government is requested to take necessary action to ensure that children are spared from the requirement to do the job and parents / guardians fulfill this vital requirement. For this purpose, active cooperation of the Education Department would be necessary. It would also be necessary to organise awareness building activities against the pernicious effect of making children work at a tender formative state of their life when they are supposed to have to avial education opportunity.

The State government sould ensure that on discontinuation of employment of the child his / her education in a suitable institution is assured. For this purpose, the State Education Departments would also be equally responsible for ensuring that each child withdrawn from hazardous employment is enabled to get education. It would be the responsibility of the State Education Department that sufficient infrastructure in the form of schools, additional teachers, and teaching / learning material etc. is provided at the places where the children withdrawn from works are normally staying. The Inspectors notified under the Act are also required to be made squarely responsible for ensuring that children withdrawn from works are given proper education.

Keeping in view the magnitude of the task, the State government should immediately create a special cell in the Labour Department. The State Labour Secretary is also expected to assume the total responsibility for monitoring the compliance of the directions of the Supreme Court at the State level.

As for as the non-hazardous jobs are concerned, the State government should ensure that the working hours of the children are not more than 4-6 hours a day and the children are enabled to receive education at least for two hours a day. This could perhaps implemented be through the non-formal education centers or evening schools or in any other manner deemed appropriate. In this area also, the State Education Department is expected to assume the overall responsibility for creating suitable mechanisms for providing education to the working children at least for two hours a day. Since the entire cost of education of the children working in non-hazardous jobs is to be borne by the employers, the State government could also consider directing the employers to provide facilities for education to the children at the work place itself. In such an event, the Inspector will ensure that the children are being imparted education for at least two hours a day.

Since the Ministry of Labour is required to monitor the compliance of the directions of the Supreme Court which are time bounded in terms of compliance's, a monthly report on the action taken in the manner indicated above may be sent on a regular basis (Ministry of Labour, Governament of India).

A conference of State/Union Territories Labour Ministers was convened on 22.1.2004 to finalize concrete action plan for the implementation of the directions of the Supreme Court on withdrawal and rehabilitation of working children. In the conference, all the participating State's / Union Territories welcomed the judgment and demonstrated their political will on the need for elimination of child labour in the light of the judgment of the Supreme Court. However, all the states pleaded for additional and a liberal financial assistance from the Central Government for giving proper effect to the judgment of the

Supreme Court. This may be viewed as the escape policy of the States and UTs. Instead of looking for the resources within their fund positions, demanding additionally fund from the central pool may be viewed as an escape mechanism. Such attitude of the local governments will never solve the present crisis of child labour.

Supreme Court Verdict on Child Labour

The Supreme Court has also deliberated the matter regarding the elimination of child labour. The court in its judgement in 1996, in a writ petition has given a judge ment in favor of directions regarding the manner in which the children working in the hazardous occupations are to be withdrawn from work and rehabilitated. The working conditions of the children working in non-hazardous occupations are to be regulated and improved upon and the judgement has directed to complete the survey of children working in hazardous employments within a period of 6 months, and a compensations amounting to Rs. 20.000/- by the offending employer of every child employed in contravention of the provisions of the Act.

Further the court has given its verdict providing alternative employment to an adult member of the family in place of the child with drawn from the hazardous occupation. If not the payment of an amount of Rs. 5,000 for each child employed in hazardous employment by the appropriate governament, payment of interest on the corpus of Rs. 20.000 to be paid by the employer and Rs. 5.000 to be contributed by the concerned

Governament to the family of the child has withdrawn from work. Provision of education in a suitable institution for the child withdrawn from work and constitution of the child labour rehabilitation-cum-welfare fund, establishment of separate cell in the labour Department. The Governament should monitor the action plan as per the court verdict.

The Governament of India has drawn up a large number of policies and programmes to deal with the problems of child labourers. Many alternative income generating programmes to the families who are sending their children to schools have been implemented. In some cases where child labour has been found to exist in concentrated form, special schools have been opened. The Ministry of Human Resource Development is running many education-related activities to the children who are compelled to work due to economic stress. Other strategies to reach out these children include running of well defined "Open Learning System (OLS) especially for girls, women, SC, ST and the poor, the unemployed and the untrained with the thrust of the OLS being acquisition of the life skills, vocational skills, directly contributing to productively and inculcation of habits of self learning" (Lillykuty, 2001). During the 10th plan, all child labour endemic districts would be covered with a substantial out lay of 668 core which is 2.7 times more of the allocation made in the 9th plan. This policy of the Governament is to ban employment of children below the age of 14 years in hazardous employments and to regulate the working conditions of children in other employments.

Action Plan- 2001: A Scheme by the Governament of Karnataka

After Andra Pradesh, Karnataka has the highest incidence of child labour. Though efforts to draw the attention of the governament and the public towards the effects on child labour were on since 1986, Karnataka alone accounted for more than 34.23 lakhs child labourers who are working in different parts of Karnataka. They are working in agricultural sector, garages, factories, beedi and agerbathi, silk, carpet, and domestic sectors and other petty establishments. Also children are engaged in rag picking, automobile, hotel, confectionery making, construction work etc.

Since child labour problem is gradually increasing in the state, state governament has implemented many polices and programmes to stop child labour. The Governament of India, ILO, UNISEF and other national and international agencies are offering all kinds of assistance to the governament in fighting against the problem. Recently, the World Bank released money to tackle the poverty in the state. Special Governament machinery has been set up. Child labour cell has also been established in 9 concerned ministries. More over, the state governament has implemented 3 vital programmes especially for child labourers: *Kooliyinda Shalege,* (From work to school) *Baa Marali Shalege*(come again to school) and *Chinnara Angala.* (A short term bridge cource)

Chinnara Angala programme has extended great opportunities for those who are deprived of normal school life. It was stared in 2001 and till now, more than 3209 children have brought to main stream (Department of Labour, Govt. of Karnataka)

Objectives of this programmes;

1. to identify the dropouts and non-enrollment of children who're in the age group of 6-14 years and the create interest in learning
2. to develop learning competencies according to their mental ability and
3. to bring them to the main stream on the basis of their achievement through bridge cource

Chinnara Angala Centers have been opened where drop out and non-enrollment rate is more and centers and will be functioning for 60 days during summer vacations.

All these programmes are specially meant for the former and present child laboures. Moreover the labour inspectors are also frequently conducting intensive raiding on the places where large number of children found to be employed. These child workers or released the children are sent to special child labour hostels. In such hostels education (Bridge cource) and lodging and boarding facilities are provided for 6 months at free of cost. After that boy or girl can join the formal schools and that too the same standard/class where he or she had left before becoming the child labourer.

Options for schooling for the released child labour

7 to 9 years 9-1212 to 14 years Direct mainstream to regular school *(Baa Marali Shalege)* Chinnara Angala to regular school (2 month) Chinnara Angala to regular school (2 month) Day bridge school (> 6 months) 0 to regular school Presidential bridge school to regular school (6 Months) Residential bridge school to regular school (6 months to 12 months)

Sources: Department of Labour, Govt. of Karnataka (2002)

An Action Plan

The Governament of Karnataka has implemented an action plan to free the state from the child labour by 2007. For this purpose an action plan has been prepared by the Karnataka Governament with due assistance from many noted NGOs working in the field. Special child labour units have been setup in the state. Many workshop and seminars have been organised by the state to sensitize all the stakeholders. Special aid programme to the NGOs also has been geared-up.

The Objectives of the Action Plan are:

1. to nsure universal primary education for all the children up to the age of 14 years
2. to ensure universal enrolment and retention of children in schools
3. to identify, release, rehabilitate and bring working children to Schools
4. to create a positive climate through massive awareness generation for elimination of child labour
5. to focus convergence of all developmental effort to alleviate the Socio economic circumstance of the child labour family.
6. to establishment of network among the community, NGO's, employers, schools and other various departments.

Strategies Adopted to Achieve the Goal are

1. Survey and planning
2. Vigorously pursue *Sarva Shiksha Abhiyan (education for all)* and DPEP and ensure mass enrollment and retention and scheme of mid day meal in all primary and higher primary schools across the state

3. Awareness generation and advocacy through all media
4. Strengthen enforcement machinery
5. Ensure effective convergence of developmental efforts
6. Open residential bridge schools to mainstream child labour
7. Involve community, NGOs, local bodies and all concerned Governament departments.
8. Make available sufficient finance on time
9. Focus on girl child and child prostitution
10. Development of effective documentation, research, monitoring and evaluation mechanism
 (From various resources).

Institutional arrangements for impemation of action plan

1. Satae level high power committee: Headed by the Chief Minster
2. State level co-ordination committe Headed by the Additional Chief Secretary to Govt of Karnataka
3. District level Advisory Committee : Elected Representatives and DC as chairman
4. District level executive committee: DC as chairman

Expectation from the NGOs

1. ensure public participation
2. participatory selection of children
3. running model transit school
4. put effort for SHG linkage
5. timely mainstreaming
6. documentation and reporting
7. Networking with various stakeholders
8. Environment building offer and media relationship
9. Inertaction with local school
10. Appropriate training and motivated teachers and others

Role of Important Departments in implementing the Action Plan

Department of Labour

- To ensure strict implementation of all the labour laws relating to employment of child labour
- To act as nodal agency and facilitate the co-ordination between various implementing agencies / departments at State level
- To facilitate the collection and compilation of data through district committees.

- Vigorous enforcement of the Minimum Wages Act, 1948
- To arrange training programmes and conducing seminars / workshops for co-ordinate efficient enforcement.

2. Department of Women and Child Development

- Responsible for rehabilitation of released child labour in co-ordination with the District Committees
- Maintain a record of each child upto the age of 6 years in the urban centers by Angnawadi workers
- The persons managing certified schools, observation homes and after care homes to be sensitized about the neglected/ withdrawn child labour including child prostitution
- Liaise with the Inspectors appointed under section 17 of the Child Labour (Prohibition and Regulation Act, 1986) to get information about the names and addresses of the child labourers withdrawn from employment, so as to rehabilitate them through bridge courses
- Accommodation be provided to the withdrawn child labourers in the observation homes of the concerned districts whenever the Inspector or any authority appointed under section 17 of the child labour temporarily.
- Nutrition supplement may also be provided to Child Labour special schools as and when required on priority basis
- To consider synchronizing the timings of Anganwadis with that of primary schools so that girl children need not miss school to take care of siblings at her home

3. Social Welfare Department

- Social welfare hostel's to be assigned the highest priority to child labour and admit them in the hostels by relaxing the existing rules of admission at any time during academic year
- Should prepare schemes to support child labour families belongs to SC, ST, OBC and Minorities etc
- Special efforts to be made to educate the families who are below poverty line and are on the evils of child labour

4. Department of Education

- To provide free, compulsory and qualitative education for all children upto the age of 14 years of age in schools as suggested in the action plan

- Liaise with the Social Welfare and Women and Child welfare departments to organise back to school programme on a regular basis through bridge schools welfare hostels during the summer months
- To Make school timings flexible to meet local requirements and needs
- To provide to all children of below poverty line families' mid-day meals, free textbooks, notebooks, uniform school bags, etc. to attract the children towards schooling
- Revamp the existing teacher's training programme to bring in the issue of child labour and its link to universalisation of the elementary education
- To make efforts to start residential schools for children of migrant labourers /bonded labourers.

5. Department of Urban Development

- All urban local bodies to ensure compulsory primary education and to monitor the progress of all children upto the age of 14 years
- The institutional mechanisms to be evolved for implementing the action plan in the Nagarapalikas vis-à-vis the targets / standards set for itself for each year of the action Plan
- Obtain an undertaking while granting any license / permission to the effect that the applicant should not engage child labour. In case of violation the licenses / permission are supposed to be cancelled
- To ensure that proper sanitation and water facilities are provided to the Child Labour Rehabilitation centers within their jurisdiction
- Sensitization and awareness training programmes against the employment of child labour to all functionaries of urban local bodies including the councilors and Corporaters etc
- Special awareness programmes to be conducted in the vulnerable sections of the community on Child Labour and Training Programmes on Child Labour be arranged at grass-root level

Department of Communication and Information

- To undertake massive publicity campaign among the public to create an environment which will encourage the children to go to school instead of work
- To play a pivital role with the active support of media and other resources groups including adverting agencies, NGOs and literacy groups in the entire social mobilization programmes for successful implementation of the action plan

- To undertake a campaign to create awareness about the government schemes specially ment for rehabilitating the child labourers and their families
- To generating public opinion against the practice of child labour by mobilizing intellectuals, artists and people having concern for child labour and also simultaneously to demand free and compulsory qualitative education

A New Step in the Child Rights Movement in Karnataka

Child rights are natural. Showing love and affection to children is also very natural. The way a family, community and society takes care of their children shows whether the children get their rights or not. When we have considered the children as future citizen of our nation, we need to question ourselves-how do we look after and support we give to their rights. Public discussion with respect to child rights began at 1919.In 1989, the UNO promulgated the child rights convention and got approval of its member countries. This resolution says that the child, by reason of his physical and mental immaturity, needs special safeguards and care, including appropriate legal protection, before as well as after birth. In 1999, the Governament of India signed the Convention on Rights of Children (CRC) declaration and agreed to provide the Indian children their rights to survive, develop, participate and get protection, provide excellent environment and develop suitable ules and regulations for the well being of the children.

So the Governament of Karnataka has initiated many steps regarding effective and immediate implement of child rights across the state. The awareness on CRC is necessary and should reach every member of the community soon. In order to reach out to the public, state has arranged/ing many workshops, training and seminars to NGO's, community leaders, parents and Government Departments and other executive agencies who are providing fundamental service to the children. Governament is also set up child right cell at each *Angnawadi* centers and each *panchyaths level.* State is also providing grants to the NGO's and other research institutes to take up research projects on local cultural norm regarding child rights and application of human rights and to introduce child rights through various methodology and mean

Evaluation and Monitoring

An independent Organisation has been set up for the monitoring and evaluation purpose. It helps in providing valuable feed back for taking mid cource corrections from time to time. This Organisation will directly to the state Governament not only in terms of programme implementation but also in terms of interest and co-operation extended by the various functionaries particularly the various Governament departments. This report first goes to the state level co-ordination committee and later on to High Power **Committee for review.**

It is the time to think about creating child labour free areas in each and every community by using a comprehensive decentralized approach which could have been developed in well partnership among children, community members and local NGO's. In these communities, children have themselves defined work they can and cannot do and their lists have been developed in connection with the various occupation children are involved in as seen within the framework of children's developmental milestones.(Gopal Bhargav).Ultimately these lists form their guidelines to declare any specific area as child labour free. Also we should note that children themselves are an integral part of the monitoring process. State and community should consolidate the local resources to implement field oriented, realistic, child centered, and innovative packages to tackle the problem from local to national level.

Draw Backs in Policies and Protective Legislation's

Probably all most all the countries have different kinds of legislation's to protect children or impose ban on child labour. But the real problem is effective implementation of the law or act by the beurocrates. Moreover effective inspection system is not adequately developed in India. Apart that, lot of different kinds occupations like agriculture, traditional occupation, pavement selling, small business doesn't comes under any specific laws and acts. Since from the beginning Governament has implemented many polices and programmes to curb child labour but, the result is only mere success. Most of the plans and schemes were not fit for the local needs or culture, and these programmes were /are not geographically and culturally specific. Governament still doing a great circus to keep alive the education market. Some of the constitutional Articles related to the welfare of the children are15, 21,23,24,38,41,42,43,47 bear ample testimony to the fact. Most antagonistic prospective is that these teeth less jaw has had the overall effect of changing the conditions of emolument of children rather than elimination or reducing child labour. And absolutely silent hiring children especially in informal sectors. Article no 24 directly relate to child labour. It proclaims that children below the age of 14 years shall not be employed to work in any hazardous or non-hazardous sectors of the economy. In 1949, the employment of children act was passed. it raised the minimum age to 14 years for employment in establishments governed act, After this, Governament brought many acts like

The child labour regulation act-1986, National policy on child labour, etc and also formed many committees of experts to suggest the Governament regarding effective tackling of the problem. Recently Governament has constituted a National Commission for Children a, statuary body set up by an act of parliament, which gives further legal protection to the children. There above mentioned child labour act 1986, does not cover all the occupations in which children employed. Also the deplorable omission is not specifying the minimum age of employment. Most unfortunate phenomenon is that the word hazardous is not clearly defined. Totally the constitutions contains provisions for protection of children from work, which is beyond their capacity, or involve long hours of work interfacing with their education, recreation, rest and overall physical and mental development.

The different acts contain various regulatory measures aimed at protecting he working children. In spite of these measures, the working children are becoming liable for exploitation and their welfare is neglected. Legislative measures taken by the Governament have largely proved to be ineffective measures taken by the problem of child labour. It is because of limitations in the act. Usha Nayer (1998) writes, "in occupations and process listed as hazardous, why should children of the family entrepreneurial activities and state managed schools be exempted and allowed to work? Once the occupations /process have been identified as hazardous for the employment of children, any exemption made thereof is to the detriment of the children. Hence is no logical and possible justification for such allowances. Thus, provisions have made child labour legitimate unless proved guilty." Resent Supreme Court verdict on child labour also high lighted this point Also Governament is not interested in creating awareness among the employers about the sprit behind all legislative measures.

More over what the policy planed by the Governament is not time bounded. Evaluation and feed back of the programmes has become nightmare. Also very implementing officials very often does not have proper inclination to deal with the problems of child labour which result in ineffective implementation. Act stands since matters relating to children receive low priority when it comes to implementation. Success of any law and act invariable depends on the its enforcement. Also all this will be mere abracadabra if society still tolerates the sacrifices of child hood that should be spent in acquiring sinews of the mind and body. Every effort should therefore be made to ban child labour in toto and not just content our selves in enacting legislation. Also we rule out legislative abolition of child labour is not the final answer and similarly, inadequate legislative protection causes problems to protecting the interests of children.

Policy failure in Ensuring Compulsory Education

There is, formal, a widespread consensus about ending child labour and establishing compulsory universal primary education for all children up to the age of 14, a commitment that can be traced back to Gopal Krishna Gokhale's effort at the turn of the last century. So perhaps we can cite, India is a very first country, which thought towards a better plan to tackle child labour problem effectively.

Spending some years during the early ages of the child hood in schools is highly essential for the effective socialization. Education is kind of immovable property of the society. Education plays a vital role in social cultural and economic progress of any society. Also cultural concept of education differs in different society. So there exists a high positive correlation between the level of educational attainment and the socio-economic standards of community life (Pati, 1992). Shandilya and Khan (2003) write "the social evil involved the employment of children is also due to illiteracy and occasionally shifting towards lack of development of child's personality which continues beyond his /her child hood adult hood. There may also be yet another causes which may force children to employment particularly when the society neglects the child and have indifferent attitude towards children". In spite of enshrine free and compulsory education in the directive principle of state polices of our constitution, the educational backwardness of India even after 50 years of independence is quite glaring. India even after 50 years of independence is quite glaring.

Compulsory primary education system is not yet fully implemented despite 93rd amendment to the constitution. Different Governments took more than 55 years to enact compulsory primary education in our country. Like western countries if, we could have brought compulsory primary education in the early periods of the independence, defiantly we would have minimize the rate of child labour atleast by this time. Prof. Dak while writing the education to all say first "the existing disparities between and within sectors and among socio economic groups must be narrowed through the increased availability of educational facilities and service in relatively deprived sectors and the provision of incentives for increased access by deprived socio-economic groups"'. But in case of India the Governament is spending million dollars on higher education and few thousand rupees on primary education. The real economic cost of schooling to the poor must to the extent possible be reduced. While the manifold benefits of primary education cannot be denied, it must be qualified with the proposition that unless there are prospects of finding employment there is like to be an apathy on the part the poor parents to send their children for education. (Datta,1991)

Perhaps one more reason that contemporary educationist is giving that inadequate motivation among poor parents is the major obstacles to universalisation of primary education. This lack of motivations probably the most continues and complexes as the issue involved range from the purely economic to border social and cultural consideration. Rather, it is the direct costs of schooling, which reduce the child's interest in education that primarily accounts for educational deprivation. In both the above phenomenon's reducing private costs of schooling and improving schooling quality and make learning is a joyful experience. The Governament has to play a crucial role over here.

Vimal Ramachandra (1999) observes "It is widely acknowledged that a significant proportion of children, especially those from underprivileged backgrounds and girls, either drop out of primary school or even if they attend school, learn very little Moreover, there is a wide gap between Governament and private school in different level of achievements. The active participation of children in primary education hinges on a plethora of factors. Besides access a range of demand and supply issue influence why children choose to attend school regularly. Thus the policy makers and education administrates should focus mainly on the formal school system and on improving access to education. The creation of backward and forward linkage is essential to creating an environment where every child not only goes to school but get some benefits from it." This is the aspect where, exactly Govt. policy makers and NGO's should focus on.

Exports have a opinion that until child get benefit from the school, Governament should seriously think about alternative income generation programme to those families or creative measures in order to lighten the burden on poor families. It is has been noted that there is no direct connection between rate if illiteracy and high incidence of child labour. Some of the countries have largely succeeded in eradicating illiteracy but remain confronted by the child labour, which some time very acute. This can be seen in some of the Middle Eastern countries.

Since 1986 India has significantly expanded its arsenal of legislation that could be used to combat exploitive child labour. It has also devoted significant expenditures to addressing some of the underlying factors driving child labour, through poverty alleviation programs and ambitious educational reform plans. These efforts are laudable, but they do not constitute the integrated strategy for combating the worst forms of child labour that India needs, and in many cases they fail to meet the test of "immediate and effective measures" required by international law. Child domestic workers are excluded from key legislation providing protection to other forms of child labour, and police, prosecutors, and judges rarely enforce protections in other legislation in cases involving child domestics. Government efforts to address child protection have largely neglected child domestic labour, and those that do address child domestic labour frequently suffer from a lack of coordination across ministries and sectors, between government and nongovernmental and international actors, and among NGOs, and a lack of a clear budget for implementation. Little detailed data exists on child labour nationally, and especially on "hidden" forms of labour like domestic work. Few programs exist to provide direct assistance for the removal of children from the worst forms of child labour, including domestic labour, and those that do exist have been largely pilot programs with limited scope and success.

Exclusion from protection of the law and failures of enforcement As noted above, all domestic workers—adults and children— are excluded from India's Labour Code and do not enjoy the minimum protections afforded to other workers in the industrial, commercial, and agricultural sectors. This exclusion leaves abusive employers free to set whatever working conditions they choose, to change those conditions at will, and to engage in abuse and exploitation of domestic workers without fear of prosecution. The impact of this exclusion falls disproportionately on women and girls, who comprise the largest percentage of household workers. While Indian criminal law contains provisions that could be used to punish child abuse, forced labour, sexual exploitation, and trafficking of children, these provisions are rarely invoked against those who abuse child domestics.

The 2003 amendments to the Labour Code provide for separate legislation governing conditions of employment for domestic workers, but as of this writing no draft of this legislation has been made public. It caused great debate among the ministries. It will take time before they are in agreement on the final draft." Activists with whom Human Rights Watch spoke also doubted the ability of the government to formulate a law regulating child domestic labour that would be consistent with its obligations under the CRC. Part of the problem is that they lack a clear definition of ill-treatment of a child, and it will be hard to define working hours."

According to the Ministry of Labour even in the absence of specialized legislation on domestic work, the Labour Code's prohibition on the employment of children under fifteen applies to all children, including child domestics. However, the Ministry has done little to enforce the current or previous minimum age legislation in cases involving child domestic workers.

The Ministry of Labour is responsible for implementing and enforcing child labour laws and regulations. However, with only a small number of labour inspectors, limited investigative powers, limited awareness of the child labour issue, and a lack of resources, the Ministry [of Employment]'s enforcement activities [on child labour] have been severely constrained. Furthermore, although the new Labour Code does empower inspectors to bring charges for employing children under age 15, inspectors have limited ability to monitor the work of children in the informal sector, including the work of child maids. Courts can take action once two witnesses file a complaint, but few employers of child maids have been prosecuted. In the few cases where legal sanctions for child labour violations are applied, they are generally insufficient to act as effective deterrents.

The greatest barrier to enforcement, government officials and activists both agree, is the Labour Code's lack of effective mechanisms for enforcement of the law in private homes. According to a Ministry official responsible for child labour issues, the ministry is unable to enforce the ban on children under fifteen working as child domestics because it lacks the legal authority to investigate violations in private homes, and even if it had the authority its resources are limited. "The only monitoring [of the Labour Code] is via the labour inspectors. The unions, social assistants, and other bodies must study the issue and come up with a way for monitoring to work in houses because the inspector doesn't have the power to do this now. The [Ministry cannot take action because the] system and the law must be in agreement."

India amended its many legislation's in 2003, strengthening provisions on child abuse and sexual exploitation, forced labour, and the sale of children. However, some of these articles are limited in scope, and activists told Human Rights Watch that police rarely intervene to protect child domestics because they lack authority to enter private houses unless they have received a complaint of severe abuse, and when they do investigate they are more likely to believe employers than children. In addition, a number of factors limit the number of complaints police receive. Child domestics themselves are unlikely to complain to police while working because they have few opportunities to do so, and may fear the police because of employers' threats to turn them over to the police for punishment. Girls who have run away from abusive employers may refuse to identify their former workplaces out of fear of being returned to their abusers, or may be unable to do so because of illiteracy and unfamiliarity with the city. Children's families also may be unable or unwilling to bring a complaint, whether because they themselves lack access to their daughters, out of fear of stigma in the case of sexual violence, or because they assume that it will lead to a time-consuming, expensive process that will provide them no benefit.

ILO-IPEC felt "We did a workshop for prosecutors. Prosecutors aren't willing to push families who aren't willing to push for trial. There is also the question of whether going to trial will do more damage to the child—it may help combat the phenomenon but it could hurt the individual child by creating a fuss around the child who will have to go back to a village where everyone knows what has happened."

NGOs Human Rights Watch spoke with said that they rarely made legal complaints on behalf of child domestics because they lacked the human and financial resources to pursue them and because judges and prosecutors were rarely interested in pursuing cases of child domestics. Amina Kamri, the vice president of an NGO working with child domestics in Bombay expressed "During the first year we were able to get some cases to court, but they were postponed or the abuser was a tourist. The problem is that there are no specialized judges for child victims. When the victim is a child the judges don't know what to do—the juvenile courts are for children who commit crimes [not for child victims]." The director of one of the few NGOs to have successfully brought legal complaints against employers who abused child domestics told us, "The procedures for implementing the laws on children are still not clear, unlike those for women. The biggest problem is implementation: there isn't implementation of the laws affecting children."

Several NGOs told us they refer cases of abuse to India's National Observatory on Children's Rights. The ONDE, created in 1995 by the central Govt. strives to promote implementation of the CRC through research, campaigns, and pilot programs. Since 1999 it has operated a telephone hotline for abused children, and its activities in this area have made it a *de facto* ombudsman for issues of child abuse. While the ONDE's close association with the rich family gives it a social weight that undoubtedly contributes to its ability to mobilize support, it lacks a clear legal mandate to play a coordinating or ombudsman role. Lack of clear legal status and authority to intervene is also a problem for social workers, NGOs, and private parties who may learn of child domestics being abused.

The problem with the status of social assistants is part of a larger problem: there is a law on public sector employees and a law on private sector employees and if you aren't in one of those sectors you don't have legal status, for example, NGO employees don't have legal status. There are four kinds of institutions that have social assistants: the Ministry of Health, and Ministry of Youth and Sport. Each has its own system and training. Also, they don't work in the same sector: some are for profit, some are not. Also, the government doesn't believe that social work is important.

India's strategy to address child labour is outlined in its 1999 National and Sectoral Plan of Action against Child Labour. Progress in implementing the plan has been slow, with the greatest progress thus far occurring in legislation addressing child labour and education. However, key provisions of the new laws exclude domestic workers or are rarely enforced, as we discuss below.

Among the major barriers to implementation of the 1999 plan of action is its generality and its emphasis on consciousness raising rather than legal enforcement. The plan provides little guidance on what specific activities should be undertaken, which agencies are responsible for them, how they would be funded, and what mechanisms would be used for coordination. In addition to general recommendations for combating child labour the plan includes child domestic labour, grouped with transport, maintenance, and marginal activities, among the six areas it prioritizes for intervention. It then lists twelve proposed activities to combat child domestic labour, and four proposed activities to improve working conditions for child domestics. Not one of the proposals calls for criminal prosecution of those who abuse child domestics or enforcement of minimum age legislation. Instead, the majority of proposals call for "sensitization" of employers, parents, children, and the general public, and for broad poverty alleviation programs in rural areas.

Child domestic labour is also likely to be excluded from the time-bound program that India is currently developing for the elimination of the worst forms of child labour. Time-bound programs are "a set of integrated and coordinated policies and interventions with clear goals, specific targets and a defined time frame, aimed at preventing and eliminating a country's [worst forms of child labour]" undertaken by countries with assistance from ILO-IPEC. According to ILO-IPEC, inclusion of child domestics is unlikely because while IPEC considers all child domestic labour to be among the worst forms of child labour, "[t]he Indian government doesn't consider child domestic labour by children over fifteen to be hazardous labour."

In case of Karnataka, Secretariat of State for Family, and Social Action is in the process of preparing a ten-year plan of Action on Childhood, which reportedly will include child labour as part of its program on child protection from abuse, exploitation, and violence, and discuss the role of brokers in trafficking of child domestics. While the details of this plan were still vague in May 2005 (and remain so as of this writing), activists we spoke with expressed concern that, like the 1999 plan of action, it lacked the specificity and mechanisms to be effective. An activist who had seen a draft told us "The [draft] National Plan is not a unified plan, and doesn't have detail or a strategic plan or a timeline or a budget." UNICEF's child protection officer told us in November 2005 that subsequent versions of the draft had been amended to include a focus on eliminating the worst forms of child labour, including child domestic labour, but that the plan still lacked a budget to implement its recommendations (The Hindu,2006).

Lack of coordination across agencies and between government and NGOs

Lack of coordination among government agencies and between the government and NGOs working on child labour is a major barrier to developing and implementing an integrated response to child labour. Since its creation in 2002, the Secretariat of State for Family and Social Action, also in charge for Family, and Handicapped Persons, has been responsible for coordination of government programs "on all areas related to children in Karnataka state. However, the Secretariat lacks legal authority to force other agencies to take action, and its small budget and staff make it reliant on other agencies and on NGOs to implement its programs. The head of the Secretariat's Division on Women Child Developmnet told us, "We don't have a ministry that has oversight over other ministries. We wrote into the [National Action Plan on Child labour] a committee to have oversight but not power and we are considering a recommendation for something like an ombudsman. We have 78 people on staff total, and the children's section is the smallest section. We would need to have more staff to have an oversight role."

These deficiencies also limit the Secretariat's ability to maximize the resources currently available for child labour work in Karnataka. Activists we spoke with stressed that there was virtually no evaluation of existing child labour initiatives, only limited training opportunities for NGOs working in this field, and no means of preventing duplication of services. Dr. Natraju director of an NGO in Bangalore with ten years of experience working with street children, child domestics, and other children in difficult circumstances, felt "We need networking and coordination of local authorities and NGO services, and a clear division of labour. We need a global approach for children, including children in difficult circumstances, that focus on prevention, and we need coordination between government agencies. The Ministry of [National] Education is in the midst of an educational reform plan but has not coordinated with literacy programs.

Donors come with their own plans without paying attention to the needs of the country. They have programs according to what is in fashion. There isn't evaluation of civil society activities. Dr. Leela told us, "We need a secretariat with a special mission to look into coordination, and a system to monitor individual children to avoid duplication of services and to follow up on what happens to them over time. The government sees NGOs as the solution. We are throwing money at associations but they need capacity building, and the government needs to take the lead."

The Committee on the Rights of the Child echoed many of these concerns in its 2006 review of Karnataka, saying that, the Committee notes the establishment of the Office of the Secretary for Family Affairs and Social

Welfare to coordinate all actions regarding children. However, the Committee, noting the information by the delegation that the change of title from Minister of State to Secretary of State does not change its level in the government hierarchy or its mandate, remains concerned that this body does not have the financial and human resources to coordinate the implementation of the Convention throughout the State party effectively.

The Committee recommends that the State party empower and provide the necessary financial and human resources to the Office of the Secretary of State for Family Affairs and Social Welfare so that it can effectively and efficiently coordinate the implementation of all areas of the Convention, both between ministries and between national, regional and local authorities.

Lack of a Strategy for Rehabilitation

Probably India lacks a clear, integrated strategy for the rehabilitation of child domestic workers, and particularly for those children under the minimum age for work. NGOs have taken up an increasingly large share of the task of rehabilitation and reintegration of child domestics, but their work is largely uncoordinated and they lack the financing, human resources, and legal status to make a significant impact. More importantly, NGOs should not be expected to resolve larger structural problems that push children to work.

Current practice is for girls who run away from abusive employers to be sent to the government's ' remand home, a closed juvenile detention facility that also accepts abandoned children, pending return to their families or their reaching majority. Detention in a closed facility is clearly an inappropriate solution for children in need of care, and in practice larger numbers of girls are now finding their way to NGOs that offer residential services for street children, child domestics, and other children in need of protection. However, information about how to access these services is not systematically provided to those likely to have contact with child domestics, and is largely dependant on NGOs' own efforts to foster relationships with police and judicial authorities. Some of the official expressed many children protection system was fraught with gaps: "There is a lack of alternatives. When a doctor sees a victim he doesn't have the number of the judge and the judge doesn't have places to send the child." She and other activists we spoke with also said that their capacity to accept children in need of residential care was limited, and that although they effectively acted as guardians to the girls in their care they lacked the legal status to do so, placing them at risk should harm befall a child. The lack of appropriate residential care for former child domestics is especially acute for girls who become pregnant as a result of rape or sexual exploitation.

The problem is with the girls under eighteen who cannot be returned to their families. We have only capacity to keep girls for six months and these girls need care for a longer period. We refer them to the Women Rehabilitation Centre. It is the NGO with a three-year programme, but it also has great difficulty in succeeding with these girls because they are too young to work and to take care of their children. Usually the problem is that the families refuse to take them back out of shame.

5

Child Labour and Health

Child labour remains a widespread problem in the world today. Although child labour can have positive effects, in some situations it has negative effects on health and development of the children. It is mainly a problem in developing countries, but it is possible to find child workers in developed countries, some of them, working in hazardous activities. In this paper we describe the child labour profile in developed and developing countries, and the principal occupations and its hazards. In addition, wesummarize the epidemiologic evidence of the grater impact of some occupational exposures on child health when compared to adults, and the theoretical concerns about the impact of child labour on health. Furthermore, we describe policies that can be used to combat harmful child labour.

The majority of the child workers live in the developing countries of Latin America, Asia and Africa, but there are also pockets of child labour in many industrialized countries. (ILO, 1998) There is a consensus that work can have positive effects on children such as the development of discipline, responsibility, self-confidence and independence; teaching children how to manage money; and providing valuable models to teach them works kills. On the other hand, it can also have a negative impact on health and development of the children. The plain fact that the children are working is not a concern in itself, but it is the type of work they perform that will determine whether work is harmful to them. Child labour will be more harmful if it interferes with school, recreation and rest; the younger the child is; the worst the nature of the work schedule, the longer the hours or the frequency of the nocturnal work; the more hazardous the occupation and the lower the wage.

Some child labour is clearly light, as the activity performed by a child delivering newspapers for two hours a day. This work is not likely to harm the

---

* Based on Various websites.

child's health or development, or reduce his attendance in school. But even in this situation there is some level of exploitation in the fact that the child probably receives a lower wage than an adult would receive to perform the same job. There are also some socially or morally in tolerable forms of exploitation, such as child prostitution, which most people would agree is necessary to eliminate. Even so, it is very difficult to get consensus on how to address this problem. However, the majority of these occupations are not extreme situations like the ones above and in these cases it is necessary to balance their beneficial and harmful aspects to define which occupations are appropriate for children.

In most countries of the world it is possible to find children working in very hazardous conditions, but is difficult to find good data about the impact of child labour on health to evaluate its harmful aspects. Some environmental epidemiological studies and research on young workers suggest that children could have higher health risks than adults have when exposed to some hazards. Moreover, several theoretical concerns about the impact of occupational exposures on child health still need to be studied. Implications of Child Labour, In this paper we intend to describe the child labour profile in developed and developing countries, to summarize the epidemiological evidence of the greater impact of some occupational exposures in child health when compared to adults, and the theoretical concerns about the impact of child labour on health. Furthermore, we will describe the policies that have been used to combat harmful child labour. We consider child labour the activities performed by persons of less than 18 years of age that contribute to the production of a marketable product, good, or service, whether that activity is done for pay or not. This includes household work performed in the parents home, in situations where such work can be assimilated to an economic activity as, for example, when a child must devote his or her entire time to that work so that his or her parents can be employed outside home and is therefore deprived of the possibility of going to school. We are also using child work as a synonym of child labour.

Though primarily a developing country problem, child labour is emerging in many East European and Asian countries, which are in transition to a market economy. When considering all forms of child labour, the prevalence in developed countries is surprisingly high. (ILO, 1997) A study in United States found that 80 percent of the high school students report that they hold jobs during the school year at some point during high school. Other research in the United Kingdom showed that between 15 and 26 percent of the 11 years old and between 36 to 66 percent of the15 years old were working. It is known that some of these workers are engaged in hazardous jobs. (UNICEF, 1997)

Therefore, in addition to the differences in the size of the problem, there are also differences in the shape of child labour between developed and developing countries. In developing countries the children start to work at a very young age, some are malnourished, work for long hours in hazardous occupations, and frequently do not attend school. They receive very low wages or are unpaid workers and their income or help is usually essential for family survival. They are mainly employed in the informal sector and bonded labour stills a problem in several places. Most part of the children works for jobs addressed to the internal markets. It is estimated that probably less than5 percent are employed in export industries. (UNICEF, 1997).

The developed countries were apparently able to eliminate bonded labour and street work; moreover, the informal sector is much smaller than in the developing countries, and child workers generally attend school. Some relatively wealthy children work for discretionary money. But child labour, including the hazardous form of it, can be found inmost rich countries and very poor people, especially ethnic minorities and migrants, can face similar child labour conditions as in developing countries. (UNICEF, 1997) As it was convened in the ILO Convention 182, the worst forms of child labour should be prohibited and eliminated. The worst forms of child labour includes all forms of slavery or practices similar to slavery; the use, procuring or offering of a child for prostitution; the use, procuring or offering of a child for illicit activities and the work which is likely to harm the health, safety or morals of children. This will be a challenge for the governments that need to prepare themselves to offer a reasonable alternative to child labour. Some of the alternatives are discussed in the section "Interventions to Combat Child Labour".

Hazardous Sectors

Many of the working children labour in very dangerous or hazardous occupations such as agriculture manufacture construction, retail and marginal activities. A quick overview won the characteristics and hazards of these activities are described in this section.

3.1 AGRICULTURE

Agriculture is the most common child occupation worldwide, and employs more working children than any other sector. This activity is consistently ranked among the most hazardous industry for mortality and morbidity. But, despite its hazards, agriculture is one of the less-regulated sectors and it is among the sectors where the existent laws are very difficult to enforce.

Moreover, most farms are not family units anymore where the children are helping their parents with the daily chores and learning their future job. There is an international trend for the introduction of mechanization, specialization (monoculture) and technological advances in the fields. These process are followed by the decrease in the numbers of 6 farms, especially small family farms, a decrease in the numbers of workers employed with an increase in the size of the farms and in productivity. Thus, there are fewer children and adolescents of the owners working on farms, and higher number of adolescents hired as farm-workers or farm-workers' children that are working along side their parents in the fields. The children generally start to work in agriculture at a very young age and usually work for long hours for little or no payment. The seasonal characteristics of the work, the long hours required, the distance from school and the lack of schools with higher grades in the rural areas are some of the reasons that reduce school attendance. In agricultural work children are exposed to dangerous farm machinery, which is a common cause of fatal and non-fatal injuries, whether they are operating it or working near these machines. Children are also exposed to strenuous labour, like carrying or lifting heavy loads and working in uncomfortable positions such as stooping in the same position or bending very frequently, which could affect the musculoskeletal development of the children. Other hazards present in the fields are pesticides and the weather, especially the heat, which can be particularly dangerous for children. Poor field sanitation contains its own hazards facilitating the transmission of communicable diseases and worsening the pesticides and the heat hazard due to the lack of water. Migrant workers can be particularly at risk since their housing conditions are frequently inappropriate.

According to the International Labour Organization's new report on child labour, the number of children working in agriculture is nearly ten times that of children involved in factory work such as garment manufacturing, carpet-weaving, or soccer-ball stitching. Yet despite their numbers and the difficult nature of their work, children working in agriculture have received little attention compared to child labour in manufacturing for export or children involved in commercial sexual exploitation.

In investigations in Egypt, Ecuador, India, and the United States, Human Rights Watch has found that the children working in agriculture are endangered and exploited on a daily basis. Human Rights Watch found that despite the vast differences among these four countries, many of the risks and abuses faced by child agricultural workers were strikingly similar.

In Egypt, Human Rights Watch examined the cotton industry, Egypt's major cash crop, where over one million children work each year to manually remove pests from cotton plants. In Ecuador, where nearly 600,000 children work in the rural sector, the organization investigated conditions for children working in banana fields and packing plants. In the United States, Human Rights Watch examined conditions for the estimated 300,000 children who work as hired labourers in large-scale commercial agriculture, planting, weeding, and picking apples, cotton, cantaloupe, lettuce, asparagus, watermelons, chilies, and other crops. In India, Human Rights Watch looked at bonded child labourers working in agriculture as part of a larger study of bonded child labour. There are as many as 15 million bonded child labourers in India, most of whom are Dalits (untouchables) or lower caste. More than half, and possibly as many as 87 percent of these bonded child labourers work in agriculture, tending crops, herding cattle, and performing other tasks for their "masters."

The International Covenant on Civil and Political Rights (ICCPR) states, "Every child shall have . . . the right to such measures of protection as are required by his status as a minor, on the part of his family, society and the State." The Convention on the Rights of the Child provides that children-all persons under eighteen "unless under the law applicable to the child, majority is attained earlier"-have a right "to be protected from performing any work that is likely to be hazardous or to interfere with the child's education, or to be harmful to the child's health or physical, mental, spiritual, moral or social development." All states parties to the Convention-every government in the world except for the United States and Somalia-are required to "undertake all appropriate legislative, administrative, and other measures for the implementation of the rights recognized in this Convention."

Abuses of Child Agricultural Workers

Ages and hours of work:

Child agricultural workers often begin work at early ages, and may work twelve or more hours a day. In India, bonded child labourers as young as eleven often work sixteen or seventeen hours a day, typically beginning at 5 or 6 a.m., and continuing until 9 or 10 at night. Some are expected to work 365 days a year. In Ecuador, children working in the banana sector typically start work at ages ten or eleven, though some begin as early as age eight. Although some work only five hours a day, Human Rights Watch found that the vast majority worked between nine and thirteen hours a day.

In the United States, children interviewed by Human Rights Watch began working in the fields as early as age twelve. They routinely worked twelve-hour days, and during peak harvest season, sometimes worked fourteen hours or more. Children may begin working as early as 4 a.m., and may spend two hours or more each morning and evening traveling to the fields where they work.

Children working in cotton pest control in Egypt are typically between the ages of seven and twelve. For periods of up to ten weeks each year, they work eleven hours a day, seven days a week.

Pesticide exposure

One of the greatest threats to the health of child agricultural workers is exposure to pesticides. In Ecuador, Egypt and the United States, children reported working in freshly sprayed fields, and even working in fields while they were being sprayed. Children interviewed reported symptoms of exposure including headaches, fever, dizziness, nausea, rashes and diarrhea. In severe cases, pesticide exposure can lead to convulsions, coma and death. Long term effects also include cancer, brain damage, sterility or decreased fertility, and birth defects.

Child agricultural workers are often not told of the dangers of pesticides, or how they can protect themselves. In the United States, not one of the children interviewed by Human Rights Watch had received training about the dangers of pesticides, safety measures, or what to do in case of exposure. Some did not even know what pesticides were. "Pesticides? Was that the medicine they put on [the crops]?" said one girl. "No, I don't know anything about that."

In Ecuador, 90 % of child banana workers interviewed by HRW stated that they continued working while fungicides were sprayed from airplanes flying overhead. They described trying to protect themselves by hiding under banana leaves, covering their faces with their shirts, or placing banana cartons on their heads. One boy said, "I went under the packing plant roof until the [fumigation] plan left-less than an hour. I became intoxicated. My eyes were red. I was nauseous. I was dizzy. I had a headache. I vomited."

In all three countries, children may participate in applying pesticides to crops. In Egypt, children sometimes operate motorized pumps that saturate cotton plants with pesticides. Half a dozen children may help carry the pump's long hose, becoming heavily contaminated with pesticides in the process. In Ecuador, children frequently handle pesticide-treated plastics used to protect banana stalks in the fields, and spray fungicides onto bananas being prepared for shipment in packing plants. Many of the children reported to Human Rights Watch that they did not use any protective equipment, even gloves, when handling the chemicals.

In Egypt, two of the five pesticides recommended for use by the government are categorized as "highly hazardous" by the World Health

Organization. In Ecuador, one pesticide in common use is the subject of over one hundred lawsuits from around the world, alleging that the chemical is responsible for serious birth defects, including cleft palate and being born with no eyes.

Pesticide risks are particularly acute for children. Because their organs are still developing, they are less able than adults to expel toxins from their body. Their breathing rate is much higher than adults, and they have more skin surface per unit of body weight than adults, allowing them to both breathe in and absorb higher concentrations of toxic chemicals.

Injuries and Disabilities

Children working in agriculture suffer high rates of injuries. They frequently suffer cuts from sharp knives and falls from ladders. They risk back injuries from hauling heavy loads of produce. They may be crushed or maimed by tractors and other heavy equipment.

In the United States, agriculture is second only to mining for occupational fatalities. Child farmworkers make up only 8% of children who work in the United States, yet account for 40% of work-related fatalities among minors. An estimated 100,000 children suffer agriculture-related injuries each year in the United States.

In Ecuador, children commonly use sharp knives and machetes to cut yellow leaves off banana plants, and curvos-short, thick, crescent-shaped blades with wooden handles-to cut bananas off their stalks, to cut plastic bags used to cover banana stalks, and for other tasks. A quarter of the children interviewed by Human Rights Watch had cut themselves with these sharp tools at least once.

In Ecuador, boys also haul heavy loads of bananas from the fields to packing plants using a harness system attached to an iron pulley riding on cables. One boy, now fourteen, reported that when he was ten years old, he would pull twenty banana stalks (each weighing 50 to 100 pounds) at one time from the field to the plant. The distance from the field to the plant was two kilometers; he would make five or six trips per day, each trip taking about one hour. Dragging the heavy fruit can cause back injuries to children. In addition, stalks of bananas or wheels on the cables sometimes fall off and strike children, causing serious injuries.

Water and Sanitation

Child agricultural workers often must work in the full sun in temperatures exceeding 100 degrees Fahrenheit or 40 degrees Celsius. Under such conditions, health experts recommend that workers drink two to three gallons of water a day. Without adequate drinking water, workers run the risk of devastating dehydration and heat illnesses that can cause death or brain damage. However, many child agricultural workers do not have access to water, or are provided with water contaminated with bacteria or pesticides.

In Egypt, some children worked from 7 a.m. until 6 p.m., but reported that only during two breaks during the day did their foremen allow them to drink. In both the United States and Ecuador, some children reported that a lack of potable water forced them to drink from canals that drain excess water from the fields. These canals are often contaminated with pesticides, fertilizers, bacteria and human waste. Children may also be forced to use their earnings to purchase water, soda or beer from their employers at inflated prices.

In the United States, agricultural employers are required by law to provide toilet facilities, drinking water, and water for handwashing. However, nearly all of the children interviewed by Human Rights Watch reported working in fields or orchards where one or more of these requirements were not met.

Lack of toilet facilities contributes to the spread of parasitic infection among workers. It is particularly dangerous and humiliating for girls, who may be forced to choose between public urination-more obvious and awkward for females-and urinary retention, which can cause severe discomfort and urinary tract infections. Some workers also report limiting their fluid intake to prevent urination, at severe risk to their health.

Lack of water for handwashing also is frequently unavailable. In addition to being unsanitary, unwashed hands virtually guarantee that pesticides will be ingested when workers eat their lunch.

Ill-treatment and Sexual Harassment:

In Egypt, Human Rights Watch found that children working in cotton fields are routinely beaten. Children typically gauged the leniency of a foreman by the severity and frequency of the beatings he administered. One ten-year-old boy worked under two foremen. "One of them I hate; the other one I like. The one I hate used to beat and kick me whenever I missed a leaf. The other one beats and kicks me lightly."

Severe maltreatment caused some children to quit work entirely or seek employment under the supervision of a different foreman. A nine-year-old Egyptian girl described a steady process of attrition from her work group. "The last work group I was in started with twenty-two [children], but you know, children don't like to be hit, so they turn up in another foreman's group. Our group ended up with twelve."

Bonded child agricultural workers in India also frequently experience physical abuse. An eleven-year old told Human Rights Watch, "I do not like work; it is hard and there is no time limit. When I'm sick, the master won't let me stay at home. If I try to take time off he will scold me and beat me and take me back to the fields. Sometimes he beats me because he says I am working slowly." A girl who began working in bondage at age nine reported that her master beats her, and yells and curses at her.

In both the United States and Ecuador, girls working in the fields reported sexual harassment by their supervisors. In Ecuador, a twelve-year-old reported that when she bent down to pick up plastic bags, her boss would say, "There is a good place to stick my balls." An adult packing plant worker in Ecuador told Human Rights experts that both supervisors and other male workers grabbed the breasts and buttocks of girls.

In the United States, girls are routinely subjected to sexual advances by farm labour contractors and field supervisors. If they refuse, they-and members of their family-face retaliation in the form of discharge, blacklisting and even physical assault and rape. An eighteen-year old said, "Everyone is scared to say anything because they threaten them. If they say something they will lose their-job."

In India, many bonded child labourers working in agriculture have never been to school. Once they are bonded-often at age eight or nine-their long hours of work frequently make schooling impossible. One thirteen-year old boy who worked from 5 a.m. to 6 p.m. tending sheep and picking mulberry leaves was enrolled in a non-formal school run at night, but told Human Rights Watch, "When I have a lot of work, I am not allowed to come to the school. . . the owners complain I am not earning enough."

Wages:

Child agricultural workers work for very low wages, and are often paid less than their adult counterparts. In Egypt, children working harvesting cotton in one region earned US $1.08 per day, while men earned US $1.63 per day and women earned US $1.36. Children working in cotton pest control-a type of work typically not done by adults -earn between US $0.68 and US $0.95 per day.

In Ecuador, the legal minimum wage for a banana worker is US $5.85 per day. Adult workers interviewed by Human Rights Watch earned, on average, approximately US $5.44 per day, while children averaged only US $3.50, 60 percent of the legal minimum wage for banana workers.

In India, children bonded into agricultural labour are working to pay off a debt. Parents or other relatives promise the labour of the child to an employer in exchange for a sum of money. The children then spend long hours over many years in an attempt to pay off these debts. Due to high interest rates charged and abysmally low wages, they are usually unsuccessful. Often the yearly or monthly sum deducted from the loan is not even one-quarter or one-third of the prevalent daily wages, let alone the legal minimum wage.

Laws and their Enforcement

In some countries, such as Egypt and Ecuador, national laws set appropriate limits on both the ages and hours at which children can work and, if enforced, would help to protect children from abusive labour conditions. In other cases, like the United States, laws are clearly inadequate and fail to protect children from violations of their rights.

In both Ecuador and Egypt, national law prohibits children from working before the age of fourteen, but allows twelve and thirteen-year olds to work as apprentices as long as the work does not threaten their health or education. Egyptian children and Ecuadorian children under the age of fifteen are not allowed to work for more than six hours a day. In Ecuador, children between fifteen and eighteen are allowed to work for seven hours a day. Other regulations and legal provisions are also intended to protect working children, and Ecuadorian law explicitly prohibits hazardous work, including handling toxic substances and tasks that are "considered dangerous or unhealthy."

In the United States, child agricultural workers receive fewer legal protections than other working children. U.S. labour law allows children in agriculture to work at younger ages, for longer hours and under more hazardous conditions than children in other jobs. While the law allows children as young as twelve to work unlimited hours in agriculture, children in other occupations cannot work before age fourteen, and can only work three hours on a school day until age sixteen. In addition, even limited protections in existing law are not adequately enforced. Only a tiny fraction of child labour violations are ever uncovered by the Department of Labour, and penalties are typically too weak to discourage employers from using illegal child labour.

Bonded labour, whether in agriculture or any other area, is illegal under India law and by law, bonded labourers are to be released and rehabilitated and their employers prosecuted. The law also prohibits children under age fourteen from handling pesticides or insecticides. However, Human Rights Watch has found that the Indian has failed to adequately enforce its own laws; even where children are identified and released from bondage, often through NGO's intervention, they often receive no rehabilitation and their employers not penalized.

Egypt, Ecuador and the United States all are party to the ILO Convention 182 on the Worst Forms of Child Labour. The Convention prohibits "work which, by its nature of the circumstances in which it is carried out, is likely to harm the health, safety or morals of children." Each country is expected to determine what constitutes such work, although the ILO's Recommendation 190 recommends that such work include "a) work which exposes children to physical, emotional or sexual abuse; b) work underground, under water, at dangerous heights or in confined spaces; c) work with dangerous machinery, equipment and tools, or which involves the manual handling or transport of heavy loads; d) work in an unhealthy environment which may, for example, expose children to hazardous substances, agents or processes, or to temperatures, noise levels or vibrations damaging to their health; or e) work under particularly difficult conditions such as work for long hours or during the night or work which does not allow for the possibility of returning home each day."

The conditions for child agricultural workers also violate the Convention on the Rights of the Child, which has been ratified by every government except the United States and Somalia. The Convention states that children have the right "to be protected from economic exploitation and from performing any work that is likely to be hazardous or to interfere with the child's education, or to be harmful to the child's health or physical, mental, spiritual, moral or social development." (Article 32) Article 24 recognizes the right of all children to a high standard of health, article 28 recognizes the right of all children to education, and article 34 states that children should be protected from all forms of sexual exploitation and sexual abuse. Finally, article 3 of the Convention states that "In all actions concerning children . . . the best interests of the child shall be a primary consideration."

Factory

Very often manufacturing uses the child-labour workforce, but the types of industry vary widely from country to country. Most of these children are employed in small workshops or in home-based work. They seldom work in medium-size or large enterprises, but such establishments sometimes contribute indirectly to child labour by subcontracting out certain production tasks to small workshops and home-workers that make extensive useof child labour and generally are not covered by child labour national laws. Industry has specific hazards linked to each production process that are specific to the tasks performed. On the other hand, there are some general hazards that arise not from the production process but from uncaring management. Examples of these problems are naked electric wires, lack of first aid facilities, poor ventilation, lack of sanitation, lack of sufficient light, heavy lifting, exposure to loud noise, proximity or operation of dangerous machines, and the lack of protective equipment. In some cases physical punishments are frequent. Specific hazards vary according to the industry type. Thus, child workers will be exposed to high temperatures, high risk of accidents caused by cuts and burns at the brassware and glass-bangle industry, to silica dust at the earthenware and porcelainfactories, and to chemical hazards and risk of fire and explosion at the matches and firework workshops. (UNICEF, 1997), (Forastieri, 1997)Child workers are also exposed to important hazards in the export sector. In the carpet industry in India the children are exposed to repetitive movements, chemical hazards, inhalation of wool dust contaminated with biological agents and inadequate working postures. In the production of soccer balls in Pakistan, children are exposed to inadequate working postures, and in the shoe industry in Portugal, Italy and Brazil, children are exposed to glue. Manufacturing is a very hazardous sector and the subcontracting practice is an issue of high concern. This practice discharges the medium-sized and large-enterprise industries of the hazardous activities, by out-sourcing this type of work to small workshops and home-based work that are frequently exempt from the existing legislation. Moreover, even if the law covered these establishments, they are much more difficult to monitor and have less economic capacity to work towards higher standards. (Bureau of International Labour Affairs, 1998).

Construction

Even for adults, the construction sector is one of the most hazardous working environments with regard to the risk of accidents. Despite this fact, this sector employs are considerable number of children in several parts of the world. In Brazil, four percent of the workers between the ages of 10 and 14 and eight percent of those between 15 and17 work in the construction sector. In the United States 2.5 percent of teen workers are employed in construction although this sector is responsible for 22 percent of the fatal work-related injuries in workers younger than 17 years. In addition to the risk of accident, there are exposures to noise, silica, asbestos, harmful dust, heavy loads, etc

Retail

The retail sector employers half of the working teens in the United States for the most partin restaurants. Retail is responsible for half of the non-fatal injuries and twenty percent of the fatal injuries. Although this type of work seems to be safe some tasks can be very hazardous and forbidden by law to be performed by teens such as working with hot grease and slicer machines. Since job titles may not reflect the nature of the tasks performed, it is difficult to divide the activities that are according to the law and the onsthat are in violation. Also, these sectors often require long hours of work and changing schedules, which can be related with leave the work late at night and difficulties to combine work and school.

3.5. SERVICES

Domestic Services

Millions of women and girls around the world turn to domestic work as one of the few options available to them in order to provide for themselves and their families. Instead of guaranteeing their ability to work with dignity and freedom from violence, governments have systematically denied them key labour protections extended to other workers. Domestic workers, who often make extraordinary sacrifices to support their families, are among the most exploited and abused workers in the world.

Abuses against domestic workers, typically taking place in private homes and hidden from the public eye, have garnered increased attention in recent years. The long list of abuses committed by employers and labour agents includes physical, psychological, and sexual abuse; forced confinement in the workplace; non-payment of wages; and excessively long working hours with no rest days. In the worst situations, women and girls are trapped in situations of forced labour or have been trafficked into forced domestic work in conditions akin to slavery.

Increased awareness has unfortunately not been matched by concerted government action. Hong Kong is one of the few places where the government guarantees equal protection under its labour laws. The norm is for governments to exclude domestic workers from these laws altogether, or to provide weaker, poorly enforced regulations that leave employers enjoying virtual impunity to exact excruciatingly long hours of work for grossly inadequate wages.

The informal and hidden nature of the domestic work makes it difficult to estimate the number of domestic workers around the world, but it is one of the most common forms of urban child labour in developing countries and employs mainly girls. In Brazil eight percent of the workers between the ages of 10 and 14 were domestic workers.

It is very difficult to study domestic workers since it is hard to contact them in order to get an interview. But it is known that domestic service does not need to be hazardous, although frequently it is. Workers often live at the workplace, are expected to work at all hours of the day with few days off, and are deprived of attending school. Far from their own families, they are very vulnerable and can receive harsh treatment from their employers, sometimes suffering physical, mental, and sexual abuse. In some cases they lack an appropriate place to sleep and do not receive sufficient food. They usually receive low or no wage; bonded labour is very common in some places.

Commercial Sex Workers

Child prostitution has been defined as "the act of engaging or offering the services of a child to perform sexual acts for money or other consideration...". This definition stresses that child prostitution is not committed by children but by the adults who engage in prostitution or offer a child's sexual services to others. NGOs estimate that at least 1 million girls worldwide are lured or forced into this scandalous form of child exploitation. Child prostitution is more frequent in developing countries such as Brazil where 200,000 children are exploited, but it can be found in developed countries such as the United States, which has at least 100,000 child prostitutes. Although girls are the most frequent targets, boys are also often exploited. There are documented cases of children as young as six or seven being exploited in Brazil. While this huge problem may be widely visible to child-prostitution exploiters, it remains virtually invisible to the people who could help these children.

Commercial sexual exploitation frequently involves trafficking of children whether theyare kidnapped or sold by their parents. The children are often recruited under the false pretense of marriage or a good job in the city. While the main media focus is sex tourism, in which persons from developed countries travel to developing countries in search of sex with children, it is important to keep in mind that local persons also exploit these children. But the new face of exploitation is transnational, with criminal networks that take place not only in neighboring countries but also across the globe. Child prostitutes suffer extreme physical and mental abuse, making this form of exploitation one of the most hazardous. They also risk drug addiction, early and unwanted pregnancies, and HIV and other sexually transmitted diseases. (UNICEF,1997), (Bureau of International Labour Affairs, 1998)The process of rescue and rehabilitation for these children is very complicated. They are frequently prosecuted by the system that should be protecting them. Even if they manage to return to their homes, they often face stigma and rejection by their families and communities.

Work for the Family

While working for their families, children can learn from a reasonable level of participation in the household chores that can develop a sense of self-worth. But sometimes, working for the family is essential to enable the parents to work outside the home. (UNICEF, 1997)This is a hidden form of exploitation that affects mainly girls and it is often not even considered work. In Brazil four percent of the children between the ages **of 10 and 14 and** nine percent of the children between 15 and 17 perform exclusively household activities without attending school. Work for the family can demand long hours, thus preventing the children from going toschool or doing well in school, perpetuating the poverty cycle. It also includes some heavy chores as taking care of siblings and carrying heavy loads of firewood and buckets of water. (UNICEF, 1997)

Children are susceptible to all of the dangerous exposures faced by adults when placed in the same environment. However, children differ biologically from adults in their anatomical, physiological, and psychological characteristics because of their process of growth and development. Thus, exposure hazards that affect adults can affect children much more strongly. In this section we examine the epidemiologic evidences and the theoretical concerns for exposures that could be particularly dangerous for children.

Epidemiological Evidence:

The impact of child labour on injuries has been studied largely in the United States. These studies show that children have a higher risk of injuries than adults. In a study inthe United States, teens between 15 and 17 have an injury rate of 4.9 per 100% full time equivalent workers, while in the group of 16 years of age and older this rate was 2.8. There is also evidence that heavy loads can be more dangerous for children the smaller they are. Parker et al. found that back injuries were more common in smaller workers than in larger workers. The other epidemiological evidence that highlights dangerous exposures for children come mainly from studies of young workers and from environmental studies. These studies show that children have higher susceptibility to lead, silica and benzene. In addition, children are more susceptible to noise, heat and ionizing radiation

Theoretical Concerns:

Work environment

The IOM report raises concerns that inappropriate assignments for children to perform tasks for which they are developmentally incapable of undertaking result in hazardous activities. The inappropriate structure of difficult work schedules (long hours, early/late hours with frequent changes) and the lack of supervision could increase the risk of work-related injuries and illnesses. Also, such characteristics of children and adolescents as inexperience, lack of physical and emotional maturity, adolescent sleepneeds and the need to balance school and work would require work environments to structure and to minimize the risks to which young people are exposed.

Ergonomic Factors

The report also focuses upon the developmental factors that could put teens at a higher risk than adults. Childhood and adolescence are periods of rapid growth in a young person's life. Thus, they could be at particularly high risk of injuring ligaments and damaging bone-growth plates. Although little research has been done on the long-term consequences of premature exposure to heavy work and to repetitive back-straining movements, ergonomic factors, nevertheless, remain a concern.

Carcinogenic Exposures

Experts have hypothesized that children are particularly vulnerable to potential carcinogens due to their rapid cell growth. (Committee on the Health and Safet y Implications of Child Labour, 1998)

4.2.4 Chemical Exposures

There are concerns that chemical exposures could have adverse effects on normal hormonal development of adolescents, altering the delicate balance of hormones and their feedback loops. Chemical exposures could result in devastating effects, given the importance of the endocrine system during this life period. Some authors also believe that exposures to toxic chemicals at a very young age could alter the body's response to future toxic exposures.

Machines

Children using machines, tools and work furniture (seats, workbenches, etc.) designed for adults may develop musculoskeletal disorders such as chronic repetitive-strain injuries, repetitive-motion trauma, back problems, tenosynovitis, vibration-induced disorders and white-finger syndrome. They could also be at higher risk for injuries due to fatigue. Moreover, personal protective equipment frequently does not fit children. Thus, they often have to work without it or use alternative devices that do not provide real protection. (Forastieri, 1997)

Education on Occupational Health and Safety

Knowing that there are hazards in most jobs, it is important to educate young workers on occupational safety and health. This initiative should raise awareness about workplace hazards and ways of preventing illnesses and injuries; raise awareness about their rights on the job and resources available to assist and encourage them to be active participants in creating and maintaining safe and healthful work environments.

Market-based Initiatives

The market-based initiatives had been playing an important rule in raising the public awareness particularly in developed countries and it is a strategy that can be explored in developing countries. These initiatives include a variety of product labelling schemes and/or corporate codes of conduct designed to inform consumers that the goods they are buying are not made or processed by children. However, to avoid the migration of the child labour to more hazardous, more hidden and worst paid jobs, these policies should be complemented by investments in schooling and the inclusion in the codes ofconduct the payment of decent wages for adults, so that the need of the families to relyon child labour may be reduced. (ILO, 1997)

Probably it is good to work, for teens, in a non-hazardous job, in low or medium intensity. It is better as higher the quality of work and as more related with the future career it is. But the child labour can have a major impact on health and development, soit is important to combat the child work in hazardous activities, the bonded labour and the work of the children in a very young age. The information system on this subject is very rudimentary. Thus the system should be built in a way that it includes the agricultural sector and the informal sector the major child employers. Also, some research is necessary to evaluate the illegal child labour, asthe work of the very young and the ones in illegal activities as prostitution and drug traffic. The impact of the child labour on health is an issue that needs further research. It is known that the children are exposed, at least, to the same exposures as the adults when performing the same activities. There are also epidemiological evidences that the children can be more susceptible to some exposures than adults are. But there is a lot to be known in this subject, many theoretical concerns about the higher child susceptibility to exposures need to be studied. The shape of child labour is very dynamic and changes in time. The new trends need to be examined to establish its impact on health. Things that already happened in developed countries start to happen in the most developed areas of the developing countries. More and more the children combine school and work, so if on the one hand the work is not depriving the school attendance, on the other it can be creating a great burden in terms of the time consumed with both activities, reducing the time to rest and play. Another trend is the exclusion of the very poor from the market. It is already established that the very poor work in more hazardous jobs than advantaged children. Moreover as the markets become sophisticated, the very poor, which are the ones in most need, have difficulties finding a job, once they do not have the minimum necessary skills. This trend reinforces the importance of the primary education as a way to decrease the number of excluded people and minimizes social inequities. Some advantaged children had been working for discretionary money. It is a relatively large amount of money to buy superfluous things without any familiar compromises orany savings addressed to future big expenses. Some authors have questioned whether it is beneficial to promote money management skills, since it could generate subsequent dissatisfaction with their living standards when they need to deal with general expenses of the real life The developing countries have some particular subjects that need to be studied. Most of the child workers in these regions are very poor and an excessive number are malnourished. Thus it is important to evaluate the impact of work exposures on malnourished children as a way to support the need of policies addressed to the adequate food intake of workers in general and child workers in particular, as the meal provision at work. Some activities that occur just in developing countries also need to be evaluated. The bonded labour is not justifiable in today's world and needs to be a priority in every place it exists. The huge informal sector is a phenomenon of current economies. In a small city in the south of Brazil 85 per cent of the child workers are in the informal sector. Thus despite the difficulties to access data on it, the informal sector with its more visible and more hidden child labour activity, street workers and domestic services, needs to be studied and covered by the policies to combat child labour. Another hidden activity in developing countries that can not be forgotten is the exclusive household activities without attendance to school. Almost nothing is known on the impact of this type of work on health. The work at home usually has a poor status, is unpaid, often is not recognized as work and besides depriving children from education, mainly girls, could also have important health consequences. The policies to combat child labour should be as comprehensive and articulated as possible and great care should be taken to avoid undesired consequences, as the migration of child workers to the worst types of jobs. The priorities and the goals should be established according to the size and shape of the problem in each place. But it 16 seems reasonable to say that, for the developing countries, the single most effective policy to combat child labour is the universalisation of a good quality primary education. On the other hand, for developed and developing countries, the combat of the illegal child work and the promotion of good quality teen job, as apprenticeships for future careers are probably policies that should be applied.

6

Child Labour and Human Rights

The history of public concern with child labour significantly predates the industrial revolution, with some restriction prohibiting the employment of children in selective dangerous areas of work having been enacted as early as 13th century. However, the process of changing limited concern regarding child labour into a broad social consensus was a slow one, involving much public debate during which the perception of the child gradually moved from one of a vital wage earner to that of a vulnerable individual to be loved and protected. Even as practical consideration have been the central force behind the modified emphasis of international child labour rededication efforts, those efforts have also been pushed in new directions by growing social science critique of the philosophies underlying abolition oriented polices and the innovative approaches of some child welfare organisations. An examination of community norms influencing child labour practices must additionally consider community perception of human rights and rights of children Hence local interoperation of human rights doctrine draw on personal biographies, community histories, and on expressions of power relations between interest groups their relationship to formal, legal versions has to be discovered, not assumed. Also human rights related meanings should be held at the multiple levels of social formation that child labour-house hold, community, and nation/world. But it will take major coalition of organisations working at grass root level (Guptha, 1999).

The international community has been concerned about child labour for along time and attempted to curb it at the first session of the International Labour Organization (ILO) in 1919 by establishing fourteen years as the

---

minimum age for children to be employed in industry. 1. In 1973, the Minimum Age Convention of the ILO (Convention 138, or C138) defined child labour as economic activity performed by a person under the age of fifteen, and prohibited it for being hazardous to the physical, mental, and moral well-being of the child as well as for preventing effective schooling. 2. The UN Convention on the Rights of the Child, adopted by the General Assembly on 20 November 1989, also included several articles against economic exploitation and abuse of children. 3. Among the human rights conventions of the United Nations (UN), the Convention on the Rights of the Child enjoys a special status and popularity. A record number of countries participated in the Convention's treaty-signing ceremony in January 1990, and the Convention broke UN records again by entering into force on 25 September 1990, less than a year after being adopted. 4. As this paper was written at the end of 2000, this Convention was the closest to achieving universal ratification with 191 state parties—the only exceptions being the United States, which signed it but did not ratify it,and Somalia, which did neither. Despite this high level of state support for the convention on children's rights, only a minority of the world's children fully enjoys the rights included in it, and many children are denied childhood. While Article 32 of the Convention obligates states to protect children "from economic exploitation and from performing any work that is likely to be hazardous or to interfere with the child's education, or to be harmful to the child's health or physical ,mental, spiritual, moral, or social development," millions of children are overburdened with adult responsibilities and work in hazardous conditions. 5. In fact, after not being able to gather enough support for the Minimum Age Convention—it is ratified by only 103 states because it is considered too complex and difficult to implement—the ILO adopted a new convention, Worst Forms of Child Labour Convention (C182), in 1999. The Convention, which entered into force on 19 November 2000, and acquired forty-nine ratification's, prioritizes the struggle against the worst forms of child labour and calls for their elimination for all persons under the age of eighteen slavery or practices similar to slavery, such as the sale and trafficking of children, debt bondage and serfdom, and forced labour or compulsory labour, including forced or compulsory recruitment of children for use in armed conflict; (b) the use, procuring or offering of a child for prostitution, for the production of pornography, or for pornographic performance; (c) the use, procuring or offering of a child for illicit activities, in particular for the production and trafficking of drugs as defined in the relevant international treaties; (d) work which, by its nature or the circumstances in which it is carried out, is likely to harm the health, safety, or morals of children (Behura,1990)

There is no way to throughly enumerate the various ways in which children around the world are economically exploited and physically mistreated. But the numbers are great — and the suffering widespread. Behind the hideous imagery — of children beaten or sexually abused by parents; ravaged beyond their years by hard living and drug abuse on the streets; maimed by landmines or turned into killers by war; stricken with AIDS — are the all-too-common struggles against disease, hardship, and family or social traditions that compromise children's humanity or subject them to physical and emotional suffering.

The Special Rapporteur's Role

To highlight the existence of the most egregious violations of international human rights law and encourage Governments to investigate particular cases, the United Nations Commission on Human Rights has appointed a Special Rapporteur on the sale of children, child prostitution and child pornography. The Special Rapporteur, an expert in the field, works to gather and analyse facts for the Commission.

The condition most common to children who suffer, or are deprived of, opportunity is the poverty resulting from economic injustice. "The most perverse form of denial of child rights is poverty, because poverty makes it impossible to satisfy those needs that are basic rights", says Tereza Albenez, Special Advisor to the United Nations Children's Fund (UNICEF) on the Convention on the Rights of the Child.

According to figures compiled by UNICEF — the United Nations organization most directly concerned with children's issues — there are now well over a dozen countries in which conditions for children are far below the norms to be expected for their levels of economic development. This includes such gauges as malnutrition levels; under-five mortality rates; percentage of children reaching the fifth grade of primary school; and low literacy rates for women.

In many poor countries, children work to supplement meagre family income or otherwise to help the family business. Although they may not always work under the most desirable conditions, most are not being intentionally exploited by their families. The real issue in such cases is not whether the children work or not, but whether the conditions under which they work are just, and whether they are being denied other basic rights because of their work — such as the right to education, to freedom from abuse, and to proper health care.

Solving a Complex Dilemma

A number of those working on behalf of child rights have come to realize that in many of the poorer countries, if children are to stop working, some form of financial compensation must be found for their families.

One creative response to this kind of complex dilemma has come from Bangladesh. In reaction to United States Congressional legislation mandating a boycott of companies in the garment industry that use child labour, companies in the garment industry in Bangladesh began ousting children from their jobs — as many as 50,000 in a four-month period. The result was that many of the children were worse off than they had been when they were working, having taken other, less desirable jobs or living in the street — but not going to school.

In July 1995, after negotiations with non-governmental organizations (NGOs), as well as UNICEF and the International Labour Organization (ILO), the Bangladesh Garment Manufacturers and Exporters Association (BGMEA) signed a Memorandum of Understanding stipulating that BGMEA would ask "that no underaged worker will be terminated until the appropriate school programmes for the workers can be put in place".

UNICEF has committed itself to supporting the education of the children, and the ILO has pledged to contribute money and technical assistance to the establishment of a labour inspection system to monitor implementation of the Memorandum of Understanding. Under the agreement, stipends will be provided to child workers attending the school programmes. All parties also agreed to take steps "to create positive public awareness" with respect to issues of child labour and education.

Injustices Perpetrated by Adults

But the more direct injustices perpetrated largely by adults — and manifested in the large numbers of children exploited as labourers and prostitutes or maimed by war — require further public exposure and protective laws that are actually enforced.

In the last decade, an estimated two million children have been killed in armed conflict, many of them by some of the 100 million landmines thought to be concealed in 62 countries. A total of perhaps four to five million more have been disabled as a result of their experience in war, and more than 12 million have been made homeless.

As for child labour, while experts agree that there are few accurate statistics available, the best estimates from the ILO are that there are nearly 80 million children under 15 working as labourers. It is also estimated that the number of children under 18 involved in prostitution exceeds two million, one million of whom are in Asia and 300,000 in the United States.

"Poverty cannot be accepted as a pretext and justification for the exploitation of children," wrote Vitit Muntarbhorn, until 1995 the Special Rapporteur on the sale of children, child prostitution and child pornography. "It does not explain the huge global demand with, in many instances, customers from rich countries circumventing their national laws to exploit children in other countries. Sex tourism has spread its illicit wings wide, and paedophiles search for their victims in all parts of the globe. The problem is compounded by the criminal networks which benefit from the trade in children, and by collusion and corruption in many national settings".

Victimizing the Marginalized

"It has become increasingly obvious that many children used for labour and sexual exploitation are lured from particular racial or social groups, rather than from the well-endowed groups in power," the Special Rapporteur went on, in a January 1994 report to the United Nations Commission on Human Rights. "In South Asia, it is the children of the 'untouchables' who are most often victimized in child labour situations".

The Special Rapporteur said a field visit to Nepal showed that "it is primarily girls from hill-tribe groups in that country who are tricked and sold into prostitution, both local and transnational. The pattern is repeated in other parts of the world, where the children of minorities, migrant workers and/or indigenous peoples, who are already marginalized, are often the main victims of such exploitation".

The Special Rapporteur — Mr. Muntarbhorn was succeeded by Mrs. O. Calcetas-Santos — has often had difficulty obtaining information from Governments in response to queries about such matters as the sale and abduction of children; bonded labour; child prostitution; or sale of child organs. But in certain cases the Rapporteur's inquiries have added an international level of accountability in otherwise domestic cases.

Abuses Against Street Children

In August 1993, to cite one example, the Special Rapporteur communicated with the Brazilian Government concerning allegations of the exploitation and abuse of street children by law-enforcement officials. The officials were alleged to have killed eight street children and injured others in Rio de Janeiro in July 1993. The allegation followed a long list of others noted in the Special Rapporteur's report on Brazil submitted to the Commission on Human Rights in 1992.

The Brazilian Government responded by acknowledging the charge. "As pointed out in your communication, this incident is not an isolated case", the Government said in its response. "The Brazilian Government is well aware that the killings of street children are not a new phenomenon and that certain elements of the policy may be implicated in the actions of 'death' squads". Three policemen and a fourth man were in prison awaiting trial for murder, and the commander of the Fifth Police Corps in Rio de Janeiro, to whom the three policemen were subordinated, was dismissed from his post.

Non-governmental organizations have played an important role in pressuring Governments to respect both international law and in many cases similar laws in their own countries, particularly when it is clear that they have been partly or largely responsible for violations of those laws.

Human Rights Watch, a non-governmental human rights organization with offices in Europe and the United States, has investigated numerous allegations. These include trafficking of women and girls from Nepal into India for use as prostitutes; the conditions of bonded labourers in Pakistan, many of whom are children; and the improper detention of juveniles by the criminal-justice system in Jamaica. Human Rights Watch recently released reports on India and Pakistan in mid-1995 that were highly critical of Government complicity.

In the United States, new tools for fighting sexual abuse of children overseas and international child pornography have been incorporated into the Mann Act, a 1910 Act of Congress originally aimed at prohibiting the interstate transportation of women "for immoral purposes". The amendments, approved after several years of lobbying by voluntary agencies, make it illegal for American citizens and resident aliens to travel abroad to engage in sexual acts with minors. The measures would bring the law into line with US domestic policy. The law — part of the Violent Crime Control and Law Enforcement Act of 1994, which was signed into law by President Clinton — also pertains to those who conspire to commit such acts, such as sex-tour operators.

A 1986 amendment to the Mann Act made it a crime to transport a person under 18 between states or abroad with the intention of having the young person engage in sexual activity.

Halting Unlawful Jailings

In response to an earlier report on conditions in Jamaica, where juvenile offenders were being unlawfully locked up with adults, some of the children were released. Local Government agencies and organizations began to explore alternatives to imprisonment for juvenile offenders, and training programmes on the rights of juveniles was begun for guards.

"If you get people out of custody or get Governments to change their policy", says Lois Whitman, Director of the Children's Rights Project at Human Rights Watch, "that is progress".

Prior to the 20th century, children were for the most part regarded as inferior and subordinate to adults, and childhood was a period of life that was often brief and regarded as a stage of passage to adulthood. Now, in the latter half of the century, childhood is regarded as a relatively sacred part of life among many of the more affluent. But it is still a period of great struggle and deprivation for children in most of the rest of the world.

Children have been included, either directly or indirectly, in most of the nearly 80 treaties and decrees on human rights in this century. The first major step on behalf of children taken by the United Nations was UNICEF's creation in December 1946.

Two years later, the Universal Declaration of Human Rights was adopted by the General Assembly. The provisions of that Declaration and its two International Covenants on human rights, adopted in 1966, recognized that child rights need protection.

The 1959 Declaration on the Rights of the Child was the first United Nations statement devoted exclusively to the rights of children, but served more as a moral rather than legally binding framework. The special plight of girls was addressed in part by the Convention on the Elimination of All Forms of Discrimination Against Women, adopted in 1979. The Working Group on Contemporary Forms of Slavery annually addresses such issues as child labour and debt bondage.

A Global Pact on Children's Rights

It took until the 1990s, however, for all of the pieces to come together in the form of the Convention on the Rights of the Child, which was adopted by the General Assembly in 1989. The Convention's 54 articles cover everything from a child's right to be free from sexual and economic exploitation, to the right to his or her own opinion, and to the right to education, health care, and economic opportunity.

By September 1995, 178 countries had ratified the Convention. A dozen more, some of which had been created since the Convention was adopted six years earlier, were considering it. As a result of this growing support, according to Ms Albenez of UNICEF, childhood is coming to be widely seen not as "some kind of probation period before becoming an adult". Instead, she said, "the child emerges as an individual with dignity who has all the rights of a full human being."

The initiative for the Convention came from the Government of Poland, which submitted a Draft Convention to the Commission on Human Rights in 1978, prior to celebration of the 20th anniversary of the Declaration on the Rights of the Child during the International Year of the Child in 1979. That led to a decade of collabouration between a small group of non-governmental organizations, including Radda Barnen of Sweden, the International Child Catholic Bureau, and Defense for Children International, and United Nations human rights experts.

After a lengthy period of careful negotiations, the Convention on the Rights of the Child was adopted in November 1989 by a vote of the General Assembly. By September of the following year, the Convention had obtained the 20 ratifications required for its entry into force as international law. Its importance as a foundation of modern human rights law was later underscored at the 1993 World Conference on Human Rights in Vienna.

Human Rights and Development

By the late 1980s, progress in attracting support for the Convention had drawn the attention of UNICEF. While the organization has always devoted itself to the improvement of social and economic conditions for children, primarily in the fields of health and education, it was not until then that it saw the potential for integrating human rights objectives with more traditional development programmes.

While UNICEF originally included the Convention as one of a number of its programme and advocacy concerns, by late 1994 UNICEF's Executive Director, James P. Grant, announced that the Convention would become the framework for all of UNICEF's programming. In May 1995, UNICEF announced a new procurement policy on child labour, pledging to purchase materials and supplies only from companies that do not exploit child labour. The UNICEF Representative in each country is required to assess the local situation and evaluate the child labour practices of local companies.

Historically there had been a conceptual divide between those who acted as advocates on behalf of human rights and those who pursued the development of economic and social policies and social welfare programmes. Because the Convention on the Rights of the Child covers so much ground, it has provided a conceptual and legislative umbrella for both traditions. The child-protection issues normally associated with human rights are included — among them those of sexual and economic exploitation, of refugee status, and of juvenile justice.

Making Needs a Matter of Rights

Advocacy for many things that had previously been considered as needs and dealt with by Government programmes, the success of which often depended upon political considerations — such as food, shelter, and access

"Poverty cannot be accepted as a pretext and justification for the exploitation of children," wrote Vitit Muntarbhorn, until 1995 the Special Rapporteur on the sale of children, child prostitution and child pornography. "It does not explain the huge global demand with, in many instances, customers from rich countries circumventing their national laws to exploit children in other countries. Sex tourism has spread its illicit wings wide, and paedophiles search for their victims in all parts of the globe. The problem is compounded by the criminal networks which benefit from the trade in children, and by collusion and corruption in many national settings".

Victimizing the Marginalized

"It has become increasingly obvious that many children used for labour and sexual exploitation are lured from particular racial or social groups, rather than from the well-endowed groups in power," the Special Rapporteur went on, in a January 1994 report to the United Nations Commission on Human Rights. "In South Asia, it is the children of the 'untouchables' who are most often victimized in child labour situations".

The Special Rapporteur said a field visit to Nepal showed that "it is primarily girls from hill-tribe groups in that country who are tricked and sold into prostitution, both local and transnational. The pattern is repeated in other parts of the world, where the children of minorities, migrant workers and/or indigenous peoples, who are already marginalized, are often the main victims of such exploitation".

The Special Rapporteur — Mr. Muntarbhorn was succeeded by Mrs. O. Calcetas-Santos — has often had difficulty obtaining information from Governments in response to queries about such matters as the sale and abduction of children; bonded labour; child prostitution; or sale of child organs. But in certain cases the Rapporteur's inquiries have added an international level of accountability in otherwise domestic cases.

Abuses Against Street Children

In August 1993, to cite one example, the Special Rapporteur communicated with the Brazilian Government concerning allegations of the exploitation and abuse of street children by law-enforcement officials. The officials were alleged to have killed eight street children and injured others in Rio de Janeiro in July 1993. The allegation followed a long list of others noted in the Special Rapporteur's report on Brazil submitted to the Commission on Human Rights in 1992.

The Brazilian Government responded by acknowledging the charge. "As pointed out in your communication, this incident is not an isolated case", the Government said in its response. "The Brazilian Government is well aware that the killings of street children are not a new phenomenon and that certain elements of the policy may be implicated in the actions of 'death' squads". Three policemen and a fourth man were in prison awaiting trial for murder, and the commander of the Fifth Police Corps in Rio de Janeiro, to whom the three policemen were subordinated, was dismissed from his post.

Non-governmental organizations have played an important role in pressuring Governments to respect both international law and in many cases similar laws in their own countries, particularly when it is clear that they have been partly or largely responsible for violations of those laws.

Human Rights Watch, a non-governmental human rights organization with offices in Europe and the United States, has investigated numerous allegations. These include trafficking of women and girls from Nepal into India for use as prostitutes; the conditions of bonded labourers in Pakistan, many of whom are children; and the improper detention of juveniles by the criminal-justice system in Jamaica. Human Rights Watch recently released reports on India and Pakistan in mid-1995 that were highly critical of Government complicity.

In the United States, new tools for fighting sexual abuse of children overseas and international child pornography have been incorporated into the Mann Act, a 1910 Act of Congress originally aimed at prohibiting the interstate transportation of women "for immoral purposes". The amendments, approved after several years of lobbying by voluntary agencies, make it illegal for American citizens and resident aliens to travel abroad to engage in sexual acts with minors. The measures would bring the law into line with US domestic policy. The law — part of the Violent Crime Control and Law Enforcement Act of 1994, which was signed into law by President Clinton — also pertains to those who conspire to commit such acts, such as sex-tour operators.

A 1986 amendment to the Mann Act made it a crime to transport a person under 18 between states or abroad with the intention of having the young person engage in sexual activity.

Halting Unlawful Jailings

In response to an earlier report on conditions in Jamaica, where juvenile offenders were being unlawfully locked up with adults, some of the children were released. Local Government agencies and organizations began to explore alternatives to imprisonment for juvenile offenders, and training programmes on the rights of juveniles was begun for guards.

"If you get people out of custody or get Governments to change their policy", says Lois Whitman, Director of the Children's Rights Project at Human Rights Watch, "that is progress".

In Jamaica, the Government has started a legislative review and, despite heavy debt payments, is increasing its expenditures for children.

In Nicaragua, the Government report to the Committee has been made public, a basis is being established for a Child and Adolescent legal code, and a public policy for children is being considered.

And in 1991, the Government of Colombia created the State Information Agency for Child Rights.

Listening to Children's Voices

In the best spirit of the Convention, the Government of Nepal is seeking input from children as part of its preparation for reporting to the Committee. In April 1995, 29 children participated in a four-day workshop on the Convention sponsored by a consortium of NGOs and UNICEF. Included were working children, a street boy, a disabled girl, children from refugee communities and those from both urban English-language schools and Nepali schools. Ultimately, they took discussion of the Convention back to their communities and met with the Prime Minister.

Even in countries where both the legality and morality of human rights covenants have been abandoned or repeatedly violated, efforts are being made in the name of the Convention. In Sudan, UNICEF and Operation Lifeline Sudan (OLS) partners have solicited support for the Convention from the Sudan Peoples' Liberation Movement (SPLM) and the South Sudan Independence Movement (SSIM), the rebel movements in control of much of southern Sudan. This is happening in an area where there are no national laws, and where military rule prevails. Relations between OLS and political authorities are governed by ground rules which OLS recently rewrote to include a statement of humanitarian principles.

These principles include a statement of support both for the Convention and the Geneva Convention, according to the Report from Sudan.

"Both rebel movements have signed the ground rules", the Report said. "This is an important step forward since it is the first time the movements have made such pledges toward child rights and will provide UNICEF/OLS with a much better opportunity to address breaches and violations."

But the realities in much of the world are that despite national laws that conform to a United Nations Convention, enforcement will be the determining factor in whether or not children's rights are protected. Even in countries with sophisticated legal systems the lack of enforcement is a problem.

"In India," according to the Special Rapporteur, "despite laws prohibiting children under 14 from working in hazardous industries, violations are widespread. They include transgressions in industries such as those producing matches, fireworks, glass and bricks, in diamond cutting and lock making, and in stone quarries."

The hope is that the Convention will continue to stimulate the kind of debate that often leads to attitudinal change. Child rights need to be actively respected rather than simply acknowledged, and advocates admit that more than the passage of laws and publicizing of the Convention will be required. "It really is a matter of a change of mentality," says Mrs. Raadi-Azarakhchi of the International Committee on the Rights of the Child.

"We believe the Convention is a wonderful instrument," says Ricardo Domenici, secretary-general of the NGO group Defense of Children International and an advocate of the Convention for more than a decade. "But unless there are really socially conscious policies in the country, the Convention won't make that much of a difference. It is still true that things are not very good for children."

Many social scientists have come to an agreement that the child labour is more a family based, rather than an economic one (wind, 2001). The issue of child labour is sometimes debated on the basis of a cultural framework. More precisely, child activities are perceived either as a socializing way for children or an apprenticeship way of life. In a certain meaning these arguments deny the value of human rights. If Sen (1999) does not focus particularly on child labour, he rejects clearly the cultural point of view. Moreover, in its discussion about human rights, Sen, establishes a distinction between substantive opportunities and freedom of processes. He focuses essentially on substantive opportunities, as the capability approach seems more in phase with this way of thinking. Human rights become entitlements to capability.

Currently an analysis of application of the capability approach to the issue of child labour has got an attention among contemporary social scientists. Firstly, they are discussing the cultural argument of child labour. Scientists arguing, on the one hand, that this point of view is not sustainable and cannot be opposite to human rights approach; and on the other hand, they continuing that the distinction between child work and child labour may be in accordance with the cultural framework, but does not constitute a rejection of human rights. Secondly, starting from the distinction made by Sen between substantive opportunities and freedom of processes, we show that substantive opportunities renews the issue of child labour by bringing critical aspects in debate. However, this aspect leads us to consider only a part of the child labour question. Freedom of processes also plays its role. Focusing on a single approach of substantive opportunities enlightens the importance of the process of decision dealt with the intrafamily issue related to children. Thirdly, social scientists go beyond this first limit to the capability approach using Nussbaum (2000) capabilities list.

to education and health care — can now be fortified by their inclusion as one of a larger number of human rights.

"Needs you can't claim," says Ms Albenez of UNICEF. "Rights you can claim. Now you have claims for each of those needs."

Social reformers and human rights lawyers have defended individual children's rights or pursued political or policy objectives deemed advantageous to children for many years. But with the Convention the concern can now be regarded as universal.

The ratification of the Convention by so many countries means that its articles and principles are now being adapted to, and becoming part of, national laws. The World Conference on Human Rights called for universal

ratification of the Child Convention by 1995. While the recent intensification of interest and concentration of resources devoted to child rights following adoption of the Convention has not yet yielded particularly dramatic or even measurable results directly affecting the daily lives of most of the world's children, it has spawned efforts at legislative reform in countries around the world — particularly in Latin America and Southeast Asia.

A Catalyst for National Action

"The Convention is our essential framework," says Mrs. Raadi-Azarakhchi of the Centre for Human Rights who serves as the Secretary of the Committee on the Rights of the Child, a United Nations body. "It's really a catalyst for action at national level. It provides universal standards — but there are ways it can be interpreted that can be suited to various cultural situations."

The Committee on the Rights of the Child was established by the Convention as a means of monitoring and aiding Governments in bringing their national laws and practices into conformity with the treaty. By late 1995, the Committee, which consists of 10 international members with backgrounds in law, education and social work, had reviewed some 40 reports on implementation plans since 1993 from countries that had ratified the Convention. Reports are required within two years of ratification, and are used as a means of opening a dialogue between members of the Committee, the Government of a ratifying state, and the public in that country.

Non-governmental organizations are invited to contribute information or comment, and in over 20 countries have published alternative reports that either add to or take issue with the Government reports. The Committee reviews the reports and releases its recommendations, which the Government is subsequently obligated to make public. A follow-up report from each

Government is required five years later. It has provided one way of measuring just how serious a Government is about honouring the Convention with legislative or social policy reform.

A Lag in National Reports

According to UNICEF's 1995 Progress of Nations, by the end of February 1995 there were 35 countries that were more than two years late in submitting their reports, and 21 that were more than a year overdue. About one-third of the 174 countries that had ratified the Convention by April 1995 had done so while lodging reservations about certain provisions with the Secretary - General of the United Nations.

In some cases countries have felt the Convention doesn't go far enough. Several countries have stated that it would be better for the Convention to stipulate 18 rather than 15 as the minimum age for participation in armed conflict. Other countries have expressed reservations about matters such as the precise definition of a child and freedom of conscience and religion. Still others have more sweeping and potentially problematic reservations, such as those of several Islamic countries that reserve the right not to apply articles in the Convention that are incompatible with shariah law.

In some cases, Government reports have been challenged as insufficient. In the Philippines, the Government report was challenged by both the National Coalition of NGOs for Monitoring the Convention on the Rights of the Child and the Committee on the Rights of the Child. The Committee noted "a lack of reliable qualitative and quantitative data, a shortcoming of means for programs of implementation, and a lack of indicators and mechanisms to evaluate the progress and impact of policies adopted." The Committee ultimately encouraged the Government to support wider participation of governmental agencies and non-governmental organizations in the process of bringing their national laws into line with the provisions of the Convention.

Progress in National Programmes

The Indonesian Government has increased budget allocations for health services to mothers and children during a period of austerity, developed manuals for law enforcement training on the Convention, and established a Child Protection Institute.

In Costa Rica, a new Legal Code for Minors is being developed using the Convention as the framework. In response to comments from the Committee on the Rights of the Child on the great number of national and international child adoptions in Costa Rica, the Legislature has started reviewing the Hague Convention on international adoption.

There is no way to throughly enumerate the various ways in which children around the world are economically exploited and physically mistreated. But the numbers are great — and the suffering widespread. Behind the hideous imagery — of children beaten or sexually abused by parents; ravaged beyond their years by hard living and drug abuse on the streets; maimed by landmines or turned into killers by war; stricken with AIDS — are the all-too-common struggles against disease, hardship, and family or social traditions that compromise children's humanity or subject them to physical and emotional suffering.

The Special Rapporteur's Role

To highlight the existence of the most egregious violations of international human rights law and encourage Governments to investigate particular cases, the United Nations Commission on Human Rights has appointed a Special Rapporteur on the sale of children, child prostitution and child pornography. The Special Rapporteur, an expert in the field, works to gather and analyse facts for the Commission.

The condition most common to children who suffer, or are deprived of, opportunity is the poverty resulting from economic injustice. "The most perverse form of denial of child rights is poverty, because poverty makes it impossible to satisfy those needs that are basic rights", says Tereza Albenez, Special Advisor to the United Nations Children's Fund (UNICEF) on the Convention on the Rights of the Child.

According to figures compiled by UNICEF — the United Nations organization most directly concerned with children's issues — there are now well over a dozen countries in which conditions for children are far below the norms to be expected for their levels of economic development. This includes such gauges as malnutrition levels; under-five mortality rates; percentage of children reaching the fifth grade of primary school; and low literacy rates for women.

In many poor countries, children work to supplement meagre family income or otherwise to help the family business. Although they may not always work under the most desirable conditions, most are not being intentionally exploited by their families. The real issue in such cases is not whether the children work or not, but whether the conditions under which they work are just, and whether they are being denied other basic rights because of their work — such as the right to education, to freedom from abuse, and to proper health care.

Solving a Complex Dilemma

A number of those working on behalf of child rights have come to realize that in many of the poorer countries, if children are to stop working, some form of financial compensation must be found for their families.

One creative response to this kind of complex dilemma has come from Bangladesh. In reaction to United States Congressional legislation mandating a boycott of companies in the garment industry that use child labour, companies in the garment industry in Bangladesh began ousting children from their jobs — as many as 50,000 in a four-month period. The result was that many of the children were worse off than they had been when they were working, having taken other, less desirable jobs or living in the street — but not going to school.

In July 1995, after negotiations with non-governmental organizations (NGOs), as well as UNICEF and the International Labour Organization (ILO), the Bangladesh Garment Manufacturers and Exporters Association (BGMEA) signed a Memorandum of Understanding stipulating that BGMEA would ask "that no underaged worker will be terminated until the appropriate school programmes for the workers can be put in place".

UNICEF has committed itself to supporting the education of the children, and the ILO has pledged to contribute money and technical assistance to the establishment of a labour inspection system to monitor implementation of the Memorandum of Understanding. Under the agreement, stipends will be provided to child workers attending the school programmes. All parties also agreed to take steps "to create positive public awareness" with respect to issues of child labour and education.

Injustices Perpetrated by Adults

But the more direct injustices perpetrated largely by adults — and manifested in the large numbers of children exploited as labourers and prostitutes or maimed by war — require further public exposure and protective laws that are actually enforced.

In the last decade, an estimated two million children have been killed in armed conflict, many of them by some of the 100 million landmines thought to be concealed in 62 countries. A total of perhaps four to five million more have been disabled as a result of their experience in war, and more than 12 million have been made homeless.

As for child labour, while experts agree that there are few accurate statistics available, the best estimates from the ILO are that there are nearly 80 million children under 15 working as labourers. It is also estimated that the number of children under 18 involved in prostitution exceeds two million, one million of whom are in Asia and 300,000 in the United States.

We argue about capabilities articulation as processes. In this vein we defend capabilities processes *of freedom*. We underline that opportunity to education needs to be completed with other capabilities like emotional capability. The capability approach is then seen as processes. This point of view implies nonetheless an opportunity to be educated but moreover non-violent processes of education is required.

Cultural framework versus child's rights

Interpretation of the cultural framework

The attempts to assert human rights or child's rights are often confronted with the accusation of violation and non-respect of countries cultural specificities. This inquisition is too excessive and most of the time does not rest on any foundation. To us, three arguments clearly reject a "caricatured" conception of defense of cultural specificities. Firstly, as Sen (1999) underlines, if we have to consider these specificities, then they indeed do not concern countries but even more restrained geographical areas and sometimes do concern only with some individuals. It is in fact impossible in most cases to consider that the individuals of the same country have homogenous cultural traits. Significative differences between regions or States, as well as within the same region or country really exist. And these differences do not limit themselves to large countries like India or the USA, but also affect countries of small size like France or Togo. The defenders of cultural specificities should agree that cultural specificities have to be maintained at the finest level that could lead to accept specificities applying to restricted individual groups. But under no circumstances, they can be considered valid for a given country.

Secondly, specificities saying "cultural" constitute a serious attack for human life. Let us imagine that a cultural specificity in a given geographical area consists in mutilating children severely at birth, for instance by cutting them a hand. On what foundation this specificity could be defended? It is clear that the defenders of cultural specificities are badly comfortable to defend cases affecting seriously human life. But they do not provide any appropriate criteria for distinguishing the specificities that can be rejected from those that can be accepted. Unless they accept that some individuals may attack human life, whereas others do not. Many countries experience dramatic practices. Let us choose two examples: the in fibulation and the cramming (force-feeding) are both practices having destructive impacts on children. The former, a deeper and serious form of excision consists of the ablation of clitoris with the suture of sex. The latter practiced essentially in West Africa consists in forcing young girls to eat a huge amount of food (more often, it is puree) in order that they gain weight substantially and become enough fat to respect the standards of beauty and perform a "good and nice" marriage. This practice leads inmost cases to serious problems of obesity and health and invalidates severely the young girls, who indeed are subjected to their husband.

Moreover, various practices, saying cultural traits, are indeed not as ancient as it appears and are the results of socioeconomic evolution. They have no only "cultural" foundations since they result from economic strategies in a context of survival or wealth rising. The dowry issue in India illustrates perfectly this specificity. Marriage and the practice of dowry are strongly embedded in a rigid social context of norms and caste rules. At the same time, new economic and development

Opportunities have a considerable impact on social organisation in Indian society. The social status of a person is determined by his caste. Within a context of economic development, particularly in urban areas, the social status takes into account of several elements: caste, education, nature of the occupation, and income. Within such context, the identity, and therefore the social status, of an individual is not determined by rigid, hereditary factors such as community and caste affiliation, but by economic factors (income, education, occupation). In well-developed urban areas, this leads to a bigger socio-economic heterogeneity within a given caste. So, a striking social change is operated across India and implies new strategies notably within the family. The changes in social status play indeed a major role in the marriage institution, which is regarded as a mean to strike up family relations and to enhance social mobility. In particular, the fact that some families pay higher dowries is for them a way of entering into a prestigious alliance and of distinguishing themselves within their own community.

This matrimonial strategy through dowry payments is associated with a strategy of differentiation and distinction, which enables the families to improve their social status and shape new identities for themselves. Thus the contemporary practice of dowry is seen for families as a strategy of investment in social status. It leads to a process of identity distinction involving spatial and social expansion of dowry and its inflation (Ballet and Radja, 2005; Ballet and Radja, 2006).The argument of cultural specificities is often a wrong argument in the hands of the conservatives finding a special interest to maintain situation in the state. This argument is not relevant taken in a broad sense which would include all practices. In this sense, it is not an opposable argument to human rights and child's rights. It does not mean that it is necessary to deny any contextual specificity. But on one hand these contextual specificities are not necessarily cultural and can be led to change with context; on the other hand they have to be confronted to human rights and to child's rights to establish if they do not constitute a fundamental violation of these rights.

The convention of the child's rights and its implications

The United Nation has implemented the convention on the rights of the child in 1989 to endow children with the same rights as adult and comfort the idea that children as human being having a fragile status must need rights, which protect them. The convention comprises 54 articles and two protocols. The convention is based on five fundamental principles stipulating that all children throughout the world regardless to its race, colour, religion, ethnic, caste, opinion, gender, wealth must beneficial of the right to survival, to develop to the fullest, to be protected from harmful influences, abuse and exploitation, to participate fully in family, cultural and social life. 187 countries except the United States of America and Somalia have ratified the convention.

UN Convention on child Rights-1989

PREAMBLE

The States Parties to the present Convention,

Considering that, in accordance with the principles proclaimed in the Charter of the United Nations, recognition of the inherent dignity and of the equal and inalienable rights of all members of the human family is the foundation of freedom, justice and peace in the world,

Bearing in mind that the peoples of the United Nations have, in the Charter, reaffirmed their faith in fundamental human rights and in the dignity and worth of the human person, and have determined to promote social progress and better standards of life in larger freedom,

Recognizing that the United Nations has, in the Universal Declaration of Human Rights and in the International Covenants on Human Rights, proclaimed and agreed that everyone is entitled to all the rights and freedoms set forth therein, without distinction of any kind, such as race, colour, sex, language, religion, political or other opinion, national or social origin, property, birth or other status,

Recalling that, in the Universal Declaration of Human Rights, the United Nations has proclaimed that childhood is entitled to special care and assistance,

Convinced that the family, as the fundamental group of society and the natural environment for the growth and well-being of all its members and particularly children, should be afforded the necessary protection and assistance so that it can fully assume its responsibilities within the community,

Recognizing that the child, for the full and harmonious development of his or her personality, should grow up in a family environment, in an atmosphere of happiness, love and understanding,

Considering that the child should be fully prepared to live an individual life in society, and brought up in the spirit of the ideals proclaimed in the Charter of the United Nations, and in particular in the spirit of peace, dignity, tolerance, freedom, equality and solidarity,

Bearing in mind that the need to extend particular care to the child has been stated in the Geneva Declaration of the Rights of the Child of 1924 and in the Declaration of the Rights of the Child adopted by the General Assembly on 20 November 1959 and recognized in the Universal Declaration of Human Rights, in the International Covenant on Civil and Political Rights (in particular in articles 23 and 24), in the International Covenant on Economic, Social and Cultural Rights (in particular in article 10) and in the statutes and relevant instruments of specialized agencies and international organizations concerned with the welfare of children,

Bearing in mind that, as indicated in the Declaration of the Rights of the Child, "the child, by reason of his physical and mental immaturity, needs special safeguards and care, including appropriate legal protection, before as well as after birth",

Recalling the provisions of the Declaration on Social and Legal Principles relating to the Protection and Welfare of Children, with Special Reference to Foster Placement and Adoption Nationally and Internationally; the United Nations Standard Minimum Rules for the Administration of Juvenile Justice (The Beijing Rules) ; and the Declaration on the Protection of Women and Children in Emergency and Armed Conflict,

Recognizing that, in all countries in the world, there are children living in exceptionally difficult conditions, and that such children need special consideration,

Taking due account of the importance of the traditions and cultural values of each people for the protection and harmonious development of the child,

Recognizing the importance of international co-operation for improving the living conditions of children in every country, in particular in the developing countries,

Have agreed as follows:

PART I

Article 1

For the purposes of the present Convention, a child means every human being below the age of eighteen years unless under the law applicable to the child, majority is attained earlier.

Article 2

1. States Parties shall respect and ensure the rights set forth in the present Convention to each child within their jurisdiction without discrimination of any kind, irrespective of the child's or his or her parent's or legal guardian's race, colour, sex, language, religion, political or other opinion, national, ethnic or social origin, property, disability, birth or other status.
2. States Parties shall take all appropriate measures to ensure that the child is protected against all forms of discrimination or punishment on the basis of the status, activities, expressed opinions, or beliefs of the child's parents, legal guardians, or family members.

Article 3

1. In all actions concerning children, whether undertaken by public or private social welfare institutions, courts of law, administrative authorities or legislative bodies, the best interests of the child shall be a primary consideration.
2. States Parties undertake to ensure the child such protection and care as is necessary for his or her well-being, taking into account the rights and duties of his or her parents, legal guardians, or other individuals legally responsible for him or her, and, to this end, shall take all appropriate legislative and administrative measures.
3. States Parties shall ensure that the institutions, services and facilities responsible for the care or protection of children shall conform with the standards established by competent authorities, particularly in the areas of safety, health, in the number and suitability of their staff, as well as competent supervision.

Article 4

States Parties shall undertake all appropriate legislative, administrative, and other measures for the implementation of the rights recognized in the present Convention. With regard to economic, social and cultural rights, States Parties shall undertake such measures to the maximum extent of their available resources and, where needed, within the framework of international co-operation.

Article 5

States Parties shall respect the responsibilities, rights and duties of parents or, where applicable, the members of the extended family or community as provided for by local custom, legal guardians or other persons legally responsible for the child, to provide, in a manner consistent with the evolving capacities of the child, appropriate direction and guidance in the exercise by the child of the rights recognized in the present Convention.

Article 6

1. States Parties recognize that every child has the inherent right to life.
2. States Parties shall ensure to the maximum extent possible the survival and development of the child.

Article 7

1. The child shall be registered immediately after birth and shall have the right from birth to a name, the right to acquire a nationality and. as far as possible, the right to know and be cared for by his or her parents.
2. States Parties shall ensure the implementation of these rights in accordance with their national law and their obligations under the relevant international instruments in this field, in particular where the child would otherwise be stateless.

Article 8

1. States Parties undertake to respect the right of the child to preserve his or her identity, including nationality, name and family relations as recognized by law without unlawful interference.
2. Where a child is illegally deprived of some or all of the elements of his or her identity, States Parties shall provide appropriate assistance and protection, with a view to re-establishing speedily his or her identity.

Article 9

1. States Parties shall ensure that a child shall not be separated from his or her parents against their will, except when competent authorities subject to judicial review determine, in accordance with applicable law and procedures, that such separation is necessary for the best interests of the child. Such determination may be necessary in a particular case such as one involving abuse or neglect of the child by the parents, or one where the parents are living separately and a decision must be made as to the child's place of residence.
2. In any proceedings pursuant to paragraph 1 of the present article, all interested parties shall be given an opportunity to participate in the proceedings and make their views known.
3. States Parties shall respect the right of the child who is separated from one or both parents to maintain personal relations and direct contact with both parents on a regular basis, except if it is contrary to the child's best interests. 4. Where such separation results from any action initiated by a State Party, such as the detention, imprisonment, exile, deportation or death (including death arising from any cause while the person is in the custody of the State) of one or both parents or of the child, that State Party shall, upon request, provide the parents, the child or, if appropriate, another member of the family with the essential information concerning the whereabouts of the absent member(s) of

the family unless the provision of the information would be detrimental to the well-being of the child. States Parties shall further ensure that the submission of such a request shall of itself entail no adverse consequences for the person(s) concerned.

Article 10

1. In accordance with the obligation of States Parties under article 9, paragraph 1, applications by a child or his or her parents to enter or leave a State Party for the purpose of family reunification shall be dealt with by States Parties in a positive, human and expeditious manner. States Parties shall further ensure that the submission of such a request shall entail no adverse consequences for the applicants and for the members of their family.
2. A child whose parents reside in different States shall have the right to maintain on a regular basis, save in exceptional circumstances personal relations and direct contacts with both parents. Towards that end and in accordance with the obligation of States Parties under article 9, paragraph 1, States Parties shall respect the right of the child and his or her parents to leave any country, including their own, and to enter their own country. The right to leave any country shall be subject only to such restrictions as are prescribed by law and which are necessary to protect the national security, public order (order public), public health or morals or the rights and freedoms of others and are consistent with the other rights recognized in the present Convention.

Article 11

1. States Parties shall take measures to combat the illicit transfer and non-return of children abroad.
2. To this end, States Parties shall promote the conclusion of bilateral or multilateral agreements or accession to existing agreements.

Article 12

1. States Parties shall assure to the child who is capable of forming his or her own views the right to express those views freely in all matters affecting the child, the views of the child being given due weight in accordance with the age and maturity of the child.
2. For this purpose, the child shall in particular be provided the opportunity to be heard in any judicial and administrative proceedings affecting the child, either directly, or through a representative or an appropriate body, in a manner consistent with the procedural rules of national law.

Article 13

1. The child shall have the right to freedom of expression; this right shall include freedom to seek, receive and impart information and ideas of all

kinds, regardless of frontiers, either orally, in writing or in print, in the form of art, or through any other media of the child's choice.

2. The exercise of this right may be subject to certain restrictions, but these shall only be such as are provided by law and are necessary:

(a) For respect of the rights or reputations of others; or

(b) For the protection of national security or of public order (order public), or of public health or morals.

Article 14

1. States Parties shall respect the right of the child to freedom of thought, conscience and religion.

2. States Parties shall respect the rights and duties of the parents and, when applicable, legal guardians, to provide direction to the child in the exercise of his or her right in a manner consistent with the evolving capacities of the child.

3. Freedom to manifest one's religion or beliefs may be subject only to such limitations as are prescribed by law and are necessary to protect public safety, order, health or morals, or the fundamental rights and freedoms of others.

Article 15

1. States Parties recognize the rights of the child to freedom of association and to freedom of peaceful assembly.

2. No restrictions may be placed on the exercise of these rights other than those imposed in conformity with the law and which are necessary in a democratic society in the interests of national security or public safety, public order (order public), the protection of public health or morals or the protection of the rights and freedoms of others.

Article 16

1. No child shall be subjected to arbitrary or unlawful interference with his or her privacy, family, home or correspondence, nor to unlawful attacks on his or her honour and reputation.

2. The child has the right to the protection of the law against such interference or attacks.

Article 17

States Parties recognize the important function performed by the mass media and shall ensure that the child has access to information and material from a diversity of national and international sources, especially those aimed at the promotion of his or her social, spiritual and moral well-being and physical and mental health. To this end, States Parties shall:

(a) Encourage the mass media to disseminate information and material of social and cultural benefit to the child and in accordance with the spirit of article 29;

(b) Encourage international co-operation in the production, exchange and dissemination of such information and material from a diversity of cultural, national and international sources;

(c) Encourage the production and dissemination of children's books;

(d) Encourage the mass media to have particular regard to the linguistic needs of the child who belongs to a minority group or who is indigenous;

(e) Encourage the development of appropriate guidelines for the protection of the child from information and material injurious to his or her well-being, bearing in mind the provisions of articles 13 and 18.

Article 18

1. States Parties shall use their best efforts to ensure recognition of the principle that both parents have common responsibilities for the upbringing and development of the child. Parents or, as the case may be, legal guardians, have the primary responsibility for the upbringing and development of the child. The best interests of the child will be their basic concern.
2. For the purpose of guaranteeing and promoting the rights set forth in the present Convention, States Parties shall render appropriate assistance to parents and legal guardians in the performance of their child-rearing responsibilities and shall ensure the development of institutions, facilities and services for the care of children.
3. States Parties shall take all appropriate measures to ensure that children of working parents have the right to benefit from child-care services and facilities for which they are eligible.

Article 19

1. States Parties shall take all appropriate legislative, administrative, social and educational measures to protect the child from all forms of physical or mental violence, injury or abuse, neglect or negligent treatment, maltreatment or exploitation, including sexual abuse, while in the care of parent(s), legal guardian(s) or any other person who has the care of the child.
2. Such protective measures should, as appropriate, include effective procedures for the establishment of social programmes to provide necessary support for the child and for those who have the care of the child, as well as for other forms of prevention and for identification, reporting, referral, investigation, treatment and follow-up of instances of child maltreatment described here to fore, and, as appropriate, for judicial involvement.

Article 20

1. A child temporarily or permanently deprived of his or her family environment, or in whose own best interests cannot be allowed to

remain in that environment, shall be entitled to special protection and assistance provided by the State.

2. States Parties shall in accordance with their national laws ensure alternative care for such a child.

3. Such care could include, inter alia, foster placement, *kafalah* of Islamic law, adoption or if necessary placement in suitable institutions for the care of children. When considering solutions, due regard shall be paid to the desirability of continuity in a child's upbringing and to the child's ethic, religious, cultural and linguistic background.

Article 21

States Parties that recognize and/or permit the system of adoption shall ensure that the best interests of the child shall be the paramount consideration and they shall:

(a) Ensure that the adoption of a child is authorized only by competent authorities who determine, in accordance with applicable law and procedures and on the basis of all pertinent and reliable information, that the adoption is permissible in view of the child's status concerning parents, relatives and legal guardians and that, if required, the persons concerned have given their informed consent to the adoption on the basis of such counselling as may be necessary;

(b) Recognize that inter-country adoption may be considered as an alternative means of child's care, if the child cannot be placed in a foster or an adoptive family or cannot in any suitable manner be cared for in the child's country of origin; (c) Ensure that the child concerned by inter-country adoption enjoys safeguards and standards equivalent to those existing in the case of national adoption;

(d) Take all appropriate measures to ensure that, in inter-country adoption, the placement does not result in improper financial gain for those involved in it;

(e) Promote, where appropriate, the objectives of the present article by concluding bilateral or multilateral arrangements or agreements, and endeavour, within this framework, to ensure that the placement of the child in another country is carried out by competent authorities or organs.

Article 22

1. States Parties shall take appropriate measures to ensure that a child who is seeking refugee status or who is considered a refugee in accordance with applicable international or domestic law and procedures shall, whether unaccompanied or accompanied by his or her parents or by any other person, receive appropriate protection and humanitarian assistance in the enjoyment of applicable rights set forth

in the present Convention and in other international human rights or humanitarian instruments to which the said States are Parties.

2. For this purpose, States Parties shall provide, as they consider appropriate, co-operation in any efforts by the United Nations and other competent intergovernmental organizations or non-governmental organizations co-operating with the United Nations to protect and assist such a child and to trace the parents or other members of the family of any refugee child in order to obtain information necessary for reunification with his or her family. In cases where no parents or other members of the family can be found, the child shall be accorded the same protection as any other child permanently or temporarily deprived of his or her family environment for any reason, as set forth in the present Convention.

Article 23

1. States Parties recognize that a mentally or physically disabled child should enjoy a full and decent life, in conditions which ensure dignity, promote self-reliance and facilitate the child's active participation in the community.

2. States Parties recognize the right of the disabled child to special care and shall encourage and ensure the extension, subject to available resources, to the eligible child and those responsible for his or her care, of assistance for which application is made and which is appropriate to the child's condition and to the circumstances of the parents or others caring for the child. 3. Recognizing the special needs of a disabled child, assistance extended in accordance with paragraph 2 of the present article shall be provided free of charge, whenever possible, taking into account the financial resources of the parents or others caring for the child, and shall be designed to ensure that the disabled child has effective access to and receives education, training, health care services, rehabilitation services, preparation for employment and recreation opportunities in a manner conducive to the child's achieving the fullest possible social integration and individual development, including his or her cultural and spiritual development

4. States Parties shall promote, in the spirit of international cooperation, the exchange of appropriate information in the field of preventive health care and of medical, psychological and functional treatment of disabled children, including dissemination of and access to information concerning methods of rehabilitation, education and vocational services, with the aim of enabling States Parties to improve their capabilities and

skills and to widen their experience in these areas. In this regard, particular account shall be taken of the needs of developing countries.

Article 24

1. States Parties recognize the right of the child to the enjoyment of the highest attainable standard of health and to facilities for the treatment of illness and rehabilitation of health. States Parties shall strive to ensure that no child is deprived of his or her right of access to such health care services.
2. States Parties shall pursue full implementation of this right and, in particular, shall take appropriate measures:
   (a) To diminish infant and child mortality;
   (b) To ensure the provision of necessary medical assistance and health care to all children with emphasis on the development of primary health care;
   (c) To combat disease and malnutrition, including within the framework of primary health care, through, inter alia, the application of readily available technology and through the provision of adequate nutritious foods and clean drinking-water, taking into consideration the dangers and risks of environmental pollution;
   (d) To ensure appropriate pre-natal and post-natal health care for mothers;
   (e) To ensure that all segments of society, in particular parents and children, are informed, have access to education and are supported in the use of basic knowledge of child health and nutrition, the advantages of breastfeeding, hygiene and environmental sanitation and the prevention of accidents;
   (f) To develop preventive health care, guidance for parents and family planning education and services.
3. States Parties shall take all effective and appropriate measures with a view to abolishing traditional practices prejudicial to the health of children.
4. States Parties undertake to promote and encourage international co-operation with a view to achieving progressively the full realization of the right recognized in the present article. In this regard, particular account shall be taken of the needs of developing countries.

Article 25

States Parties recognize the right of a child who has been placed by the competent authorities for the purposes of care, protection or treatment of his or her physical or mental health, to a periodic review of the treatment provided to the child and all other circumstances relevant to his or her placement.

Article 26

1. States Parties shall recognize for every child the right to benefit from social security, including social insurance, and shall take the necessary measures to achieve the full realization of this right in accordance with their national law.
2. The benefits should, where appropriate, be granted, taking into account the resources and the circumstances of the child and persons having responsibility for the maintenance of the child, as well as any other consideration relevant to an application for benefits made by or on behalf of the child.

Article 27

1. States Parties recognize the right of every child to a standard of living adequate for the child's physical, mental, spiritual, moral and social development.
2. The parent(s) or others responsible for the child have the primary responsibility to secure, within their abilities and financial capacities, the conditions of living necessary for the child's development.
3. States Parties, in accordance with national conditions and within their means, shall take appropriate measures to assist parents and others responsible for the child to implement this right and shall in case of need provide material assistance and support programmes, particularly with regard to nutrition, clothing and housing.
4. States Parties shall take all appropriate measures to secure the recovery of maintenance for the child from the parents or other persons having financial responsibility for the child, both within the State Party and from abroad. In particular, where the person having financial responsibility for the child lives in a State different from that of the child, States Parties shall promote the accession to international agreements or the conclusion of such agreements, as well as the making of other appropriate arrangements.

Article 28

1. States Parties recognize the right of the child to education, and with a view to achieving this right progressively and on the basis of equal opportunity, they shall, in particular:
   (a) Make primary education compulsory and available free to all;
   (b) Encourage the development of different forms of secondary education, including general and vocational education, make them available and accessible to every child, and take appropriate

measures such as the introduction of free education and offering financial assistance in case of need;

(c) Make higher education accessible to all on the basis of capacity by every appropriate means;

(d) Make educational and vocational information and guidance available and accessible to all children;

(e) Take measures to encourage regular attendance at schools and the reduction of drop-out rates.

2. States Parties shall take all appropriate measures to ensure that school discipline is administered in a manner consistent with the child's human dignity and in conformity with the present Convention.

3. States Parties shall promote and encourage international cooperation in matters relating to education, in particular with a view to contributing to the elimination of ignorance and illiteracy throughout the world and facilitating access to scientific and technical knowledge and modern teaching methods. In this regard, particular account shall be taken of the needs of developing countries.

Article 29

1. States Parties agree that the education of the child shall be directed to:

(a) The development of the child's personality, talents and mental and physical abilities to their fullest potential;

(b) The development of respect for human rights and fundamental freedoms, and for the principles enshrined in the Charter of the United Nations;

(c) The development of respect for the child's parents, his or her own cultural identity, language and values, for the national values of the country in which the child is living, the country from which he or she may originate, and for civilizations different from his or her own;

(d) The preparation of the child for responsible life in a free society, in the spirit of understanding, peace, tolerance, equality of sexes, and friendship among all peoples, ethic, national and religious groups and persons of indigenous origin;

(e) The development of respect for the natural environment.

2. No part of the present article or article 28 shall be construed so as to interfere with the liberty of individuals and bodies to establish and direct educational institutions, subject always to the observance of the principle set forth in paragraph 1 of the present article and to the requirements that the education given in such institutions shall conform to such minimum standards as may be laid down by the State.

Article 30

In those States in which ethnic, religious or linguistic minorities or persons of indigenous origin exist, a child belonging to such a minority or who is indigenous shall not be denied the right, in community with other members of his or her group, to enjoy his or her own culture, to profess and practise his or her own religion, or to use his or her own language.

Article 31

1. States Parties recognize the right of the child to rest and leisure, to engage in play and recreational activities appropriate to the age of the child and to participate freely in cultural life and the arts.
2. States Parties shall respect and promote the right of the child to participate fully in cultural and artistic life and shall encourage the provision of appropriate and equal opportunities for cultural, artistic, recreational and leisure activity.

Article 32

1. States Parties recognize the right of the child to be protected from economic exploitation and from performing any work that is likely to be hazardous or to interfere with the child's education, or to be harmful to the child's health or physical, mental, spiritual, moral or social development.
2. States Parties shall take legislative, administrative, social and educational measures to ensure the implementation of the present article. To this end, and having regard to the relevant provisions of other international instruments, States Parties shall in particular: (a) Provide for a minimum age or minimum ages for admission to employment;
   (b) Provide for appropriate regulation of the hours and conditions of employment;
   (c) Provide for appropriate penalties or other sanctions to ensure the effective enforcement of the present article.

Article 33

States Parties shall take all appropriate measures, including legislative, administrative, social and educational measures, to protect children from the illicit use of narcotic drugs and psychotropic substances as defined in the relevant international treaties, and to prevent the use of children in the illicit production and trafficking of such substances.

Article 34

States Parties undertake to protect the child from all forms of sexual exploitation and sexual abuse. For these purposes, States Parties shall in particular take all appropriate national, bilateral and multilateral measures to prevent:

(a) The inducement or coercion of a child to engage in any unlawful sexual activity;

(b) The exploitative use of children in prostitution or other unlawful sexual practices;

(c) The exploitative use of children in pornographic performances and materials.

Article 35

States Parties shall take all appropriate national, bilateral and multilateral measures to prevent the abduction of, the sale of or traffic in children for any purpose or in any form.

Article 36

States Parties shall protect the child against all other forms of exploitation prejudicial to any aspects of the child's welfare.

Article 37

States Parties shall ensure that:

(a) No child shall be subjected to torture or other cruel, inhuman or degrading treatment or punishment. Neither capital punishment nor life imprisonment without possibility of release shall be imposed for offences committed by persons below eighteen years of age;

(b) No child shall be deprived of his or her liberty unlawfully or arbitrarily. The arrest, detention or imprisonment of a child shall be in conformity with the law and shall be used only as a measure of last resort and for the shortest appropriate period of time;

(c) Every child deprived of liberty shall be treated with humanity and respect for the inherent dignity of the human person, and in a manner which takes into account the needs of persons of his or her age. In particular, every child deprived of liberty shall be separated from adults unless it is considered in the child's best interest not to do so and shall have the right to maintain contact with his or her family through correspondence and visits, save in exceptional circumstances;

(d) Every child deprived of his or her liberty shall have the right to prompt access to legal and other appropriate assistance, as well as the right to challenge the legality of the deprivation of his or her liberty before a court or other competent, independent and impartial authority, and to a prompt decision on any such action.

Article 38

1. States Parties undertake to respect and to ensure respect for rules of international humanitarian law applicable to them in armed conflicts which are relevant to the child.

2. States Parties shall take all feasible measures to ensure that persons who have not attained the age of fifteen years do not take a direct part in hostilities.
3. States Parties shall refrain from recruiting any person who has not attained the age of fifteen years into their armed forces. In recruiting among those persons who have attained the age of fifteen years but who have not attained the age of eighteen years, States Parties shall endeavour to give priority to those who are oldest.
4. In accordance with their obligations under international humanitarian law to protect the civilian population in armed conflicts, States Parties shall take all feasible measures to ensure protection and care of children who are affected by an armed conflict.

Article 39

States Parties shall take all appropriate measures to promote physical and psychological recovery and social reintegration of a child victim of: any form of neglect, exploitation, or abuse; torture or any other form of cruel, inhuman or degrading treatment or punishment; or armed conflicts. Such recovery and reintegration shall take place in an environment which fosters the health, self-respect and dignity of the child.

Article 40

1. States Parties recognize the right of every child alleged as, accused of, or recognized as having infringed the penal law to be treated in a manner consistent with the promotion of the child's sense of dignity and worth, which reinforces the child's respect for the human rights and fundamental freedoms of others and which takes into account the child's age and the desirability of promoting the child's reintegration and the child's assuming a constructive role in society.
2. To this end, and having regard to the relevant provisions of international instruments, States Parties shall, in particular, ensure that:
   (a) No child shall be alleged as, be accused of, or recognized as having infringed the penal law by reason of acts or omissions that were not prohibited by national or international law at the time they were committed;
   (b) Every child alleged as or accused of having infringed the penal law has at least the following guarantees:
      (i) To be presumed innocent until proven guilty according to law;
      (ii) To be informed promptly and directly of the charges against him or her, and, if appropriate, through his or her parents or

legal guardians, and to have legal or other appropriate assistance in the preparation and presentation of his or her defence;

(iii) To have the matter determined without delay by a competent, independent and impartial authority or judicial body in a fair hearing according to law, in the presence of legal or other appropriate assistance and, unless it is considered not to be in the best interest of the child, in particular, taking into account his or her age or situation, his or her parents or legal guardians;

(iv) Not to be compelled to give testimony or to confess guilt; to examine or have examined adverse witnesses and to obtain the participation and examination of witnesses on his or her behalf under conditions of equality;

(v) If considered to have infringed the penal law, to have this decision and any measures imposed in consequence thereof reviewed by a higher competent, independent and impartial authority or judicial body according to law;

(vi) To have the free assistance of an interpreter if the child cannot understand or speak the language used;

(vii) To have his or her privacy fully respected at all stages of the proceedings. 3. States Parties shall seek to promote the establishment of laws, procedures, authorities and institutions specifically applicable to children alleged as, accused of, or recognized as having infringed the penal law, and, in particular:

(a) The establishment of a minimum age below which children shall be presumed not to have the capacity to infringe the penal law;

(b) Whenever appropriate and desirable, measures for dealing with such children without resorting to judicial proceedings, providing that human rights and legal safeguards are fully respected.

4. A variety of dispositions, such as care, guidance and supervision orders; counselling; probation; foster care; education and vocational training programmes and other alternatives to institutional care shall be available to ensure that children are dealt with in a manner appropriate to their well-being and proportionate both to their circumstances and the offence.

Article 41

Nothing in the present Convention shall affect any provisions which are more conducive to the realization of the rights of the child and which may be contained in:

(a) The law of a State party; or

(b) International law in force for that State.

PART II

Article 42

States Parties undertake to make the principles and provisions of the Convention widely known, by appropriate and active means, to adults and children alike.

Article 43

1. For the purpose of examining the progress made by States Parties in achieving the realization of the obligations undertaken in the present Convention, there shall be established a Committee on the Rights of the Child, which shall carry out the functions here in after provided.
2. The Committee shall consist of ten experts of high moral standing and recognized competence in the field covered by this Convention. The members of the Committee shall be elected by States Parties from among their nationals and shall serve in their personal capacity, consideration being given to equitable geographical distribution, as well as to the principal elegal systems.
3. The members of the Committee shall be elected by secret ballot from a list of persons nominated by States Parties. Each State Party may nominate one person from among its own nationals.
4. The initial election to the Committee shall be held no later than six months after the date of the entry into force of the present Convention and thereafter every second year. At least four months before the date of each election, the Secretary-General of the United Nations shall address a letter to States Parties inviting them to submit their nominations within two months. The Secretary-General shall subsequently prepare a list in alphabetical order of all persons thus nominated, indicating States Parties which have nominated them, and shall submit it to the States Parties to the present Convention.
5. The elections shall be held at meetings of States Parties convened by the Secretary-General at United Nations Headquarters. At those meetings, for which two thirds of States Parties shall constitute a quorum, the persons elected to the Committee shall be those who obtain the largest number of votes and an absolute majority of the votes of the representatives of States Parties present and voting.

6. The members of the Committee shall be elected for a term of four years. They shall be eligible for re-election if renominated. The term of five of the members elected at the first election shall expire at the end of two years; immediately after the first election, the names of these five members shall be chosen by lot by the Chairman of the meeting.
7. If a member of the Committee dies or resigns or declares that for any other cause he or she can no longer perform the duties of the Committee, the State Party which nominated the member shall appoint another expert from among its nationals to serve for the remainder of the term, subject to the approval of the Committee.
8. The Committee shall establish its own rules of procedure.
9. The Committee shall elect its officers for a period of two years.
10. The meetings of the Committee shall normally be held at United Nations Headquarters or at any other convenient place as determined by the Committee. The Committee shall normally meet annually. The duration of the meetings of the Committee shall be determined, and reviewed, if necessary, by a meeting of the States Parties to the present Convention, subject to the approval of the General Assembly.
11. The Secretary-General of the United Nations shall provide the necessary staff and facilities for the effective performance of the functions of the Committee under the present Convention.
12. With the approval of the General Assembly, the members of the Committee established under the present Convention shall receive emoluments from United Nations resources on such terms and conditions as the Assembly may decide.

Article 44

1. States Parties undertake to submit to the Committee, through the Secretary-General of the United Nations, reports on the measures they have adopted which give effect to the rights recognized herein and on the progress made on the enjoyment of those rights:
   (a) Within two years of the entry into force of the Convention for the State Party concerned;
   (b) Thereafter every five years.
2. Reports made under the present article shall indicate factors and difficulties, if any, affecting the degree of fulfilment of the obligations under the present Convention. Reports shall also contain sufficient information to provide the Committee with a comprehensive understanding of the implementation of the Convention in the country concerned.

3. A State Party which has submitted a comprehensive initial report to the Committee need not, in its subsequent reports submitted in accordance with paragraph 1 *(b)* of the present article, repeat basic information previously provided.
4. The Committee may request from States Parties further information relevant to the implementation of the Convention.
5. The Committee shall submit to the General Assembly, through the Economic and Social Council, every two years, reports on its activities.
6. States Parties shall make their reports widely available to the public in their own countries.

Article 45

In order to foster the effective implementation of the Convention and to encourage international co-operation in the field covered by the Convention:

(a) The specialized agencies, the United Nations Children's Fund, and other United Nations organs shall be entitled to be represented at the consideration of the implementation of such provisions of the present Convention as fall within the scope of their mandate. The Committee may invite the specialized agencies, the United Nations Children's Fund and other competent bodies as it may consider appropriate to provide expert advice on the implementation of the Convention in areas falling within the scope of their respective mandates. The Committee may invite the specialized agencies, the United Nations Children's Fund, and other United Nations organs to submit reports on the implementation of the Convention in areas falling within the scope of their activities;

(b) The Committee shall transmit, as it may consider appropriate, to the specialized agencies, the United Nations Children's Fund and other competent bodies, any reports from States Parties that contain a request, or indicate a need, for technical advice or assistance, along with the Committee's observations and suggestions, if any, on these requests or indications;

(c) The Committee may recommend to the General Assembly to request the Secretary-General to undertake on its behalf studies on specific issues relating to the rights of the child;

(d) The Committee may make suggestions and general recommendations based on information received pursuant to articles 44 and 45 of the present Convention. Such suggestions and general recommendations shall be transmitted to any State Party concerned and reported to the General Assembly, together with comments, if any, from States Parties.

PART III

Article 46

The present Convention shall be open for signature by all States.

Article 47

The present Convention is subject to ratification. Instruments of ratification shall be deposited with the Secretary-General of the United Nations.

Article 48

The present Convention shall remain open for accession by any State. The instruments of accession shall be deposited with the Secretary-General of the United Nations.

Article 49

1. The present Convention shall enter into force on the thirtieth day following the date of deposit with the Secretary-General of the United Nations of the twentieth instrument of ratification or accession.
2. For each State ratifying or acceding to the Convention after the deposit of the twentieth instrument of ratification or accession, the Convention shall enter into force on the thirtieth day after the deposit by such State of its instrument of ratification or accession.

Article 50

1. Any State Party may propose an amendment and file it with the Secretary-General of the United Nations. The Secretary-General shall there upon communicate the proposed amendment to States Parties, with a request that they indicate whether they favour a conference of States Parties for the purpose of considering and voting upon the proposals. In the event that, within four months from the date of such communication, at least one third of the States Parties favour such a conference, the Secretary-General shall convene the conference under the auspices of the United Nations. Any amendment adopted by a majority of States Parties present and voting at the conference shall be submitted to the General Assembly for approval.
2. An amendment adopted in accordance with paragraph 1 of the present article shall enter into force when it has been approved by the General Assembly of the United Nations and accepted by a two-thirds majority of States Parties.
3. When an amendment enters into force, it shall be binding on those States Parties which have accepted it, other States Parties still being bound by the provisions of the present Convention and any earlier amendments which they have accepted.

Article 51

1. The Secretary-General of the United Nations shall receive and circulate to all States the text of reservations made by States at the time of ratification or accession.
2. A reservation incompatible with the object and purpose of the present Convention shall not be permitted.
3. Reservations may be withdrawn at any time by notification to that effect addressed to the Secretary-General of the United Nations, who shall then inform all States. Such notification shall take effect on the date on which it is received by the Secretary-General

Article 52

A State Party may denounce the present Convention by written notification to the Secretary-General of the United Nations. Denunciation becomes effective one year after the date of receipt of the notification by the Secretary-General.

Article 53

The Secretary-General of the United Nations is designated as the depositary of the present Convention.

Article 54

The original of the present Convention, of which the Arabic, Chinese, English, French, Russian and Spanish texts are equally authentic, shall be deposited with the Secretary-General of the United Nations.

If only it was sufficient to illustrate by an example that the non ratification of the convention of the child's right does not stem from the defense of the cultural specificities, the fact that two different countries like the USA and Somalia do not sign this convention would be significant. Even if the convention is largely ratified and accepted by governments, it remains nonetheless problematical concerning its application in developing countries particularly when it challenges the issue of child labour. Developing countries have lately recognized the existence of child labour. Therefore, all the countries having ratified the convention take the engagement to include it in their constitutions and they accept to implement all the means to protect children. The refusal to sign this convention on behalf of the United States is rather linked to their will not to compromise the practices of multinationals in terms of exploitation operating in South. The signature of this convention can indeed be meant systematically so that the governments act against the practices of these companies.

Nonetheless, the fundamental principles of the convention raise some main issues of discussion. The survival of children is the main problematical issue. In the literature on child labour the survival of a child depends on that of the household living standard. The poverty approach stipulates that a child for the survival purpose has to work as long as the family income is unable to ensure his living (see for instance Basu and Van 1998). Hence, child labour becomes a mean for the household survival. The policy implication of such a principle consists in improving the household income particularly those of the parents and denies the problem of children of the street who have to work for their survival on the street (Ballet et al. 2005). If this aim is easily attainable in developed countries and in wealthier household, it is not the case in developing countries. Thus the fundamental constraint for applying this convention is not cultural but economic. A number of studies deals with this issue, for instance the papers of Ray (2000a, 2000b,and 2002) examine cases of several single countries (Ghana, India) but also comparative analyses studies (Peru and Pakistan, Pakistan and Nepal). The empirical studies reveal the fact that child labour is directly and indirectly related to poverty depending on the structures of the economies.

The second problem faced by the convention is its objective of "to develop to the fullest". This objective is the main core of the millennium goal led by the United Nations. For the harmonious development of children, the States members of the UN must educate their children, give health services, as well as social services. In most of the low-income countries the rate of enrolment is under 50% and the gap between boys and girls enrolment is quite high and particularly in rural areas. UNESCO has implemented in 1992 the programme "education for all (EFA)" in order to attain the millennium goal. The objective of such a programme is to have 100% of enrolment for both boys and girls. Two difficulties have to be considered to reach this goal. The first one is of economic nature. The reason for non-enrolling children at school is explained by income poverty, lack of parents' education, worst school infrastructures, and lack of school in rural areas. In such an environment it is very difficult to fulfil the objective of EFA. The second dimension is cultural. Some countries count in the rate of access to education the children who are registered in schools always not offering basic programmes allowing a "normal" schooling. For instance, some coranic schools only supply coranic teaching without any consideration of other subjects or disciplines. It is a wrongly cultural feature since these schools, in addition to the coranic teaching, can also offer basic teachings required for a normal schooling. Moreover, a number of them and probably the best make it.

The third problem addressed by the UN convention is those of exploitation and child abuse. The convention forbids the recruitment of children for the industry of sex, pornography, and prostitution and also for armed conflicts. Lately in 1999, the ILO has adopted the convention on the worst forms of child labour. The convention C182 challenges the issue of child rights and the ILO makes its priority to eradicate the worst form of child labour as it is detriment to the child development for the fullest. Hence, the ILO distinguishes between child labour and child work. If the former is seen as dangerous for the physical and mental development of the child, the latter is considered as beneficial to children as it can be a way of socialisation (Fyfe 1989). Acknowledging the possibility for children to exercise a socialising activity (for instance to milk cows in rural area) does not however justify to put them in work during long hours, even if this activity does not present any danger in itself.

Socializing activity from what dealt with economic constraint affecting the household. The economic conditions such as the lack of family resources time constraint for women, etc. Often imply children occupations for completing these resources or for freeing women's time. And if some activities, more or less traditional, can be linked to apprenticeship, it is also necessary to distinguish them from the economic constraints. From this point of view, the number of the performed hours, the conditions in which they are executed are significative elements. It is the obvious, under these conditions of boundary that traditions do not enter in contradiction with the child's rights but can favour their promotion. In the sense, the argument of cultural specificities cannot be opposed to human rights and child's rights. If it is necessary to take it into account, it is it is because cultural specificities reinforce the implementation of these rights.

Child labour and the concept of childhood

In society, a child is a passive person without having any possibility to express his desires. The convention gives children the possibility to voice their wishes and to participate actively in the family decision particularly when they are directly concerned with. A child becomes an active person inside the family. Nevertheless, the perception of childhood is quite different in most developing countries.

The convention on the child rights gives a universal concept of childhood. Every child in every part of the world must have the same childhood, which consists in going to school for basic education, playing game for the physical and mental development. The UN defines a child as a person being under the age of 18. This definition of a child does not allow a child to work as long as it is detrimental to her/his development. The ILO convention 138 fixes the minimum age of work at 15 years old and encourages the States ratifying the convention to take actions to fight against child labour and to raise gradually the minimum age of work. Moreover the convention stipulates that the national legislations must not be in conflict with the compulsory education.

Considering the real economic state of a lot of low income countries, the ILO accepts that the age of work can be decreased to the age of 13 and 12 in non detrimental activities and the age of work in dangerous activities is maintained at 18 years old. However, derogation can be given of working in dangerous activities to children of 16 years old belonging to the poorest household. Meanwhile, the ILO has engaged a lot of means to fight against child labour and in 1999 a special convention has been ratified aiming to fight against the worst forms of child labour. The convention on the worst forms of child labour has been widely ratified contrarily of the convention 138 which is more in debate; especially because it is more difficult to find a consensus about the minimum age of work among States. The concept of childhood is not universally accepted and concepts of childhood and adulthood depend on societies. According to Aries (1969) the concept of childhood is a recent creation; it is a transitional step common to Every child which is characterised by basic physical changes. Therefore according to James and James (2001) if childhood is common to all children, it is not the same for all, it varies due to cultural factors and generations. And according to Punch (2001) within a country all the children do not have the same childhood whether they are issued from a wealthier or poorer milieu. The concept of childhood cannot be understood outside its local and social context and not as global Sub-Saharan Africa the transition from one state to another depends on rituals. (ILO. 1991)

We cannot deny that cultural factors influence the place of a child in society. Each society considers differently a child; norms and traditions influence the perception of childhood. However, it is not a reason to justify the precocious working age of children in bringing the cultural argument. In several cases, economic considerations determine the child labour decision and not cultural factors. For proof, numbers of industrial countries have recently revised their legislation in a worrying way in reducing the minimum age to work. It is the case of France that has just lowered the age of work for apprenticeship from14 years to 13 years. If this measure aims to favor the insertion of young persons in the professional life, we have to consider the negative repercussions of this policy. It reduces for instance the professional trajectories of the young persons by “formatting” them too much early. Moreover, some firms could find cheap, malleable and not unionized labour force, and from which they can part without any Compensation. As stated earlier, childhood is a transition step towards a stable state of adulthood. However, if all the children do not have the same childhood, the convention gives a conceptual framework for reaching this aim. The question is what is the best mean to reach the state of adulthood? The UN considers that schooling is the best way to attain adulthood, which increases human capital and has a positive impact on growth and development. All the children must have the same childhood, which consists in going to school and to endow their free time on leisure. It is necessary to acknowledge the apprenticeship as an intermediary form but it is also necessary to differentiate two aspects of the apprenticeship taken in the broad sense. The first aspect is an effect of socialisation. It can be applied to younger children, since it concerns none dangerous activities and since it is limited to a low level of working hours. It can be quite in relation with some cultural traditions if they do not present danger for children. The second aspect is an effect of training in a professional perspective. Therefore, in this case, the age must be absolutely the highest as possible. Indeed, the aspect of training is not the same nature as the dimension of socialization. It involves a defined trajectory of the child's activity for his future and in these senses restrains his space of future freedom. The assimilation of these two effects without any precaution drives the defenders of cultural specificities to admit any type of activity in name of the respect of traditions. In reality, they refuse to accept economic constraints affecting child labour. This pressure is not only the prerogative of developing countries, as confirms it the legal measures taken recently by several industrialized countries in favor of a reduction of the age of apprenticeship which is viewed as a violation of the convention 138. Therefore, what is behind apprenticeship is not really in relation with the question of childhood (wind, 2003)

2. Substantive opportunities versus freedom of processes

On the distinction between substantive opportunities and freedom of processes

In his recent works, Sen (2004, 2005) establishes a link between capability approach and human rights. In this approach, human rights are seen as the entitlements of capabilities. To underline the

Role-played by this approach in the defense of human rights, Sen evokes the distinction between substantive opportunities and freedom of processes. This latter distinction is expressed by Sen through the example of a woman called Natasha. We suppose that Natasha is constrained by any authority to go out in the evening. This situation implies that she is not free to decide if she wants to go out or not. And even if she wants to go out, then the constraint is in correspondence with her choice, she has no freedom to make a choice. We are therefore in a situation of violation of freedom of choice,

---

* Based on Website.

what Sen names a violation of the freedom of processes. Moreover, this situation underlines a lack of opportunities since precisely there is no choice. The capability approach focuses on the second aspect namely the absence of alternatives in the achieved choice and deals with the issue of substantive opportunities. The capability approach seems over demanding since it involves the real possibility of alternative choices, which includes the possibility to evaluate freely the alternative choices.

Hence, whereas the freedom of processes limits itself to the absence of freedom on a choice decided by another one, substantive opportunities is related to make something that has been chosen by another one and which would not be chosen if the freedom of choice has been given. However, as Sen (2005) underlines, if the capability approach allows to give a foundation to human rights by stressing on the aspect of "opportunity of freedom", it is hardly adapted to treat in a adequate manner the process of freedom. The capability approach deals with the individual advantages and gives up partly the issues of equity or justice in the process of choice. In other words, it is interested in the alternatives of choice and not in the process which lead to achieve these choices. Thus, this approach can be used for instance as a way to defend democracy by stressing on the importance of the electoral choices, but does not allow examining properly the democratic process in itself (Gupta, 2003)

Implications of the distinction for child labour and child's rights

The distinction between freedom of processes and substantive opportunities permits to reveal three very different aspects in the moral valuation of situations. The first aspect is the possibility to do, namely this is the means to accomplish actions. The capability approach examines the issue beyond means since it is necessary to take into account of the freedom of choice e.g. to consider the real presence of alternative opportunities. In this sense, the capability approach is an approach in term of freedom of choice. It is the second aspect there. The third aspect concerns the process by, which the choice is made, or the procedural aspect of choice. It refers to the valuation of the importance of the freedom of processes. These three aspects have different implications in the debate on child labour and child's rights. Concerning the distinction between the two first aspects, e.g. doing and the freedom to choose for doing, it is clear that the issue of choice between education and work is central regarding the freedom of choice and that child labour may be seen as a serious negative externality in the freedom of choice. But the freedom of choice has some implications beyond the dichotomy between work and education. First, freedom does not limit itself to a dichotomic choice and it assumes to enlarge the choice to other alternatives for instance to apprenticeship. There is a list of questions relative to apprenticeship such as the minimum age at the beginning of apprenticeship, the conditions in which it is realised, etc. From this point of view, the capability approach can certainly be useful, for instance by establishing a link with health, but seems unsatisfactory. It does not permit to answer on the whole to such questions. However, we can underline by emphasizing the freedom of choice (in terms we have defended earlier) that economic constraints determine essentially choices and then the capability approach becomes a strong argument to lay on the real absence of freedom of choice and to re-question about the diminution in the age of in apprenticeship. Then the freedom of choice repositions the distinction between child labour and child work. In comparison with the first one, the second category is considered possible because it does not constitute an "aggression" against the moral and physical development of children. However, as the first one, it reveals an absence of freedom of choice. Child work (eve light activities) cannot be considered as a choice that they have made. Much worse, the longer hours of work affected to these working activities reduce seriously the future alternatives for children in terms of choice of life. In this perspective, the child work is also reprehensible. The tolerance of child work can certainly be recovering from a principle of reality but enters in spite of in contradiction with a vision of child's rights would give all its importance to the freedom of choice. If we now consider the distinction between freedom of choice and freedom of processes, it seems to us that the aspect of freedom of processes brings a complementary light but also a moreover demanding argument in the field of child's rights. Indeed, it is not only the question to know if the child's rights are respected on the basis of the freedom of choice, but to consider the process by which choices are made. Therefore this aspect is particularly important concerning children since it is often parents or tutors who decide for them. Even if these choices comply with children's expectations, the aspect of freedom of processes requires that children be involved in the choice and that they can reveal their preferences in a context of freedom of choice. Finally it comes to examine the power of decision within the family. Regarding the debate on child labour and the child's rights, there are some direct implications. On one hand, education must be a freely approved choice and for which the child acts substantially. The educative rules must themselves be founded on voicing and the involvement of children must be encouraged in the definition of rules. On the other hand, if the choice is made for exercising an activity, the gains perceived have to be freely used by children. This perspective repositions completely the debate in the field of children's freedom in the definition of their own life and decisions involving them. This framework can appear over demanding but it is the price to pay for taking seriously in account the child's rights as a space of freedom regarding them. Then we can easily understand the decisive role played by the right to voice for children.

These results present a great interest because they give importance to what children consider as important and not what the adult in charge of children's wellbeing consider as important to them. Moreover, the study confirms clearly that education is the capability that is the most in consideration. Such a result seems to confirm the policies of development based on education as a cure of child labour. Biggeri et al. (2005), reveal five essential aspects of the capability approach dealing with children's wellbeing. First, the set of parents' capabilities affect directly or indirectly the set of

Children's capabilities. Thus, there would be a kind of intergenerational transfer of capabilities. The first aspect presents a particular interest in the case of debt bondage performed by parents which is finally transferred to children. Secondly the possibility to convert the capabilities into functioning depends on the behaviour of parents and other adults because children being generally dependant to parents, they do not have an entire autonomy and their choice is more or less severely constrained by the parental decisions and parents attitude. The degree of autonomy increases in average with age. Thirdly, every capability has certainly an intrinsic value, but it has also, particularly in the case of children, an instrumental value for the development of autonomy and of freedom of choice. Fourth, the evolution of the life cycle and more specifically the age of children have to be linked with different capabilities. The importance of some capabilities then does not appear to be identical at every stage of the life cycle and for different age of childhood (child, teenager). The relevance of every capability must be consequently examined according to age and stage of the life cycle. Fifth, children constitute the keystone of future changes. In other words, as being strongly influenced by the intergenerational transfers of capabilities from their parents, they are also considered as future parents future transmitters of capabilities. Then, they play a very important role in changes and in the possibilities of conversion of capabilities with time. (Weinner, 2001)

The normative considerations we bring constitute a direct reaction to the approach proposed by Biggeri et al. (2005). In comparison with this approach we want to underline two critical points. On the one hand, it seems to us that the overlapping between the five aspects of the list of capabilities developed by these authors is more important than their distinction. Considering the overlapping dimension leads to modify the prominence of certain capabilities. However, the authors are essentially concentrated on the distinction aspect and not on the embedding structure. From a heuristic point of view, if the distinction between these aspects is appropriate, it raises some serious difficulties for understanding some issues such as children of streets (Ballet et al.2005). On the other hand, the authors finally lean essentially on the forth aspect of the capability. This issue of the intergenerational transfer of capabilities is central in the debate on socially sustainable development; see Ballet and al. (2005). approach enunciated earlier, namely the relevance of capabilities in the life cycle and according to age. But several nuances can be enlightened. Firstly, the distinction between intrinsic value and instrumental value of capability is not emphasized. It is indeed possible that children give more importance and then give a better consideration during interviews for the intrinsic value of capabilities and minimise the instrumental value. That means they underestimate the importance of some capabilities for reaching those whose intrinsic value seems the most important to them. For instance, it raises the question on the necessary capabilities capable to develop the capability dealt with education. It means from a point of view of policies, that instrumental capabilities maybe more important than others. Moreover, the result underlined by the authors does not emphasize the link with the second aspect enunciated in the capability approach namely the role of parental attitude and constraints imposed by parents. This result refers partly to this link since children are be able to value either capabilities transferred by their parents or capabilities that children could not have been able to enhance because of constraints from their parents. But the difference between both aspects is worth being raised since the conditions of achievements are not always constant in terms of intergenerational transmission of capabilities. It seems to us that these difficulties are mostly related to the methodology chosen by the authors. It is a static method where children of different ages are interviewed for a given period of time. Adia chronic method reflecting the trajectory of children would be more fruitful because it would permit to have the opinion of children themselves on the revaluation of the capabilities to which they had given an importance in a previous time. Let's take the example of a capability for which the relevance is judged very weak by children: religion and identity. This capability cans be underestimated because the moral development of children is insufficient and because they do not perceive the importance of such a capability. For instance the works of Kolhberg (1981) show particularly that the moral development of children followed different stages. Hence, to children, religion and identity can appear at different stages of childhood as a secondary matter and without having any intrinsic value compared to education. But taken over long period, beyond childhood, religion and identity can take a higher and substantial value whereas education will take also an instrumental value through its achievement. A diachronic analysis could be able to capture precisely these changes. We apply now these considerations to the issue of children of streets. On the one hand, the attitude and the constraint imposed to children by their parents determine the phenomenon.

The family violence is the main factor. Eradicating the phenomenon supposes to act on violent practices. But an interview of children at some point of time would give some results in favor of education. However, education is not the solution since some forms of education through the institutional violence are also at the origin of the phenomenon. In terms of intergenerational transmission, violent practices reduce considerably the identity trajectory of children (Ballet and Radja 2005) and restrain the freedom of future choice, affecting also a set of capabilities comprising those linked to social relationships. Hence, from a static point of view of children embedded in a given situation, the affective relationships may not be seen as the essential capability whereas it determines the other capabilities. Affective relation's influence also Of course, we understand that this methodology has been chosen for reasons of its practicability. But it is however necessary to underline some limits. Educative performances (Leibowitz 1974) and in the case of children of streets, it constitutes the main motor of the dynamics of the phenomenon (Ballet et al. 2004).

Children rights and the capabilities approach as capabilities processes of freedom

The capability approach remains essentially static. Even if Biggeri et al. (2005) introduce temporal aspects, their approach remains static through their methodology. Some works have however already attempted to make the approach dynamic. It appears that the aspect of freedom of processes constitutes an appropriate way to integrate dynamics in this approach. Hence, contrary to Sen (2004, 2005), who puts in opposition the capability approach to the approach of freedom of processes; it seems to us that the latter could improve substantially the former. Evoking freedom of choice, if this freedom precisely concerns only the choice and not the process by which the choice is done constitutes a restrictive view which is surely acceptable from a static point of view, but insufficient when it comes to include dynamic considerations in the analysis. Regarding children, the dynamic dimension is essential because if normative considerations are taken into account, it is certainly to consider their present situation but also in the perspective when they will be adults themselves. The freedom to achieve a valuable life of dignity, through a set of positive choices depends also on the capacity to express the choices in question. From a dynamic point of view, substantive opportunities cannot be opposed to the freedom of processes.

They are both complementary. Choices have not to be only performed on actions to do or not, but also on rules permitting to achieve these choices.

This last aspect constitutes a meta-choice in relation with the choice of doing or not. We then name the approach as a capability approach of processes of freedom, in the sense that the processes of decision freely defined determine themselves the choices of actions among different opportunities. This approach has a major impact regarding the choice between education and work. It is not only a question of offering education as an alternative for work. The forms of education must permit to children to voice freely, assuming two conditions. On the one hand, within the family children have to be able to freely express their preferences. On the other hand, educative rules are themselves jointly defined between adults and children as well as within the family as at school. These considerations imply to go beyond the Millennium objectives in terms of rate of enrolment. A higher rate of enrolment is indeed not significative because it does not mean necessarily a for of education freely accepted. A higher enrolment rate can be even compatible with some very violent forms of education. On the contrary, taking into account of children in the definition of procedures and rules of education themselves calls to a not violent form of education.

Beneficiaries and violators of children's rights

Child labour is sustained by a triangular foundation formed by three corners players: the employers, parents, and the state. Its critics tend to recognize the first two as the immediate violators and hold the state responsible for failing to protect children's rights by allowing the employers and parents to exploit child labour. Employers use child labour because it is profitable. Governments of then, turn a blind eye to the practice because they are willing to welcome any form of investment. Employers prefer children because they are docile, willing to work for lower wages and in undesirable work conditions, incapable of collective bargaining, and easier to manage. Child labour is particularly favored in industries such as carpet weaving, silk production, synthetic gemstone manufacturing, and jasmine picking due to a belief that nimble fingers, small hands, and thin arms can do the delicate jobs better (Dube,1991). Powerful investors—individuals as well as national or transnational corporations—usually use their power to bribe officials to ignore violations, pressure governments to relax employment restrictions, and encourage or support governments to restrict labour rights and union activities. More importantly, what many employers fail to provide for adult workers—e.g., "living wages," disability benefits, a healthy and safe work environment, health care coverage, and childcare allowances—create the conditions that increase the family dependency on child labour. Parents, who normally care about the welfare and future of their children, participate in the process by allowing, or even forcing, their children to work. Poor parents who are unable to make an adequate living rely upon the contribution of the youngsters, either in the form of un paid labour in family farms and businesses or as wage labour paid by other employers. Usually the poorest parents, unable to pay bills for a medical emergency or funeral, sign up their children to work in bondage for their creditors.28 However, it is important to note that parents usually resort to child labour when they have no other options. While the options are generally limited by the resources of the country, even in the poorest countries, the children of the well-to-do families do not share the fate of the poor children. Child labour is provided by lower classes and poor households which are un proportionally high among immigrant and ethnic minority groups (Johari,1990).

Most countries also have laws that ban child labour, but governments often fail to enforce these laws. The state contribution to the child labour problem, however, is not limited to its failure in law enforcement or regulations. Most governments deny the existence of the problem, and some of the actually sustain the practice by hiring child labourers in state-owned enterprises. India is an "exemplary" case that demonstrates all of these problems. While the Constitution and nearly a dozen laws forbid both forced labour and child labour, Indian governments have been unsuccessful in enforcing these laws, several officials have insisted that there were no child labourers in their provinces, and the government itself has been using child labourers. While the law specifically forbids the employment of children in the carpet industry due to its hazardous nature, the government runs a Schooling in among government officials, caste and class biases, obstruction by employers, lack of accountability, and the lack of adequate enforcement staff are listed as obstacles for enforcement. "training" program for child carpet weavers and recruits children as young as six. The critics note that by ignoring the educational provisions of the program, the Indian government in effect runs a business that is entirely based on child labour (Muller, 1986).

Many adults in developing countries are unemployed or underemployed, and consequently are not able to make a decent living for themselves or their families. For example, in a village near Bihar with 50,000 people, more than 30 percent of the adult males are unemployed, while others work for low wages in rice, wheat and cornfields. The cotton fields of the village, however, including that owned by the state, are full of child labourers picking cotton. Even though children are paid no more than $1.50 for an eight-hour day, their earnings provide a major source of income for their families (Kumar,1999).

According to Human Development Report 2000, "About 790 million people are hungry and food insecure," and more than half of the population in nearly a dozen countries lives for less than one dollar a day(in 1993 PPP$).46 The Human Poverty Index, developed by the UNDP shows that nearly 1.2 billion people live on less than a dollar a day and cannot meet their basic needs. According to the ILO reports, children commonly contribute around 20–25 percent of family income. Since more than four fifths of private income is spent on food in developing countries, 49% them eager earnings of children are critical to their survival.

Having a high percentage of young population means that more people depend on the work of fewer people. As we know developing countries, especially those in Sub-Saharan Africa and South Asia, have larger youth populations and higher dependency ratios. In order to avoid starvation, countries that have high dependency ratios would need to either increase the productivity level of the working age population or allow some of the under-aged to participate in the work force. The extreme poverty prevalent in many of these countries with high dependency ratios is a factor that works against the prospect of increasing (Parish, 2001).

While there has been a considerable global interest in curbing the population increase in developing countries, most of the effort and money have been devoted to population control programs that turned out to becoercive and ineffective. Although studies repeatedly show that the increase in women's education is directly related to the decline in fertility rates, education in general, and girls' education in particular, has been neglected by governments and many internationally sponsored development programs. Less than 4 per cent of national income is spent on education in developing countries. The World Bank, while recognizing education and health as crucial to eliminating poverty in its development reports, has been allocating only about a combined 8 per cent of its development assistance funds to projects on primary health care, education, clean water and sanitation. National laws that declare primary education as mandatory are noten forced, especially beyond the perimeter of urban centers (Smithu, 2001). Rural areas tend to lack schools, and most village schools have been severely under funded. Overcrowded schools, with inadequate staff and supplies, offer poor quality education, which promises very little in terms of improved prospects. Thus, from the perspective of impoverished parents, sending children to school isseen as nothing but a waste of time and money.

In addition to its opportunity cost (the time the child could use to earn some money instead of spending it at school), keeping a child in school imposes an extra financial burden on parents (even if schools were available and properly equipped). While "modest" school fees actually constitute large sums for the poor, in many countries "free" education means only the absence of tuition and fees; the cost of uniforms, books, and supplies still has to be absorbed by the family. Given these problems, it should not be surprising that more than 260 million of the primary and secondary school-age children of the world are out of school. Enrollment rates are particularly low in least developed countries and in Sub-Saharan Africa Moreover, enrollments are not stable or continuous; the UN data for 1992–1995 show that, in developing countries, 22 percent of all primary school enrollees fail to reach grade five. 59 In some countries the figure rises to 60 percent. (Stevar, 1994)

HUMAN RIGHTS,AND ECONOMIC POLICIES*

The advocates of the Universal Declaration of Human Rights have repeatedly emphasized the interrelatedness and interdependency of human rights. At least since the Proclamation of Teheran in 1968, these principles havebeen accepted and underscored in various international declarations and conventions. The Vienna Declaration and Programme for Action of 1993asserts: "All human rights are universal, indivisible, and interdependent andinterrelated. The international community must treat human rights globallyin a fair and equal manner, on the same footing, and with the sameemphasis."

The issue of child labour shows not only that the full enjoyment of one right by an individual depends on his ability to enjoy other rights, but also that the fulfillment of children's rights depends on the recognition and realization of their parents' rights. Denying the right to employment or the right to livable wages for adults inevitably results in the violation of children's rights. Improving the parents' economic conditions would certainly provide better opportunities for the children and free them from labouring. International finance and development agencies, however, tend to ignore human rights and their interdependency in their dealings with the developing world. The conditions that the IMF and the World Bank set for lending, commonly referred to as the "structural adjustment policies," do exactly the opposite of what is necessary to promote the rights of the poor and improve the lives of poor people. Although these policy formulationshave no direct reference to children, their adverse impacts are probably most remarkable on the children from poor households. As well put by UNICEF, "the real cost of adjustment is being paid disproportionally by the poor and by their children."(Singh,1998).

In the name of economic stability, these agencies require governments to implement measures of "fiscal discipline" which involve freezing wages, reducing government spending, and privatizing government enterprises.

* Based on Various Resources.

While the reduction in government spending typically means cutting down social expenditures (e.g., health and education) and eliminating government subsidies on basic goods, privatization almost always results in major lay offs. Facing increasing unemployment levels, declining wages, and the increase in out of pocket expenditures for essential food items, utilities or transportation, the low income households in recipient countries find themselves tightening their belts more and more. Through the reduction of aggregate demand, the IMF may be successful in curbing inflation (although it has not been always as successful as expected even in meeting that objective), but it does so at the expense of poor households, which are likely to turn to child labour for additional income (Kapaia,1998).

The experience of India in the 1990s provides an illustrative case. As a result of its agreement with the IMF in 1991, the Indian government slashed social spending, especially on food subsidies, education, and health, while simultaneously making every effort to increase its exports as it liberalized itseconomy. 64 The reduction in government services, combined with and regulated economy and economic policies catering to business interests, not only increased poor households' dependency on child labour but also enabled the local elite who employed poor children to run exploitative and unsafe businesses that subsequently escaped government regulations and law enforcement. According to the Commission on Labour Standards(2001) and International Trade, child labour in India grew at an annual rate of 4 percent in the 1990s, as the cost of living and unemployment increased adjustment. It is noted that during the debt crisis of the 1980s, government cuts in social spending hit education particularly hard, and in all regions spending per student declined. In addition to pushing government spending down, the structural adjustment policies adversely affect children's education by forcing parents to rearrange their priorities. Trying to cope with the shrinking family income, poor parents stop sending children to school or take the mout of school to reduce household expenses, to send children to work, or to keep them at home to watch their younger siblings, since their mothers have to enter the labour market or increase their work hours. Given the patriarchal nature of the societies, the education of the female child is likely to be sacrificed first. (Kapoor, 1979). A study of seventeen countries that had implemented the structural adjustment programs in the 1980s identified "a clear tendency for a deterioration in the ratio of girls to boys in secondary education after the onset of recession, reflecting decisions by families to remove girls from schools at a greater rate than boys." As a response to its persistent critics, the IMF has demonstrated as sensitivity to the situation of the poor, and starting in the late 1980s it included the development of "safety nets" in its loan packages.

However, the IMF notion of safety nets (e.g., distributing free milk in some urbanslums) appears to be too small to fill the big hole that its other "adjustment" policies open. Even Joseph Stiglitz, who has subscribed to the same neoliberal economic theories followed by the IMF and shaped the policies of the World Bank as its chief economist, finds himself agreeing with the protestors of the IMF: "They'll say the IMF's economic 'remedies' often make things worse—turning slowdowns into recessions and recessions in to depressions. And they'll have a point."(IMF,2001).

Moreover, the aid from the developed world has shown a steady decline itself. The World Bank notes that while donor countries' economies grew after 1992, their development assistance shrank.72 The net official development assistance received by developing countries dropped from an early $48 billion in 1991 to about $35 billion in 1997; and again, the countries of Sub-Saharan Africa experienced the largest decline, from $42.6to $33.5 in per capita values. The net capital transfer through loans, exports and other means also marked a net benefit for the industrial world. UNIFEM noted that while the net transfer of funds from the North to South was $19.1 billion in 1980, by 1990 the direction of the flow had changed and $27.5 billion was transferred from South to North.73 In fact, the last century demonstrated steady and unprecedented levels of increases in 1989 (UNISEF, 2002).

In addition to its poor economic policies, Director of the IMF for being undemocratic: "In theory, the fund supports democratic institutions in the nations it assists. In practice, it undermines the democratic process by imposing policies. Officially, of course, the IMF doesn't 'impose' anything. It'negotiates' the conditions for receiving aid."75 What he fails to mention, however, is that the World Bank has also been guilty of imposing the very same structural adjustment policies—policies that are also known as "austerity measures" because of their negative economic and social impacts. Of course, with its development mission and programs geared toward fighting poverty, the World Bank, when compared to the IMF, presents amore complex picture in terms of its approach to the issues of poverty and development. Numerous studies conducted by the Bank staff or published by the Bank have repeatedly pointed to the persistent nature of the poverty problem (some households experience chronic poverty, although there is atransient component), the need to invest in human resource development, and the enormous social gains promised by improving education and income opportunities for women (e.g., improved nutrition and health of children, higher labour and land productivity, lower fertility rates) since theate 1960s.76 In case of funding, however, the Bank has been slow in incorporating these findings into project designs and policy formulations (Stain,1986).

Moreover, it has been reluctant to acknowledge the violations of human rights caused by some of its grandiose projects and stubborn in denying the negative impact of its adjustment policies on health, nutrition, and education. When confronted by critics about the social ramifications of its policies, including accusations about enabling the trends that contribute to child labour, the Bank officials have been rejecting the notion that the Bank had any responsibilities in devastating the poor and insisting on the argument that the recipient countries would have been worse off and The report also notes that a "study of worldwide income distribution among households shows a sharp rise in inequality—with the Gini coefficient deteriorating from 0.63 in global poverty and poverty reduction efforts.

A more direct undesirable impact of the Bank's work on child labour canbe best observed in its financing of the silk industry in India. In an effort tohelp India increase its silk exports, the Bank has been lending India millions of dollars since the 1980s. The Bank's support, which was intended to create jobs and alleviate poverty began with loans of $54 million to supports sericulture (the raising of silkworms) in Karnataka in the 1980s. In the1990s, the lending was extended to the state of Uttar Pradesh and involvedthe overall modernization of the industry (UNDP,2001).

The fact that the silk industry in India has been largely dependent on child labour and that in Karnataka alone there might have been the Bank has overlooked "as many as 100,000 bonded children in every stage of silk production". In 1997, it was confronted by critics who argued that the Bank had failed to monitor labour conditions, and "in effect, underwritten an industry which relied on bonded child labour at all stages of operation."78 The Bank responded to thesecharges with a range of statements: "The Bank does not condone the use of child labour," yet "in some areas child labour is essential for families to survive"; also that India's silk projects have been "regularly appraised" by the Bank, but the problem of child labour "has not shown up in any of ourreports."79 Although an official of the Bank claimed that "the Bank has tried to look in terms of providing the environment to discourage child labour," the mechanisms used for creating such an environment were not specified (IMF,2001).

Human Rights Watch, on the other hand, called on the Bank to suspend funding until the Indian government fully implemented its law against bonded labour and worked on the rehabilitation of the children working in the industry. The Bank was also urged to set up educational and other programs that would allow the bonded child labourers to attend school. As a result of this pressure, the Bank hired an official in 1998 to oversee the process to avoid lending to businesses that use child labour. This and other recent changes in the approach of the World Bank, e.g., moving away from large scale projects and increasing funding for education and health care, are all promising developments. However, they are not likely to be effective if the Bank, the IMF, and other international agencies heavily influenced by the US continue to subscribe tothe policy principles that are known as the "Washington Consensus"—a set of neoliberal economic policies that require developing countries to limit government spending, eliminate subsidies, privatize state enterprises, deregulate private businesses, protect property rights, broaden the tax base but reduce the marginal tax rates, encourage direct foreign investment, devaluate their currency, and liberalize trade.83These requirements clearly weaken government control over the economy and favor the freedom of capital. Their implications for the poor and working classes are all-negative and point to a tacit mission of resource allocation. Forced to follow these prescriptions, governments with reduced budgets and declining regulatory power, cannot enforce laws on minimum working age, healthy and safe work conditions, or mandatory education, even if they had the will to do so (Ali,1987) Moreover, the price competition in international markets, along with the desire to attract foreign capital, constantly pushes governments in developing countries to find ways to reduce the cost of labour. In order to increase their country's competitiveness in global market, the executive and legislative bodies, both in developing and industrial countries, have been busy redefining their welfare policies, social security systems, retirement policies and labour laws.

Historical data show that unionization in a country increases as the country becomes more industrialized. The IMF and the World Bank employ a "cookie-cutter approach" to economic stability, and require all loan applicants to implement essentially the same structural adjustment policies. These policies are supported and promoted by the US Treasury Department as well, and the Department has been influential in formulating the lending policies of the two international financial agencies. Since they are all located in Washington, D.C., the underlying economic philosophy of the structural adjustment policies is commonly referred to as "the Washington Consensus" by the critics. Although they all uphold the principles of neo-liberalism, the key players in these agencies may have some min differences on the specifics (Roy,1998).

***Corporal Punishment in Schools: A Legal form of Child Rights Violation?**

After home, children like schools. Parents think schools are very much important in the overall growth and development of any child. These schools

---

* Based on Govt. of Kenya Report Resources are acknowledged.

play a vital role in molding their future. But these schools are violating child rights in the name of disciplines.

Caning

Caning is the one of the most common form of corporal punishment permitted far the most common kind of corporal punishment. As discussed in the earlier background sections of this report, many laws strictly regulate basically caning. Corporal punishment is reserved for the most serious disciplinary infractions; no more than six strokes may be given, and only by or in the presence of the head teacher; a full inquiry must have been conducted before corporal punishment is administered; a written record must be kept; and children can only be hit on the buttocks or the palm, and not in the presence of other children.

As noted, despite the regulations permitting corporal punishment, the Ministry of Education has sent mixed messages as to whether teachers should cane at all. Although the 1972 regulations allow corporal punishment under particular circumstances, the reported Director's statement of 1996 was touted as prohibiting the practice as a matter of policy.

Nonetheless, our research indicates that caning is regularly imposed, and it is often administered in a manner inconsistent with the regulations. In most schools, virtually every classroom teacher has a cane, and uses it. In many schools, teachers routinely carry canes with them, or have them easily accessible in their classrooms; canes lean against the walls in many head teachers' offices, and adorn teachers' desks in some classrooms.

Although the regulations only permit caning in the presence of or by the head teacher, students at nearly every school visited by Human Rights Watch reported that in practice, every classroom teacher had the independent authority to cane students. Some teachers chose not to cane, however, and some teachers caned more than others.

Most of the head teachers we interviewed appeared to be familiar with the Education (School Discipline) Regulations on corporal punishment, and when pressed as to why caning was administered by classroom teachers independently, many simply shrugged, and told us that the regulations were impractical. As one head teacher told us, "Discipline is supposed to be done by the headmaster but he can't because there are so many students, so he delegates his authority to junior teachers who do it." Similarly, the Mysore municipal education officer told us that "we have in our Education Act procedures for how a child is to be punished, but in most cases, because the procedure is a bit long, most of the heads don't follow it."

Reasons for Caning

Teachers caned students for a wide range of infractions, some serious, some extraordinarily minor. As reasons for punishment, students, teachers and head teachers frequently cited tardiness, making noise or talking in class, truancy or absenteeism, bullying, fighting, stealing, disobedience or rudeness, and leaving the classroom or school when the teacher is away. Less frequent grounds for punishment include selling or using drugs, smoking cigarettes, jumping on tables, not paying attention or falling asleep in class, and using profanity. A Standard Two boy told us that all the Standard One through Three students had once been caned for "spoiling the toilet." Failure to complete homework and not being prepared for class were other common reasons for punishment. Other behaviour that was sometimes cause for punishment included "wearing an improper uniform," having an "unkempt appearance" or being "dirty," and "failure to clean the classroom in the morning."

Missing extra "tuition classes," classes that are given after school and for which students pay extra fees, was also cited as a cause for caning. Such classes are theoretically voluntary, but students reported that they were punished for failing to enroll in the extra classes, as well as for failure to attend, once enrolled.

Children are beaten whether their behavior is under their control or not. For example, students who work after school may not have time to prepare for the next day's classes. Their homes may not have electricity to allow them to study in the evening, and the children may lack the books and supplies necessary to complete their assignments. They and their parents may not have enough money to pay for a proper uniform or to keep a clean appearance at all times. Furthermore, exhaustion may overcome them during school hours.

If you couldn't pay fees, you would be caned six times, and sent home to bring the money from your parents. You would go home, and there is no money, and then you would go back to school because you still want to learn, and you would be caned again. I kept going back to school and home again. The headmaster would come to class with a list of students who had not paid, and would cane them all, then move on to the next class with the list. You would lie down on the floor, and he would hit you. Hit you on the back, between the shoulders and the buttocks. It would shock the kids... they were fearing the cane.

Number of Strokes

The severity of punishments also varied greatly, and many children viewed the number of strokes as somewhat arbitrary: while most children agreed that the more serious the infraction, the higher the number of strokes, the most important factor seemed to be the "harshness" of the particular teacher. A gentle teacher might cane rarely, and give only a few light strokes even for relatively serious offenses, while a harsh teacher might routinely administer six or more heavy strokes.

A particularly harsh teacher, some children told us, might even hit harder or administer more strokes to a child who cried when hit. In a way, expressing pain is viewed as an act of further disobedience, an expression of a child's unwillingness to silently accept punishment. Suresh S., fifteen, a student at a poor rural primary school in Central Province, told us, "If you are beaten very hard, sometimes you cry, and then they are angry and beat you harder still." James E., a boy at a suburban Central Province primary school, reported, "There are some that when you cry, they hit you more. There are some that try to make you hurt."

While we were able to see no particular patterns in the incidents of severe caning, many of the cases of high numbers of strokes seemed to occur during incidents of collective punishment, when several students were being punished at once by several teachers. Collective punishments are common, according to the children we interviewed: "For example, if there is noise in the class, then sometimes the whole class is caned-so you will be caned even if you have done nothing wrong," twelve-year-old girl Leela from a rural Mysore school explained.

Size of the Cane

The size of the cane used in corporal punishment varies significantly. In most cases, children indicated that the canes used were about two to three feet long, and about one half to three quarters of an inch thick. Other descriptions of canes included "a cane made of wood that doesn't break, sometimes a guava tree," "a blackboard ruler" used "until it gets broken," and a "bamboo stick" that "may have little thorns in it." Three students at a secondary school indicated that the cane used there was quite large, describing it as "a broomstick, maybe one inch thick," "about 1.5 meters long," and "four feet long, made of wood."

Parts of the Body Hit

The regulations governing corporal punishment also state that children may only be hit on the buttocks, if a cane is used, or on the palm, if a strap is used. In practice, we found that boys were mostly caned on the backside, and girls were mostly caned on the palm or back of the hand. Nonetheless, several teachers and head teachers openly acknowledged that they hit children on parts of the body, as well, and children at schools throughout Kenya reported that at times they are hit on the back, the calf muscles, the soles of the feet, the toes, the shoulders, the front and back of the thighs, the knees, and even on the face and head.

Other Forms of Corporal Punishment

Although caning is the only form of corporal punishment in Kenya permitted under the Education (School Discipline) Regulations, many children told Human Rights Watch that at times they are slapped, pinched, hit, whipped or kicked by their teachers. Teachers and head teachers also acknowledged that such "unofficial" punishments are used at times.

After caning, slapping was the most commonly reported form of school corporal punishment. Children recalled being slapped on the face, the head, the back, and on "every part" of the body. Slapping was considered by some to be less severe than caning: "sometimes also they slap in the face, but that is a less serious punishment."

Many students also reported that teachers pinched them, and one at primary school in a city explained that they were pinched on the cheeks. Fifteen-year-old boy reported being elbowed in the back by her teachers, and in several cases children said that the teachers "boxed" and "hit" in addition to slapping. One teacher told us that she sometimes punished students by "snatching," which she described as grabbing the students.

Whipping is also not infrequent as a form of corporal punishment. A deputy head teacher at Mary Primary school in Nanjunagoodu told us that "even this morning I had to punish eighty students" by whipping them. He showed the researcher the whip, which was made of heavy rubber, cut from a car tire. The whip was about three feet long and three inches wide, and he demonstrated its use by slamming it down on his desk. At an urban secondary school in Central Province, a whip adorned the head teacher's desk, and several students told us that the head teacher both whipped and caned to punish students.

Failure to Conduct Inquiries and Keep Records

The Ministry of Education's regulations stipulates that caning can only be administered after a full inquiry, but a common complaint from children was that teachers caned them without even waiting for an explanation of the perceived misbehavior. Similarly, the Ministry of Education's regulations require each school to keep a record of every incident of corporal punishment. We were able to review the punishment logbook at only a few schools, and found that a few punishments were actually recorded. For the most part, interviews with children made it clear that caning was far more frequent than the logbooks showed.

At other schools, the head teachers openly acknowledged that not every incident of caning is recorded. "We delegate the authority to teachers to do it. They don't report back to me, and it's not recorded," admitted one rural primary school head teacher. One student at a rural primary school in Coastal part of Karnataka told us that school does not keep a punishment log at all, and the deputy head teacher at another school acknowledged the same: "We don't write it down. We don't keep a register." At least one head teacher seemed to think that recording was only necessary for "serious" cases of corporal punishment; in that case, he told us, "then we shall have a record."

Resulting Physical Injuries, Including Deaths

Well-meaning teachers who were taught no other means of maintaining classroom discipline and promoting academic performance inflict much corporal punishment in Kenyan schools. For the most part, there is little reason to doubt that most teachers administer corporal punishment in a manner that seems to them to be fair, reasonable, and pedagogically valuable. Nonetheless, when the use of corporal punishment becomes an acceptable and regular part of the teaching process, severe injuries and abuses inevitably occur.

First, accidents happen: a stroke of the cane aimed at a child's backside may in advertently strike another part of the body-the head or the kidneys, for instance-causing severe injuries. Similarly, some children have medical conditions that render them vulnerable to serious injuries from strokes of the cane that would not seriously injure another child: a child with a heart or lung condition, for instance, may faint or even die out of a combination of pain and fear.

Second, when corporal punishment is permitted, there is virtually no way to prevent some teachers from inflicting corporal punishment in a fashion that is sadistic, cruel, and intended to cause grievous injury. At virtually every one of the twenty Kenyan schools visited by this researcher it was clear from interviews with children that some teachers, at least, inflicted corporal punishment in a disproportionate, arbitrary, and cruel manner.

It is Human Rights violation that all school corporal punishment constitutes cruel, inhuman, or degrading treatment, notwithstanding the benign motives alleged by some of those who inflict it. In some cases, corporal punishment may even rise to the level of torture. School corporal punishment involves violence inflicted by public officials or persons performing a public function against people under their control, and the violence is deliberately calculated to cause physical pain and humiliation. Since children are physically and psychologically undeveloped, relative to adults, they are especially vulnerable to the negative effects of corporal punishment.

Government Response

Government responses to serious incidents of corporal punishment have been wholly inadequate to combat abuses. The Ministry of Education is doing little to educate its teachers on appropriate methods of discipline and the harms of corporal punishment. When children are injured by corporal punishment, schools-or individual teachers-at times provide or pay for medical assistance for the child, but teachers who injure children are rarely disciplined, let alone dismissed or prosecuted. Some parents press charges against abusers, and there have been a number of well-publicized prosecutions; in almost every case known to Human Rights Watch, however, teachers have either been acquitted, the cases have been dismissed, or teachers have been convicted but handed extremely light penalties-generally just a small fine. Most continue to have children in their care, teaching in the same schools in which they have previously abused children. In practice, children are left with little remedy against corporal punishment, and in many cases, children respond to severe punishments and injuries by transferring from abusive schools, if they are able to, or by dropping out of school altogether.

Judicial Remedies

Head teachers and teacher who cane children may be criminally prosecuted for assault or murder as a verdict given by the Kereal High Court. According to an Advocate, there are several barriers to effective criminal prosecution for corporal punishment. If a teacher is in fact convicted of assault, the punishment is typically minimal; in the case of described above, the teachers responsible received a small fine, although they could have been liable to several years' imprisonment.

The severity of the assault charge depends largely on whether the doctor who examines the victim and fills out the required police medical form, the "A3" form, classifies the injury as "harm" or "grievous harm." According to the A3 form, "[h]arm means any bodily hurt, disease or disorder whether permanent or temporary. [g]rievous harmmeans any harm which amounts to main, or endangers life or seriously or permanently injures health, or which is likely so to impair health, or which extends to permanent disfigurement, or to any permanent or serious injury to any external or internal organ." Assaults resulting in harm are misdemeanor offenses; those resulting in grievous harm are felonies.

No statistics on criminal prosecutions for crimes related to corporal punishment are available, but attempts to prosecute are increasing in frequency. A Principal Magistrate believes that, when corporal punishment leads to severe injury, "generally you find that the teachers are charged. Cases are going down. Parents and children are more aware of their rights." One experienced police official, the officer-in-charge of a Police Station, reports that he's seen about two cases each year involving parents who wish to press charges. However, he says that he's been able to handle most of the cases without involving the courts: "most of them we've been able to handle at the station level." He says they do prosecute in cases where the punishment is clearly excessive.

In many cases, according to Senior Principal Magistrate felt assault charges were supposed to be filed against the teachers after the murder charges were dismissed, but they were never filed and the teachers went free. Some time it is attributed to the absence of an eyewitness, highlighting another difficulty with prosecuting teachers for corporal punishment: if the victim is dead, it is difficult to find any eyewitness testimony. "If before she died she made a dying statement as to who beat her, then it could have been produced as evidence. Without such a statement, it makes it very difficult to convict."

Finally, most parents are simply unwilling to engage the legal system in cases of severe corporal punishment., a magistrate in Bangalore explains that corporal punishment "is an accepted practice in schools. People aren't aware they can complain against a teacher, or fear that if they complain, the child will not get the proper attention in school from teachers, and will do poorly." Therefore, most people would not think to bring charges in the first place.

Administrative Remedies

The Education Department has the responsibility for hiring, firing, and disciplining government-employed teachers in Karnataka. Despite widespread media coverage of injuries resulting from excessive corporal punishment, the commission does not undertake investigations unless complaints are brought to it, and rarely disciplines teachers over incidents of corporal punishment.

In a interview with the deputy director of the Teacher Services Commission, who told us that the commission only occasionally deals with cases of excessive corporal punishment, but that "if a teacher violates, then a teacher is disciplined." Such cases are "very rare," according to him: "we receive them once in a while, once every two or three years." He claims that "most of the caning is as per the regulations," and explains that the commission rarely investigates or disciplines teachers for incidents of corporal punishment, because "we cannot act on those things that we do not know about."

Responses from Head teachers

None of the students, teachers, head teachers, or parents interviewed by Human Rights Watch said they knew of incidents where a head teacher had taken action against a teacher who injured a student through corporal punishment. The school might provide medical assistance to help a student, but would typically try to resolve the matter through negotiations with the parents rather than disciplinary proceedings against the teacher.

At several schools, students reported that if they were injured as a result of corporal punishment, the teacher or the school would pay for their medical expenses and/or take them to the hospital; some, but not all, parents corroborate this. The head teacher at a rural primary school told us that he collects 2 Rs per child each week to be used for a fund to pay for any injuries suffered at school (including injuries from corporal punishment). He or a teacher would take the child to the hospital and call his or her parents in the event of an injury: "It's our responsibility."

Negotiation with Parents

In most cases, students, parents and head teachers reported that complaints of excessive corporal punishment were dealt with through quiet negotiation, sometimes including an apology to the parents. One head teacher told us that in cases of injuries where the parents "even threaten to go to the police," she would simply tell them that it was an accident; she went on to say that generally "parents are very understanding because they also cane their children at home. They are used to this." Another head teacher told us, "if a child goes back home and complains about punishments, the parents are not happy. Sometimes they come in to see me, but if I explain they usually accept it."

While corporal punishment is the most obvious violation of fundamental children's rights in Kenyan schools, it is not the only school practice that threatens the basic rights of children. In addition to inflicting corporal punishment upon children, teachers also give children a wide variety of other punishments, many of which, if sufficiently severe, would violate provisions of the Convention on the Rights of the Child and be cruel, inhuman, or degrading.

These punishments include hard physical labour such as uprooting tree stumps, slashing long grass with a stick, and digging pits, physically exhausting punishments such as running for long distances, humiliating practices such as forcing children who misbehave to kneel in front of the classroom for lengthy periods, and requiring work that can be both demeaning and a health risk, like forcing children to clean pit latrines that are covered with urine and feces, without providing protective gloves, cleaning materials, or running water.

These strenuous, humiliating and unsafe punishments should be distinguished from ordinary chores which students in some schools are called on to perform on a regular basis. A student's shared responsibility in the performance of light chores does not place him or her under the same physical or emotional strain, or health risks, as the punishments described below.

Kneeling

Many children and teachers told us that being forced to kneel in front of the class was a routine punishment for minor infractions (kneeling was often accompanied by caning, but also used on its own). Julia R. from Coast Province reported that "sometimes you must kneel in class for a full lesson as punishment."

Digging

Digging was a commonly reported punishment, especially at rural primary schools, where many students reported being made to dig ditches or pits. In some cases, students reported that digging was, in their opinion, the worst punishment, and others considered it second only to caning.

At some schools, only boys were punished by digging. A rural primary school head teacher told us that normally only boys are punished with digging, which he considered to be a particularly effective punishment, since students find it particularly degrading: "it looks to be kind of a job, a kind of slavery."

Slashing

"Slashing," which entails cutting grass or clearing fields by slashing with a long stick, was another form of manual labour commonly given as a punishment. Children generally did not perceive slashing to be as severe a punishment as digging; like digging, some students reported that slashing was predominantly given as a punishment for boys.

Other Manual Labour

Many other forms of manual labour were assigned to students as punishments. Students told us that they might be made to cut trees as a punishment, to uproot trees, to pull out weeds, "to work in the teacher's shamba," or to plow the school's fields. One student in Kisumu reported that he was made to do other forms of work for teachers: "I was told to bring firewood, or grass for thatching teachers' houses. If you don't have it, they would ask you to bring it again."

Toilet Cleaning

Many of the schools visited by researcher used toilet cleaning and/or sewer system cleaning as a punishment, which was almost universally despised by the students. Many students told us that toilet cleaning was the worst form of punishment, some insisting that it was worse than caning. Twelve-year-old Sarah J. from Central Province said "I prefer being caned to washing the latrines. That is not good, I am thinking that you can be getting diseases from it." One schoolgirl enrolled at a suburban Central Province primary school told us that girls are made to wash the toilets more often than boys.

Public Shaming

At several schools, forms of public embarrassment and shaming were sometimes used as punishments. Seventeen-year-old boy from Mysore city told us that in addition to handing out corporal punishment, teachers "call you out in the assembly so people will see you and know you and that you have done wrong. Sometimes they laugh at you." Other head teachers also described using this sort of punishment in a school parade; one of them called it "humiliation."

Some of these punishments can be abusive, depending on their severity and context. Hard physical labour can lead to serious injuries; hard labour or forced exertion in the hot equatorial sun can leave children dehydrated, exhausted, and suffering from sunstroke. Similarly, toilet-cleaning can be both degrading and hazardous when imposed as a punishment and when children are forced to come into contact with urine and feces, without protective gear or the opportunity to wash throughly afterwards. Digging and cleaning as a punishment can be also exploitative, and publicly shaming a child can be abusive, if the humiliation and ridicule are sufficiently severe.

NOTE: This chapter is based on the various reports and publications mainly of Human Rights Watch (International NGO) and other Internet resources. Resource are greatly acknowledged-Author

7

Policy Implications

One view is that in certain economies child labour in unavailable and bound to portion as a harsh reality' (GOI, 1995) and that withdrawal of children from the workforce is possible only when the economic status of the families improve. Legislative measures are unlikely to succeed in this situation and the principle effort would have to be directed towards amelioration of work conditions rather than elimination of child labour. Any effort at eliminating child labour would have to focus on the more exploitative forms prevalent in the hazardous sectors.

The inevitability of child labour is essentially a consequence of what can be broadly termed as the 'Poverty Argument'. In its simplest from the argument states that children work because they belong to poor families which cannot survive without the income which accrues to them an account of child labour. Analyzing the causes of child labour, the Report of the Committee on child Labour notes:

Stronger than tradition is the factor of chronic poverty responsible for the prevalence and perpetuation of child labour. Nearly healf of India's population subsists below poverty line... In these families, the child since his very appearance in this world is endowed with an economic mission. The child is compelled to shed sweat of brow to keep the wolf away from the door (GOI, 1979).

Child labour is viewed as a harsh reality and as long as poverty continues to exist, it would be difficult to totally eliminate it. Any attempt to abolish it through legal recourse would, under the circumstances, not be practical since this would lput already poor families under acute economic stress. In this situation, the only alternative that is left is to ban child labour lin hazardous areas and to regulate and ameliorate the conditions of work in other areas. This assessment of the child labour situation is one which many governments, including India, have adopted.

A similar approach to the elimination of child labour in developing countries has been adopted by many international agencies,. Notably the ILO and UNICEF.

In the latest statement of Union India, in which all children outside the School system are identified as child labourers or potential child labourers, but in terms of priority for action, the UN system believes it is imperative to abolish the most exploitative and intolerable forms of child labour as a first priority'(UN 1998).

A variation of the above approach is the view that child labour simply cannot be wished away. It is argued, notably by Ben White (1994), that irrespective of any industrial or agricultural legislation or even compulsory education that may have been responsible for the eradication of child labour, the simple fact is that child labour still exists in practically every society. It exists because children them selves want it. As long as the various intervention agencies including the state insist on treating children as passive spectators who need to be rescued from work, or as an 'empty bucket' to be filled with whatever the current value system thinks fit, there is little scope for success. Children have to be treated as active agents of change, capable of demanding and exercising rights and in general what they want is precisely what intervention agencies want to rescue them from. Thus, although most agencies assume that non wage work for children in a family environment is 'good' while paid work for outside employers is 'bad' children themselves prefer the latter. Under the circumstances, it is unlikely that any measure,

In Indian family system traditional women is a real leaving force of the family. She is the strength of the family. She plays a major and final role in every house holds decisions. Hence there is a need to create socialization and consciousness among rural and urban women, because the worst enemies have been *traditional female* and *conservative female*. There is the need for change in social attitude and in this context mass media can a play a vital role.

Since social and cultural background of the family plays a vital role in taking house hold decision to send children to work all anti child labour and poverty eradication programmes should emphasize on the following aspects: 1value, norms and social solidarity of the community, 2 integrative forces in the people's life, 3 minimum and maximum resistance to innovations in their culture, 4 recognizing vital linkage in people's cultural fabrics.

The definition and scope of the term child labour should be throughly revised. It should include all small, house old and cottage industry in to the circumference of the definition. State should consult experts before excluding any occupation out of the scope of the term. State should encourage more Anthropological research where, purely social and cultural reasons has dominated on the incidence of the problem.

Since it is big country having different culture and tradition all polices and programmes should be geographically and culturally specific. All polices should have lot of waitage to the local cultural norms. Enough flexibility is highly desirable. Governament should consult Anthropologists before framing any polices, because they are well versed with the different cultural aspects of the people.

No specific legislation is required it is ensured that existing laws are effectively implemented. For example, the manner in which the National Authority on Elimination of child labour proposes to implement its scheme generate a measure of skepticism. Not only is the scheme excessively bureaucratic-there is no mention of NGO', but it also does not take in to account the usual sloth, red tape and corruption which plague endeavors of this kind

Constitutional prohibition of child labour, no child below the age of 14 must engage in labour should be completely implemented. Effective decentralization and encouragement to local civic bodies to take principal responsibility for prevention and eradication is central (CACL). Central sectors and conditions of work need to be targeted for immediate eradication, example, child prostitution, and children working in conditions of bondage and children in the hotel and domestic sectors.

A comprehensive integrated approach is required to address sector-specific issues, rural/ urban regional and cultural specificity. This necessitates the active participation of civil society and a synergy between the various government programmes, which are dealing separately with aspects that impinge on child labour (Nayer, U). Local self-government should be activated and have the central responsibility in the elimination of child labour.

Importanst and necessary alternative is the implementation of free, relevant, quality, compulsory elementary education for all children up to 14 years as soon as possible. This, if implemented, would certainly deter the process of children being drawn into the work force. The task of reorganizing or restructuring the education system and experimenting with different approaches should go hand in hand with the enlisting of children into the education system Ongoing efforts need to be address development issues of the communities from where children come into employment (Verma, S).

Initiatives for child labour eradication must be combined with community development and social mobilization. There should be a lot provisions be made for health, education, loan and credit facilities and ensuring minimum wages for adult employment.

State should make sure every child must have access to education, which should be relevant in terms of language, dialect, socio cultural conditions, and history of the region and opportunities prevalent in the region. A special effort must be made to provide education in those areas where it has been historically absent.

Crèches attached to primary schools in rural and urban centers are necessary. Young children who are otherwise forced to take care of siblings will be encouraged to attend school if such facilities are provided. Successful programmes have been conducted for the children of construction workers (combining education for older children and crèches for younger siblings) by different NGO, and are worthy of emulation.

Education must be of high quality in terms of teachers, infrastructure and educational aids. An active programme to control school dropouts is necessary. It can be seen that though enrollment is high, many children are forced to drop out of school for several reasons including poor teaching methods, lack of infrastructure, etc. Teachers need to be further trained to make education interesting and attractive- it should be such that children should miss school if they dropped out

At present we are following a uniform system of education though out the country. The schools need to change their time and yearly schedule to cater the need of girls in terms of attracting more girls from poor families. The school time should be completely modified according to the local cultural and requirements of the people.

Single point entry system should be revised. Instead of one final exam state should think in reforming a new criteria to promote from one standard to another. The provisions of multiple point entry in schools would be very useful to the working girls and may prevent heavy drops out rate.

Education as a bridge towards rehabilitation: It is necessary to look at the kinds of jobs that children are doing for the formulation of appropriate strategies for eradication of child labour. Strategies must address sector specific issues, for instance, children in garage, children in the construction children working in hotels, domestic work, street children, etc. It is necessary to involve the community, parents and employers to design a comprehensive rehabilitation programme so as to have an impact in the context of a widespread campaign against the employment of children (CACL).

Also some reformations in educational market is required, such as improving the quality of the Governament Schools, and reducing direct and indirect cost of schooling. The strategy must aim at getting the nowhere children into school and attempting to retain a much larger proportion of children in primary to middle school stage. (Aggarwal, 2004). Efforts also need to be made to simultaneously provide non-formal education, vocational education and training to the child workers. Income increasing incentives need to be combined with school incentives, especially for girls, in order to increase household well-being and children's human capital attainment

Governament shout target poverty as a vital point embeds with this problem. Polices and programs should be implemented in a decentralized manner and there should be enough scope for grass root level development. This kind of programme should be more suited to the local conditions.

Urban anti poverty programmes mainly should cover slum dwellers, people belongs to depressed class, causal workers, etc. More Anthropological research is needed on cultural analysis of poverty and its particular context and local settings.

The urban anti poverty programme should be threefold: poverty reduction, construction of productive assets and promoting mainstream employment subsequently .We stonily believe that the act needs to includes this long term focus of the programme as the strategies use of surplus manpower for sustainable development has to be an important component of any new programme.

Cost effective health care measures must be put in operation, seeking in particular reduction in infant mortality rates, that will reduce the social pressure on families to have many children as possible as way to insure against high rate of child mortality and more over family planning service must be made available to all at easily and affordable cost.

All anti child labour programmes need to be improved in case of information, communication, decentralization, skill training, and capacity building for the ensuring better result.

Today growing majority of children population falls in context of deprivation, "which is born not necessarily so much from economic poverty-but to appropriate technologies to infrastructure and managerial ability. This sort of poverty can not be successfully overcome by improved GNP and per captia income measures to expand the availability, efficiency as well as the utilization of service and to make them more responsive to children and their developing needs" (Mittal, M).

To formulate and execute a big project related to child labour organizational capacity of institutions and departments must be strengthen.

The responsibility of setting priority, coordinating activates promoting private sectors participation and, launching pilot schemes, etc should be entrusted to this institutions and departments.

Providing free food grain rations to families who send children to school, and promoting savings and credit groups or micro credit schemes among women would be highly desirable.

In all developmental programmes there should be some special provision foe child labour families. Identifying beneficiaries must be the sole responsibilities of local governament. Speedy dispersal of benefits is also important to save the children from going off from schools. Also, the efficacy of anti child labour campaign will be weakened unless it is backed up by firmer safety nets and enhanced income for the poor.

In order to prepare the children future adult life it becomes absolutely necessary to equip them with certain skills suited to their aptitude. So, it would be desirable to cultivate suitable aptitude among the children who are doing part time work along with the study and who are completely involved in work. Free and advanced level of vocational education at the primary or higher primary level should be given to children. It may provoke parents to send children to school up to that level.

Government should establish a separate control unit to maintain co-ordination role among all different departments, which are working on anti child labour programmes.

More Anthropological study on child labour should be under taken on a large scale in different parts of the Bangalore City to reveal regional variations in different aspects of child labour. This help in making uniform polices which perfectly suitable to the different cultural and geographical areas. Also it ensures flexibility to suit regional variations. Through this method we can suppress the voice of *regional differences* more speculated especially after blue, white and green revolution.

The prevalence of child labour in any geographical are is inversely related with its development The incidence of child labour is invariable prepositional to the overall development of the specific area. So the Governament should take initiatives to improve the conditions of the section of the people who are living in those areas. This plan would attack the problem at its root level.

The ultimate objective of the child labour programme is to convert working children into productive and participate members of the society. This needs generation of public awareness and simultaneously gearing up of the enforcement machinery to meet the challenge. Introduction of new methods of monitoring and evaluation of child labour programmes and projects will help to implement a programme in a specific, time-bound, cost-effective and result-oriented manner

Seminars, workshops, symposia etc should be organised on various aspects of the problem. All findings and new inventions should be easily assessable to the last lay man of the society. The issue should have publicity to create awareness among the community. Every citizen from deferent walks of the society should think about this visible social tragedy from the mind.

Recommendations:

The extraordinary numbers of children working in agriculture -some 170 million worldwide- and the severe abuses they endure demand that governments, employers and trade unions prioritize protections for child agricultural workers as part of their strategies to end child labour.

Human Rights Watch recommends that all governments:

Ratify the ILO 182 Convention on the Worst Forms of Child Labour, if they have not already done so, and ensure that their national laws are consistent with the Convention and Recommendation 190. National laws should explicitly prohibit all individuals under the age of eighteen from using dangerous tools, from hauling heavy loads, from working long hours, from handling pesticides, and from being exposed to pesticides in the workplace. National laws should also explicitly prohibit sexual harassment in the workplace, establishing separate and more stringent penalties for cases in which the victim is a minor.

Take measures to ensure the effective implementation of Convention 182. Such measures should include the allocation of resources to provide for a sufficient number of labour inspectors targeting child labour in agriculture, proactive monitoring, and unannounced on-site inspections.

Ensure that restricted-entry intervals (REIs)-the time after pesticide application when entry into the treated areas is banned or limited -are clearly established in government regulations and vigorously enforced. Special REIs for children should be established, taking into consideration the greater risks they face from exposure to toxic chemicals.

Government regulations and vigorously enforced. Special REIs for children should be established, taking into consideration the greater risks they face from exposure to toxic chemicals.

Ensure that all workers, including children, receive full information and training from their employers about occupational illnesses and injuries related to agricultural work, including those associated with exposure to pesticides. Such training should be conducted regularly and be understandable by children. Employers should also provide all workers, including children, with appropriate protective equipment and train them in methods of protecting themselves from workplace hazards.

Ensure that children and their families are aware of the rights of children. Undertake comprehensive surveys to determine the scope and scale of child labour in the agricultural sector, the number and nature of injuries or illnesses suffered by children working in agriculture, and disaggregate the data by sex and age.

Ensure that all children receive free and compulsory primary education. School fees and other associated costs of education, including costs for books and uniforms, should be waived, or scholarship programs developed for children whose families are unable to afford them. Special educational or vocational programs should be developed for child farmworkers who have dropped out of school.

Violators of child labour laws should be sanctioned to the fullest extent of the law. Governments should consider increasing fines for child labour violations and dedicating a portion of the fine to the rehabilitation of child workers.

Ensure that child agricultural workers who labour in hazardous conditions in violation of ILO Convention 182 and suffer workplace accidents or illnesses are provided with free health care.

Establish mechanisms to monitor the treatment of children working in agriculture and ensure that effective complaint mechanisms are available to children and their families.

Human Rights Watch recommends that all corporations who employ children or with suppliers who employ children:

Ensure that children's human rights are respected on all directly owned and supplier farms and plantations by adopting effective monitoring systems to verify that labour conditions on these facilities comply with internationally recognized child labour standards and relevant national child labour laws, reporting annually on compliance, and, where the facilities fall short, by providing the economic and technical assistance necessary to bring them into compliance.

Ensure that pesticides potentially harmful to children are neither sanctioned for use nor applied in practice on directly owned or supplier farms and plantations.

Immediately turn over to the appropriate national authorities any information regarding violations of national child labour laws or international child labour standards on supplier farms and plantations.

Provide adequate support for underage workers, as defined by the ILO Minimum Age Convention, to attend school or an appropriate academic alternative in lieu of working.

Suggestions by the Economists

Unions and grassroots groups are increasingly recognizing direct connections between worker rights and the fight against child labour. Recognizing child labour as a violation of children's and workers' rights, trade unions are joining with families and community organizations to combat child labour, to move children out of work and into school, and to support core labour standards. Historically and in today's global economy:

- strong unions are an important protection against child labour
- when parents are able to improve conditions through effective unions, children are much less likely to have to work
- active struggles against child labour tend to strengthen unions and workers' rights in general

Many workers and unions in the U.S. and other countries are supporting efforts to end child labour by forging alliances with unions in other countries. These alliances work to achieve enforceable global labour standards, such as ILO Convention 182, and hold transnational companies accountable for labour practices.

Supporting workers' struggles to organize unions and reject child labour

In 2001 factory monitors confirmed illegal union-busting and other violations—including employment of 13-15 year-old children—at a Mexican factory sewing clothing with university logos for Nike and other U.S. companies. Thousands of American students, workers, and consumers wrote letters to corporate CEOs protesting worker treatment. The international solidarity campaign helped factory workers overcome violence, intimidation, and mass firings when they tried to organize, and after months of struggle, workers won an independent union.

In 2002, as news of child labour abuses and attacks on workers in Ecuador's banana plantations spread around the world, workers, consumers, and students contacted Los Alamos plantation owner Alvaro Noboa to demand that he recognize the workers' union and cease using illegal child labour. Presidents of the AFL-CIO, the International Union of Food and Allied Workers (IUF), the Teamsters, and many other labour leaders also issued letters in support of Los Alamos workers' struggle.

Campaigning for institutions to adopt and enforce codes of conduct

Pressure from human rights groups, consumers, and international trade unions led the group overseeing the World Cup (FIFA—Federation Internationale de Football Association) to adopt a Code in 1998 stating it would cease using soccer balls made with child labour. This year, when reports indicated that children were still working in the soccer ball industry and that adult workers were not being paid a living wage, activists launched a new publicity and letter-writing campaign, mobilizing soccer fans, consumers, and politicians to demand FIFA improve factory monitoring and live up to the promises in its Code.

Implementing and supporting fair trade or labeling initiatives

Through programs developed by non-profit organizations, export goods like coffee or cocoa can now be certified as "Fair Trade" products if producers adhere to basic labour standards—including ILO conventions on child labour—and pay farmers fair prices so families can meet basic living needs without having children work for wages. Groups like TransFair USA and others help to publicize Fair Trade initiatives and educate consumers about Fair Trade products.

When the use of child labour in the rug-making industries of Pakistan and India gained international publicity in the 1990s, consumer groups—building on the history of effective "union label" initiatives—worked with manufacturers to begin phasing out the use of child labour and licensing companies to use "no child labour" labels if production facilities were regularly inspected by independent monitors. The resulting "RUGMARK" label program uses licensing fees to fund monitoring programs and education and rehabilitation for children removed from carpet jobs. Consumer groups and unions play a role in educating the public about the label program and ensuring it maintains strict standards for licensed companies.

Using collective bargaining strategies

The International Federation of Chemical, Energy, Mine and General Workers' Unions (ICEM) signed in 2000 and recently renewed a "global agreement" with the multinational Freudenberg corporation, which owns chemical and rubber manufacturing plants all over the world. Freudenberg is headquartered in Germany/Japan, but the agreement covers all Freudenberg workers in the U.S. and 40 other countries. Among other recognitions of workers' rights, the agreement commits Freudenberg to a ban on "child labour according to the definitions included in ILO Convention 138."

Promoting global labour standards in trade agreements

The International Confederation of Free Trade Unions continues to propose adding a "social clause" covering seven core labour standards, including prohibitions on child labour, to WTO rules governing international trade; this proposal has so far been rejected by WTO leaders.

Filing suit against corporations for labour rights abuses abroad

The International Labour Rights Fund and other groups have begun pursuing legal action against companies for alleged labour abuses in other countries. In 1996, for example, ILRF filed a suit against Unocal for using slave labour to build pipelines in Burma; and with the support of U.S. labour unions, ILRF recently filed a suit against Coca-Cola for using paramilitary forces to suppress organizing and assassinate union leaders in Colombia (these suits are still pending). If effective, this strategy could be used in the future to hold transnational corporations accountable for child labour abuses.

Promoting access to education

Increasing children's access to public education is a fundamental strategy for ending child labour. An example of promoting access to education is the Bangladesh Building and Woodworkers' Federation and the Metal Workers' Union that seeks to remove children from hazardous workplaces and enroll children in education and assistance programs. On a larger scale, the Global Campaign for Education is a coalition involving teachers' unions, Global March Against Child Labour, Oxfam, and Action Aid.

Suggestions to Improve the Organizational Capacity of NGOs

Child labour has long been both an economic and social problem in our country. India has one third of the total child labour population of the world. Numerous NGO's have been working towards find a solution to the child labour problem. Many NGO's have grown in size and capabilities conducting research and training's while developing effective and innovative programmes to shift children from work to school. The work of NGO's in the fields of primary education, micro-financing, and alternative income generation programmes have also made important contribution in the effort to eradicate child labour in both urban and rural India. However, unless NGOs make significant improvement in their performance in promoting sustainable livelihood for the poor their best efforts may not prove sufficient for ending child labour. Here in this paper an attempt has been made, how NGOs still effectively can work towards the eradication of this social stigma. Despite the formation of specific polices and projects for dealing with child labour, and the implementation of a large number of programmes by the Governament and NGOs in pursuance of these policies, the impact on child labour in the country has not been minimal. The basic reason for the failure of many programmes is that they are simply is not designed to do so. All programmes that will be implemented by the NGOs should be geographically and culturally specific.

As long as poverty continues to exist it would be difficult to eliminate it. Simple legislation is not enough. Since acute economic crisis is the prime reason behind this problem the only method of withdrawing a child from work is by compensating the family adequately for the loss of income. In this corner point, all NGOs must and should think rather than to provide some alternative income generation programme to assisting producers organizations. If NGOs seriously wants to be in this field and, if so, necessary specialize and they should think much larger scale programmes and project. Not only this, they should have high quality of human resource to mange themselves as organizations and their operations in a more effective manner. Most impordent is all NGOs should have a good relation ship each other and they should establish complimentary links with technology institutes, employer's, banks, financial institutions and Governament agencies.

Although at policy level NGOs have been perceived as developmental agents, yet the scene at the grassroots level is not always in consonance with this subjectivity. It is so because base level Governament functionaries some time see NGOs workers as outside encroaching/ occupying their space. (Baland and Robinson, 2001) And on other side few NGOs thinks different Governament

Agencice are the main hurdles in their way. This may be the major weakness of many NGO's. Their mutual interactions and even good Collabouration makes the effort more effective.

Here both Governament and voluntary agencies should change their attitude and should be complimentary to each other and must take confidence in each other. The NGOs should make lot of homework in making people's participation in educating and training to improve their of professional skills, overcoming behaviour and cultural resistance of communities may be preferably involved in tackling the problem of child labour and always they should try to became closer to the local people. Many NGOs believe economic compulsion is not only the reason for child labour. The recent survey shows that more than 29.27% of working children is the need to supplement the family income while only 7.56% of child worker were required to gain employment to earn a minimum living for their families. Only 3.56% are working part time, to finance their own education besides contributing to the inadequate family income. So all NGOs must think in the way of giving more and more low cost job oriented education and their by encouraging more women joining the work force besides empowerment of women would go a long way in elimination of child labour.

Apart from the poverty, the second main reason is the present education system in our country. Many children are working because their parents want them to work for the reasons other than economic crises. For example child might lost his interest in the education, failed in the same class many times, corporal punishment by the teachers, parents might wanted to continue their family occupations in the early age, hanging with bad friends, threat of probable unemployment in the future, earn additional income to the family-etc. In short time any NGOs /Governament cannot eradicate poverty, so NGOs should think about present education scenario and better concentrate on these topics.

Since many parents do not under stand the significance of the education, NGOs have to work to create awareness about the value of the education. As soon as possible NGOs should open *Home work centers* where any school going child can come and get help to complete his home work under the guidance of a trained teacher, and *Community play centers* where all children come and can play any games like carom, chess and volleyball-etc. if so few educational aspects of child labour can be solved. All children would have certain inherent skills. It is necessary to equip with certain skills suited their aptitude, NGO's should conduct most advanced type vocational training courses and must be more suitable to the dropout children because these dropout children are potential child labourers. These courses should be suited for child worker in general and in vocations for those working children who combine their work with studies. Also in order to provide opportunity to working girls for supplementing the family income NGO's should take some step to develop co-operative societies Through this, young working girls having responsibility for organizing training, making raw material, available and selling the products goods to the market.

The NGOs should initiate a dialogue with trade unions in order to prepare institutional framework necessary for collective bargaining with regard to improvement in working conditions and to control the magnitude of child labour. If possible NGOs should try to open children club, libraries and reading rooms fully equipped with necessary material suited to the local children. So children may get awareness about their rights and exploitations by the owners etc.

Learning from others

Organizations like CRY, CWC, APSA,. ROAD, CROSS, PLAN and CACL are some of the important NGO's working on child labour Issues in Bangalore City. They have valuable lesson from the field to others. Especially Rural Organization For Appropriate Development (ROAD) a Mysore based NGO has successfully implemented all above mentioned programmes in its working area. But before learn any thing from others they have to concede that the work being done by agencies is addressing the same child labour issues as the NGO's are trying to grapple with. But it is important to note that, each

NGO's will have different ideas regarding poverty focus, community acceptance, beneficiary owner ship, funds, human resource, planing strategies-etc.

Resources from the Mainstream

1. Finances

Since almost all NGO's is totally depend on either foreign or Indian grants for their activities, it is necessary to rise capital from mainstream sources, such as the development

Financial institutions and the bank. If so it will have two benefits; first it will make NGO's more accountable in terms of effective use of money and also it opens much larger sources of funds that foreign and Indian grants. Almost all-financial institutions like SIDBI, ICICI, NABARD, IDIBI have by accumulated years of experience in funding NGO's through grants for experimental projects NGO's can approach these institutes to get fund as loans with longer than normal repayment and moratorium periods and lower interest rate or they can rise money from the corporal sectors like CRY (Bombay) and CWC (Bangalore) NGO's.

2. Human resources

NGO's are known to have highly experienced and committed individuals. Many NGO's have good grassroots worker but not at middle levels. If so, the grassroots worker may not get any guidance and support. So, NGO's should hire more experienced persons in child labour, Anthropologists and experts in other related field. If NGO's would like to move from direct implementing agencies to supporting producers organization, they need to have higher caliber of people at all levels is accentuate. Those in support roles have to be more versatile, having broad-based knowledge of various fields that impinge on child labour eradication programme. (Basu and Van, 1998)

3. Technology

As another step towards effectiveness in child labour eradication programmes NGO's need to have link with various technology generation institutions blessed with a very large scientific and technological research infrastructure in India. For example ICAR, ICMR, CFTRI, IVTC (Institute of Vocational Training Center) etc in addition to state level research and training institutes. Since child labour issue is related to more than one field NGO's should get lot of technical support from these institutions. The presence of professionally trained staff in NGO's greatly facilitates this process of acquiring technology and adaptation to the local situation and to the poor child labour families.

4. Expertise

NGO's should have a vast pool of technical experts and professionals specialized in project finance, socio-economic analysis, micro finance, training and capacity building, technical aspects, computing, rural infrastructure, rural financial institutions, planning, monitoring, evaluation-etc

5. Knowledge

As child labour is a complex phenomenon all NGO's should have certain useful concepts which have a bearing on successful child labour eradication programmes like,

1. NGO's should understand social structure, caste and class problem, dynamic of social changes, political economy of resources and police analysis-social science.
2. communication theory; diffusion of innovation; group dynamics and collective action; training and organization development; and any appropriate technology.
3. competitive behaviour of firms; resource and ecological economics; social cost benefit analysis-economics (Mahajan).

Through this research study it is strongly recommended that Child labour related NGO's should re-examine their approaches in this field due to it's inherent complexity and difference rather than relief and welfare programmes. They should exclusively focus on child labour related issues. If these kinds of NGO's could succeed in promoting sustainable livelihood for the poor, so that they can develop requisite level of expertise in child labour related sub sectors. And NGO's must think of much larger scale projects and draw financial and human resource from the mainstream. Polices and projects should adopt a holistic approach, taking in to the consideration socio economic set-up of working area. They should also enter into collabourative relation ships with Governament agencies and other NGOs. NGOs try hard to solve grass-root level of problem and they should think in up gradation of living standards and education status more particularly of the women and child. More than this, NGOs should learn in employment generation in non-agricultural sectors will go a long in curbing the demand and supply of child labour

Conclusion

The study of child labour has attracted considerable attention is recent times, much more so in India which accounts for a significant proportion of the world's child labour force. Most of these studies have attempted to give detailed descriptions of the various manifestations of child labour. A few have attempted to understand the underlying causes for the persistence of child labour despite its universal condemnation and the various legislative and administrative policies adopted by governments to deal with the problem. While some have treated child labour as an evil to be eliminated others have viewed it from the perspective of its socio economic significance to a society at a particular stage of transformation. They would assert that the very persistence of child labour is indicative of the crucial role it plays and consequently it cannot be wished away merely by enacting legislation. There is no uniformity of opinion on what constitutes child labour, or for that matter, to what extent it is necessary to prevent children from working. To a large extent, the diversity is views is reflective of the wide variations in the socio economic context in which child labour survives. We shall try to examine some of the issues raised with specific reference to their relevance to India and set this work in relation to the ideas currently prevailing.

The term child labour defines, any child between the age of 5 and 14 years is directly or indirectly forced to work at home or outside it. It may be for money or for the sake of apprentice. As a consequence, children are not only deprived of their dignity but also their freedom to play and spend some time as they spend. More over there scope to develop physically, mentally and emotionally is lost. These children are also denied education, which is a fundamental right and should be available to them under any circumstances. It is very unfortunate that even today the problem of child labour is greatly existing in our country and in many part of the world. These child labourers are paid some money for all their hardships, which generally fails to get one square meal a day. Driven to work at a crucial formative age and burdened which hard labour these ill-fated children are deprived of nutritious food, play time and education. They lead a pathetic life, devoid of simple childhood pleasures and do not even get the opportunity to develop into valuable human resource. There by their precious childhood seems to be stolen by the different problems of the respective families.

Children are important assets of any nation, they are the future builders of any society. The destiny of a country depends directly on how its children are nurtured to fulfill the requirements of its society. In India, education is the joint responsibility of both the state and central governments, and the constitution of India envisages free and compulsory education for all children until the age of 14. Ironically, in reality, large numbers are denied this fundamental right and are subjected to backbreaking labour in pathetic conditions. The result is illiteracy—heart and soul of the problem after the poverty, which is linked with child labour.

Child labour policy in India concentrates more on amelioration than on total abolition. Only 3.9 percent of India's gross national product (GNP) are spent on education. And only 1.4 percent on primary education. It is quite miracle and unfortunate that the same country spends 65 thousand corer rupees of money for *Defense* in a year. Lack of social and cultural based anthropological study of the problem, strong political will, under use of available resources, low economic growth are some of the basic factors that lead to the failure of anti child labour programme as per as India is concerned. Lacks of educational facilities, inadequate supervision, lack of trained anthropologists and neglect of disadvantaged regions/communities are also responsible for this dismal performance.

Recent World bank report has reveled that there are more then 9 corer working children in India, which is largest in terms of any country in the world. These nine corer working children the one and a half crore bonded working children. No doubt, the elimination child labour is a big challenge for the country. The federal Governament is keep-framing number polices and programmes to eliminate or just to control the problem atlest. Progressive as well as integrated approach has bean adopted by the Governament In order to resolve this intense socio economic problem, a multidimensional action plan to create awareness among all section of the society is most essential (Bhandari,j).with the heralding of the new millenium, the burning challenges that have appeared globally, the problem of child labour stands as one of he most acute among them. From this research study it is evident that Social and Cultural factors, Poverty, Big size families, and legal failure are the major reasons for the existence of child labour problem as per as Bangalore City is concerned.

The existence of poverty in different forms is one major and most vital reason behind this problem. Also lot of cultural and social factors are embedding around the poverty. The cultural analysis of the poverty is most urgently needed phenomenon. Because of wide spread poverty may leads to the big size of the family. Of cource, many cultural believe plays a major role in the increasing of the family size. These twin problems continue to exist, it will not be possible to affectivity tackle the problem of child labour. Since India is a big country having different cultural and traditional factors at each and every segment of the society with 103 crore people it is highly impossible to eradicate or control the spreading of poverty. Or, it is not so easy as we thought. So "it hardly of any use to talk about abolition of child labour Which is not only unrealistic but is also likely to do more harm than good to the millions of poverty stricken people in the county who are forced by their awfully poor economic condition to seek the help of their children to come out and work for their existence" (Mittal, M). Perhaps along with other effort the most vital and most urgent need is a wind of *cultural change* must blow through society and through the men and their by community, for it is only if community adopt a radical change and brand new out look on the child labour that the ultimate objective, probably the elimination of child labour up to certain extent can be possible.

Another major problem is that difficulty is inherent I the fact that children working in rural areas, in urban informal sector in domestic service are not readily visible. An integrated and effective measure to save children from hazardous or abuse should, therefore, begin by exploring the invisible visible. As long as the community more particularly middle and higher classes, consider that child labour is part of the harsh reality that makes good economic sense, the conditions for change will not be met (Narasaiah, N).

A Balanced Approach

As per as India is concerned Child labour problem is a complex of both social and economic one. This problem requires an analysis from the different angle is highly essential today. Lot of research work has been done /or still going on this topic. But an intensive social and cultural factors which embed in household fertility behaviour, cultural concept of risk, house hold decision making, labour market and advanced technology should be explored as soon as possible. A conventional research provides a useful framework for integrating these variables and analyzing childlabour problem.

Cultural and traditional background, economic strength and demographic characteristics feature are largely affects the supply of child labour as per as Bangalore city is concerned, where this proposed research work had conducted. It is evident that parental education level, employm status of the family members, also affects on the supply of the child labour. When number of family member increases, invariably it increases the dependency ratio, both the factors that increases the likelihood that a child will need to generate income to maintain the household. But it depends on age physical stamina, mental maturity and gender of the child (Lloyd 1992, Pattrions 1997).

In this situation each house old will allocate the time of its children to whatever activities are perceived to have the highest private return, until the marginal return is equalized across all uses of a child's time. As Grootaert and Patrons observe "the crucial question is whether, at that point, equally is achieved with the marginal social return. When the private return of child labour exceeds the social return, there is arguably too much child labour and interventions are called for. It can be occur in the labour market itself, in the market for education, or elsewhere. Depending on where the market failure occurs."

This is the most fertile time to go beyond the poverty argument and move towards why the education market more or less failed in India. The dynamics of household behavior in spending on education depends on a verity of factors relating to the households. As Tilak* observed that it is not true to hold the view that households in economically advanced states spend more on education, though thy may have higher ability to spend. In other words we can interpret that the ability to spend and the actual level of spending do not go together. Also it has been reveled that Public spending on education positively influences on the household decision to spend money on education.

Since the Governament spending crores together money on higher education primary education market has gradually been to the state of failure. Along with poverty it has been proved that failure of the education market also plays a major portion for perpetuating of this problem in the Indian society. Low quality of education, poor learning achievements by the children, excessive cost, employment lack of educated roll models in the community, absence of forward and backward linkage hat strengthen primary education, failure of market for educators, less investment by both state and households on education, a mere success of universalisation of primary education are different reasons for great failure of the Indian education market. If Governament decided to impose ban on child labour or by any new proposed (Not yet) law which contains provision to punish the parents who sends their children work will absolutely lead to a further detritus the of the child's already limited opportunity set Just imposition ban on the child labour is not quite logic and it will be a meaning less move by the state. Also this move may affect on the basic structure of welfare economics of the family. Because on one hand child cont work and other hand child may doesn't want to go to the school. This kind of forceful imposition on child labour issue is likely to be failed, because it would threaten the survival of the entire household in the community.

So, *we have to search for the needle where we had lost it.* The most vital task before The Governament, community and NGO's should be that restoration of education market soon. The Governament should revise its National Policy on Education. All its educational programmes should be culturally and geographically specific. A uniform type of education system is not good for the whole country. Governament should fill the gap between the learning achievements between Governament schools and private schools children. Studies have shown that an alarmingly large number of children do not become literate even after four years of schooling. Hence, school effectiveness and actual learning have to be central rather then secondary concerns for universal elementary education (Sharma, R). Next, how effective schools are and success in learning depend not only on school level inputs but also on factor outside the school. So, the impact of the wide context of schooling has to be understood better. More than this it should seriously think about improving the quality of education especially in Governament schools, more than that it should bring some radical changes in teachers education It should invest more of its GDP on primary education and social development. Indirect cost on the education on the parents must and should be reduced. Alternative Income Generation Programme to parents who sends there children to school should be the vital initiative and it is very crucial in the retention of the children in schools until the end of the cource. Universalisation of primary education, compulsory primary education all these schemes would be very suitable to write on the white paper unless, the Governament should think about to fill the income gap of the family because of school. Many families are neither working nor participating in welfare to work programmes for a variety of reasons, and more families are likely to join their numbers as the economy slows. Welfare programmes need to develop better strategies for identifying families with serous barriers to employment and healthy family functioning, and to explore new ways of helping these families, by using integrated approach. Also it would be very interest to know that some poor family would like to send their children to school, and some of them are not. This is the most transition point where more Anthropological based action research is highly required. Governament should think new approaches to strengthen the forward and backward linkage, which gives a new life to job market. There should be lot of scope for vocational education after certain level of the primary education. Once the Government could address all these issues the next step should not be the ban on child labour. Because Government and NGO's should make sure with respect to 3 aspects (1) designing special delivery mechanisms for reaching the unreached and marginalised sections of the society, (2) designing and demonstrating innovative and workable models for providing quality of education (3) identifying through field experimentation, basic parameters for ensuring an efficient delivery system for primary education, formal and non formal. As Grootaert* argued, "the functioning of the labour market could be less than efficient and contribute to child labour, in which case labour market interventions are called for, such as the removal of regulations that prevent wage flexibility and artificially enhance segmentations".

Education and eradication of child labour are more or less closely linked. But the problem is in our country poverty reduction programmes don't have any strong linkage with education for all. Education is a key element in prevailing child labour. The route of power, social justice, gender equity, decentralization, better democracy, good administration and prosperity has to be through classroom's and schools. The policy maker should understand child labour issue and education is pre requisites to development.

More Anthropological research would be desired to revel why some of the poor family spends considerable amount of money on education and why not some of the financially sound family would not.? Also it is very interesting to know that, of cource, a *missing link* in search of a solution for this problem that why many households gives most priority to the income from the child'work and less weightage to the child's schooling than the social optimum. In this situation the only way before the state will be improve the living conditions of families depending on the wage of children. A new type of public distribution system should be brought in to these people. Urban poor also brought within the circumstance of the Employment Guarantee Programme. Small premium-based health insurance would be an asset to these families. Totally polices designed to reduce poverty, make school more attractive, encourage household industry, these kind of multiple policy interventions for eliminating child labour is more essential today. More over income-increasing incentives need to be combined with schooling incentives, especially for girls, in order to increase household well being and children's human capital attainment.

Child labour is socio economic problem required multi prolonged strategies should be adopted as a long-term basis basis. As much as possible all polices and programmes should be culturally and geographically specific. Programmes should be need based one. Under standing the problem from poor peoples point of view is half done in the long way. An innovative well-balanced welfare economics, legislative, a social intervention is the most likely to succeed in eliminating child labour as per as India is concerned. And more over all these programmes should be on continuous basis with the sole participation of concerned local people. Based on the detailed field study on the different aspects of the problem the researcher has got some suggestions. All these suggestions have operative base. This new findings and results may be useful to the policy makers, economic planners, administrators' researchers, demographers, and NGO's social and women activists, who are fighting against this social evil.

It is a well-researched truth that there exists a vicious cycle of poverty and child labour as well as illiteracy and child labour. The main problem is that poverty alleviation programmes in our country do not have strong linkage with education and child labour. All Governament polices and programmes and NGO's Efforts is narrow because they do no analyze and link them with board context of economic environment in families and comminutes, poverty related polices, the existing development paradigms and the process of globalization. So a concrete solution to this problem is not yet been possible till today. A multi dimensional approach consisting of creation of awareness, community participation, alternative and viable social and economic rehabilitation, and enforcement of legal instruments in relate to the children and other similar plans is needed for linking child labour with overall poverty reduction program. Involvement of anthropologist will definitely gives a cutting edge to the successes.

Governament should bring more jobs into hazardous sectors. Linking of anti poverty program with education may prove to be the cornerstone of an effective child labour policy. International convention and national banning on child labour need it be consider local enforcement capacity and are best directed to types of child labour almost universally unacceptable on ethical and social ground regardless of economic considerations, such as prostitution, rag picking, bounded labour-etc. Efforts to create awareness among community members about child labour can round out the policy approach. What is need is the creation of an environment where the comminute would not tolerate child labour in any form. It is only then child labour can be eliminated totally and permanently. If parents or children are to be commenced monetarily or in some other way, the cost of the programme will increase enormously and it may even tempt others to withdraw their children from school jus to get the compensation package.

The child labour problem is an intense socio-economic problem that requires a long-term multi prolonged strategy to be carried out on a continuous basis Poverty alleviation programmes should have strong linkage with education and child labour. As for the project on the child labour undertaken by civil society organisations and Governament institutions, the vision is narrow. They do not analyze and link them with the border context of economic environment in families and comminutes, poverty related polices, the existing development paradigms and the process of liberalization, privatization and Globalisation. In this situation, a long-lasting solution to the birth and perpetuate of child labour cannot be ascertained (Satyarthi, K). Multidimensional approaches that have a direct linkage with the poverty alleviation programme may give a cutting edge to the success. Also it is true that child labour cannot be wished away with a magic wand. Of cource, normal growth and development of children can be protected, absolute poverty overcome, population growth slowed down and environmental deterioration arrested, improved physical and social infrastructure development. For decades now, this has not been a question of possible, but of priorities. Whatever be the particular cause, be it democracy or human rights, development or equality, gender equality or environmental protection, the growth, developmental and education of the children is central to long term success. Lost but not least, this study has reveled that majority of the poor families consider children is one of the meanse for economic development of the families since long time. It requires a radical change particularly in our society where traditional precipitin on children is not favourable for their well being. A commitment to people centered development requires purposeful efforts to weaken such culturally bounded traditional perception and to bring about more enlightened social attitudes towards innocent children. A police approach that balance economic, legislative, and social interventions are most likely to minimizing child labour. Governament should bring more jobs into hazardous sectors. Linking of anti poverty program with education may prove to be the cornerstone of an effective child labour policy. International convention and national banning on child labour need it be consider local enforcement capacity and are best directed to types of child labour almost universally unacceptable on ethical and social ground regardless of economic considerations, such as prostitution, rag picking, bonded labour-etc. Efforts to create awareness among community members about child labour can round out the policy approach. If we set time-bound goals and follow, of cource, with the continues assistance and participation of national and international community, it is possible to eliminate or atlest minimize the exploitative child labour within our life time

Children are the blooming flowers of garden of our society. So it is everyone's responsibility to protect these flowers from the damaging effects of excessive exposure to any natural calamities. They must and should be put on the right track always, as they are the seeds of future national growth more who passes our tradition, culture and customs to our next generation without fail.

Appendix-I

Universal Declaration of Human Rights, G.A. res. 217A (III), U.N. Doc A/810 at 71 (1948).

PREAMBLE

Whereas recognition of the inherent dignity and of the equal and inalienable rights of all members of the human family is the foundation of freedom, justice and peace in the world,

Whereas disregard and contempt for human rights have resulted in barbarous acts which have outraged the conscience of mankind, and the advent of a world in which human beings shall enjoy freedom of speech and belief and freedom from fear and want has been proclaimed as the highest aspiration of the common people,

Whereas it is essential, if man is not to be compelled to have recourse, as a last resort, to rebellion against tyranny and oppression, that human rights should be protected by the rule of law,

Whereas it is essential to promote the development of friendly relations between nations,

Whereas the peoples of the United Nations have in the Charter reaffirmed their faith in fundamental human rights, in the dignity and worth of the human person and in the equal rights of men and women and have determined to promote social progress and better standards of life in larger freedom,

Whereas Member States have pledged themselves to achieve, in cooperation with the United Nations, the promotion of universal respect for and observance of human rights and fundamental freedoms,

Whereas a common understanding of these rights and freedoms is of the greatest importance for the full realization of this pledge, *Now-therefore,*

The General Assembly

Proclaims this Universal Declaration of Human Rights as a common standard of achievement for all peoples and all nations, to the end that every individual and every organ of society, keeping this Declaration constantly in mind, shall strive by teaching and education to promote respect for these rights and freedoms and by progressive measures, national and international, to secure their universal and effective recognition and observance, both among the peoples of Member States themselves and among the peoples of territories under their jurisdiction.

Article I

All human beings are born free and equal in dignity and rights. They are endowed with reason and conscience and should act towards one another in a spirit of brotherhood.

Article 2

Everyone is entitled to all the rights and freedoms set forth in this Declaration, without distinction of any kind, such as race, colour, sex, language, religion, political or other opinion, national or social origin, property, birth or other status.

Furthermore, no distinction shall be made on the basis of the political, jurisdictional or international status of the country or territory to which a person belongs, whether it be independent, trust, non-self-governing or under any other limitation of sovereignty.

Article 3

Everyone has the right to life, liberty and security of person.

Article 4

No one shall be held in slavery or servitude; slavery and the slave trade shall be prohibited in all their forms.

Article 5

No one shall be subjected to torture or to cruel, inhuman or degrading treatment or punishment.

Article 6

Everyone has the right to recognition everywhere as a person before the law.

Article 7

All are equal before the law and are entitled without any discrimination to equal protection of the law. All are entitled to equal protection against any discrimination in violation of this Declaration and against any incitement to such discrimination.

Article 8

Everyone has the right to an effective remedy by the competent national tribunals for acts violating the fundamental rights granted him by the constitution or by law.

Article 9

No one shall be subjected to arbitrary arrest, detention or exile.

Article 10

Everyone is entitled in full equality to a fair and public hearing by an independent and impartial tribunal, in the determination of his rights and obligations and of any criminal charge against him.

Article 11

1. Everyone charged with a penal offence has the right to be presumed innocent until proved guilty according to law in a public trial at which he has had all the guarantees necessary for his defence.
2. No one shall be held guilty of any penal offence on account of any act or omission which did not constitute a penal offence, under national or international law, at the time when it was committed. Nor shall a heavier penalty be imposed than the one that was applicable at the time the penal offence was committed.

Article 12

No one shall be subjected to arbitrary interference with his privacy, family, home or correspondence, nor to attacks upon his honour and reputation. Everyone has the right to the protection of the law against such interference or attacks.

Article 13

1. Everyone has the right to freedom of movement and residence within the borders of each State.
2. Everyone has the right to leave any country, including his own, and to return to his country.

Article 14

1. Everyone has the right to seek and to enjoy in other countries asylum from persecution.
2. This right may not be invoked in the case of prosecutions genuinely arising from non-political crimes or from acts contrary to the purposes and principles of the United Nations.

Article 15

1. Everyone has the right to a nationality.
2. No one shall be arbitrarily deprived of his nationality nor denied the right to change his nationality.

Article 16

1. Men and women of full age, without any limitation due to race, nationality or religion, have the right to marry and to found a family. They are entitled to equal rights as to marriage, during marriage and at its dissolution.

2. Marriage shall be entered into only with the free and full consent of the intending spouses.
3. The family is the natural and fundamental group unit of society and is entitled to protection by society and the State.

Article 17

1. Everyone has the right to own property alone as well as in association with others.
2. No one shall be arbitrarily deprived of his property.

Article 18

Everyone has the right to freedom of thought, conscience and religion; this right includes freedom to change his religion or belief, and freedom, either alone or in community with others and in public or private, to manifest his religion or belief in teaching, practice, worship and observance.

Article 19

Everyone has the right to freedom of opinion and expression; this right includes freedom to hold opinions without interference and to seek, receive and impart information and ideas through any media and regardless of frontiers.

Article 20

1. Everyone has the right to freedom of peaceful assembly and association.
2. No one may be compelled to belong to an association.

Article 21

1. Everyone has the right to take part in the government of his country, directly or through freely chosen representatives.
2. Everyone has the right to equal access to public service in his country.
3. The will of the people shall be the basis of the authority of government; this will shall be expressed in periodic and genuine elections which shall be by universal and equal suffrage and shall be held by secret vote or by equivalent free voting procedures.

Article 22

Everyone, as a member of society, has the right to social security and is entitled to realization, through national effort and international co-operation and in accordance with the organization and resources of each State, of the economic, social and cultural rights indispensable for his dignity and the free development of his personality.

Article 23

1. Everyone has the right to work, to free choice of employment, to just and favourable conditions of work and to protection against unemployment.

2. Everyone, without any discrimination, has the right to equal pay for equal work.
3. Everyone who works has the right to just and favourable remuneration ensuring for himself and his family an existence worthy of human dignity, and supplemented, if necessary, by other means of social protection.
4. Everyone has the right to form and to join trade unions for the protection of his interests.

Article 24

Everyone has the right to rest and leisure, including reasonable limitation of working hours and periodic holidays with pay.

Article 25

1. Everyone has the right to a standard of living adequate for the health and well-being of himself and of his family, including food, clothing, housing and medical care and necessary social services, and the right to security in the event of unemployment, sickness, disability, widowhood, old age or other lack of livelihood in circumstances beyond his control.
2. Motherhood and childhood are entitled to special care and assistance. All children, whether born in or out of wedlock, shall enjoy the same social protection.

Article 26

1. Everyone has the right to education. Education shall be free, at least in the elementary and fundamental stages. Elementary education shall be compulsory. Technical and professional education shall be made generally available and higher education shall be equally accessible to all on the basis of merit.
2. Education shall be directed to the full development of the human personality and to the strengthening of respect for human rights and fundamental freedoms. It shall promote understanding, tolerance and friendship among all nations, racial or religious groups, and shall further the activities of the United Nations for the maintenance of peace.
3. Parents have a prior right to choose the kind of education that shall be given to their children.

Article 27

1. Everyone has the right freely to participate in the cultural life of the community, to enjoy the arts and to share in scientific advancement and its benefits.
2. Everyone has the right to the protection of the moral and material interests resulting from any scientific, literary or artistic production of which he is the author.

Article 28

Everyone is entitled to a social and international order in which the rights and freedoms set forth in this Declaration can be fully realized.

Article 29

1. Everyone has duties to the community in which alone the free and full development of his personality is possible.
2. In the exercise of his rights and freedoms, everyone shall be subject only to such limitations as are determined by law solely for the purpose of securing due recognition and respect for the rights and freedoms of others and of meeting the just requirements of morality, public order and the general welfare in a democratic society.
3. These rights and freedoms may in no case be exercised contrary to the purposes and principles of the United Nations.

Article 30

Nothing in this Declaration may be interpreted as implying for any State, group or person any right to engage in any activity or to perform any act aimed at the destruction of any of the rights and freedoms set forth herein.

Appendix-II

International Covenant on Economic, Social and Cultural Rights

Preamble

The States Parties to the present Covenant,

Considering that, in accordance with the principles proclaimed in the Charter of the United Nations, recognition of the inherent dignity and of the equal and inalienable rights of all members of the human family is the foundation of freedom, justice and peace in the world,

Recognizing that these rights derive from the inherent dignity of the human person,

Recognizing that, in accordance with the Universal Declaration of Human Rights, the ideal of free human beings enjoying freedom from fear and want can only be achieved if conditions are created whereby everyone may enjoy his economic, social and cultural rights, as well as his civil and political rights,

Considering the obligation of States under the Charter of the United Nations to promote universal respect for, and observance of, human rights and freedoms,

Realizing that the individual, having duties to other individuals and to the community to which he belongs, is under a responsibility to strive for the promotion and observance of the rights recognized in the present Covenant,

Agree upon the following articles:

PART I

Article 1

1. All peoples have the right of self-determination. By virtue of that right they freely determine their political status and freely pursue their economic, social and cultural development.
2. All peoples may, for their own ends, freely dispose of their natural wealth and resources without prejudice to any obligations arising out of international economic co-operation, based upon the principle of

mutual benefit, and international law. In no case may a people be deprived of its own means of subsistence.

3. The States Parties to the present Covenant, including those having responsibility for the administration of Non-Self-Governing and Trust Territories, shall promote the realization of the right of self-determination, and shall respect that right, in conformity with the provisions of the Charter of the United Nations.

PART II

Article 2

1. Each State Party to the present Covenant undertakes to take steps, individually and through international assistance and co-operation, especially economic and technical, to the maximum of its available resources, with a view to achieving progressively the full realization of the rights recognized in the present Covenant by all appropriate means, including particularly the adoption of legislative measures. ▶▶▶*General comment on its implementation*
2. The States Parties to the present Covenant undertake to guarantee that the rights enunciated in the present Covenant will be exercised without discrimination of any kind as to race, colour, sex, language, religion, political or other opinion, national or social origin, property, birth or other status.
3. Developing countries, with due regard to human rights and their national economy, may determine to what extent they would guarantee the economic rights recognized in the present Covenant to non-nationals.

Article 3

The States Parties to the present Covenant undertake to ensure the equal right of men and women to the enjoyment of all economic, social and cultural rights set forth in the present Covenant.

Article 4

The States Parties to the present Covenant recognize that, in the enjoyment of those rights provided by the State in conformity with the present Covenant, the State may subject such rights only to such limitations as are determined by law only in so far as this may be compatible with the nature of these rights and solely for the purpose of promoting the general welfare in a democratic society.

Article 5

1. Nothing in the present Covenant may be interpreted as implying for any State, group or person any right to engage in any activity or to perform any act aimed at the destruction of any of the rights or freedoms

recognized herein, or at their limitation to a greater extent than is provided for in the present Covenant.

2. No restriction upon or derogation from any of the fundamental human rights recognized or existing in any country in virtue of law, conventions, regulations or custom shall be admitted on the pretext that the present Covenant does not recognize such rights or that it recognizes them to a lesser extent.

PART III

Article 6

1. The States Parties to the present Covenant recognize the right to work, which includes the right of everyone to the opportunity to gain his living by work which he freely chooses or accepts, and will take appropriate steps to safeguard this right.
2. The steps to be taken by a State Party to the present Covenant to achieve the full realization of this right shall include technical and vocational guidance and training programmes, policies and techniques to achieve steady economic, social and cultural development and full and productive employment under conditions safeguarding fundamental political and economic freedoms to the individual.

Article 7

The States Parties to the present Covenant recognize the right of everyone to the enjoyment of just and favourable conditions of work which ensure, in particular:

- (a) Remuneration which provides all workers, as a minimum, with:
  - (i) Fair wages and equal remuneration for work of equal value without distinction of any kind, in particular women being guaranteed conditions of work not inferior to those enjoyed by men, with equal pay for equal work;
  - (ii) A decent living for themselves and their families in accordance with the provisions of the present Covenant;
- (b) Safe and healthy working conditions;
- (c) Equal opportunity for everyone to be promoted in his employment to an appropriate higher level, subject to no considerations other than those of seniority and competence;
- (d) Rest, leisure and reasonable limitation of working hours and periodic holidays with pay, as well as remuneration for public holidays

Article 8

1. The States Parties to the present Covenant undertake to ensure:

(a) The right of everyone to form trade unions and join the trade union of his choice, subject only to the rules of the organization concerned, for the promotion and protection of his economic and social interests. No restrictions may be placed on the exercise of this right other than those prescribed by law and which are necessary in a democratic society in the interests of national security or public order or for the protection of the rights and freedoms of others;

(b) The right of trade unions to establish national federations or confederations and the right of the latter to form or join international trade-union organizations;

(c) The right of trade unions to function freely subject to no limitations other than those prescribed by law and which are necessary in a democratic society in the interests of national security or public order or for the protection of the rights and freedoms of others;

(d) The right to strike, provided that it is exercised in conformity with the laws of the particular country.

2. This article shall not prevent the imposition of lawful restrictions on the exercise of these rights by members of the armed forces or of the police or of the administration of the State.

3. Nothing in this article shall authorize States Parties to the International Labour Organisation Convention of 1948 concerning Freedom of Association and Protection of the Right to Organize to take legislative measures which would prejudice, or apply the law in such a manner as would prejudice, the guarantees provided for in that Convention.

Article 9

The States Parties to the present Covenant recognize the right of everyone to social security, including social insurance.

Article 10

The States Parties to the present Covenant recognize that:

1. The widest possible protection and assistance should be accorded to the family, which is the natural and fundamental group unit of society, particularly for its establishment and while it is responsible for the care and education of dependent children. Marriage must be entered into with the free consent of the intending spouses.

2. Special protection should be accorded to mothers during a reasonable period before and after childbirth. During such period working mothers should be accorded paid leave or leave with adequate social security benefits.

3. Special measures of protection and assistance should be taken on behalf of all children and young persons without any discrimination for reasons of parentage or other conditions. Children and young persons should be protected from economic and social exploitation. Their employment in work harmful to their morals or health or dangerous to life or likely to hamper their normal development should be punishable by law. States should also set age limits below which the paid employment of child labour should be prohibited and punishable by law.

Article 11 General comment on its implementation

1. The States Parties to the present Covenant recognize the right of everyone to an adequate standard of living for himself and his family, including adequate food, clothing and housing, and to the continuous improvement of living conditions. The States Parties will take appropriate steps to ensure the realization of this right, recognizing to this effect the essential importance of international co-operation based on free consent. *General comment on its implementation*
2. The States Parties to the present Covenant, recognizing the fundamental right of everyone to be free from hunger, shall take, individually and through international co-operation, the measures, including specific programmes, which are needed:
   (a) To improve methods of production, conservation and distribution of food by making full use of technical and scientific knowledge, by disseminating knowledge of the principles of nutrition and by developing or reforming agrarian systems in such a way as to achieve the most efficient development and utilization of natural resources;
   (b) Taking into account the problems of both food-importing and food-exporting countries, to ensure an equitable distribution of world food supplies in relation to need.

Article 12 General comment on its implementation

1. The States Parties to the present Covenant recognize the right of everyone to the enjoyment of the highest attainable standard of physical and mental health.
2. The steps to be taken by the States Parties to the present Covenant to achieve the full realization of this right shall include those necessary for:
   (a) The provision for the reduction of the stillbirth-rate and of infant mortality and for the healthy development of the child;

(b) The improvement of all aspects of environmental and industrial hygiene;

(c) The prevention, treatment and control of epidemic, endemic, occupational and other diseases;

(d) The creation of conditions which would assure to all medical service and medical attention in the event of sickness.

Article 13 General comment on its implementation

1. The States Parties to the present Covenant recognize the right of everyone to education. They agree that education shall be directed to the full development of the human personality and the sense of its dignity, and shall strengthen the respect for human rights and fundamental freedoms. They further agree that education shall enable all persons to participate effectively in a free society, promote understanding, tolerance and friendship among all nations and all racial, ethnic or religious groups, and further the activities of the United Nations for the maintenance of peace.

2. The States Parties to the present Covenant recognize that, with a view to achieving the full realization of this right:

   (a) Primary education shall be compulsory and available free to all;

   (b) Secondary education in its different forms, including technical and vocational secondary education, shall be made generally available and accessible to all by every appropriate means, and in particular by the progressive introduction of free education;

   (c) Higher education shall be made equally accessible to all, on the basis of capacity, by every appropriate means, and in particular by the progressive introduction of free education;

   (d) Fundamental education shall be encouraged or intensified as far as possible for those persons who have not received or completed the whole period of their primary education;

   (e) The development of a system of schools at all levels shall be actively pursued, an adequate fellowship system shall be established, and the material conditions of teaching staff shall be continuously improved.

3. The States Parties to the present Covenant undertake to have respect for the liberty of parents and, when applicable, legal guardians to choose for their children schools, other than those established by the public authorities, which conform to such minimum educational standards as may be laid down or approved by the State and to ensure the religious and moral education of their children in conformity with their own convictions.

4. No part of this article shall be construed so as to interfere with the liberty of individuals and bodies to establish and direct educational institutions, subject always to the observance of the principles set forth in paragraph I of this article and to the requirement that the education given in such institutions shall conform to such minimum standards as may be laid down by the State.

Article 14 General comment on its implementation

Each State Party to the present Covenant which, at the time of becoming a Party, has not been able to secure in its metropolitan territory or other territories under its jurisdiction compulsory primary education, free of charge, undertakes, within two years, to work out and adopt a detailed plan of action for the progressive implementation, within a reasonable number of years, to be fixed in the plan, of the principle of compulsory education free of charge for all.

Article 15

1. The States Parties to the present Covenant recognize the right of everyone:
   (a) To take part in cultural life;
   (b) To enjoy the benefits of scientific progress and its applications;
   (c) To benefit from the protection of the moral and material interests resulting from any scientific, literary or artistic production of which he is the author.
2. The steps to be taken by the States Parties to the present Covenant to achieve the full realization of this right shall include those necessary for the conservation, the development and the diffusion of science and culture.
3. The States Parties to the present Covenant undertake to respect the freedom indispensable for scientific research and creative activity.
4. The States Parties to the present Covenant recognize the benefits to be derived from the encouragement and development of international contacts and co-operation in the scientific and cultural fields.

PART IV

Article 16

1. The States Parties to the present Covenant undertake to submit in conformity with this part of the Covenant reports on the measures which they have adopted and the progress made in achieving the observance of the rights recognized herein.

2. (a) All reports shall be submitted to the Secretary-General of the United Nations, who shall transmit copies to the Economic and Social Council

for consideration in accordance with the provisions of the present Covenant;

(b) The Secretary-General of the United Nations shall also transmit to the specialized agencies copies of the reports, or any relevant parts therefrom, from States Parties to the present Covenant which are also members of these specialized agencies in so far as these reports, or parts therefrom, relate to any matters which fall within the responsibilities of the said agencies in accordance with their constitutional instruments.

Article 17General comment on its implementation

1. The States Parties to the present Covenant shall furnish their reports in stages, in accordance with a programme to be established by the Economic and Social Council within one year of the entry into force of the present Covenant after consultation with the States Parties and the specialized agencies concerned.
2. Reports may indicate factors and difficulties affecting the degree of fulfilment of obligations under the present Covenant.
3. Where relevant information has previously been furnished to the United Nations or to any specialized agency by any State Party to the present Covenant, it will not be necessary to reproduce that information, but a precise reference to the information so furnished will suffice.

Article 18

Pursuant to its responsibilities under the Charter of the United Nations in the field of human rights and fundamental freedoms, the Economic and Social Council may make arrangements with the specialized agencies in respect of their reporting to it on the progress made in achieving the observance of the provisions of the present Covenant falling within the scope of their activities. These reports may include particulars of decisions and recommendations on such implementation adopted by their competent organs.

Article 19

The Economic and Social Council may transmit to the Commission on Human Rights for study and general recommendation or, as appropriate, for information the reports concerning human rights submitted by States in accordance with articles 16 and 17, and those concerning human rights submitted by the specialized agencies in accordance with article 18.

Article 20

The States Parties to the present Covenant and the specialized agencies concerned may submit comments to the Economic and Social Council on any general recommendation under article 19 or reference to such general recommendation in any report of the Commission on Human Rights or any documentation referred to therein.

Article 21

The Economic and Social Council may submit from time to time to the General Assembly reports with recommendations of a general nature and a summary of the information received from the States Parties to the present Covenant and the specialized agencies on the measures taken and the progress made in achieving general observance of the rights recognized in the present Covenant.

Article 22General comment on its implementation

The Economic and Social Council may bring to the attention of other organs of the United Nations, their subsidiary organs and specialized agencies concerned with furnishing technical assistance any matters arising out of the reports referred to in this part of the present Covenant which may assist such bodies in deciding, each within its field of competence, on the advisability of international measures likely to contribute to the effective progressive implementation of the present Covenant.

Article 23

The States Parties to the present Covenant agree that international action for the achievement of the rights recognized in the present Covenant includes such methods as the conclusion of conventions, the adoption of recommendations, the furnishing of technical assistance and the holding of regional meetings and technical meetings for the purpose of consultation and study organized in conjunction with the Governments concerned.

Article 24

Nothing in the present Covenant shall be interpreted as impairing the provisions of the Charter of the United Nations and of the constitutions of the specialized agencies which define the respective responsibilities of the various organs of the United Nations and of the specialized agencies in regard to the matters dealt with in the present Covenant.

Article 25

Nothing in the present Covenant shall be interpreted as impairing the inherent right of all peoples to enjoy and utilize fully and freely their natural wealth and resources.

PARTV

Article 26

1. The present Covenant is open for signature by any State Member of the United Nations or member of any of its specialized agencies, by

any State Party to the Statute of the International Court of Justice, and by any other State which has been invited by the General Assembly of the United Nations to become a party to the present Covenant.

2. The present Covenant is subject to ratification. Instruments of ratification shall be deposited with the Secretary-General of the United Nations.
3. The present Covenant shall be open to accession by any State referred to in paragraph 1 of this article.
4. Accession shall be effected by the deposit of an instrument of accession with the Secretary-General of the United Nations.
5. The Secretary-General of the United Nations shall inform all States which have signed the present Covenant or acceded to it of the deposit of each instrument of ratification or accession.

Article 27

1. The present Covenant shall enter into force three months after the date of the deposit with the Secretary-General of the United Nations of the thirty-fifth instrument of ratification or instrument of accession.
2. For each State ratifying the present Covenant or acceding to it after the deposit of the thirty-fifth instrument of ratification or instrument of accession, the present Covenant shall enter into force three months after the date of the deposit of its own instrument of ratification or instrument of accession.

Article 28

The provisions of the present Covenant shall extend to all parts of federal States without any limitations or exceptions.

Article 29

1. Any State Party to the present Covenant may propose an amendment and file it with the Secretary-General of the United Nations. The Secretary-General shall thereupon communicate any proposed amendments to the States Parties to the present Covenant with a request that they notify him whether they favour a conference of States Parties for the purpose of considering and voting upon the proposals. In the event that at least one third of the States Parties favours such a conference, the Secretary-General shall convene the conference under the auspices of the United Nations. Any amendment adopted by a majority of the States Parties present and voting at the conference shall be submitted to the General Assembly of the United Nations for approval.
2. Amendments shall come into force when they have been approved by the General Assembly of the United Nations and accepted by a two-

thirds majority of the States Parties to the present Covenant in accordance with their respective constitutional processes.

3. When amendments come into force they shall be binding on those States Parties which have accepted them, other States Parties still being bound by the provisions of the present Covenant and any earlier amendment which they have accepted.

Article 30

Irrespective of the notifications made under article 26, paragraph 5, the Secretary-General of the United Nations shall inform all States referred to in paragraph I of the same article of the following particulars:

(a) Signatures, ratifications and accessions under article 26;

(b) The date of the entry into force of the present Covenant under article 27 and the date of the entry into force of any amendments under article 29.

Article 31

1. The present Covenant, of which the Chinese, English, French, Russian and Spanish texts are equally authentic, shall be deposited in the archives of the United Nations.

2. The Secretary-General of the United Nations shall transmit certified copies of the present Covenant to all States referred to in article 26.

References

Alston, P. (1994), The Best Interest of the Child, Clarendon Press-UK

Arnason Jonson, 1995. Nationalism, Globalization and Modernity New Delhi: Sage Publication.

Burra, N., (1999), Born to Work: Child Labour in India, Oxoperd University press, New Delhi.

Bhargava, Gopal. (2003), Child Labour (Vol-I and II), Kalpaz Publication, New Delhi.

Bose. B., (2003), The State of Children in India, Mnoher Publications, New Delhi.

Dak, et.al, (2002), Child Labour in India Serials Publications, New Delhi.

Joshi, 1999. Manifestation of Globalisation, Bangalore: Nanda Publication\

Jha, Mhaken 1993. Social Anthropology Vikas Publishing House, New Delhi. pp. 23-45

Kulshreshtha, (1978), Child labour in India, Ashish Publication, New Delhi.

Litten., (1999), Small Hands in South Asia, Manoher Publications, New Delhi.

Mohan Jan, 1997. Towards Understanding of the Phenomenon of Globalisation. New Delhi: DK Publishers. pp. 123-234

Murthy, et.al, (2001), Child Labour in India: Causes, Consequences and Cures, RBSA Publication, Delhi.

Mital, Mukta., (1994), Child Labour in Unorganised Sector, Anmol Publication, New Delhi.

Nieuwennuy, (2003), Children life World: Gender Welfare and Labour in the Developing World, Social Science Press, New Delhi.

Pathak, B., (1991), Road to Freedom, M B Publishers New Delhi

Patrions, and Hearry., (2003) The Policy Analysis of Child Labour, St Martins Press, USA.

Prasad N, (2001), Population, Growth and Child Labour; Indian Prospective, Kanishka Publications, New Delhi.

Pandey, M.K(1999), Child labour in India, SLP Press, Punjab.

Sharma, I., (1993), Child Labour in India An Anatomy B R Publishing House, Delhi.

Singh, B, and Mahanty, S, (1998), Children at Work: Problems and Polices, B R Publishing, Delhi.

Tripathy, and Pradhan, (1993), Girl Child in India, Discovery Publication, Delhi.

Weiner, Myron., (1994), The State and the Child in India, Oxoford University Press, -Delhi.

Zelizer, Vivianna 1985, Princing the Priceless Child: The Changing Social Value of Children, New York: Basic Books.

Ahlawat, rose (2004), Anthropology of Small Hands, *Participative Development,* Vol. 21, pp. 12-20.

Boyden and Myers, W (1998) What Works for Working Children. *Stockholm Radda Barmen.*

Basu, Kaushik., (1999), Child Labour: Cause, Consequence and Cure, *Journal of Economic Litrature*, Vol. 37,1083-119.

Basha, Chand., (2001), Living and Work Conditions of Child Labou,r *Man and Life* , Vol.27 No 3-4

Duraisamy, M., (1997), *Changes in Child Labour Over space and Time* in India, Indian Journal of Labour Economic, 40 (4): 809-18.

Liten,, (2005), Child Land Work: Number From the General to the Specific, *The Indian Journal of labour Economic*, Vol. 48, No. 1.

Mead, M.and M. Wolfenstein, (1955), Child hood in Contemporary Culture, *Chicago University Press*-USA.

Mehendalke, Archana., (2004), Children's Right Lessons on Monitoring, *Economic and Political Weekly (EPW)*, pp. 1568-1570.

Nicuwenhuys., (1996), The Paradox of Child Labour and Anthropology, *Annual Review of Anthropology,* 25:237-51.

Neera Burra, 1990, Out of Sight and out of Mind: Working Girls in India, International Labour Review, Vol. 128, No. 5, ILO-Geneva.

Ramachandran, Vimal., Backward and Forward Linkages that Strengthen Primary Education, *EPW* , March-2003, pp. 959-962.

Rao, and Rao., (1998), Employers View on Child Labour, *Indian journal of Industrial Relation* , Vol. 34, No.1.

Reddy, B.S. 'Financing of Education and Health in India', Journal of Education and Planning in India Vol. 5 361-81. 1991.

Roy, P.K., (1998), Child labour legislation and Polices, *Legal News* and Views, pp. 22-24.

Sharma, Rao., Universal Eliminatory Education, The Question of How ? *EPW*, pp. 1640-1644.

Woodhead, M.(1998),Children Perspective on Their Working Lives. *Stockholm Radda Barmen.*

Wood head, and Martin. 1998, 'Combating Child Labour Listen What the Children Say', The Childhood, Vol. 6(1): 27-49,

Wiener, Myron 'Child Labour in India: Putting compulsory

Primary Education on the Political Agenda, EPW, Nov. 9-161996.

Wind Steven, 2003. 'Globalization: Can We Survive?', *Critique Anthropology,* Vol. 24 No 10 , pp. 134-34.

Index